The War People

This book uses the transnational story of a single regiment to examine how ordinary soldiers, military women, and officers negotiated their lives within the chaos and uncertainty of the seventeenth century. Raised in Saxony by Wolf von Mansfeld in spring 1625 in the service of the King of Spain, the Mansfeld Regiment fought for one and a half years in northern Italy before collapsing, leaving behind a trail of dead civilians, murder, internal lawsuits … and copious amounts of paperwork. Their story reveals the intricate social world of seventeenth-century mercenaries and how this influenced how they lived and fought. Through this rich microhistorical case study, Lucian Staiano-Daniels sheds new light on key seventeenth-century developments like the military revolution and the fiscal-military state, which is supported by statistical analysis drawn from hundreds of records from the Thirty Years War. This pathbreaking book unifies the study of war and conflict with social history.

Lucian Staiano-Daniels is a research and teaching fellow at the Hoover Institution at Stanford University.

The War People
A Social History of Common Soldiers during the Era of the Thirty Years War

Lucian Staiano-Daniels

Stanford University

CAMBRIDGE
UNIVERSITY PRESS

Shaftesbury Road, Cambridge CB2 8EA, United Kingdom

One Liberty Plaza, 20th Floor, New York, NY 10006, USA

477 Williamstown Road, Port Melbourne, VIC 3207, Australia

314–321, 3rd Floor, Plot 3, Splendor Forum, Jasola District Centre, New Delhi – 110025, India

103 Penang Road, #05-06/07, Visioncrest Commercial, Singapore 238467

Cambridge University Press is part of Cambridge University Press & Assessment, a department of the University of Cambridge.

We share the University's mission to contribute to society through the pursuit of education, learning and research at the highest international levels of excellence.

www.cambridge.org
Information on this title: www.cambridge.org/9781009428408
DOI: 10.1017/9781009428415

© Lucian Staiano-Daniels 2024

This publication is in copyright. Subject to statutory exception and to the provisions of relevant collective licensing agreements, no reproduction of any part may take place without the written permission of Cambridge University Press & Assessment.

First published 2024

A catalogue record for this publication is available from the British Library

Library of Congress Cataloging-in-Publication Data
Names: Staiano-Daniels, Lucian, author.
Title: The war people : a social history of common soldiers during the era of the Thirty Years War / Lucian Staiano-Daniels, Colgate University, New York.
Other titles: Social history of common soldiers during the era of the Thirty Years War
Description: Cambridge, United Kingdom ; New York, NY : Cambridge University Press, 2024. | Includes bibliographical references and index.
Identifiers: LCCN 2024018170 (print) | LCCN 2024018171 (ebook) | ISBN 9781009428408 (hardback) | ISBN 9781009428422 (paperback) | ISBN 9781009428415 (epub)
Subjects: LCSH: Mansfeld Regiment–Military life. | Mansfeld, Wolfgang von, 1575-1638. | Thirty Years' War, 1618-1648–Regimental histories. | War and society–Germany–History–17th century. | Saxony (Germany)–History, Military–17th century.
Classification: LCC D260 .S74 2024 (print) | LCC D260 (ebook) | DDC 943/.041–dc23/eng/20240506
LC record available at https://lccn.loc.gov/2024018170
LC ebook record available at https://lccn.loc.gov/2024018171

ISBN 978-1-009-42840-8 Hardback

Cambridge University Press & Assessment has no responsibility for the persistence or accuracy of URLs for external or third-party internet websites referred to in this publication and does not guarantee that any content on such websites is, or will remain, accurate or appropriate.

I hadn't cried until now ... presently the temperate tempered air dried my tears as it dries the spit in your mouth and the seed in your body.
—Graham Greene, *The Quiet American*

Contents

List of Figures	*page* ix
List of Tables	x
Acknowledgments	xi
Notes on Money, Dates, Ranks, and Measurements	xiii
List of the People	xv

	Introduction: The War People	1
1	Display All Good Will and Keep Moving: The Mansfeld Regiment and the 1625–1627 Campaign	8
Scene I	Hieronymus Sebastian Schutze and Hans Devil	21
2	The Italian Dance: Early Modern Military Finance and the Mansfeld Regiment	24
3	Righteous Guys: Military Society	41
4	The Spinner-Lords of Saint Gallen: Small Group Cohesion and Military Social Networks as Seen through a Theft of Fabric	58
5	The Kind of People I Know You Will Like: Social Structure in the Saxon Army and the Mansfeld Regiment	77
6	Elizabeth Sanner and the Dead Men: Mansfeld Interactions with Their Surroundings	98

7	To Be Happy Doing What You Want: The Death of Victoria Guarde and the Life of Theodoro de Camargo	118
Scene II	Hieronymus Sebastian Schutze, Felix Steter, and Wolfgang Winckelmann	135
8	Making It in This Thing: Money and Payment within Saxon Regiments in the 1620s	146
9	And to My Son the Breaking Wheel: The Mansfeld Regiment Falls Apart	164
	Conclusion: A Beautiful Regiment	191
	Bibliography	200
	Index	220

Figures

3.1 Origins of Saxon soldiers, all decades of the Thirty
    Years War *page* 44
3.2 Origins of Saxon soldiers, 1620s 45
3.3 Origins of Saxon soldiers, 1630s 46
3.4 Origins of Saxon soldiers, 1640s 46
3.5 Origins of members of the Mansfeld Regiment, 1625–1627 55
4.1 Who passed fabric to whom: Winckelmann company,
    Mansfeld Regiment 68
6.1 Baptisms, marriages, and burials, Busto Arsizio,
    1620–1629 107
6.2 Baptisms, marriages, and burials, Legnano, 1620–1629 109
6.3 Baptisms, Pontestura, 1620–1628 109
8.1 Common infantry pay in gulden/month by specialization,
    1619–1625 149
8.2 Noble and common infantry pay in gulden/month
    by specialization and social background, 1619–1625 152

Tables

3.1	Number of soldiers with non-German origins in the Saxon army by decade	page 49
3.2	Number and percentage of soldiers by population of hometown and branch of service	52
4.1	Total value of missing cloth as enumerated by Schobinger and Beyer, December 3, 1625	61
4.2	Total value of cloth that Steiner found in Winckelmann Company, January 11, 1626, in Milanese lire	73
5.1	Number and percentage of nobles in Saxon cavalry, 1620s	86
5.2	Number and percentage of nobles in Saxon cavalry, 1630s	86
5.3	Number and percentage of nobles in Saxon cavalry, 1640s	87
5.4	Number and percentage of nobles in Saxon infantry, 1620s	87
5.5	Number and percentage of nobles in Saxon infantry, 1630s	88
5.6	Number and percentage of nobles in Saxon infantry, 1640s	88
6.1	Infantry strength, Mansfeld Regiment, September 1626–July 1627	103
6.2	Cavalry strength in horses, Mansfeld Regiment, August 1625	104
6.3	Baptisms, marriages, and burials, Busto Arsizio, 1620–1629	108
6.4	Baptisms, marriages, and funerals, Cremona, 1620–1629	111
8.1	Infantry officers' pay, 1619–1625	147
8.2	Common infantry pay in gulden/month by specialization, 1619–1625	148
8.3	Noble and common infantry pay in gulden/month by specialization and social background, 1619–1625	151
8.4	Cavalry officers' pay, Hoffahne rolls, 1624	154
8.5	Infantry officers' pay, 1631	158
8.6	Cavalry officers' pay, Franz Albrecht von Sachsen's regiment, 1632	159

Acknowledgments

Like the men I study, my life relies on outspread social networks; unlike most of them, a deep shyness and reticence often prevents me from expressing out loud my love for others. I would like first to thank my advisors at the University of California, Los Angeles (UCLA), David Sabean and Geoffrey Symcox. Peter Baldwin recruited me, and Richard Rouse taught me palaeography. Unfortunately, he is dead, so my thanks are extended to Mary Rouse in his absence. Kathryn Norberg helped me investigate Victoria Guarde's death. Gadi Algazi was not only a great help while I was based in Tel Aviv, he was also kind to me. I enjoyed Perry Anderson's classes. At my post at Colgate University I benefited from the close support of the Peace and Conflict Studies program and its director Jake Mundy, as well as Ray Douglas's keen sardonic eye.

At Oxford, my thanks go to David Parrott and Peter Wilson; at Cambridge, Joachim Whaley; at the University of Aberdeen, Karin Friedrich and Robert Frost; and at Texas A&M, Adam Seipp. I also thank my colleagues and friends Ilya Berkovich, Noor Khan, Sascha Moebius, Hannah Murphy and the King's College early modern reading group, Tobias Roeder, and Adam Storring.

I would also like to thank scholars in Italy and specialists of Italy for their generous aid, including Giuseppe de Luca, who was pleased to host me at the Università degli Studi in Milan; as well as Emanuele Colombo, Stefano Damico, Gregory Hanlon, Davide Maffi, and Mario Rizzo. Archives in Italy are small and dispersed, and many of their staff members are volunteers, including Don Paolo Fusar in the archives of the Cathedral of Cremona; Manuela Meni, at Casale Montferrato; Antonella Ricci, who found and scanned baptism records from tiny Pontestura; and above all, the archivists in the churches in Busto Arsizio, Gallarate, and Legnano. I would also like to thank the archivists in Alessandria, Casale, Cremona, Mantua, and La Trivulziana in Milan – and the Battle of Tornavento reenacting company, one member of which wrote to Samarate himself on my behalf.

In Germany, my thanks go to Gerd Schwerhoff at the Technische Universität Dresden, and the archivists at the Sächsisches Hauptstaatsarchiv Dresden. I also did research at archives in Darmstadt, Karlsruhe, Ulm, and Würzburg. I would like to specially mention the Green Brigade reenacting regiment and its most honorable colonel, Nico Baumgärtel.

Historians of conflict are fortunate in that we interact professionally with non-academics a great deal. I would like to thank James Palmer at *Foreign Policy*, as well as all my friends.

For bringing this manuscript to completion, I thank Michael Watson at Cambridge University Press, as well as Rosa Martin and the editorial team. I also thank my sister, whose wry sense of humor is a light in dim times.

I am also grateful to everyone at St. John's College, most especially my tutor Barry Goldfarb.

Notes on Money, Dates, Ranks, and Measurements

Most dates for the Mansfeld Regiment and its Spanish/Italian overlords were originally given in the new (Gregorian) calendar, and they still are. All dates for non-Mansfelder Saxon units were originally given in the old (Julian) calendar, which at the time was ten days behind the new calendar. Some Mansfelder and Imperialist documents from the late summer and fall of 1627 use both dates. I have changed old calendar dates to new in this book.

Coinage was complex and unstable during this period. Much commerce was handled in "money of account," for which no physical coin existed, such as lire (in the Italian lands) or gulden (in the German speaking world).

Pay in Saxon rolls was given in gulden and thalers. Theoretically, one ducat was four gulden. Ideally, one gulden (abbreviated R or f) was worth sixty kreutzer after the Reichsmünzordnung of 1559. From 1623 onward one thaler (abbreviated Rth with one or two horizontal strokes through the letters, or #) was worth ninety kreutzer or one and a half gulden.[1] One batzen was four kreutzer. One groschen was three kreutzer. One kreutzer was four pennies, which in the early seventeenth century was still written *denarii*, singular *denarius*. One *denarius* was two heller. These are ideal values; during the economic crises of the early 1620s, the value of money fluctuated wildly.

Much of the Mansfeld Regiment's finances were recorded in Milanese money. Official documents often used "scudi da 110 soldi," in which one scudo was counted as five and a half lire, and one lira was 20 soldi. Yet the value fluctuated, and that of a scudo of gold was more often five and a half to six lire, which makes about 120 soldi. The latter is the calculation I have used. The exchange rate was not constant: For the Mansfelders, one soldo was worth one-fifth batzen, slightly less than a kreutzer. There was no lira coin.

---

[1] Eduard Döring: *Handbuch der Münz-, Wechsel-, Mass- und Gewichtskunde* (Koblenz: J Hölscher, 1854), 19–20.

Members of the Mansfeld Regiment said "Zick" or "Zeck" for a coin worth one and a half scudi or three gulden, but that looked like a ducat from a distance.[2] This meant "nanny goat" in the German of the south but was probably a corruption of *zecchino*, the Venetian gold ducat, or *zecca*, Italian for mint.

All distances and weights have been translated from seventeenth-century Saxon measurements to modern American measurements. Until 1839 the Saxon pound was about 467.2 grams as opposed to the American 453.6. The Saxon hundredweight was 110 Saxon pounds.

I have translated ranks into their English-language equivalents whenever I could, but these are sometimes not now synonymous with what they meant in seventeenth-century Germany. *Feldwebel* is "sergeant" and *Gemeinwebel* is "corporal," but at the time these were both officers – while sergeants (*Chargants*) and corporals (*Corporals*) are also listed in documents from the 1630s and 1640s. I have translated *Führer*, an officer responsible for direction, order, overseeing the company surgeon and medicine chest, and doubling up the flag-bearer's duties at need, as "commander."

An artisan in Milan could expect to earn one lira per day; a peasant perhaps half that, on days he worked.

It took four gulden and twelve groschen to buy dry fodder for one horse for one month. It took six gulden for one soldier to feed and support himself for one month.

---

[2] Sächsisches Hauptstaatsarchiv Dresden (hereafter SHStADr) 10024 9239/2, 64v.

The People

The Mansfeld Regiment (1625–1627)

Wolfgang von Mansfeld (Wolf): Colonel of the Mansfeld Regiment, Captain of the most honorable companies in it, of horse and foot
    Bernhard Lauerwald: His agent
    Andreas Medringer: Captain-Lieutenant and frequent legal witness, later Captain, later von Mansfeld's master of horse
    Michael Meder, Michael the Surgeon, Master Michael: Surgeon of von Mansfeld's Life Company
        His brother
            His brother's wife
                Her sister: beaten with rods
                Her sister's man: broken on the wheel

Mattheus Steiner: Regimental Bailiff and Secretary
    Elizabeth Sanner: His wife

Hans Wolf von Schingo: Regimental Provost (until December 1626)
Gottfried Reichbrodt: Regimental Provost (after December 1626)

Hans Georg Heyl: Master of provisions

Vratislav Eusebius von Pernstein: Lieutenant Colonel, Cavalry
Eustachius Löser (Stach): Lieutenant Colonel, Cavalry

Captain Ulleben: Cavalry captain

Christoff Kettel: Cavalry captain
    Hans Devil: Cavalry trooper
        His boy

Theodoro de Camargo: Lieutenant Colonel, Infantry; Infantry Second-in-Command, Captain of its second-most-honorable company; godfather to infants
    Victoria Guarde: His wife
        Margarita Pellegrini: Her maid
        Wilhem Stum: Her page
        Anna Luisa Ségers: Her maid
    Juan Gammert: His flag-bearer
    Theodoro de Camargo: His son

Wolfgang Winckelmann: Infantry Third-in-Command, Regimental Quartermaster, Captain of the infantry's third-most-honorable company
    Hieronymus Sebastian Schutze: Flag-bearer
    David von Bernleben: Flag-bearer
    Felix Steter: Lieutenant
    Christof Hubrich: Steward
    Hans Heinrich Tauerling: Shot in the eye
    Andreas Melchior von Schneeberg: Sergeant
    Heinrich Teichmeyer: Muster-writer, died
    Christof the Drummer
    David Schmidt: Squad leader
    Jacob Fritzsch: Sick

Captain Dam Vitzthum von Eckstedt
Captain August Vitzthum von Eckstedt
    Wolf Heinrich von Dransdorf: Lieutenant
        His wife: beaten with rods
            Her child
            Her previous man: hanged
    Hans Reinhardt Kochstetter: Commander
    Barthel Golzer: Fourier
    Georg Lauren: Sergeant

Captain Moser
    His flag-bearer
    Simon Löhr: Lieutenant
    Christian Hendel: Commander
    Heinrich Deckert: Sergeant
    Hans Gebler: Ordinary soldier
    Hans Albrecht: Musketeer

The People

Captain Hans von Ponickau
    Nicholas Korn: Lieutenant
    Michael Andreas: Drummer
    The piper
    Urban Beyer: Soldier who heard Korn beat Andreas
    Christoff Pfeiffer: Soldier who heard Korn beat Andreas
    Christoff Frederick: Soldier who heard Korn beat Andreas
    Hans Werner: Soldier who heard Korn beat Andreas

Captain Daniel von Schlieben
    Zdenko Sigmund von Wallenstein: Flag-bearer
    Justus Wilhelm Lipsius: Lieutenant
    Hans Kley: Menacing soldier
    Barthel Meylig: Menacing soldier
    Michael Kleiben: Made a pact with the Devil
    Hans Pönischen: Menacing soldier

Michael Hevel: Flag-bearer, legal witness
Johann Silbernagel: Sergeant

Stach Krakow: Flag-bearer, later promoted to cavalry captain. Godfather to infants

Valentin von Treutler: Corporal, duelist
Jonas Eckert: Ordinary soldier, duelist

Georg Schmaliner: Agitated for pay
Lucas Paz: Agitated for pay

Georg Reinsberger: Ordinary soldier
    Maria: His legal wife
Hans Jungnickel: Ordinary soldier
    His wife

Noc Münch: Cavalryman

Heinrich Lehnfeldt: Trumpeter who saw a rape
Christof Heschler: Cavalryman who saw a rape

Bartolomeo Gattone, The Bag: Translator

The Sulz Regiment (1625–1627)
Alwig von Sulz: Colonel
Johann Beck: Lieutenant Colonel
The Third-in-Command

Introduction
The War People

Their word for themselves was *People.* Early seventeenth-century common soldiers were *Die Leute, Das Volk, les gens,* or *la gente.* They were *Das Kriegsvolk, Die Kriegsleute, les gens de guerre,* the War People. Neutral outsiders called them mercenaries, *Söldner,* or soldiers, *Soldaten.* When a warlord ordered them by the head in a contract they were "persons," *Personen.* To a quartermaster charged with supplying their bread, they were "mouths." When they call themselves *Kriegsleute* I translate it as War People. This phrase echoes classic works of ethnography like *The Harmless People* (1959), *The Forest People* (1961), *The Mountain People* (1972), and *The Fierce People* (1968).[1] It is deliberately defamiliarizing.

This is a social history of common soldiers in and from Electoral Saxony during the Thirty Years War, primarily from the 1620s. It aims to present the interactions of these men in their depth and intricacy, in order to argue that the concepts of the military revolution and the fiscal-military state should be separated from the question of social relationships within early seventeenth-century military units.

Discussions about the growth and centralization of modern armies and the modern state share the assumption that new political philosophies and new governmental structures were intertwined with a change in daily practice in early modern European armies.[2] The thesis that war and the needs of the military led to the development of the modern state is well-developed.[3] Arguments relating to this thesis are

---

[1] Elizabeth Marshall Thomas, *The Harmless People* (New York: Alfred Knopf, 1959); Colin Turnbull, *The Forest People: A Sudy of the Pygmies of the Congo* (New York: Simon and Schuster, 1961); Napoleon Chagnon, *Yanomano: The Fierce People* (New York: Holt, Rinehart, and Winston, 1968); Colin Turnbull, *The Mountain People* (New York: Simon and Schuster, 1972). None of these works is without controversy.

[2] Otto Hintze, "Military Organization and the Organization of the State," in *The Historical Essays of Otto Hintze,* trans. F. Gilbert (Oxford: Oxford University Press, 1975), 178–215. Gerhard Oestrich, *Neostoicism and the Early Modern State,* ed. Brigitta Oestrich and H. G. Koenigsberger, trans. David McLintock (Cambridge: Cambridge University Press, 1982).

[3] Samuel Finer, "State and Nation-building in Europe: The Role of the Military," in *The Formation of National States in Western Europe,* Charles Tilly, ed. (Princeton: Princeton University Press, 1975), 84–163; Charles Tilly, "Reflections on the History of European State-Making," in *The Formation of National States in Western Europe,* Charles Tilly, ed.

varied.[4] State developments from the sixteenth to the eighteenth century varied substantially, but in the classic formulation fiscal-military states funded increased military spending through taxation and financial infrastructure.[5] The social disciplining of soldiers was supposedly one element of this complex of processes: In this argument, early-modern states increased their control over their civilian populations in part to raise tax money for larger armies, that were inhabited by soldiers who were themselves increasingly well-disciplined.[6] Military changes not only had an impact on society in general, they had an impact on the society of soldiers. A soldier's daily routine would have changed. The way he interacted with his fellows would have been different. Since this contains a microhistorical argument, it can be investigated by microhistorical means.

Historians study how seventeenth-century armies were supplied and how they traveled.[7] We study how they were raised and financed,

---

(Princeton: Princeton University Press, 1975), 73–76; Richard Bean, "War and the Birth of the Nation State," *Journal of Economic History* 33 (1973), 203–221; William McNeill, *The Pursuit of Power: Technology, Armed Force, and Society since AD 1000* (Oxford: Oxford University Press, 1982); Brian Downing, *The Military Revolution and Political Change: Origins of Democracy and Autocracy in Early Modern Europe* (Princeton: Princeton University Press, 1992).

[4] For an introduction to state-building theories, see Thomas Ertman, *Birth of the Leviathan: Building States and Regimes in Medieval and Early Modern Europe* (Cambridge: Cambridge University Press, 1997), 1–34; Benno Teschke, *The Myth of 1648: Class, Geopolitics, and the Making of Modern International Relations* (Brooklyn: Verso, 2003), chapter 4.

[5] Michael Duffy, ed., *The Military Revolution and the State, 1500–1800* (Exeter: University of Exeter Press, 1980); M. S. Anderson, *War and Society in Europe of the Old Regime, 1618–1780* (Leicester: Leicester University Press, 1988); John Brewer, *The Sinews of Power: War and the English State, 1688–1783* (London: Unwin Hyman, 1989); Jan Glete, *War and the State in Early Modern Europe: Spain, the Dutch Republic, and Sweden as Fiscal-Military States* (New York: Routledge, 2001); Christopher Storrs, ed., *The Fiscal-Military State in Eighteenth-Century Europe: Essays in Honor of P. G. M. Dickson* (Aldershot: Ashgate, 2009).

[6] Michael Roberts, "The Military Revolution, 1560–1660," reprinted in Clifford J. Rogers, ed., *The Military Revolution Debate: Readings on the Military Transformation of Early Modern Europe* (Abingdon: Routledge, 1995) 13–36, 14.

[7] Geza Perjés, "Army Provisioning, Logistics and Strategy in the Second Half of the 17th Century," *Acta Historica Academiae Scientiarum Hungaricae* XVI (1970); Bernhard Kroener, *Les Routes et les Étapes: Die Versorgung der französischen Armeen in Nordostfrankreich (1635–1661): Ein Beitrag zur Verwaltungsgeschichte des Ancien Régime* (Münster: Aschendorff Verlag, 1980); Jürgen Pohl, *"Die Profiantirung der Keyserlichen Armaden Ahnbelangendt:" Studien zur Versorgung der Kaiserlichen Armee 1634/1635* (Horn: F. Berger & Söhne, 1994); Cordula Kapser, *Die bayerische Kriegsorganisation in der zweiten Hälfte des dreissigjährigen Krieges 1635–1648/49* (Münster: Aschendorff Verlag, 1997); Erik A. Lund, *War for the Every Day: Generals, Knowledge, and Warfare in Early Modern Europe, 1680–1740* (Westport: Greenwood Press, 1999); John Lynn, *Giant of the Grand Siècle: The French Army, 1610–1715* (Cambridge: Cambridge University Press, 2006); Guy Rowlands, "Review of *Giant of the Grand Siècle* and *The Wars of Louis XIV*, by John Lynn," *French History*, 14 (2000), 450–454.

especially in the second half of the century.[8] We study their operations and the battles they fought.[9] But discussions of the way these soldiers lived with one another and their superiors are often based on inference from normative texts. For instance, Peter Burschel used articles of war to argue that discipline and control over the common soldier seemed to increase from the sixteenth to the seventeenth century.[10]

Arguments like these sit oddly alongside other impressions of early seventeenth-century military life, like Fritz Redlich's classic presentation of German "military enterprisers" or the diary of the mercenary Peter Hagendorf.[11] Geoffrey Parker's seminal early work on the Spanish Army of Flanders presented proud soldiers willing to agitate for their rights through mutiny, and who did so successfully.[12] The social relations apparent in these accounts include command and obedience, but in this context the frequent calls for military discipline by officers seem more like contemporary non-military laws: Made in profusion but often disobeyed.[13] Meanwhile, David Parrott pointed out that early seventeenth-century French soldiers do not appear to have been trained by drilling but learned how to fight gradually through participation in the military

---

[8] Hubert Salm, *Armeefinanzierung im Dreißigjährigen Krieg: Die Niederrheinisch-Westfälische Reichskreis 1635–1650* (Münster: Aschendorff Verlag, 1990); David Parrott, *Richelieu's Army: War, Government, and Society in France, 1624–1642* (Cambridge: Cambridge University Press, 2006); Guy Rowlands, *The Dynastic State and the Army under Louis XIV: Royal Service and Private Interest 1661–1701* (Cambridge: Cambridge University Press, 2002).

[9] To cite only some recent books, William P. Guthrie, *Battles of the Thirty Years War: From White Mountain to Nördlingen, 1618–1635* (Westport: Greenwood Publishing Group, 2001); William P. Guthrie, *The Later Thirty Years War: From the Battle of Wittstock to the Treaty of Westphalia* (Westport: Greenwood Publishing Group, 2003); Pavel Hrncirik, *Spanier auf dem Albuch: Ein Beitrag zur Geschichte der Schlacht bei Nördlingen im Jahre 1634* (Maastricht: Shaker, 2007); Peter Wilson, *Europe's Tragedy: A New History of the Thirty Years War* (London: Penguin Books, 2009); Lothar Höbelt, *Von Nördlingen bis Janckau: Kaiserliche Strategie und Kriegführung 1634–1645* (Vienna: Heeresgeschichtliches Museum, 2016); Peter Wilson, *Lützen* (Oxford: Oxford University Press, 2018).

[10] Peter Burschel, *Söldner in Nordwestdeutschland des 16. und 17. Jahrhunderts* (Göttingen: Vandenhoeck & Ruprecht, 1994). See also Jan Willem Huntebrinker, *"Fromme Knechte" und "Garteteufel:" Söldner als soziale Gruppe im 16. und 17. Jahrhundert* (Konstanz: UVK, 2010).

[11] Fritz Redlich, *The German Military Enterpriser and his Work Force*, 2 vols. (Wiesbaden: Franz Steiner Verlag, 1964–1965). Peter Hagendorf, *Ein Söldnerleben im Dreißigjährigen Krieg: Eine Quelle zur Sozialgeschichte*, ed. Jan Peters (Berlin: Akademie Verlag, 1993); Geoff Mortimer, *Eyewitness Accounts of the Thirty Years War 1618–1648* (New York: Palgrave Macmillan, 2002), chapter 3.

[12] Geoffrey Parker, *The Army of Flanders and the Spanish Road 1567–1659: The Logistics of Spanish Victory and Defeat in the Low Countries' Wars* (Cambridge: Cambridge University Press, 1972); Geoffrey Parker, "Mutiny and Discontent in the Spanish Army of Flanders, 1572–1607," *Past & Present* 58 (1973), 38–52.

[13] Jürgen Schlumbohm, "Gesetze, die nicht durchgesetzt werden: ein Strukturmerkmal des frühneuzeitlichen Staates?," *Geschichte und Gesellschaft* 23.4 (1997), 647–663.

way of life. If two armies of comparable size met in the field, the deciding factor was probably the length of service of the troops.[14]

Seventeenth-century soldiers and minor officers were often feared and hated by non-soldiers. Whether or not their commanders received glory and honor in the profession of arms, these people were forgotten. Most did not get the chance to articulate their own history. They are therefore an ideal topic for history from below.[15] But, although historians have explored the daily lives of common soldiers, most have focused on the eighteenth century to the present day, not the seventeenth century.[16] On the other hand, many German works on war and society in the early seventeenth century explore non-soldiers' experiences of war or interactions between soldiers and civilians, rather than soldiers' interactions with one another.[17]

This book aims to present this history from below through the microhistorical account of a single regiment raised in Saxony by Wolf von Mansfeld in spring 1625 in the service of the King of Spain. The infantry had 2,545 men on the rolls at its highest recorded point and the cavalry comprised 979 horses.[18] This regiment traveled from Dresden to northern Italy in summer 1625, where it settled near Milan. Because the governments of Alessandria and Cremona could not obtain financing at the right time, it mutinied and fell apart in 1627.

---

[14] David Parrott, "Strategy and Tactics in the Thirty Years War: The 'Military Revolution'," in *The Military Revolution Debate: Readings on the Military Transformation of Early Modern Europe*, Clifford J. Rogers, ed. (New York: Routledge, 1995); Parrott, *Richelieu's Army*.

[15] E. P. Thompson, "History from Below," *The Times Literary Supplement* (1966), 279; Tim Hitchcock, Peter King, and Pamela Sharpe, eds. *Chronicling Poverty: The Voices and Strategies of the English Poor, 1640–1840* (Basingstoke: Macmillan, 1997); Tim Hitchcock, "A New History from Below," *History Workshop Journal* 57 (2004), 294–298.

[16] Stephen Brumwell, *Redcoats: The British Soldier and War in the Americas, 1755–1763* (Cambridge: Cambridge University Press, 2006); Ilya Berkovich, *Motivation in War: The Experience of Common Soldiers in Old-Regime Europe* (Cambridge: Cambridge University Press, 2017).

[17] Benigna von Krusenstjern and Hans Medick, eds. *Zwischen Alltag und Katastrophe: Der Dreißigjährige Krieg aus der Nähe* (Göttingen: Vandenhoeck & Ruprecht, 1998); the works put out by the Arbeitskreis Militär und Gesellschaft in der Frühen Neuzeit eV; Maron Lorenz, *Das Rad der Gewalt: Miliär und Zivilbevölkerung in Norddeutschland nach dem Dreißigjährigen Krieg* (Cologne: Böhlau Verlag, 2007); Huntebrinker, *"Fromme Knechte" und "Garteteufel."*

[18] Figures derived from lists in SHStADr 10024 9239/2, *Die Beiden in Italien Stehenden Regimenter des Graffen Wolfgang von Mansfeld: Schreibem Desselben An die Unterbefehlshaber, des Rechnungswerk, die Abdankung d.a. bet 1626-28*, 54–82; StadtA Ulm Kriegsamtes A [5556], *Verzeichnis des Kriegsvolks zu Pferd und Fuß* by Wachmeister Christoph Revelheimer, Aufstellung der Mansfeldischen Kavallerie.

This unimportant regiment happens to be unusually well-documented. Its passage and its quartering are recorded in primary-source documents from southern Germany and northern Italy, while I analyze the effect of its presence on local Italian communities by tracking demographic data from unpublished parish archival records. Strikingly, most of this regiment's internal legal documents also survive. Mattheus Steiner, regimental secretary, not only copied the transcripts of the trials over which he presided, but also records of inquests, soldiers' IOUs, letters to members of the regiment relating to legal cases, last testaments, criminal investigations, and tickets certifying the bearer was honorable. The first two of these three *Gerichtsbücher,* "court books," handle the legal matters of the Mansfeld infantry. The third, incomplete, covers the cavalry. The historian Jan Wilem Huntebrinker cited the first book, but the investigation of this regiment, and what a Saxon regiment was doing in Philip IV's service, was outside the scope of his work.[19] The other two Mansfeld Regiment books were filed separately from the first and may never have been seen after 1628. Although these three are the only regimental legal books I have seen, they were almost certainly not the only ones that were produced.

These big flat Mansfeld legal books seized and still seize me with what Arlette Farge described when encountering eighteenth-century Paris police archives. "It is a rare and precious feeling to suddenly come across so many forgotten lives, haphazard and full, juxtaposing and entangling the close with the distant, the departed." The ordinary records of a working legal apparatus like eighteenth-century Paris police records or early seventeenth-century regimental documents (regiments were legal establishments) are not the same as documents which were deliberately framed for some posterity: "Even the most intimate personal notebook ... nonetheless presupposes that whoever wrote it was in some fundamental way looking for it to be discovered, in the belief that the events of his or her life called for a written record. There is none of this in the archives." The Mansfelders wanted to leave written records, like last testaments. Their trial transcripts, their lawsuits and squabbles, like Farge's subjects' records, "were recorded for an altogether different reason. This changes everything ... the relationship we have to it, particularly our feeling of being in contact with the real." Whether or not it is accurate, this feeling "is intense and stubborn, perhaps even invasive."[20]

---

[19] Huntebrinker, *"Fromme Knechte" und "Garteteufel,"* 40. Mansfeld's Italian expedition is also documented in Barbara Stadler, *Pappenheim und die Zeit des Dreissigjährigen Krieges* (Winterthur: Gemsberg-Verlag, 1991), 154–156.

[20] Arlette Farge, *The Allure of the Archives* (New Haven: Yale University Press, 2013), 7–9.

Supplementing these sources, I also use seventeenth-century documents which describe other soldiers and other armies. These works are variegated and idiosyncratic; they were produced for many reasons and cannot be constrained in a single genre. They are rich sources for early modern society and the lives of ordinary human beings.[21] Although the writings of ordinary people are not clear windows on the past, if we read them actively and critically, they enable us to analyze the interactions of the people recorded in them. Through close reading, I attempt to piece together the lives of the Mansfelders and other soldiers to analyze common soldiers' words and actions within the social and economic contexts of central Europe in the 1620s.

All the human chatter on which I eavesdrop here took place in German, French, Latin, Spanish, and Italian, the native language of the civilians in the area, and the administrative language of many Spanish officials. The snappy polyglot sizzle of seventeenth-century soldiers' German is difficult to translate. The Mansfeld Regiment had its own slang. To *pull from leather* is to draw your sword, to *take care of your own earthworks* is to mind your business. On Christmas Eve 1626, Stefan Spizer was sitting in front of the door to his quarters when a tailor came running down from the village. As Mattheus Steiner recorded it, the tailor yelled what sounded like *"Für dich, Soldat, Becce futui:"* "For you, soldier, I fucked your mouth!" in German, Italian, and perfect Latin. As the tailor had probably said it, it was "becco fottuto," the billy goat, a common slur in this region for soldiers. In any language, the tailor had been looking for a fight, and he got one. The two chased each other through town until Spizer cornered him behind a woodpile and killed him.[22]

These were violent men. If soldiers were not becoming more disciplined during the early seventeenth century, we might be able to conclude that they were the rootless, marauding thugs of stereotypes of the Thirty Years War. However, a statistical analysis of soldiers from the entire Saxon army during the entire war indicates that most Saxon soldiers were recruited near their homes and, unlike the Mansfelders, probably served

---

[21] The literature on ego-documents, self-writing, and self-narrative is vast. See, for instance, Mary Fullbrook and Ulinka Rublack, "In Relation: The 'Social Self' and Ego-Documents," *German History* 28.3 (2010), 263–272; Kaspar von Greyerz, "Observation on the Historiographical Status of Research on Self-Writing," in *Mapping the "I": Research on Self-Narratives in Germany and Switzerland*, Claudia Ulbrich, Lorenz Heiligensetzer, and Kaspar von Greyerz, eds. (Leiden: Brill, 2015), 34–57; Lorenz Heiligensetzer, "Swiss-German Self-Narratives: The Archival Project as a Rich Vein of Research," in *Mapping the "I": Research on Self-Narratives in Germany and Switzerland*, Claudia Ulbrich, Lorenz Heiligensetzer, and Kaspar von Greyerz, eds. (Leiden: Brill, 2015), 58–75.
[22] SHStADr 10024 9739/6, 110.

nearby. This large statistical study also enabled me to analyze pay in the Saxon army in the 1620s. Since soldiers' pay can be used as a proxy for their social status within the regiment, my study of pay also functions as an analysis of the unexpectedly high social complexity within military units.

This book follows the Mansfeld Regiment from mustering-in to dissolution, with breaks for topics like soldiers' places of origin, pay, religion, or social class, and with flash-backs and flash-forwards. The "thick descriptions" of the interactions of Mansfelders with one another and outsiders demonstrate social organization within the regiment, and personal relationships at the intersection of structural organization and individual emotion.

The story of these men suggests that some older interpretations of early seventeenth-century military life need revision. While the Mansfeld Regiment's career and statistical studies of the Saxon army demonstrate the expanding and ramifying networks of international military finance that developed during the sixteenth and seventeenth centuries, I found neither an intensification of military discipline nor unadulterated thuggishness. The military community was made up of systems of relationships that were subtle, intricate, and disorganized. Changing opinions of elites about drill and discipline rarely touched daily life in the regiment, but the Mansfeld Regiment's career and its collapse were influenced by developments in Italian and German finance, which were broad and spreading, but deeply imperfect.

1 Display All Good Will and Keep Moving
The Mansfeld Regiment and the 1625–1627 Campaign

Months later, after he stabbed his wife twelve times but before the Mansfeld Regiment mutinied and disbanded itself, Theodoro de Camargo told the enigmatic regimental bailiff Mattheus Steiner he had never wanted to go to Lombardy in the first place.

Theodoro de Camargo was a nobleman from Brabant, and the lieutenant colonel of the Mansfeld infantry.[1] He had been an officer for a long time. Four years previously at the Battle of Neuhäusel, the Count of Buquoy, commanding the Imperial army, took two lance blows and died in Camargo's arms.[2] Camargo was with the Spanish at the siege of Breda and after the city fell in summer 1625, the Governor of the Spanish Netherlands entrusted him to take the news to the Emperor.[3] It was to repeat this success, according to a chronicler in Alessandria, that the Imperialist-Spanish campaign into northern Italy was launched.[4] When Camargo arrived in Vienna, Wolf von Mansfeld was canvassing a regiment for this campaign and wanted him to take command of the foot. Camargo answered that he was already serving Infanta Isabella and could not accept another office, but after Ferdinand II wrote to Brussels the Infanta released him from her service and Ferdinand ordered him to take command of Mansfeld's infantry. Camargo had no further excuse and joined the regiment in late 1625. His wife, Victoria Guarde, followed:

---

[1] Joseph van den Leene, *Le theatre de la noblesse du Brabant, representant les erections des terres, seigneuries, & noms des personnes, & des familles titrées, les creations des chevaleries, & octroys des marques d'honneurs & de noblesse: Accordez par les princes souverains ducs de Brabant, jusques au roy Philippe v. a present regnant. Divisé en trois parties, enrichies des genealogies, alliances, quartiers, epitaphes, & d'autres recherches anciennes & modernes* (Liege: J. F. Broncaert, 1705), 359.

[2] Milos Kouřil, *Documenta Bohemica bellum tricennale illustrantia*, Tomus III: *Der Kampf des Hauses Habsburg gegen die Niederlande & ihre Verbündeten: Quellen zur Geschichte des Pfälzisch-Niederländisch-Ungarischen Krieges, 1621–1625* (Prague: Academica, 1976), No. 140, 66.

[3] SHStADr 10024 9119/38, 125–127; Herman Hugo, "The Siege of Breda by the Armes of Philip, 1627," in *English Recusant Literature 1558–1640*, vol. 261, D. M. Rogers, ed. (London: Scolar Press, nd), 141–142.

[4] "Ripiando i sucessi del la Patria, dico, che vennero mese di giugno in Alessandria tre Regimenti de Alemania ..." Girolamo Ghilini, *Annali di Alessandria, overo Le Cose Accadvte in esta Città: Nel suo, el Circonvincino Territorio dall'Anno dell'Origine Sua Sino al M.DC.LIX* (Milan: Gioseffo Marelli, 1666), 204.

By now, she was openly cuckolding him.[5] He killed her less than six months later.

Officers who served the Spanish Habsburgs commonly moved into the service of the Imperial Habsburgs and vice versa.[6] Theodoro de Camargo was a subject of the King of Spain and Infanta Isabella who went to Lombardy in the King of Spain's service because the Emperor requested it. His colonel, Wolf von Mansfeld, was the feudal subject of the Elector of Saxony and an Imperial civil servant, and his regiment, raised in Saxony, was going to war for the King of Spain.

For years the Spanish Monarchy and its allies had been fighting France and its allies over northern Italy. The little war that preceded this one had been over control of the Valtelline. This was the shortest and most comfortable route between Tyrol, which belonged to the Archduke of Further Austria, and Milan, second only to Flanders in the system of the Spanish Monarchy in Europe: An exposed synapse between two Habsburg territories north to south. It was an important node on the braid of routes by which Spain sent money, supplies, and troops back and forth between the Netherlands and Milan. East to west the Valtelline was also a trade route between the Kingdom of France and its ally the Republic of Venice, and it abutted land belonging to Venice for thirty miles.[7] The Valtelline had been a focus of French and Spanish foreign policy for decades. For Spain it was the "gate and outer wall of Milan," the doorway to the Alps, and it was controlled largely by heretics.[8]

But not entirely. The Valtelline had been controlled by the Three Leagues or *Bünde*, three Swiss associations called the League of God's House, the League of the Ten Jurisdictions, and the Gray League, or *Grisons*. Spain and France had been cultivating different factions in this federation since the late sixteenth century. Sometimes the pro-Habsburg Catholic faction predominated in local politics, sometimes the anti-Habsburg Calvinist faction. Whoever was on top established rigged courts to punish prominent members of the other side.[9] In 1618, radical young Protestant clerics in the anti-Habsburg faction set up a court in Thusis to purge the region of Habsburg hegemony and Catholics. Some

---

[5] SHStADr 10024 9119/38, 128–129.
[6] Gregory Hanlon, *The Twilight of a Military Tradition: Italian Aristocrats and European Conflicts, 1560–1800* (London: Routledge, 2014).
[7] Parker, *Army of Flanders and the Spanish Road*, 62–63; C. V. Wedgwood, *The Thirty Years War* (New York: New York Review Books Classics, 2005), 33.
[8] Andreas Wendland, *Der Nutzen der Pässe und die Gefährdung der Seelen: Spanien, Mailand und der Kampf ums Weltlin (1620–1641)* (Zürich: Chronos Verlag, 1995).
[9] Silvio Färber, "Bündner Wirren," *Historisches Lexicon der Schweiz/Dictionaire Historique de la Suisse/Dizionario Storico della Svizzera* (Basel: Schwabe Verlag, 2001).

of the Catholic notables in the region, in contact with Milan and Rome, conspired against them and, on the night of July 18, 1620, armed Catholics marched down the valley, killing every Protestant they found. The governor of Milan sent troops to seal off the valley and the killings lasted for fifteen days. Habsburg troops garrisoned the valley, which was lost to the Three Leagues.[10]

During his lifetime, Henri IV had secured the Valtelline passes for French use; that access cut off, his successor Louis XIII pursued a diplomatic approach at first. In 1621, the French diplomat François de Bassompierre went to Madrid to negotiate, but, although the Spanish government agreed in the ensuing Treaty of Madrid to recognize the sovereignty of the Three Leagues over the Valtelline, it used the treaty's guarantee of free worship for Catholics as an excuse to keep troops in the area. Louis threatened military intervention in 1622; in response, papal troops were brought in, supposedly to protect the religion of local Catholics, and Spanish troops continued to use the passes with impunity.[11] On February 7, 1623, France, Venice, and the Duke of Savoy formed an alliance to put the Three Leagues back in control. Richelieu became Louis XIII's chief minister in April 1624. That summer he began preparations for a military expedition into the region.[12]

This expedition, under François-Hannibal d'Estrées, Marquis de Coeuvres, has been overshadowed by the later French incursion under Henri de Rohan in 1635. But these armies were not inconsiderable. De Coeuvres had more than seven regiments under him: One of Three Leaguers recruited secretly in Zürich, two Three Leagues regiments recruited in their own dominions, three Swiss regiments, one French regiment of infantry, and ten companies of French cavalry.[13] Venice sent a battery of guns all the way from the arsenal in Brescia.[14] On the Spanish side, Milan was the center of Spanish power in Italy, and the nexus and training ground of Spain's army in the region. The small Mansfeld Regiment was added to a total military force numbering six or seven

---

[10] Parker, *Army of Flanders and the Spanish Road*, 64; Wendland, *Der Nutzen der Pässe und die Gefährdung der Seelen*, 111–116.

[11] John H. Elliott, *The Count-Duke of Olivares: The Statesman in an Age of Decline* (New Haven: Yale University Press, 1986), 62, 72, 83; A. Lloyd Moote, *Louis XIII, The Just* (Berkeley: University of California Press, 1989), 134–135.

[12] Jacques Humbert, "En Valtelline avec le Marquis de Coeuvres," *Revue Historique de l'Armée* 14 (1958) 47–67, 49.

[13] Ibid., 49.

[14] Giulio Ongaro and Simone Signaroli, *I cannoni di Guspessa. I comuni di Edolo, Cortenedolo e Mu alle soglie della Guerra dei Trent'Anni (1624–1625)* (Valle Camonica: Pubblicazioni del Servizio Archivistico Comprensoriale di Valle Camonica, 2016).

tercios, more than 20,000 men.[15] This force embarked on October 26. The roads were iced over by November, but this force managed to liberate the Valtelline by mid-December and drive the papal troops out of their fortresses.[16]

The Duke of Feria, Governor of the Duchy of Milan, said "the water was up to his neck." He withdrew units from Sardinia and Naples, took out a loan from Genoa, and raised troops with the Emperor's help. A captain's patent for this endeavor survives from December 6, 1624.[17] One of the Imperial colonels raising and leading troops for the Spanish army was the Count of Pappenheim, looking for an opportunity to take Spanish service.[18] He may have already had a reputation in Italy. Peter Hagendorf mentioned him while he was fighting for Venice in 1625: "in the Valtelline, there the King in Spain was our enemy, how now count Pappenheim arrived, he powerfully harried us with fieldpieces and drove us out of the Valtelline from our positions, so we had to give way all the way to Turin ..."[19]

In March 1625, French and Savoyard forces struck Spain's client state Genoa as part of a coordinated action which was also supposed to include contingents from England and the United Netherlands. In response, Spain brought troops north from Naples and mobilized its allies. Both Parma and Modena sent troops to Lombardy; the ships carrying the Neapolitan reinforcements were Tuscan.[20] Imperial German reinforcements arrived that summer.

Wolfgang, Count of Mansfeld (1575–1638), was one of the Imperial colonels who raised troops for the defense of Milan.[21] Mansfeld was a member of a large and powerful family with ties to both Electoral Saxony and the Imperial administration. The dynasty hailed from Eisleben, birthplace of Martin Luther – to be precise, the fortress of Mansfeld,

---

[15] Alessandra Dattero, "Towards a New Social Category: The Military," in *A Companion to Late Medieval and Early Modern Milan: The Distinctive Features of an Italian State*, Andrea Gamberini, ed. (Leiden: Brill, 2015), 465.
[16] Humbert, "En Valtelline," 51–55.
[17] Stadler, *Pappenheim*, 156. The patent from December 6, 1624 is cited in footnote 34 on the same page.
[18] Ibid., 154–156.
[19] "In feltlin, da Ist *der köngnieg In spangen*, vnser feindt gewessen, wie nun graff *pabpenheim* Ankommen Ist, hat er vns mit stugken mechtig zugesedtzet vndt vns aus feltelin von vnser posten vertrieben, das wir haven must weichen bis nach turan ..." Hagendorf, *Ein Söldnerleben im Dreißigjährigen Krieg*, 37.
[20] Hanlon, *Twilight*, 106–110.
[21] Stadler, *Pappenheim*, 160. The other Imperialist colonels who raised troops on behalf of the Spanish Monarchy for the 1625–1626 conflict in northern Italy were Christian von Ilow, Hannibal von Schauenburg, Wilhelm Salentin von Salm, Alois von Baldiron, and Alwig von Sulz.

perched above the little city Tal Mansfeld, five and a half miles from Eisleben.[22] Called "one of the most important, if now forgotten, commanders of the middle stage of the war" by Peter Wilson, Mansfeld was an Imperial Privy Councilor and a member of the Imperial Chamber.[23] Two of his four brothers were also Imperial officers: His younger brother Bruno von Mansfeld was the Imperial master of the hunt, an influential position in the court of an Emperor who hunted as much as Ferdinand II. Ferdinand died in Bruno's arms.[24] Bruno and the rest of Wolf's brothers converted to Catholicism by the turn of the century. Wolfgang himself was a Catholic sympathizer by the time his regiment went to Italy, and he converted a few years later.

Multiple and possibly conflicting loyalties like these were not unusual for Saxons. Saxony was the most powerful Protestant state in the Empire. It repeatedly acted as a broker in negotiations or attempted negotiations, a center of gravity for smaller moderate Protestant political entities. Elector Johann Georg I's policies can appear enigmatic or indecisive. Although Wedgwood is broadly sympathetic to him, he did not come off well in nineteenth-century historiography.[25] But this deeply conservative man pursued a consistent policy from his point of view, attempting to uphold the constitution of the Empire as he saw it. On the other hand, some of his nobles did not agree with his decision to go to war against the rebellious Bohemian Estates, "their dear neighbours, their friends through blood and other ties, and also their co-religionists."[26]

The Elector of Saxony's irenic viewpoint explains why early seventeenth-century Electoral policy – and the actions of some Saxons, like Mansfeld and some of his officers – was not only pro-Imperial but also pro-Habsburg and pro-Spain. Saxony had been the birthplace of the Lutheran Reformation and most of the Electors, until Augustus the Strong, were devoutly Lutheran. But to contemporaries, including many Saxons, early seventeenth-century Electoral Saxon policy sometimes ended up looking more "Catholic" than "Protestant" because of its support for both sections of the Habsburg dynasty.[27] Despite the feelings

---

[22] Robert J. Christman, *Doctrinal Controversy and Lay Religiosity in Late Reformation Germany* (Leiden: Brill, 2011), 15–17.
[23] Wilson, *Europe's Tragedy*, 398–399.
[24] Felix Stieve, "Mansfeld, Graf Bruno III Von," *Allgemeine Deutsche Biographie*, Vol. 20 (Leipzig: Duncker & Humblot, 1884), 221.
[25] Wedgwood, *The Thirty Years War*, 62–65.
[26] F. L. Carsten, *Princes and Parliaments in Germany from the Fifteenth to the Eighteenth Century* (Oxford: Oxford University Press, 1959), 229.
[27] Axel Gotthard, "'Politice seint wir bäpstisch.' Kursachsen und der deutsche Protestantismus im frühen 17. Jahrhundert," *Zeitschrift für Historische Forschung* 20 (1993), 275–319.

of some of their nobles, Saxon Electors maintained a good relationship with Spain from 1575. This served the interests of both Saxony and Spain since Spanish foreign policy during the reign of Philip II sought to maintain the balance of power within the Empire. The King of Spain pursued relationships with several important Protestant powers if they were not Calvinist, like Saxony or Brandenburg. Philip II thought Saxony would be able to foster peace within the Empire and hoped that Elector August of Saxony (1526–1586) would influence the Palatinate. August did not support the Dutch against the Monarchy of Spain, even though one of his daughters married William the Silent in 1561. Regular written exchanges between August and Philip II began after April 1576, when Emperor Maximilian II visited Dresden.[28]

Caught between conflicting obligations, Saxony pulled hard for peace at the start of the Thirty Years War but failed; the Electorate entered the war on the Emperor's side, despite a lack of enthusiasm on the part of his more Bohemian-oriented nobles. During the 1620s the Imperialist coalition including Saxony won a series of victories. Wolf von Mansfeld commanded the Saxon army in successful campaigns in Upper and Lower Lusatia, conquering them from the Bohemian Estates.

The last Saxon troops were demobilized in March 1625 and the Electorate did not raise another army until early 1631, several months before it re-entered the war, this time against the Emperor.[29] This changing alignment was informed by Johann Georg I's distrust of both Catholic absolutism and the threat Calvinism posed to the Imperial constitution: Saxony's 1631–1634 alliance with Sweden was an aberration in an otherwise pro-Imperial foreign policy. In early to mid-1625 Saxony was not at war, and Saxons who were familiar with fighting would have been available for this expedition to Italy. So was Mansfeld himself, the Elector's former lieutenant general.

According to Wolf von Mansfeld, the Duke of Feria promised him his regiment would only be in Lombardy for a short time. It came in as a reinforcement "to refresh [*rafrescar*] the others."[30] One Italian chronicler believed that, had the Mansfelders not arrived to cover the Spanish

---

[28] Friedrich Edelmayer, *Söldner und Pensionäre: Das Netzwerk Philipps II im Heiligen Römischen Reich* (Vienna: R. Oldenbourg Verlag, 2002), chapter 6.

[29] Lucian Staiano-Daniels, "Determining Early Modern Army Strength: The Case of Electoral Saxony," *Journal of Military History* 83.4 (2019), 1000–1020, tables 1, 2, and 3.

[30] SHStADr 10024 9737/13, 80. Rough draft of letter from Wolf von Mansfeld to the Duke of Feria, April 1, 1626.

retreat, they would not have been able to withdraw from the siege of Verrua without risking the artillery and losing many men.[31]

Although they were not yet legally a regiment, since they had not sworn their sacred oaths to their flags, their officers, and the King of Spain, the Mansfelders began to travel in late May 1625.[32] The infantry looped southwest from Dresden around the mountains separating Bohemia from southern Germany, then south. On June 26, Mansfeld wrote the Bishop of Bamberg from Dresden requesting passage. "About Yr. Gr.'s land, part of my officers of horse as well as of foot must stir themselves to march in it" he said obsequiously,

> and therefore I find the need hereunder to obediently entreat Yr. Grace with my entirely obedient plea to graciously condescend to the same, to let your officials and subordinates [*Undtanen*] allow this, with which my officers with the soldiers they have with them will not only pass freely through your land and territories but also the same would display all good will and keep moving, and where they might be allowed to overnight.[33]

The Bishop of Bamberg forwarded a copy to the Bishop of Würzburg on July 8 and gave the regiment a pass since Mansfeld was upholding the constitution of the Reich.[34]

By mid-July many Mansfeld infantry were south of Bamberg and Würzburg. Amid local stories like the birth of a large baby the size of a

---

[31] "Ma doue con la celerità si sarebbe portato via felicemente questa Piazza; pero lentamente caminando, cagione, che il Principe Tomaso infestasse la Retroguardia con danno di vn Regimento Alemano del Lillo [sic: Ilow], Feria stimando più la Piazza di quello, che in sostanza era, il tempo che spese in fortificarsi, diede tempo al Duca di Sauoia di entrare in Crescentino, di doue introdusse in Verruua soldati, e munitioni: e si riduceua ad impossibilita poco meno, cauare frutto dall'assedio di Verruua, se non si assicuraua di Crescentino. Essendo in elettione del Duca di Feria per la carica di Maestro di Campo Generale il pigliare o D. Gonzalo di Cordoua, o'l Marchese di Montenegro, mostrò d'inchinare più nel Cordoua suo Cognato, et era appunto all'hora arriuato di Fiandra doppo la resa di Bredà D. Gonzalo, ad eßercitare questa carica; e però hauendo il Cordoua disposto quell'assedio, ne eßendo riuscita l'impresa, corse voce, ch'egli hauesse trascurato, ne si sà perche, la gloria del Conato; Sia com'eßere si voglia, l'assedio duro molto tempo, e vi si persero tanti huomini per le sortite delli Assediati malamente riparate, per la infirmità introdotte da i patimenti, e per la disubidienza de' Capi Alemani, ch'erano in maggior numero del resto dell'Eßercito, che bisognò senza pericolo levarsene, et è certo, che se non giongeva il Conte di Masfelt di Germania con vn Regimento fresco, con che si spallegiò la ritrata, era difficil' il poterlo fare senz' arrischiare l'Artiglieria, e perdere molti Soldati." Giovanni Francesco Fossati, *Memorie historiche delle guerre d'Italia del secolo presente* (Milan: Filippo Ghisolfi, 1639), 89–90.

[32] SHStADr 10024 9119/38, 8.

[33] Copy of letter from Wolf von Mansfeld to Bishop of Bamberg, June 16/26, 1625, StAWu Lehensachen 3087.

[34] Letter from Bishop of Bamberg to Bishop of Würzburg, July 8, 1625, StAWu Lehensachen 3087.

two-month-old child, one Nuremberg chronicle noted that 2,500 infantry and a portion of the cavalry "under the Colonel Count Wolffen von Mansfellt" came through the city in little groups from July 14 to 19, bound for Günzburg, between Augsburg and Ulm. One hundred and fifty horses and 150 foot soldiers came by a day later on July 20, and 300 more horses on the 29th. This chronicler knew this regiment was intended to "form a force of 3,000 on foot, and 1,000 horse, for the Estado de Milan."[35] Unlike the bishops of Bamberg and Würzburg, the city of Nuremburg did not want Mansfeld's *"Undisciplinirt[es] Volck"* anywhere near them.[36] They eventually decided to give the cavalry bread and beer, but no money.[37]

On July 19, Leopold, Archduke of Further Austria, reported he had heard from the Mansfeld Regiment's quartermaster Wolf Winckelmann that 800 men had arrived near Lindau.[38] By August 1625 both infantry and cavalry were in towns near Ulm.[39] Late that month, some of the infantry were near Lake Constance: The deserters Phillip Appelt and Jacob Bötger thought they could make it there from the tiny nearby town of Taubenhof.[40]

The infantry and cavalry traveled in small groups, and dispersed into small towns by company or smaller units.[41] Even the best roads were little more than dirt tracks and would be ruined by a big convoy, nor could the soldiers support themselves off the land in their full numbers.[42]

---

[35] "Der 4. 5. bis 9 Juli sint bey 2500 man zu fus troppenweis vhnbroche [...] volk vnter der Obristen Graff Wolffen von Mansfellt fur Italia gehörich hier fierüben auff der Musterblatz nach Güntzburg zwischen Augspurg vnd Ulm *marsiert* ... 10 Jul: 150 pfert Mansfeldisch volk fierüber *marsirt*, vnd gleich des fus volks weg vnd Quartier genomen ... den 19 Juli sint abermahl 300 pfert Mansfeltisch hier fürüber vff der Musterplatz marsirt, welcher eine *armee* vor 3000 zu fus, vnd 1000 pferd solle richten, vor der Mayländischen *Stato*." UCLA Library Special Collections MS *170/355, *Der Anndre Thaill Nurembergische Cronica*, 348v. Personal chronicles seem to have been popular in Nuremberg; numerous examples survive either of chronicles entirely made up by individuals or families, or commercially available chronicles with space for the owner to add his or her own records.

[36] SHStADr 10024 9205/3, *Der Stadt Nürnberg Schreiben an den Kaiserl. General Grafen Wolfgang Mansfeldt, die Durchmarsche, Einquartirungen ü Kriegs [...] 1625 Dergl. an den Herzog v. Friedland 1627*, Document 2, June 29, 1625.

[37] SHStADr 10024 9205/3, Document 4, July 18, 1625.

[38] SHStADr 10024 9734/8, *Allerhand bestallunge vor Graff Wolffen von Mannsfeld theils von Keysser Rudolfo, Matthia, Ferdinando II, Churfurst Christiano II und Johann Georg I zu Sachsen, 1597–1626,* July 19, 1625.

[39] StadtA Ulm Kriegsamtes A [5556], *Verzeichnis des Kriegsvolks zu Pferd und Fuß* by Wachmeister Christoph Revelheimer, Aufstellung der Mansfeldischen Kavallerie.

[40] SHStADr 10024 9119/38, 25.

[41] Alessandro Buono, *Esercito, istituzioni, territorio: Alloggiamenti militari e "case herme" nello Stato di Milano (secoli XVI e XVII)* (Florence: Firenze University Press, 2009), 22.

[42] Lund, *War for the Every Day*, 107–108.

Towns along the way were usually too small to house more than a little contingent of soldiers.[43] Mansfelders were strung out in dribs and drabs along the roads between southern Germany and northern Italy for months that summer *truppenweise*, "in troops." Individuals would have traveled between these little groups constantly: Deserters, whores, children, officers carrying information back and forth, soldiers visiting friends in other companies, running errands for themselves or their superiors. The frequent passage of units like the Mansfelders along the military roads between northern Italy and southern Germany devastated local communities, and country priests moved services from one chapel to another because the transit of soldiers desecrated them.[44]

Letters about quartering circulated. Conflicts between mercenaries and non-soldiers sharing a small dwelling against their will were inevitable, but Mansfeld's soldiers were not given enough money to cover their expenses. They extorted supplies from their hosts.[45] "When I arrived today in this city I understood with the greatest displeasure and perturbation of spirit the coldness with which my cavalry was received in their bands, wanting (after having shared much work, and ~~employed great expense~~) (done more than obligation carried) to maintain them in the quarters on four batzen a day," Mansfeld wrote the Duke of Feria on September 17.[46]

Research has been done on local support for military transit and quartering in Spanish Lombardy. The *egualanza generale*, instituted in 1590, guaranteed a system in which Milanese provinces all contributed to the same extent to maintain troops; areas where soldiers were quartered were reimbursed.[47] Confraternities and charitable organizations were founded and provided with tax-exempt capital, which offered liquidity to occupied communities.[48] Villages also formed corporations to provide specialized military housing and equipment like bedding.[49]

---

[43] Parker, *Army of Flanders and the Spanish Road*, 87.
[44] Luca Gianna, 'Frammenti di luoghi. Le valli Belbo e Bormida di Spigno nel Piemonte dell'età moderna', in *Lo spazio politico locale in età medievale, moderna e contemporanea. Atti del Convegno internazionale di studi*, Renato Bordone, Paola Guglielmotti, Sandro Lombardini, and Angelo Torre, eds. (Alessandria: Edizioni dell'Orso, 2007), 177–190.
[45] Lorenz, *Das Rad der Gewalt*.
[46] Rough draft of letter from Wolf von Mansfeld to the Duke of Feria, September 17, 1625, SHStADr 10024 9737/13, 24.
[47] Giulio Ongaro, *Peasants and Soldiers: The Management of the Venetian Military Structure in the Mainland Dominion between the 16th and 17th Centuries* (New York: Routledge, 2017), 180–181.
[48] Ibid., 188. [49] Buono, *Esercito, istituzioni, territorio*, 179–187.

Although Spanish military officials oversaw and directed this process, these communities managed supplies and lodging themselves.[50]

Venetian territories were like Spanish Lombardy in social and institutional structures.[51] As in Lombardy, armies in the Terraferma were housed through public–private action, which Giulio Ongaro has analyzed in detail. Under the state's aegis, communities sold hay to soldiers, or rented housing, bedding, and pallets to them. Military commissions were also important to the local labor market: Locals worked as drivers or gunsmiths, or on military construction projects. Effects were specific. In the small Piedmontese village of Pancalieri, requests from armies had a negative effect on agriculture for personal consumption but incentivized production for the military market.[52] Similarly, quartering in the Veneto resulted in burdens for some and advantages for others, like non-soldiers who were already locally important or members of families that were. Cooperation with military demands kept money within communities in the provinces Ongaro studied, and redistributed assets within those communities, but most of the profit was concentrated in the hands of a few families, who invested what they made.[53]

Military developments in Spanish Lombardy took place within a Eurasia-wide growth, development, and complication of human networks. Administrations knitted themselves together through cooperation with local elites: Similar public–private interaction happened in Spanish Lombardy, Venice, Piedmont, France, the Holy Roman Empire, and the Ottoman Empire. Traditional means of obtaining military resources remained, but changed; for instance, many contributions changed from in-kind to cash.[54] Government interventions increased. In general, early modern political entities "developed an increasingly greater capability of *imposition* of burdens and of *supervision* of the functioning of fiscal and military structures, while the day-to-day practicalities of *management* remained unseen by the eyes of the state" and handled by private agents.[55]

But actions and interactions like the ones that supplied, fed, and housed the Mansfeld Regiment were also regionally specific, even individually specific.[56] Although the documents created by Mansfelders themselves give the impression almost of a regiment in a bubble, Italian

---

[50] Ongaro, *Peasants and Soldiers*, 207.   [51] Ibid.,180.   [52] Ibid., 191.
[53] Ibid., ch. 6, 143.   [54] Ibid., 185.   [55] Ibid., 207.
[56] I make this argument for Hesse rather than northern Italy in Lucian Staiano-Daniels, "Two Weeks in Summer: Soldiers and Others in Occupied Hesse-Cassel 14–25 July 1625," *War in History* 30.2 (2022), 1–25.

sources reveal that Wolf von Mansfeld and his officers were in regular contact not only with the world around them, but with their superiors in Milan and local officials like Camillo Capoletto, paymaster of the office of soldiers' lodging in Cremona.

The Mansfeld infantry settled in Busto Arsizio, Gallarate, Samarate, and Legnano, just northwest of Milan, surrounded by low mountains, right before the valley opens and sweeps down to that great unlovely city, heaped inside its double walls and smoke over it.[57] Busto Arsizio was a big fortified town, an *oppidum* in Latin, known for its wire-drawing, and some of its wire was exported as far as the Levant.[58] Gallarate was a market town five miles northwest, a crossroads like Domodossola to the north. Many of its people were artificers, and a market was held every Sunday with commodities from Milan, the provinces of Novara and Vercelli, towns and villages in Lugano, and the Bergamasque.[59]

The Mansfeld cavalry was quartered south of Milan, moving among Casale Montferratto, Alessandria, and towns and rural territory near these cities. On November 12, they left for the siege of Verrua to cover the Duke of Feria as he raised an army.[60] After that, three of its companies remained in Pontestura and seven companies took quarters in Cremona.[61] Although it is better documented in external German and Italian sources, the cavalry is less well attested in the Mansfeld Regiment's own sources than the infantry, with one incomplete legal book to the infantry's two complete ones, perhaps because Mattheus Steiner had traveled with Wolfgang Winckelmann's infantry company. A Mansfelder cavalry secretary of unknown rank died in a fire in Rammingen on the night of August 10/11, 1625.[62] His death may be another reason for the slim documentation.

---

[57] For discussions of Florence as "beautiful" and Milan as "great," see Stefano D'Amico, *Spanish Milan: A City Within the Empire, 1535–1706* (London: Palgrave Macmillan, 2012), 9.

[58] Ibid., 17.

[59] Domenico Sella, *Crisis and Continuity: The Economy of Spanish Lombardy in the Seventeenth Century* (Cambridge, MA: Harvard University Press, 1979), 14.

[60] "Alli 12 si partirolo andato sotto Verrua per aiutare il detto Duca di Feria che non ardiva levare il suo esercito, per paura di essere assalito dai nemici, quali si trovavano più avantagiosi degli spagnuoli. Il detto Duca di Feria si è fatto portare a Pontestura sotto pretesto di essere infermo due giorni avanti che giungessero al campo li detti soldati Allemanni del Conte di Mansfelt." Gioanni Domenico Bremio, *Cronaca monferrina (1613–1661) di Gioanni Domenico Bremio speciaro di Casale Monferrato*, ed. Giuseppe Giorcelli (Alessandria: Societa poligrafica, 1911), 78.

[61] Ghilini, *Annali di Alessandria*, 208; AST Archivio Sola Busca, Serbelloni, box 48, letter from Camillo Capoletto, March 10, 1627.

[62] StadtA Ulm Kriegsamtes A [5556], *Verzeichnis des Kriegsvolks zu Pferd und Fuß* by Wachmeister Christoph Revelheimer, Aufstellung der Mansfeldischen Kavallerie.

Milanese documentation on local housing of soldiers during the period that overlaps with the Mansfeld Regiment's time in Italy is sparse.[63] The commune of Busto Arsizio put down a deposit on a property in the Basilica district in 1620 to house soldiers, although the balance was not paid until after the Mansfelders left.[64] Regimental sources mention soldiers quartered in local houses: One official recommended that the Mansfeld cavalry be quartered in "houses of the *padroni* instead of barracks," which may have been an attempt to lessen the impact of their presence by splitting them up. "Houses of the *padroni*" refers to the most substantial and capacious dwellings of landowners, with more amenities. Housing was managed at every step not only by agents of the Spanish governance in Milan but also by important locals who participated in that governance, such as Pietro Paolo Lumello in Pontestura. Billets survive for the housing Lumello provided, scrap-paper tickets inscribed by him and sometimes countersigned by the soldier receiving the billet – like Red Vincent or Bernardo the Cat – in his own hand.[65]

On November 2, 1625, after the Mansfeld Regiment's terrible October, when they had been ambushed and had murdered the residents of two local estates, its infantry assembled on the moor outside Gallarate.[66] The Mansfelders were there to swear their oaths to their Articles of War. Although they had already fought several times that fall, and although the war that brought them to northern Italy was almost over, with this act they formally became a regiment.

The copy of these articles stuck between the first pages of one of the regiment's legal books is written in Mattheus Steiner's neat hand; Mansfeld's signature is at the bottom of the last page above black/red ribbons and his slick red seal. As of November 1, when this document is

---

[63] Dattero, "The Military," 470–471; Buono, *Esercito, istituzioni, territorio*, 185.
[64] Franco Bertolli and Umberto Colombo, *La Peste del 1630 a Busto Arsizio: Riedizione commentata della "Storia" di Giovanni Battista Lupi* (Busto Arsizio: Bramante Editrice, 1990), 233.
[65] AS-AL Archivio Storico Comune Alessandria Serie II, Busta N. 194/9, Alloggiamenti militari, packet *1625 Giugnio 13–1625 Aprile 9 Ordine e distinte per provvigioni date alle truppe Militari firmata de Lumello [1] No 198/237*. I argue that soldiers were more literate than historians have believed in Lucian Staiano-Daniels, "Scribes and Soldiers: A Brief Introduction to Military Manuscripts and Military Literacy," *Manuscript Studies* 5.1 (2021).
[66] Antonio Rasini, ed., Ettore Tito Villa, "Alloggi militari, carestia, e peste nelle due notai galleratsi 1," *Rassegna Gallarattese di Storia e d'Artte* XXXI.118.4 (1972), 131–140, 132–133.

dated, Mansfeld was still in Italy. He was in front of his infantry on horseback on November 2, his retinue and staff officers, the paymasters, the Marquis de Val de Fuentes, and Steiner at his elbow. He did not stay long. After Wolf von Mansfeld received his people's oath, after the battles were over, he traveled back north to Leipzig and his estates, leaving his regiment behind.

Scene I   Hieronymus Sebastian Schutze and Hans Devil

At 8 PM on August 7, 1625, in southern Germany near Ulm, Hieronymus Sebastian Schutze, flag-bearer in the Mansfeld Regiment's third most honorable infantry company, was shooting his pistols out the window of the upstairs room where he and his friends had been dining. They were wheellock cavalry pistols, barrels longer than a man's forearm, and Schutze had at least two. Two soldiers stood beside him at the window and fired their muskets at his command. A drummer stood next to the little group of shooters and banged his drum with each volley. These were common soldiers and Schutze was an officer, but he ate with them and partied with them.

As during a cannon salute in a fortress or ship, as the musket salvoes they fired in the regiment every time a high officer left his quarters, the noise slammed around the walls and the pistol spat flaming bits of wadding and specks of unburnt powder like red-hot sand. Black powder smoke filled the room, choking and sulfurous. Schutze was drunk.

He sent his servant to find his winding key: Wheellocks are fired with a big solid wheel snapping burred teeth against iron pyrite wrapped in lead and wound with a key like a watch. The servant went through the building, each room crammed with soldiers, and found it in Heinrich Gauert's room downstairs. Then Schutze reloaded the first pistol. When Schutze leveled it out the window, tipped it sideways with his knuckles toward the ceiling, and pulled the trigger, the hammer snapped forward with a heavy click and shot sparks but did not fire. He wound the pistol again and left the safety off. Either when he allowed the dog to fall forward into the cocked position or shortly before, the pistol discharged, shooting his good friend Hans Heinrich Tauerling "through the head into the right eye and directly out the back."

The Mansfelder infantry in this room took Schutze's actions casually until he killed someone. A witness said later he did not know how Tauerling got shot because he had been talking to someone else at the time; he had kept on socializing through the musket and pistol shots. When he saw Tauerling fall, he thought the barrel had exploded. Schutze threw himself on Tauerling's body, screaming, and begged the onlookers to kill him too.¹

The Mansfelder cavalry, less well documented most of the time, is more precisely located in early August 1625. They were quartered in towns around Ulm, skirting the city itself, heading southwest then due south. On August 11, Christoff Revelheimer, the master of Ulm's city watch, recorded the strength of their companies and their locations, and the times of their coming and going around Rammingen, Oberelchingen, and Unterelchingen.² Rammingen is thirteen miles northeast of Ulm. These companies were fanning out as they traveled, to towns about a mile and a half apart.

At 10:30 at night, Captain Christoff Kettel's company had been preparing to head out under halflight, first quarter moon. Ten at night was the beginning of their working day. Between 10 and 11, a hue and cry went up in Rammingen. "As is the common rumour," said Revelheimer, "and which the cavalrymen themselves told me," a boy servant (*Jung*) who served a trooper named Hans Devil got "completely plastered" and, while they were breaking up quarters, close together, the troopers went to the stable and the boy was looking after the horses. "He fell asleep in the stable and left the light standing, the fire was due to that: the Jung himself burned too, with all his tack." Forty-one infantrymen were burned to death, along with six cavalrymen and a company muster writer. The fire burned until 4 in the morning.

It had been two days since Schutze shot Tauerling, when the Mansfeld infantrymen in Langenau saw Rammingen burning on the horizon under the light before dawn. Two Mansfeld companies of horse were there, and they marched out at 2 in the morning while the fire was burning: Goldacker out of the territory of Ulm to Oberechlichen, then over the bridge to Kirchberg, and Kettel to Underechlichen. They put out the fire on their way.³ This was August and the sun rose early; moving out by 2 in

---

¹ SHStADr 10024 9119/38, 27-39.
² "Räimingen. Rittmeister Hartman Goldacker, den 1. August. ankommen, 10. Tag stillgelegen, den .11. August. Hernach in der Nacht um 2 Uhr Zu Oberehlichen über Peuelichen, auß dem Ulmichen, nach under Kirchberg gemarsiert." "Räming. Rittm. Christoff Kettel, den 1 Aug: ankommen, 10 Tag stillgelegen, den. 11. dito hernach In der Nacht, Um .2. Uhr gemarsieret und Zu Unterechlingen." StadtA Ulm Kriegsamtes A [5556] *Verzeichnis des Kriegsvolks zu Pferd und Fuß* by Wachmeister Christoph Revelheimer, Aufstellung der Mansfeldischen Kavallerie, 3-4.
³ "Mitwoch abents, den 10. Augusti, 1625./ Ist Zu Räimingen, Zwischen 10. und 11. Uhr Vor Mitternacht, Ein heüe aufgangen, und wie die gemeine Sag, und mir die Reütter selbst anZeigt, hab ein Reütters Jung, So bey einem Reütter, nahmens Hannß Teüfel, gedient, sich wollgesoffen, und weilen die quartier das lost, Eng gefallen, die Reütter Ihr Pferd in die Städl gestelt, und der Jung Zu den Pferdten gesehen, In dem Stadl eingeschlaffen, das liecht stehen laßen, dauon hernach dz feur außkhomen, der Jung

the morning these companies would have made good distance by the time the heat rose.

Schutze was tried, of course. The regimental bailiff had to make sure it was not murder and determine the status of Schutze's honor and his soul. When the witnesses said that Schutze and Tauerling had nothing against each other, the court decided it had been an accident. Schutze had to take an oath purifying himself of the sin in the name of Jesus's suffering. He was deprived of his office for seven days. The tribunal also told him he should take better care of his weapons, so he could further the interests of their colonel Wolfgang von Mansfeld, and their noble lord, King Philip IV of Spain.[4]

---

auch selbst verprunnen, und aller Zeüg. Item in dem dorff auch 41. fuest, von 10. und 11 Uhr an biß Morgens Umb .4. Uhr, alle abgebrandt gewest, In solcher brunst, den Reüttern an Stiffeln, Sattl, Pistollen und andern will verprunen, auch 6 Roß und ein Veldt schreiber verprunen, auch den Armen Leüthen, über die waßer will heüehte, dann sie erst Endten Zeit gehabt, Im feür gebliben, beide Compagn: so da gelegen, als Rittmeister Gold Acker und Rittmeister Köttel sein mit den Compagn: Ins Veld geruehet, die in Langenau ligente Reütter, haben auch Zu Pferdt geblaßn, auch die Zu Underelchingen ligente Reütter in Armis gewest, Zu gemelten Langenau, hat man auch Sturmb schlagen, und die Pauren Zusamen lauffen wollen, und über die Reütter gewolt, so aber verhüettet und abgeschlafft worden, NB: Die Zwo Compagnia aber, seind umb .2. Uhr in der Nacht ge marsieret, Rittmeister Goldackher, auß den Ullmischen, Zu Ober Elchingen über die Pruckhen nach Kirchberg, und Rittmeister Köttl, nach Und/ Elchingen, daßelbst auch bald ein feur von dißen, Köttls Reüttern aufgangen, wo mit solches durch Rittmeister Schennfelsers Compagn:/ so auch da gelegen, gelöscht were worden." StadtA Ulm Kriegsamtes A [5556], 4–5.

[4] SHStADr 10024 9119/38, 27–39.

2 The Italian Dance
Early Modern Military Finance and the Mansfeld Regiment

Between 1610 and 1622, the economy collapsed almost everywhere in Europe.[1] The seventeenth century was catastrophic for Eurasia, although the existence of a single crisis during this century has been debated, as well as the periodization, extent, and causes of the century's ramifying environmental, economic, political, and social upheavals.[2] The concept of a single seventeenth-century crisis is resilient; after controversy in the history of Europe, it has returned as a concept in global and environmental history as a Eurasian or world-wide phenomenon. Geoffrey Parker linked it to colder temperatures causing harvest failures, scarcity, collapse, and war, arguing that climate change caused a single global crisis.[3] Even historians who believe that it would be too broad to speak of one general crisis agree that the European economy regressed or began to stagnate in the early seventeenth century.[4]

Yet the Italian economic situation was ambiguous. Expenses rose in rural communities in the dominions of the Republic of Venice because of military expenditures as well as wider economic factors.[5] In Milan, taxes increased to meet the demands of war. After 1627 debts increased rapidly.[6] Costs for Milanese defense also fell on other polities in the Spanish Monarchy, like Naples. Between 1550 and 1638, government revenue from the kingdom of Naples rose steadily despite fluctuations in

---

[1] David Hackett Fischer, *The Great Wave: Price Revolutions and the Rhythm of History* (Oxford: Oxford University Press, 1996), 95.
[2] Geoffrey Parker and Lesley Smith, eds., *The General Crisis of the Seventeenth Century*, 2nd ed. (New York: Routledge, 2005); Jan de Vries, "The Economic Crisis of the Seventeenth Century after Fifty Years," *Journal of Interdisciplinary History* 40.2 (2009), 151–194.
[3] Geoffrey Parker, *Global Crisis: War, Climate, and Catastrophe in the Seventeenth Century* (New Haven: Yale University Press, 2014).
[4] Niels Steensgaard, "The Seventeenth-Century Crisis and the Unity of Eurasian History," *Modern Asian Studies* XXIV (1990), 683–697, 684; de Vries, "Economic Crisis," 156.
[5] Ongaro, *Peasants and Soldiers*, 27–30.
[6] Giuseppe Bognetti and Giuseppe de Luca, "From Taxation to Indebtedness: The Urban System of Milan during the Austrias' Domination (1535–1706)," in *Taxation and Debt in the Early Modern City*, Michael Limberger and José Ignacio Andrés Ucendo, eds. (New York: Routledge, 2016), 36, 38, 42. For Spanish military endeavors in Lombardy after 1630, see Davide Maffi, *Il Baluardo della Corona: Guerra, esercito, finanze e società nella Lombardia seicentesca (1630–660)* (Florence: Le Monnier Università Storia, 2007).

the population and a decline in the silk trade, because indirect taxes went up substantially.[7] In Piedmont, Lombardy, and the Veneto, economic problems are associated with an historiographical debate over whether or not northern Italy was "re-feudalized" during the Thirty Years War.[8] However, recent studies of Italian finance have interpreted this period as one of resilience and development rather than catastrophe alone. During the late sixteenth and early seventeenth centuries, more people became involved in loans and banking, public banks were founded, and the private credit market grew.[9]

The Mansfeld Regiment's transnational operation was made possible by the growth and development of international military finance, which was both public and private. Historians have traditionally believed that this kind of finance and administration was inferior to the way armies were raised and administered later, in the late seventeenth and eighteenth centuries. In contrast, David Parrott has demonstrated that private military enterprise did not shrink during the early modern period but expanded. He also argued that private military enterprise – more precisely, the cooperation of public and private activity – filled the gaps that political entities of the time could not.[10] Military housing in Milanese territory was provided by local notables in cooperation with the State of Milan. Wolfgang Winckelmann, the Mansfeld Regiment's quartermaster and captain of its third most honorable company, contracted for fabric as a semi-independent agent, supported by his regiment and the heads of state he served. Military enterprise expanded and changed along with Italian finance more generally. This enabled the Mansfeld Regiment's expedition to Italy, but also shaped its disintegration.

The daily lives and decisions of individual Mansfelders were enmeshed in this economic context. Armies were a safer berth than many; the rising price of food compelled Hungarian soldiers to enlist, and young nobles in the Kingdom of Hungary signed up as common soldiers to pick up some money.[11] Soldiers also engaged in little negotiations to get the best

---

[7] Antonio Calabria, *The Cost of Empire: The Finances of the Kingdom of Naples in the Time of Spanish Rule* (Cambridge: Cambridge University Press, 1991), 67.
[8] de Vries, "Economic Crisis," 151–194, 167–170.
[9] Giuseppe de Luca and Marcella Lorenzini, "Conflicts, Financial Innovations, and Economic Trends in the Italian States during the Thirty Years War," in *Financial Innovation and Resilience: A Comparative Perspective on the Public Banks of Naples (1462–1808)*, Lila Constable and Larry Neal, eds. (London: Palgrave Macmillan, 2019), 165–186.
[10] David Parrott, *The Business of War: Military Enterprise and Military Revolution in Early Modern Europe* (Cambridge: Cambridge University Press, 2012).
[11] Zoltán Péter Bagi, "The Life of Soldiers during the Long Turkish War (1593–1606)," *The Hungarian Historical Review* 4.2 (2015), 384–417, 396, 387–388.

economic outcome for themselves, such as mutiny, irregular work, or theft. This chapter describes a mutiny within the Mansfeld Regiment in detail.

The lives of individual men were also entangled within global economic changes in more unexpected ways. For instance, some cases recorded in the regimental legal books took place within the context of a Europe-wide crisis in coinage. This crisis reached a zenith between 1619 and 1622.[12] In central Europe this is known as the *Kipper- und Wipper Zeit*, a period of runaway debasement and inflation of small currency. Signs of Empire-wide instability appeared in the 1570s, and edicts against devalued small currency went out in 1589, 1592, and 1594 without success.[13] The debasement and re-minting of small coins spiraled out of control. As each political entity within the Empire attempted to gain seignorage by minting coinage with less silver and exchanging it outside its borders for better money, debasement cascaded and spread. Trade broke down and prices rose sharply.[14] In Milan, the quantity of gold and silver coins declined while that of copper coins rose: The money supply fluctuated from 1607 to 1609, and again from 1619 to 1622.[15]

In Saxony, small-denomination coins were dropping in value by around 1600 and, by the first decade of the seventeenth century, payment of debts and collection of taxes were already difficult. Attempts to fix the ratio of *Reichsthaler* to smaller coins failed, and political relationships within the Upper Saxon Kreis deteriorated. In February 1620 another edict to fix monetary ratios was published, and failed. This was the last act of the Upper Saxon Kreis for a long time.[16] The Saxon crown compounded the effects of this economic crisis by unsuccessful speculation on the copper market.

Customary or "interim" money (*Usualmünze, Interimsmünze*) began to appear in Saxony in 1619 and was minted in great quantity from autumn 1620. From 1620 to 1623 there were so many mints throughout

---

[12] Ruggiero Romano, "Between the Sixteenth and Seventeenth Centuries: The Economic Crisis of 1619–22," in *The General Crisis of the Seventeenth Century*, Geoffrey Parker and Lesley Smith, eds. (Abingdon: Routledge, 1997), 165–225, 190. The landmark work is W. A. Shaw, *The History of Currency* (New York: G. P. Putnam's Sons, 1896).
[13] Robert Wuttke, "Zur Kipper- und Wipperzeit in Kursachsen," *Neues Archiv für Sächsische Geschichte und Altertumskunde* 15 (1894), 119–156, 124–125.
[14] Charles P. Kindleberger, "The Economic Crisis of 1618 to 1623," *The Journal of Economic History* 51.1 (1991), 149–175.
[15] Romano, "Sixteenth and Seventeenth Centuries," 188–189; Carlo Cipolla, *Mouvements monétaires dans l'Etat de Milan (1580–1700)* (Paris: Librairie Armand Colin, 1952), 43–44.
[16] Wuttke, "Kipper- und Wipperzeit," 135, 138.

Electoral Saxony it is impossible to say how many existed.[17] Just three of these mints produced customary money with the face value of 12.5 million gulden, which was far above the quantity of good money minted in Saxony. In twenty years Augustus I minted 8.5 million gulden, and in the twenty-eight years from 1628 to 1657, Johann Georg I minted 3.5 million more.[18] In the early 1620s, trust in state money was so deeply shaken that in place of electoral coins, authorities in Leipzig and other cities issued coins of sheet tin.[19] Beginning in winter 1622 and into spring 1623, mints began to stop producing bad money since people no longer took it.

Mansfeld Regiment sources do not mention bad small change, since soldiers were paid in non-debased money. Instead, tied to full-value coinage, the interactions of the soldiers and officers in them reveal a lack of low-denomination coins altogether.

Sergeant Johann Silbernagel and flag-bearer Michael Hevel, one of the witnesses to the muster-writer Heinrich Teichmeyer's eventual death, argued on February 14, 1626, when Hevel asked Silbernagel to make change for him and Silbernagel refused. "Because the Sergeant had wanted to get a drink of wine," he said Hevel should let it go until they got to the tavern, "then I'll shoot money at you." Since Silbernagel knew Italian, Hevel asked him to buy thread with him after lunch. Silbernagel poured a Zick and some batzens and half-batzens onto the table. Hevel took a ducat and a Zick out of his own purse and said "Sergeant, you have lots of half-batzens, give me something for both of these because up until now I've had to pay my servant back in my quarters and I can't get this broken." Silbernagel said he'd give him something for one of them, not both. Hevel answered, "Didn't you put a Zick in your stuff?" implicitly accusing him of theft in the tavern. Silbernagel denied it.[20]

Michael Hevel had money but lacked useful coins: Ducats were too big to buy wine and thread with, or to pay his servant back. Early-modern European society did not have enough small change until the late nineteenth century. Much business was reckoned in money of account such as lire or gulden, for which there may not have been an equivalent physical coin. Accounts ticked along in tidy *Reichsgoldgulden* or lire while the real physical coins that clattered in your purse were more or less clipped, debased, battered, or counterfeit; or almost pure copper, "black money," the low-denomination fiat coinage of Spain, Venice, or Saxony. Small-denomination coins that were not debased were scarce. While

---

[17] Ibid., 138–139. [18] Ibid., 144. [19] Ibid., 152.
[20] SHStADr 10024 9119/38, 206–210.

minting thalers enabled seignorage, smaller coins had a face value below their value in silver and cost money to produce.[21] Small coins were debased even outside the *Kipper- und Wipperzeit*, as governments attempted to ameliorate their scarcity by devaluing them and minting more. A soldier could – if he was paid in coins that were too valuable – have a purse full of silver but not enough usable cash to buy necessities.[22]

If a government wanted to pay its soldiers in silver, an immense effort was required to transport that much metal: In 1676, 200,000 écus came to 11,989 pounds of silver. To move a big siege gun of this weight needed twenty-five horses, crawling down the road at a few miles a day. Le Tellier wrote that it took 800 horses to haul cash over land to French troops in Italy in 1641. Shipping 86,000 livres from Brittany to Paris in 1606 took eighteen pack horses and twenty-four days. Larger-denomination gold coins weighed less and took up less space, but changing them into smaller coins in an occupied territory was difficult and local financiers charged money to do it.[23] If the place where the soldiers were quartered used a different currency from the government that sent them there, local authorities could also attempt to make money off a commander by manipulating the exchange rate when he tried to cash a bill of exchange. This happened to the Mansfeld Regiment's Dam Vitzthum von Eckstedt.

Except for Theodoro de Camargo, who bought his wife a palace full of rich possessions and drove away with them all the night he killed her, soldiers probably had fewer goods than everyone else but more cash. Sometimes a great deal more – common soldiers might carry several thalers at a time. Estate inventories reveal that non-soldiers kept little money and stored their wealth in material objects instead.[24] Objects were harder to steal and non-soldiers did not have to think about how easy their possessions were for a woman to carry on foot. Peter Hagendorf called his things "his linens" (*Weißzeug*), and he was limited to how much his wife or boy servant Bartelt could carry on a horse. Everything else, like the belts and pitcher his wife brought out of Magdeburg, was flipped for cash as quickly as possible.[25] When Heinrich Teichmeyer lay

---

[21] Wuttke, "Kipper- und Wipperzeit," 126–127.
[22] Thomas J. Sargent and François R. Velde, *The Big Problem of Small Change* (Princeton: Princeton University Press, 2002).
[23] Parrott, *Richelieu's Army*, 244–246.
[24] James C. Riley, "A Widening Market in Consumer Goods," in *Early Modern Europe: An Oxford History*, Euan Cameron, ed. (Oxford: Oxford University Press, 2001), 257.
[25] Hagendorf, *Ein Söldnerleben im Dreißigjährigen Krieg*, 145, 147.

dying his wife and children got all his goods that were "lying to hand or far away" and his wife received his salary, which was in arrears, but he left the twenty-five ducats he had on him to Wolfgang Winckelmann.[26]

The inventory of Winckelmann's possessions when he was arrested in 1631, after he had moved on from the Mansfeld Regiment, amounted to "one cuirass, one Hungarian saddle, another saddle with leather inserts, a tent made of multicolored stuff, a saddle-cushion [*Postkussen*]," and "in a yellow clothes cupboard," one pair of old black cloth breeches with a mantle and stockings of the same, one pair of old black silk samite breeches with broad brown silk piping, one pair of old black silk atlas breeches with silk stockings, one "mourning hat" (*Trauerhut*), one small Italian hat with a black feather, one old embroidered sword hanger with the belt, and one old sword hanger with red embroidery.[27] At the time Winckelmann was the former quartermaster for a regiment, which is not an inconsiderable position. He had a multicolored tent and two different saddles but no bed, or books; the single doublet he wore daily but no other; not a spoon to eat with. The saddle-cushion may have gone under his head at night. When indoors and not in someone else's bed he may have folded up the tent and slept on that.

Armies were nodes of circulation for weapons or goods, and some Mansfelders sold their weapons when the regiment collapsed. When Augsburg was occupied Jakob Wagner saw

> whole herds of cattle, big and small, large numbers of horses, numerous wagons loaded with copper, tin, bedding, clothes, linen, and all kinds of other things which had been plundered from the countryside or other towns offered for sale on every street and square in the city, where they were sold for miserable little sums of money. And this went on for weeks on end.[28]

Soldiering could also have been a part-time job for some of the people on seventeenth-century muster rolls who left their companies and came back. When Peter Hagendorf was between enlistments in northern Italy he and a friend worked for a luthier.[29] During the eighteenth century, soldiers with craft skills worked independently or for the company. For instance, captains saved money on uniforms by getting a tailor in the company to make or alter them. Even though armies of this period were

---

[26] SHStADr 10024 9119/38, 88–90.
[27] Jan de Vries, *The Industrious Revolution: Consumer Behavior and the Household Economy, 1650 to the Present* (Cambridge: Cambridge University Press, 2008), 1–4. SHStADr 10024 9678/12, *INQUISITION Acta CONTRA Den Vorhafften Wolffen winckelmann 1631*, 185.
[28] Quoted in Mortimer, *Eyewitness Accounts*, 82–83.
[29] Hagendorf, *Ein Söldnerleben im Dreißigjährigen Krieg*, 38.

more organized than they were during the seventeenth century, soldiers found guard duty a good opportunity to work at their side jobs.[30]

Mansfelders may have worked for their own units for extra cash. Soldiers could be paid extra for digging and entrenching, although this regiment was scattered around existing towns rather than encamped. They may have been paid to gather firewood or chop down trees and vines around their towns to create fields of fire. Some soldiers burned furniture to get away with not collecting wood, but I have not seen this recorded for the Mansfelders, who gathered wood in many sources. When Hans Jungnickel's woman crowded in front of the hearth and hammered a nail into the wall over the fire to hang her pot upon, knocking soot into the "little bit of green herbs" Georg Reinsberger's "legal wife" Maria was cooking, Reinsberger shoved Jungnickel's woman onto the bed, then Jungnickel grabbed a blade and cut Reinsberger behind the left ear. (That night all four of them ate those greens. Reinsberger ate half an egg and said little. He died twelve days later and Maria woke beside the corpse.) Maria, who prepared food, called this implement "a cleaver" when the investigator asked her what happened; the men in the room, who cut wood, called it "an Italian woodcutting knife."[31]

Women performed irregular work to a disproportionate extent.[32] Early-modern women's economic activity is more difficult to see than men's, like their activity as debtors or creditors.[33] Large numbers of women traveled with German military units, and military women did legal, quasi-legal, and illegal work to live. They bought and sold goods, hawked food and alcohol, and exchanged sex for money. They also sold or recirculated plundered goods, an essential part of what John Lynn called "the pillage economy."[34] Those who hired mercenaries

---

[30] Jutta Nowosadtko, "Soldiers as Day-Laborers, Tinkers, and Competitors. Trade Activities in the Garrisons of the Eighteenth Century Using the Example of Prince-Bishopric Münster," in *Shadow Economies and Irregular Work in Urban Europe: 16th to Early 20th Centuries*, Thomas Buchner and Philip R. Hoffmann-Rehnitz, eds. (Münster: LIT Verlag, 2011), 165–181.

[31] SHStADr 10024 9119/38, 189–198. The verbal distinction between a soldier's "woman" or "partner" ("Weib") and his "legal wife" ("Eheweib") is clear in this account.

[32] Thomas Buchner and Philip R. Hoffmann-Rehnitz, "Irregular Economic Practices as a Topic of Modern (Urban) History: Problems and Possibilities," in *Shadow Economies and Irregular Work in Urban Europe: 16th to Early 20th Centuries*, Thomas Buchner and Philip R. Hoffmann-Rehnitz, eds. (Münster: LIT Verlag, 2011), 22.

[33] Elise Dermineur, ed., *Women and Credit in Pre-Industrial Europe* (Turnhout: Brepolis Publishers, 2018).

[34] John Lynn, *Women, Armies, and Warfare in Early Modern Europe* (Cambridge: Cambridge University Press, 2008), chapter 3.

disapproved: The phrase William of Orange used for soldiers' families was "useless followers," *onnutte naeloop*.[35] In March 1574, a Dutch captain wrote his superior to say that his men were unhappy because their families were no longer supposed to accompany them on the march; instead, they were to be "dispersed over villages and make themselves useful by spinning." The order came from William himself.[36] But what looked like idleness included labor.

Soldiers could mutiny to try to secure their livelihoods when food and pay were unsure. Their willingness to mutiny in this period has been well known since a pioneering essay by Geoffrey Parker. Mutinies were a form of workplace protest.[37] The sixteenth-century Landsknechts regarded their service as a free choice and expected payment; if they were not paid punctually, they threatened to leave.[38] Like food riots, military protests rested on a view of the world in which social relationships had to be "fair," and the recognition that this fairness required active defense.[39] The best-explored early modern mutinies in English-language sources are probably the ones in the Spanish Army of Flanders. Once these soldiers resolved to mutiny, they elected their own leaders, swore to obey them, and submitted their grievances to the military authorities. The matter was settled by negotiation. In contrast to the belief that military justice in this period was harsh and arbitrary, the mutineers' demands – arrears of pay – were usually met.[40] This also happened when units in Hungary threatened to mutiny.[41] Mutineers wanted no more than their due as they saw it, but it had to be wrested away from others. In this way they protected their material interests and affirmed themselves as people who deserved respect.[42]

There was at least one big mutiny in the Mansfeld Regiment before its final collapse. Soon after mustering-in, the Moser Company was supposed to receive meat as part of their food allotment but got sausage

---

[35] Erik Swart, "From 'Landsknecht' to 'Soldier': The Low German Foot Soldiers of the Low Countries in the Second Half of the Sixteenth Century," *International Review of Social History* 51 (2006), 75–92, 89.

[36] Ibid., 91.

[37] Parker, "Mutiny and Discontent;" Julius R. Ruff, *Violence in Early Modern Europe 1500–1800* (Cambridge: Cambridge University Press, 2001), 55.

[38] Reinhard Baumann, "Protest und Verweigerung in der Zeit der klassischen Söldnerheere," in *Armeen und ihre Deserteure: Vernachlässigte Kapitel einer Militärgeschichte der Neuzeit*, Ulrich Bröckling and Michael Sikora, eds. (Göttingen: Vandenhoeck und Ruprecht, 1998), 16–49.

[39] E. P. Thompson, "The Moral Economy of the English Crowd in the Eighteenth Century," *Past and Present* 50 (1971), 76–136.

[40] Parker, *Army of Flanders and the Spanish Road*, chapter 8. For officers' mutinies, see Redlich, *German Military Enterpriser*, 445.

[41] Bagi, "Life of Soldiers," 394. [42] Parker, *Army of Flanders and the Spanish Road*, 170.

instead. When they were fed, soldiers ate more meat than contemporary non-soldiers, according to analysis of chemical residues on the teeth of soldiers in early seventeenth-century mass graves.[43] If they had been short of protein before they enlisted, these soldiers would have felt themselves grow stronger and seen the change in their skins and hair when they ate more protein, and perceived themselves to be different from non-soldiers in that way. This happened to police recruits in early twentieth-century Papua New Guinea when they began eating meat regularly.[44] But often soldiers were not supplied.

On January 11, 1626, Captain Moser's sergeant, Heinrich Deckert, "was sent to the company with the commissary of bread, wine, cheese, and sausage." According to Deckert, the food was to be shared out by the corporals. When Deckert got there, a soldier named "Hans Gebler asked, where is the meat … the Sergeant answered, there was no meat, but sausage in its place, at which Gebler said again, people promise a lot but hold to it little [*mann sagte viel zu, hielte aber wenigk*]." He threw the bread back into the basket. The captain sent Lieutenant Simon Löhr "to ask them whether they wanted to go on or not;" "to go on" meaning to remain with the army or remain on campaign, similarly to the way "to go out" meant to go to war. "They answered no, they did not want to go on, but to have money."[45] Sergeant Deckert turned away "and was going to go back to the captain, but there was a shot behind him, so that the smoke blew out around him, but he doesn't know who did it."[46] The culprit was musketeer Hans Albrecht, who also attacked a transport boat with a pike. After his corporal took his musket from him Albrecht ripped his bandolier off and dashed it against the stones of the pavement, and the wooden powder-bottles broke.[47] The rest of the mutineers held fast to their demands. They had been mustered-in back in November and they wanted a month's pay as promised. Löhr listened to their demands and told them, "You should be taken care of," calling them his "brothers." When he said it looked like they "did not want to follow their flag," "they answered they wanted money." "What money?" blurted Löhr.[48]

After Captain Moser spoke to the soldiers himself and realized there was nothing he could do, he withdrew to a tavern called The Angel,

---

[43] *1636 – ihre letzte Schlacht*, 111–113; Bettina Jungklaus, "A Mass Grave from the Thirty Years War on Friedländer Tor Neubrandenburg," in the conference *Battlefield and Mass Grave: Spectra Interdisciplinary Evaluation of Locations of Violence*, Brandenburg an der Havel, November 21, 2011.

[44] August Kituai, *My Gun, My Brother: The World of the Papua New Guinea Colonial Police, 1920–1960* (Honolulu: University of Hawaii Press, 1998), 106.

[45] SHStADr 10024 9119/38, 91. [46] SHStADr 10024 9119/38, 92.

[47] SHStADr 10024 9119/38, 97. [48] SHStADr 10024 9119/38, 92.

losing his nerve. The other officers reassured him that they had 400 men to order, and if Moser's company "did not want to go on they'd bring them on," and also they wanted him to notify the commander of the garrison in Milan at the Castello of the Jove Gate.[49] The mutiny eventually fizzled out. Although the exact terms are not recorded, the Mansfeld Regiment was not mustered-in for pay until the better part of a year later. Only Hans Albrecht, who had attacked a boat and fired on his officer, was executed, on February 24.[50] The rest of the mutineers were not prosecuted, even Hans Gebler, who had begun it. Experienced soldiers were too valuable to treat harshly without cause, and observers recognized that unpaid soldiers could be expected to protest.

Desertion was another strategy for soldiers to navigate military life. This was ubiquitous and could destroy entire regiments. Manuals warned against letting a regiment remain idle too long before taking it into the field, since everyone in it would leave. Soldiers were more likely to desert when not paid or fed, and might desert from one company to enroll in another for the enlistment bonus. Soldiers left for many reasons, and believed they were entitled to desert if they wanted. Sometimes they came back: Since the expression used was *Außreisen* or *Entloffen* (to run away or stray away) rather than the later *Desertion*, muster-roll entries were often unclear about the difference between deserters and men who took a break for a while. Sometimes their companies knew where they went. One cuirassier roll from the 1630s lists troopers spread out around Saxony and Bohemia as far as Zeitz in one direction and Cheb and Plzen in the other.[51] Sometimes the difference between temporary and permanent absence blurred for reasons beyond a soldier's control. In 1635, Jobst Steinnetze from Hermannsacker, infantryman in H. E. Koenig's company, "wanted to go home but never got there, whether he had fallen into the hands of the enemy or was slain by peasants, nobody knows."[52] The other members of the company were close enough to his hometown and familiar enough with its inhabitants that they went there and asked. They were not concerned about his capture: Enemy forces would just take Steinnetze prisoner or enroll him in their army. Peasants probably would have killed him. (The word the roll uses for "slain" is *erschlagen*, literally "bludgeoned to death.")

---

[49] SHStADr 10024 9119/38, 96.   [50] SHStADr 10024 9119/38, 97–98.
[51] SHStADr 11237 10841/2 2.
[52] SHStADr 11237 10841/3 3. Jobst Steinnetze, new soldier, recruited in Stolberg in 1635: "nach hause gehen Wollen, aber nichtt dahin kommen, ob er in Feindes haende kommen oder Von bauern erschlagen sey, Weiss niemandt."

34   The Italian Dance

Yet, in his list of deserters from the Mansfeld Regiment, Mattheus Steiner wrote that if any came back, he would have them hanged from a withered tree. Since they were not around, he nailed a piece of paper with their names on it to a withered tree instead.[53] In this regiment they used dead trees for gallows. Armies hanged their condemned from trees when gallows were unavailable, but several Mansfelders stressed the tree had to be dead. Specifically, "withered" (*dürr*). Johann Silbernagel skipped town instead of letting his dispute with Michael Hevel go to trial. He had been allowed his choice of dates and showed up to none of them. Steiner wrote "Silbernagel's name ... as an honor-forgetting, oathbreaking rogue and thief, is publicly nailed to the gallows. Both here and in whatever place and location he may enter, it is hung on a withered tree: well-deserved punishment for him, and a frightening and marked example for others."[54] When Juan Gammert deserted, Camargo wrote that he should "be hanged from a withered and no green tree."[55] Hans Geyer, Hans Heimberger, and Mattheus Blanckenberg, who stole a sheep, "shall be hanged either from the gallows [*Justiciani*] or from a withered tree."[56]

This was rhetoric and custom; in reality, only a few deserters were hanged. We probably cannot track early seventeenth-century desertion rates systematically, but they were almost certainly higher than in the eighteenth century. That century was called "the century of the deserter" not because of its prevalence, but because desertion became a topic for discussion then, a problem that might be solved, which was not yet the case when the Mansfeld Regiment was in operation.[57]

For seventeenth-century military authorities, desertion was something a commander simply had to deal with, like bad weather or disease. People left constantly and casually, and absent soldiers who came back were often received without comment. One cuirassier roll contained a request to the Elector to issue patents to the officers to force absent troopers to come back, implying not only that casual absence was common but also that these soldiers respected military norms enough that this strategy might work. That company's horsemen had no armor and were "mostly terribly clothed" (*meistentheils Vbel bekleidet*).[58]

But the relationship between employer and soldier was not solely financial; it was also tinctured with soldiers' sense of their emotional relationships to their superiors, and to their own honor within these relationships. *Arbeit*, "work," was not used to describe what soldiers

---

[53] SHStADr 10024 9739/6, 239.   [54] SHStADr 10024 9119/38, 226.
[55] SHStADr 10024 9739/6, 155.   [56] SHStADr 10024 9739/6, 109.
[57] Berkovich, *Motivation in War*, chapter 2.   [58] SHStADr 11237 10841/2 3.

did. They did not refer to themselves as laborers. It was *Dienst* or *Pflicht*: "service" or "duty." This came with moral obligations. "If Your Grace were not my paymaster," wrote Johann Wolf von Schrauttenbach to the Margrave of Hesse in knotty language, "you could order me into the street or the alley … to attack" the man von Schrauttenbach was suing. A mercenary with a paymaster (*soltener*) did not simply jump people in the street.[59] "If you had no lord, you could go from one fair to another with your wife and cut purses," sneered Sergeant Georg Lauren to Lieutenant Wolf Heinrich von Dransdorf, both of the Mansfeld Regiment.[60] When Maz Japsch was questioned by his company authorities about whether he actually thought it was legitimate for soldiers to fight one another whenever they felt like it, he answered he had been wrong to say that. "It would have to be someone who was lordless and who had enough cause."[61] A mercenary "without a lord" was *auf dem garten*, "on the guard," and civilians feared and loathed a *Garteknecht*.[62] Soldiers who "had a lord" were responsible for a level of honorable behavior that masterless men were not.

"Receiving money from the lord" was a phrase mercenaries used for the practice of soldiering; Theodoro de Camargo said that when Juan Gammert deserted, he stole from the purse of the king of Spain. There were specific words for specific kinds of payment. *Sold* or *Besoldung* is pay: One colonel was given his salary *zu Leibesbesoldung*, "payment to support his body."[63] *Liefergeld* or *Laufgeld*, "delivery money" or "walking money," was the sum given to recruits to pay their expenses while they traveled from the place where they signed up to the place where they were supposed to muster-in. They were expected to do this without supervision. The Spanish never could get their mouths around this word and

---

[59] "Oder aber damit Ihg. nicht meiner soltener, das ich mich für Johan Wersen fürchtete, möchten Ihg. ihme befehlen mich auf Straßen oder gaßen Zur *attacquiren*." SHStADr 10024 9119/30, doc 1.
[60] SHStADr 10024 9739/6, 162.
[61] SHStADr 10024 9121/5, 47r. Lucian Staiano-Daniels, "Masters in the Things of War: Rethinking Military Justice during the Thirty Years War," *German History* 39.4 (2021), 497–518.
[62] The etymology of this phrase, which dates from the fourteenth century, is the French *garde*, "watchman/servant," since masterless soldiers often had to work privately. From this comes a host of dissolute, rowdy meanings: *gardede* or *garden* also meant "to go foraging," and *garren*, "to fence." *Deutsches Wörterbuch von Jacob Grimm und Wilhelm Grimm*. Trier center for Digital Humanities/Kompetenzzentrum für elektronische Erschließungs-und Publikationsverfahren in den Geisteswissenschaften an der Universität Trier 1998–2011, available at http://woerterbuchnetz.de/cgi-bin/WBNetz/wbgui_py?sigle=DWB entry for "Garten, garden" (last accessed January 16, 2024).
[63] SHStADr 11237 10798/4, *Niedereingegebene Feld-Kriegs-und Andere Bestallungen*, de Ais 1618, 19, 20, 21, 22, 23, 24, 28, 32, 35, 39, 53r.

wrote it as *Aufgeld* when they wrote about paying German regiments in Milanese service. *Werbegeld* was "enlistment money." *Verpflegung* was the amount necessary to support a soldier for one month, his room and board. Some high-ranking cavalrymen got *Umritsgeld*, "circuit money." *Lehn* meant pay when a soldier said it (*Vorlehn*, "prepayment," was the month's pay a soldier received as a lump sum when he signed up) but to non-soldiers it meant feudal beneficence. This word was used in solemn contexts: *Lehn* should be given out in the presence of the Captain and the Elector's clerk, one contract said, shared out by the soldiers hand to hand.[64]

Like other communities, the Mansfeld Regiment was pervaded by networks of credit and debt. The Mansfelder use of the word *honored* to describe payback of a debt illustrates what one historian called the "moral economy" of early-modern credit: Like soldiers' pay, credit was not solely economic but depended on interpersonal relationships, reciprocity, and mutual trust.[65] Michael Hevel was in debt to his own servant. Some soldiers of Winckelmann's company gave cloth to other soldiers or to women as payback for debts. Officers were creditors to their men. One document from 1681, on the eve of the development of a standing army in Saxony, recorded the debts owed to a regiment's lieutenant-colonel: More than 200 thalers for equipment (*Mundierung*), accrued over about ten years. The debt belonged to the office, not the individual, and it had been tallied because the incumbent lieutenant-colonel was leaving and the new one would inherit it.[66]

When soldiers in the Mansfeld Regiment lent one another money, they testified before Mattheus Steiner while he wrote the amounts down. The accounts in the legal books are copies. Soldiers may have carried the originals, like they carried their housing tickets and their honorable discharge papers.[67] If they had been civilians, this might never have been written down: Record-keeping on paper was important when one party

---

[64] "Gleichfalls sollen alle die werordnenten lehen in beisein des hauptmans und höchstermelter Irher Churf. Gn. Feldtschreibers, den knechten selbst von hand zu hand ausgeteilet, und darüber ordentliche register erhaltten warden." SHStADr 11237 10798/4, 5r.
[65] Laurence Fontaine, *The Moral Economy: Poverty, Credit, and Trust in Early Modern Europe* (Cambridge: Cambridge University Press, 2014).
[66] SHStADr 11241 000001, see Oberst-Lieutnant Gateschi's company in the Life Regiment of Foot, January 1681.
[67] SHStADr 10024 9119/38, 203–207, legal tickets of Hans Munderler and Hans Großman; Michael Schreiber and Feldwebel Heinrich Rabenau. For common soldiers' interactions with paperwork, see Lucian Staiano-Daniels, "A Brief Introduction to Seventeenth-Century Military Manuscripts and Military Literacy," *Manuscript Studies* 5.1 (2020), 142–163, 155.

to the transaction might leave or die at any time. Common soldier Franz Beer owed Friedrich Zeckel, also a common soldier, eighteen thalers for his medical bills, "a cure for his thigh." He also borrowed thirty-two thalers from Zeckel on a different occasion. Then Beer died. Twenty thalers were found on him, from which two were given to a soldier named Samuel Aschenbacher, to whom Beer was also in debt. The remaining eighteen went to Zeckel. The challenge was finding thirty-two more thalers to cover Beer's entire debt. Zeckel got a promise from his company's officers that they would eventually pay it back. In this case the written document from the regimental secretary was a receipt for Zeckel as well as written assurance from the officers. The members of Beer's and Zeckel's company worked out a sort of insurance – *Versicherung* was the word they used – for loans among themselves, backed by the officers' commitment to cover the debts of dead men.[68]

Irregularities in funding for the Spanish army in northern Italy in 1625 became apparent early in the Mansfeld Regiment's operation. On September 22, the Alessandrian representative Giovanni Battista Castone wrote that the Genovese banker Giovanni Salvaterra had found a source for a loan for 300,000 scudi to pay the regiment.[69] However, it was difficult for Milan, Cremona, and Alessandria to secure this loan.[70] The negotiations were complex. On October 8, the King of Spain ordered the Duke of Feria to promise the great Genoese financier Steffano Balbi that the debt would be repaid.[71] Alessandrian officials proposed "a new request to facilitate the payment" on November 6.[72] "The later this doling-out [*partitio*] is secured, the more delayed Mansfeld will be," wrote Castone.[73]

This loan was intended to cover payments mediated through Milanese, Cremonese, and Alessandrian officials. Some funding made it to the Mansfeld Regiment: The Cremonese paymaster Camillo Capoletto reported that he paid the seven companies of cavalry quartered in Cremona the real equivalent of 71,242 lire between February 3, 1626 and March 8, 1627, in addition to housing, hay, fodder, and

---

[68] SHStADr 10024 9119/38, 201–203.
[69] AS-AL Serie II, *Lettere de 1625 del Sig. Grat. Castone, Tomus 50*, 254r–254v. Letter from G. Castone, September 22, 1625.
[70] AS-AL Serie II, *Lettere de 1625 del Sig. Grat. Castone, Tomus 50*, 254–255. Letter from G. Castone, September 12, 1625.
[71] AS-AL Serie II, *Lettere de 1625 del Sig. Grat. Castone, Tomus 50*, 270r–270v. Printed letter from Philip IV to Duke of Feria, October 8, 1625.
[72] AS-AL Serie II, *Lettere de 1625 del Sig. Grat. Castone, Tomus 50*, 308. Letter from G. Castone, November 6, 1625.
[73] AS-AL Serie II, *Lettere de 1625 del Sig. Grat. Castone, Tomus 50*, 265–266. Letter from G. Castone, October 9, 1625.

straw.[74] However, the full 300,000 scudi loan appears to have been delayed.

In late January 1626, the papers in Castone's files began mentioning other units.[75] In order to raise and support these units, Castone wrote, on February 2, 1626, that he would send 134,000 scudi, then 200,000 more.[76] The total is about 300,000 scudi, possibly including the 71,242 lire that went to the Mansfeld cavalry in Cremona. On March 6, Steffano Balbi promised to send out this full amount at once.[77] I do not know if most of this money ever reached the Mansfeld Regiment. From early 1626 to spring 1627, the discussions in Castone's files concern Italian and Spanish regiments, not the German ones raised in 1625: Having been delayed, funding may have been diverted to new regiments when it became available. For several crucial months, most of a year, the Mansfelders may simply have been forgotten. Discussing finance was "the Italian dance – I will not say Spanish dance," wrote Castone. "One step forward, and one step back."[78]

In fall 1627, after everything had unraveled, Dam Vitzthum von Eckstedt claimed that the Governor of Milan owed the officers of the Mansfeld Regiment 63,521 scudi. Vitzthum von Eckstedt, who went on to become a Saxon general but was then one of Mansfeld's captains, wrote the paper in his own hand and at some speed; although the document is unsigned, his distinctive handwriting is unmistakable.[79] But an earlier document, when its figures are added up, claimed the Mansfeld Regiment actually owed the Governor of Milan, at the end of its tour, a total of 1,501 scudi.[80] By this point, the Governor of Milan was the Duke of Feria's successor Gonzalo de Córdoba, formerly the commander of Spanish troops in the Palatinate. His claims were false: In fact, Mansfeld and his officers had paid to raise the regiment themselves. They

---

[74] AST Archivio Sola Busca, Serbelloni, box 48. Letter from Camillo Capoletto, March 10, 1627.
[75] AS-AL Serie II, *Lettere de 1626 del Sig. Grat. Castone, Tomus 51*, 32.
[76] AS-AL Serie II, *Lettere de 1626 del Sig. Grat. Castone, Tomuss 51*, 33–34. Letter from G. Castone, February 2, 1626.
[77] AS-AL Serie II, *Lettere de 1626 del Sig. Grat. Castone, Tomus 51*, 46–47. Printed letter from Steffano Balbi, March 6, 1626.
[78] AS-AL Serie II, *Lettere de 1625 del Sig. Grat. Castone, Tomus 51*.
[79] SHStADr 10024 9239/5, *Allerhand Schriften, das aus italien zurückgekehrten Regiment zu Fuß des kais-generals grafen wolfgang mansfeld, dessen übler Zustand, aufenthalt zu frantfurt a. m. samt u.d.a*, 63r–63v.
[80] SHStADr 10024 9239/2, *Die beiden in italien stehenden regimenter des Grafen Wolfgang von Mansfeld: Schreiben desselben an die Unterbefehlshaber, des Rechnungswerk, die Abdankung u. a.bet, 1626–28*, 24–82.

had been hoping that someone associated with the Duchy of Milan would reimburse them since at least July 1625.[81]

The actions and interactions of early seventeenth-century soldiers took place within the socioeconomic context of early seventeenth-century Europe. Not only would contemporary economic catastrophes have made military service an attractive alternative to non-military life, even in relatively stable times many lives scraped along near the margins of supportability. Yet although soldiers' daily lives were inextricable from their economic context, they were more than mercenary in the narrow or pejorative sense. We can see this from soldiers' statements that what they did was a form not of work, but of service.

These attitudes are visible in the single largest wave of desertion in the Mansfeld Regiment, which also demonstrates how shambolically run this regiment and its financing were, even in its first months in being. Of 249 recorded deserters from the Mansfeld Regiment, 40 left a month before Salvaterra found a source for the regiment's ill-fated loan, on August 27, 1625. When the soldiers were near Lake Constance, a rumor went around they were going to be sent to Spain and given Spanish officers, and the deserters sneaked away.[82] Two officers deserted at the same time, and wrote letters explaining their decision.[83] Mattheus Steiner copied them into the legal book.

Georg Dressler from Dresden believed Lieutenant Stach Löser was leaving; since Löser had recruited him, he felt no obligation to stay. (Actually Löser had switched from lieutenant-colonel of infantry to lieutenant-colonel of cavalry.[84]) The regiment was five weeks out of Dresden and Dressler still had no idea where they were going: "we have received the Ordinance that we must march away from my people, but we do not know where we will have our last Muster-place, but instead march all the time, God knows where there will be an end of it." "I want solemnly to vow to you that as long as God gives me luck, I will provide your wife with wood this winter, when I can get there," he said to one of the Mansfeld officers; not only did he know this man, but their families also knew each other.[85]

---

[81] SHStADr 10024 9737/13, *Italienische und französische* Concepta *derer Schreiben Graf Wolffgangs Zu Mansfeld an den Herzog zu* Feria, *Spanische Bottschafter, und andere Ao 1625–26*, 15, 18. Rough draft of letter from Wolf von Mansfeld to unknown recipient, probably the Duke of Feria, July 29, 1625.
[82] SHStADr 10024 9119/38, 20–27.   [83] SHStADr 10024 9119/38, 15–19.
[84] StadtA Ulm Kriegsamtes A [5556], *Verzeichnis des Kriegsvolks zu Pferd und Fuß* by Wachmeister Christoph Revelheimer, Aufstellung der Mansfeldischen Kavallerie, 3–4.
[85] SHStADr 10024 9119/38, 17–19.

An unnamed Fourier, an officer responsible for arranging troops' lodging, wrote the other letter to flag-bearer Stach Krakow.

To the honorable and manly flag-bearer and my most honored friend. Because as everyone knows, I have received no money from the lord, and I did not imagine that I would be thus betrayed, I also ask your honor and manliness to pardon me in this case, because I have done what is due and expected to every righteous guy [*Rechtschaffener Kerl*].

Like Michael Hevel, this officer was in debt to his own servant, and wrote that he left enough cash to pay him back.

I really liked marching with you ... I had really hoped to have better opportunities in this thing than this, and to serve in my office as promised. But now I see that I was only leading an empty name ... I have spent a great deal on the men [respectfully: *Knechte*, "landsknechts"]: effort, work, and money I have spent, so that it really seems to me, as I had hoped, that I should have been better repaid.[86]

The same night as these officers deserted, common soldiers Phillip Appelt and Jacob Bötger told Sebastian Schlüssel that he and his comrades would make themselves scarce in the morning [*sich davon machen*] and desert: Because he was a righteous guy, he was going with them to Ulm. Appelt and Bötger urged Augustus Roth that if he was a righteous brother he'd stay back in the woods when the army moved on and desert with them.[87]

These officers and common soldiers spoke about desertion as a kind of negotiation, as one strategy within a complex range of possible actions. These actions took place within an implicit social contract as well as a group of personal relationships. If Wolf von Mansfeld did not uphold his end of this deal, if the soldiers were not paid or told what was going on, if the officers were not repaid for their effort and for the payments they had made out of pocket, desertion was justified.

These men saw themselves as "righteous guys," men with a code. Being a righteous man involved both tangible and intangible relationships with superiors and inferiors. The next chapter analyzes the origins of these righteous men, and probes more fully the local, regional, familial, and social ties that bound them to the military community.

---

[86] SHStADr 10024 9119/38, 15–16.   [87] SHStADr 10024 9119/38, 21–22.

3 Righteous Guys
Military Society*

A soldier who lived the way you were supposed to – who was brave, dueled or scrapped when he was called out, paid for his share of the drinks, and deserted if his friends told him to – was a *rechtschaffener Kerl*, a "righteous guy." This was the jargon in the Mansfeld Regiment and in other units. The word has an implication of playing by the book, doing what is expected, but soldiers did not use it to describe people who obeyed orders. An obedient soldier, who followed orders and could be relied upon by his superiors, was *redlich*, "upright." *Rechtschaffen* was a word soldiers and officers used when they were standing up for themselves.

These men's description of themselves as righteous, both officers and men, is unexpected given the longstanding belief that seventeenth-century soldiers were rootless marginals. Soldiers were supposedly recruited from drifters, vagabonds, and outcasts disconnected from their communities: Poor and working-class men criminalized by the state, then used as cannon fodder and a catchment for surplus labor.

However, existing statistical and demographic research on the armies of the Thirty Years War does not support the contention that soldiers were immiserated or rootless before they enlisted. Cordula Kapser notes in her study of the Bavarian army after 1635 that fewer than 30 percent of soldiers were listed as unemployed or without occupation.[1] She concluded that mercenary soldiers could not "simply be classified as 'criminals' or branded as the 'scum of society'."[2] Although the jobs of the Scottish soldiers in Swedish service James Fallon studied were not listed systematically, he mentions some recruits whose previous occupation he was able to find, including smiths, tailors, a cooper, a

---

* Part of this chapter, in a modified form, appeared as "Most Saxon Soldiers Are Saxon: The Myth of the Rootless Mercenary and the Origins of Soldiers in Electoral Saxony, 1618–1651" in the panel *Everything Old Is New Again: Historical-Statistical Studies of Central European Armies 1618–1789* at the 2017 Annual Meeting of the Society for Military History, Jacksonville, FL, April 1, 2017. Thanks to Nick Klein and Efron Licht for their assistance with the maps in that presentation. Thanks to Efron Licht for assistance with the maps in this chapter.

[1] Cordula Kapser, *Die bayrische Kriegsorganisation*, 68–73. [2] Ibid., 72.

mason, and a gardener.[3] These men may have been solidly employed before their enlistment. After the war ended, Peter Hagendorf moved to Görzke in Brandenburg, where he may have already had relatives, became a judge, served a term as mayor, and died in 1677 at the age of seventy-nine.[4] This was not an outcast's life.

If Saxon soldiers were rootless, their places of origin would be distributed throughout the Empire, maybe throughout Europe, but this is not the case. The statistical analysis in this chapter is based on the surviving muster rolls for regular mercenaries in the Saxon State Archives in Dresden. It is derived from 170 company muster rolls, 3 monthly payrolls from the Saxon Hoffahne, and 2 housing lists. Two of the muster rolls are copies of other rolls on file, leaving 168. Total sources number 173. This analysis is based on every muster roll in the archive except the duplicates, not on a sample. Most of these sources date from the 1620s and late teens: Although Saxony was only involved in the first stage of the war until 1625, there are 115 from that decade. Many rolls from the 1620s survive from each company, year by year or month by month. Later decades are less well-covered: Forty-seven rolls and the two housing lists are from the 1640s, but only nine rolls survive from the 1630s, even though the Saxon army was largest then. In contrast to some other armies' rolls, or Saxon rolls from the 1680s, Saxon muster rolls from the Thirty Years War recorded only a few things: Each soldier's full name, his rank or office, and often but not always his place of origin. Cavalry rolls were less well-organized than infantry rolls, but almost all cavalry rolls recorded the number of horses each trooper had and sometimes the health of these horses, which was more important to the cavalry than the number of troopers. These sources contain about 30,000 entries, but many soldiers show up in more than one entry and many soldiers have no place of origin listed. Once I removed duplicate entries for the same person and those with no origin listed, or an origin that could not be located, there remained 13,480 individual soldiers whose places of origin are known, both listed in the original documents and locatable now. These men can be mapped.

Military recruitment in early seventeenth-century Europe was enacted through social networks which were both local and international. Recent research has demonstrated the importance of the international military

---

[3] James A. Fallon, "Scottish Mercenaries in the Service of Denmark and Sweden, 1626–1632" (PhD dissertation, University of Glasgow, 1972), 90–91.
[4] Hans Medick, *Der Dreißigjährige Krieg: Zeugnisse vom Leben mit Gewalt* (Göttingen: Wallstein Verlag, 2018), 115–122.

market.[5] A mass grave at the location of the 1636 battle of Wittstock demonstrates that soldiers came from across Europe, which archaeologists can tell from the isotopes in their teeth.[6] Certainly the people traveled a great deal. During twenty-five years of service, Peter Hagendorf covered at least 25,000 kilometers.[7] Mercenaries themselves knew their way of life entailed travel: "To march," "march out," or "go out" were the usual terms for going on campaign. "I really liked marching with you," wrote the unnamed fourier to Stach Krakow the night before he deserted.[8] Archaeology shows their joints were terrible: Knees and ankles worn from long walking, hip bones and lower backs marked from hours in armor, in the saddle. Only the dead were immobile. Soldiers paused when they went into winter quarters, but nobody used the word "remain" for this. People in winter quarters were "in," as opposed to "going out" in the spring. Imperial *Kriegscommissarius* Wolf Rudolf von Ossa zu Dehla said they "lived at home."

Soldiers in the Saxon army came from across Germany, and places as far away as Ireland, northern Italy, Sweden, and what is now Slovakia. They came from cities on the shore of the Baltic Sea from northern Germany all the way up to Reval, modern Tallinn. However, while the networks and flows in the trade in soldiers spanned nations, most soldiers in the Saxon army came from an area centered on Saxony.[9]

Figure 3.1 shows the origins of Saxon soldiers in all decades of the Thirty Years War. Each dot is a location from which one or more soldiers came. A larger penumbra around the dot means more soldiers came from that place. The region most Saxon soldiers came from looks like a flattened diamond, with Mühlhausen roughly on the left point, the Bohemian city of Eger (modern Cheb) on the bottom, Magdeburg

---

[5] Peter Wilson, "Foreign Military Labor in Europe's Transition to Modernity," *European Review of History: Revue européenne d'histoire* 27.1–2 (2020), 12–32. Peter Wilson, "'Mercenary' Contracts as Fiscal-Military Instruments," in *Subsidies, Diplomacy, and State Formation in Europe, 1494–1789: Economies of Allegiance*, Svante Norrhem and Erik Thomson, eds. (Lund: Lund University Press, 2020), 68–92. Peter Wilson and Marianne Klerk, "The Business of War Untangled: Cities as Fiscal-Military Hubs in Europe (1530s–1860s)," *War in History* 29.1 (2020) 1–24.
[6] Brandenburgisches Landesamt für Denkmalpflege und Archäologisches Landesmuseum Brandenburg, *1636 – ihre letzte Schlacht: Leben im Dreißigjährigen Krieg* (Stuttgart: Konrad Theiss Verlag, 2012), 178–180.
[7] Peter Burschel, "Himmelreich und Hölle: Ein Söldner, sein Tagesbuch, und die Ordnung des Krieges," in *Zwischen Alltag und Katastrophe: Der Dreißigjährige Krieg aus der Nähe*, Benigna von Krusenstjern and Hans Medick, eds. (Göttingen: Max-Planck-Institut für Geschichte, 1999), 181.
[8] SHStADr 10024 9119/38, 15.
[9] This study is similar to Hanlon's of the army of Parma. Gregory Hanlon, *The Hero of Italy: The Duke of Parma and the Thirty Years War* (Oxford: Oxford University Press, 2014), 67–69.

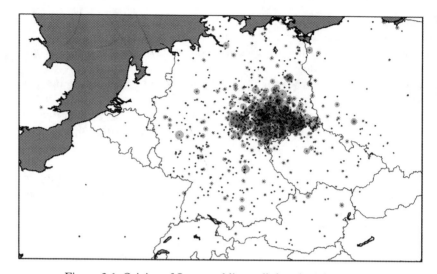

Figure 3.1 Origins of Saxon soldiers, all decades of the Thirty Years War.
SHtsADr 11237 series 1040, 1041, 10821, 10831, 10839, 10840, 10841 (n = 13,480)

roughly at the top point, and Görlitz on the right point. Electoral Saxony is thickly populated with dots; the city most soldiers came from is Dresden.

These soldiers shared a common place of origin; most came from Electoral Saxony or the Thuringian duchies. This is consistent with men joining the Saxon army based on regional ties, native language (even native dialect), and how likely they were to meet a recruiter, rather than religious beliefs, political opinions, or the goals of their feudal overlords. Subdividing the results by decade makes their origins clearer.

Figure 3.2 depicts the origins of Saxon soldiers during the first decade of the Thirty Years War. For Saxony this began in 1618 with the Bohemian Revolt and ended in 1625, when the last Saxon regiments were mustered out.[10] The overall distribution of soldiers is not different from the pattern for the war as a whole; this is unsurprising, since this decade accounted for 115 out of 172 sources.

The origin of these soldiers is interesting in the political context of the 1620s. Although Saxony spent this decade as the Emperor's loyal vassal, regions that owed their allegiance to prominent anti-Imperialists

[10] SHStAD 11237 10831/1.

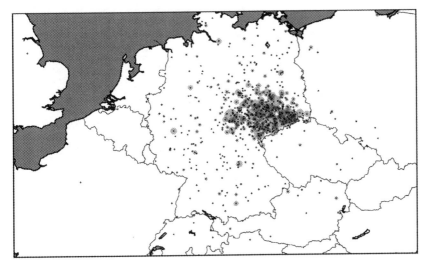

Figure 3.2 Origins of Saxon soldiers, 1620s.
SHtsADr 11237 Loc 1040, 1041, 10821, 10831, 10839, 10840, 10841 (n = 9,720)

are well-represented in this map. Duke Christian of Brunswick-Wolfenbüttel, the famous "mad Halberstadter" and staunch anti-Imperial paladin, was also the Margrave of Magdeburg. Territory belonging to Magdeburg extended in a little tongue of land into Electoral Saxony as far south as Halle, but more than 200 men from Magdeburg lands filled Saxon muster rolls in the 1620s. Bautzen was the largest and most important city in Upper Lusatia, that, along with Lower Lusatia, rebelled alongside the rest of the Bohemian lands in 1618. Saxon troops under Wolf von Mansfeld besieged Bautzen and took it in the fall of 1620.[11] Fifty-three men from Bautzen alone appear in Saxon muster rolls of the 1620s, most after the city had fallen, not to mention men from throughout Upper and Lower Lusatia.

Data from the 1630s are idiosyncratic, probably because the number of surviving records is so small. Here the diamond is weighted toward its north-western corner, and the south and east are less well represented (Figure 3.3).

Figure 3.4 depicts the origins of Saxon soldiers during the 1640s. The same diamond shape is visible, although more strongly represented this time toward the eastern side, Electoral Saxony proper more than Thuringia.

---

[11] Peter Wilson, *Europe's Tragedy*, 301.

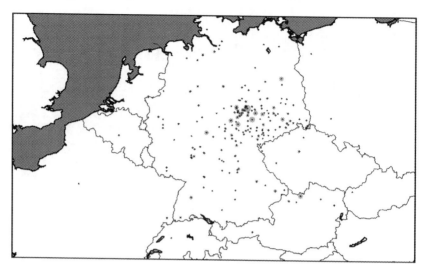

Figure 3.3 Origins of Saxon soldiers, 1630s.
SHtsADr 11237 Loc 10841 (n = 916)

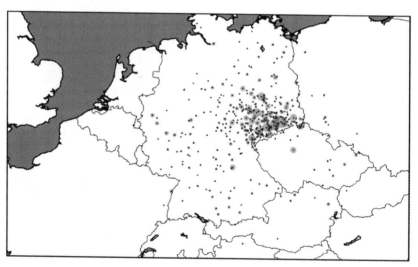

Figure 3.4 Origins of Saxon soldiers, 1640s.
SHtsADr 11237 Loc 10841 (n = 2,844)

Soldiers joined their units based on regional ties. This is why the limited number of available records from the 1630s makes the map from that decade lopsided. Only eight company rolls from this decade survive in the Saxon Hauptstaatsarchiv, three from the same regiment. These soldiers came from a relatively narrow area of Thuringia, while only three soldiers during this decade came from the major city of Dresden. Similarly, but with a far more extreme effect because it rested on a different social structure, Scottish colonels recruited from carefully delineated areas, allowing them to draw on clan ties to obtain their men.[12]

Ordinary soldiers were active participants in the recruiting process, and their political opinions were mediated in a complex manner through local and regional interactions. This is visible when we compare maps from before and after the 1635 Peace of Prague. Small Protestant political entities near Saxony provided many recruits to the Saxon army in the 1620s despite the fact that they were anti-Imperialist: Potential soldiers living there would enlist for the Imperialist side if a recruiter was nearby. After the Peace of Prague, this recruitment dropped off. This treaty not only established the neutrality of the small Protestant states, it also prohibited quartering in their territories, making it less likely for non-soldiers to interact with armies. It is likely that Saxony was also forbidden from recruiting there.

Local relationships are evident in some companies like Carl von Krahe's, in which 24 out of 222 common soldiers came from the small Thuringian city of Suhl.[13] Most of these men are listed one after the other in two large blocks: Infantry rolls did not list soldiers strictly by seniority but in a more casual order which varied slightly from roll to roll. This may have been the order in which they stood in line while the muster was being written, which would mean that these soldiers from Suhl stood next to one another.

We cannot conclude that common soldiers during the 1620s and the 1640s were especially peripatetic before signing up. To judge from their mobility alone, these men do not appear to have been marginal members of their societies. But many soldiers may have been younger sons or apprentices who never made master: Those who could neither marry as civilians nor inherit. Although lack of opportunity did not make a man an outcast, soldiering was a viable choice for men blocked from non-military ways of life.

These Saxon and Thuringian soldiers in the army of Electoral Saxony are like the soldiers in the army of the Duchy of Parma during the 1630s,

---

[12] Fallon, "Scottish Mercenaries," chapter 6.   [13] SHStADr 11237 10840/4 2.

who were primarily northern Italian, and like soldiers in some armies in the English Civil War, which were numerically dominated by specific ethnicities.[14] The information in Saxon muster rolls also allows us to test the longstanding belief that the longer the war continued the more "internationalized" it became. Like the belief that mercenaries had been criminalized or immiserated before they enlisted, the belief that they came from everywhere in Europe is both a statement of fact and a value judgment: When the war became "internationalized," in this argument, it also grew more cruel. Nineteenth-century German representations of the horrors of the Thirty Years War framed the conflict as foreign invaders violating the bodies of German victims, by extension Germany itself. Kevin Cramer observed, "Working through the trauma caused by German religious division and political fragmentation, these narratives dwelled on the violation of Germany by foreign mercenary armies of Italians, Walloons, Spaniards, Hungarians, Croats, and Cossacks."[15] Gregory Hanlon argued soldiers were not "wantonly destructive" before 1630, because, during the first decade of the war, "soldiers and civilians understood that they lived in a shared 'imagined community' and that peace would soon return." Only after "the internationalization of the German war following 1631 and especially with the arrival of the Croat dragoons, gratuitous destruction taught populations that there were no such things as 'friendly' troops."[16] These arguments imply that individuals who belonged to the same religious and cultural groups could not commit atrocities against one another.[17] Foreign troops are a synecdoche for social breakdown.

But, although most Saxon soldiers were Saxon, central European mercenary soldiers had also always been international. Though the Thirty Years War metastasized as non-Imperial powers like France and Sweden intervened or regional spats like Sweden's struggle with Sigismund Vasa got dragged into its orbit, this international element was present from the beginning. The Saxon army did not simply grow more diverse as the war went on. Instead, the shifting regional makeup of the men who ended up in the ranks reflected the course of the war. Table 3.1 lists by decade the raw number of soldiers in the Saxon army

---

[14] Mark Stoyle, *Soldiers and Strangers: An Ethnic History of the English Civil War* (New Haven: Yale University Press, 2005); Hanlon, *Hero of Italy*, 67–69.
[15] Kevin Cramer, *The Thirty Years War and German Memory in the Nineteenth Century* (Lincoln: University of Nebraska Press), 181–182.
[16] Gregory Hanlon, *Italy 1636: Cemetery of Armies* (Oxford: Oxford University Press, 2016), 155.
[17] Quentin Outram, "Demographic Impact of Early Modern Warfare," *Social Science History* 26 (2002), 245–272; 261–264.

Table 3.1 *Number of soldiers with non-German origins in the Saxon army by decade*

Decade	1620s	1630s	1640s
Total soldiers	13,462	1,628	3,956
Total with unknown origin	3,742	712	1,112
Total with known origin	9,720	916	2,844
Upper and Lower Lusatia	301	15	165
Bohemia and Moravia	274	28	247
Switzerland	30	10	5
Poland–Lithuania	26	7	24
Ottoman territories and Hungary	13	3	4
England	12	–	3
Sweden	11	3	17
Scotland	10	–	11
United Netherlands	9	2	3
Denmark	8	3	9
France	8	1	5
Livonia	6	–	4
Spanish Netherlands and Burgundy	5	3	3
Italy	3	2	1
Croatia	2	–	1
Romania	1	2	1
Ireland	–	–	8
Finland	–	1	–

whose places of origin are known and who were not from the non-Swiss parts of the German lands: The German part of the Holy Roman Empire (including Silesia), the Hereditary Lands of the House of Austria, territories of the Teutonic Order, and the Duchy of Pomerania.

It is imprecise to say Saxon forces grew "more diverse" during the war. Instead, they grew more Bohemian and Lusatian, specifically in the 1640s. The percentage of Saxon soldiers from the Lusatias was 3 percent in the 1620s, about 1.5 percent in the 1630s, and just under 6 percent in the 1640s, while the percentage of soldiers from Bohemia and Moravia was slightly under 3 percent in the 1620s, slightly over 3 percent in the 1630s, and skyrocketed to just over 8.5 percent in the 1640s. As the war began, the Bohemian Estates, along with both Lusatias, were rebelling against the Emperor, which meant that soldiers recruited by agents working for the Bohemian Estates and soldiers recruited by Saxon agents were fighting on opposite sides. But Ferdinand II began consolidating his hold over Bohemia after 1621.[18] Although both Lusatias had been

[18] Wilson, *Europe's Tragedy*, 357–358.

granted in pawn to the Elector of Saxony in 1623, the Emperor only awarded them formally to Saxony after the Peace of Prague in 1635. Saxon possession of these lands entailed many changes of ownership, and some Saxon captains and colonels eventually obtained Lusatian fiefs.[19] By the 1640s, Lusatians would have been available to be recruited by Saxon officers directly, while Bohemians and Saxons were serving in two factions of an allied Imperial/Saxon force and could have easily gone from one army to the other.

By percentage, the Saxon army also became more Livonian, more Polish–Lithuanian, more Scottish, more Irish, and more Swedish during the war, but not by much. That is, it incorporated soldiers from Sweden's army and from regions associated with Sweden's sphere of influence. Likewise, the percentage of people from French territories shows a steady increase not entirely attributable to the fact that parts of Alsace were taken over by France after 1639. This process reflects Sweden's entry into the war; Saxon forces spent the late 1630s and the 1640s fighting Swedish forces in the east of central Europe.[20] Soldiers with Nordic last names appear in some rolls that did not record place of origin, like Hendrickson, Erickson, and Leonardson, all from 1644.[21] The Saxon and Swedish armies drifted around the same territory for a long time during the late 1630s and 1640s, drawing from the same pool of potential soldiers. The origins of the forty-three infantrymen listed in one of Dam Vitzthum von Eckstedt's company rolls (undated, approx. 1635) as "received from the Swedes" were not reported, but it would have been interesting to compare their backgrounds to their comrades who had begun their careers in the Saxon army.[22]

The percentage of soldiers in the Saxon army from Denmark, Italy, the Ottoman territories, Royal and Ottoman Hungary, Switzerland, and both the Spanish Netherlands and the United Provinces rose in the 1630s and fell again in the 1640s. This is less easy to explain and may be due to the small surviving number of soldiers from the 1630s amplifying the statistical visibility of any change. The total number of English soldiers in the Saxon army in the 1620s was twelve: Eleven of them, mostly pikemen, served in a single regiment. Meanwhile three Englishmen served in the Saxon Life Regiment in 1645. In both cases they would have been fighting for Imperial-aligned troops, a tiny

---

[19] SHStAD 11237 10831/1.
[20] Peter Wilson, "Meaningless Conflict? The Character of the Thirty Years War," in *The Projection and Limitation of Imperial Powers 1618–1850*, F. C. Schneid, ed. (Leiden: Brill, 2012), 28.
[21] SHStAD 11237 10841/13.   [22] SHStAD 11237 10841/3 doc 1.

reminder that the English did more during this conflict than support Protestants abroad. The smallest numbers may be statistical noise, like the single Finn, squad leader Heinrich Hennig, recorded in Jonas Ernst Koenig's infantry company in 1635.[23]

Most of the soldiers from Slovenia have German names, like the Tyroleans. Most of the Bohemians came from German-speaking areas in Bohemia or Moravia like the Sudetenland, Prague, or the area around Znaim. The soldiers from what is now Romania may have been Saxons like their comrades further west. German-speakers were scattered throughout central Europe, so these men may have been able to speak at least a little German of some kind when they joined up. On the other hand, the cuirassier Georg Ungar from Győr was probably Magyar, and Ungar, "Hungarian," was probably not his real family name.[24] There is a clear line between Habsburg areas of south-eastern Europe, from which several Saxon soldiers came, and Ottoman regions, from which only a few came.

Written records become vaguer about location the further away from Saxony, Thuringia, Bohemia, and Silesia they got; the same muster-writer who specifies hamlets of ten or twenty in east-central Europe writes merely "England" or "Sweden" for more exotic places. Thomas Hartung, English pikeman in Adam Adrian von Walnitz's company of von Schlieben's Regiment, came from "Salop:" a nickname for Shropshire, which the muster-writer wrote down not knowing the difference.[25] Sometimes these brief entries reveal connections between soldiers from across Europe. William Mellin was a musketeer from 1619 to 1624 in a free company which belonged first to Eustachius Löser then to Hans von Taube. Mellin came from Kingston, England, which his muster-writer recorded accurately at first. By the fourth and last roll in which Mellin appears, the syllables of his hometown have morphed into Königstein: Whether the muster-writer did this consciously or unconsciously the effect is as though Mellin had come not from a distant country, but from the massive fortress just up the Elbe from Dresden.[26]

Historians argue that cavalrymen came from a more rural background than infantry, since peasants had more experience with horses.[27] This reveals unfamiliarity with work in cities or towns until well after the

---

[23] SHStAD 11237 10841/3 doc 3. [24] SHStAD 11237 10841/2 2.
[25] SHStAD 11237 10840/4 10.
[26] SHStAD 11237 10840/1-1, 11237 1040/1-2, 11237 10840/9, and 11237 10840/11-1.
[27] For example, see Peter-Michael Hahn, "Kriegserfahrungen im Zeitalter des Dreißigjährigen Krieges," in *Kinder und Jugendliche in Krieg und Revolution: vom Dreißigjährigen Krieg bis zu den Kindersoldaten Afrikas*, Dittmar Dahlman, ed. (Paderborn: Schönigh, 2000), 13–14.

Table 3.2 *Number and percentage of soldiers by population of hometown and branch of service*

	Cavalry/ Dragoons	Infantry
Total Soldiers with Known Origin by Number: Size of Hometown	1,451	10,106
>10,000	261	1,634
5,000–10,000	250	1,568
1,000–5,000	490	3,740
<1,000	405	2,977
thinly settled	18	85
estate/Schloss	27	101
Total Soldiers with Known Origin by Percentage: Size of Hometown		
>10,000	18%	16%
5,000–9,999	17%	16%
1,000–4,999	34%	37%
<1,000	28%	29%
thinly settled	1%	1%
estate/Schloss	2%	1%

internal combustion engine. Transport and heavy work like construction required the labor of horses in even the largest cities; horse carcasses, hair, body parts, hides, and manure were valuable commodities. Large numbers of horses living and dead were a routine presence in the crowded urban landscape into the early twentieth century.[28] Not only did the rural/urban composition of the Saxon army's horsemen not differ significantly from the foot, both horse and foot were more urban than civilians (Table 3.2).[29]

---

[28] Clay McShane and Joel A. Tarr, *The Horse in the City: Living Machines in the Nineteenth Century* (Baltimore: The Johns Hopkins University Press, 2007); Ann Norton Greene, *Horses at Work: Harnessing Power in Industrial America* (Cambridge, MA: Harvard University Press, 2008).

[29] Early modern census information for central Europe is complicated. A single documentation of the population of what is now Germany did not exist before 1867 (Rolf Gehrmann, "German Census-Taking before 1871," working paper for the Max Planck Institute for Demographic Research WP 2009-023, August 2009, 4). Although local or regional counts were made in what is now Austria from the sixteenth century onward, Maria Theresa had the first overall census in the Austro-Hungarian Empire taken in 1754 (Peter Teibenbacher, Diether Kramer, and Wolfgang Göderle, "An Inventory of Austrian Census Materials, 1857–1910. Final Report," working paper for the Max Planck Institute for Demographic Research WP2012-007, December 2012, 1). The information that produced Table 3.2 was taken from local enumerations which were as close in time to the early seventeenth century as possible, supplemented with data

Contrary to the assumptions of military theorists like Wallhausen (for instance, that peasants were less likely to fear death because they knew little of good living to begin with), Saxon soldiers were more likely to come from cities or towns than the countryside.[30] They were unusually urban: In the Empire at this time there were only 3,500 to 4,000 "cities," with roughly 85 percent having fewer than 1,000 inhabitants.[31] The percentage of the general population in the Empire that lived in urban settings with more than 10,000 inhabitants was small: 3 percent in the year 1500, 5.4 percent by 1700.[32] Townspeople and city dwellers were not bound to landlords like peasants. They were vulnerable to sudden shifts in the labor market or changes in the price of food and goods, strong incentives for men and their families to take the chance on enlisting. (John Lynn said that famines coincided with spikes in French enlistment in 1694 and 1709.[33]) Soldiers were more urban before they joined up and, once they enlisted, they lived in the middle of more humans and animals in one place than all but the largest metropolis. As of 1574, Gallarate numbered 2,300 souls, out of which were 470 heads of household, making the entire town about 200 less than the Mansfeld Regiment's infantry at its highest recorded strength.[34] The number of soldiers in Table 3.2 differs from the total number with known origin because I could not find the sizes of some Saxon towns but, even if every soldier whose hometown's size is unknown came from a small village, the proportion of Saxon soldiers who came from larger towns or from cities would still be comparatively high.

These results confirm Gregory Hanlon's results for soldiers from neutral Italian territories in the Duke of Parma's army, and for soldiers in that army from France: "About a third of them came from cities of more than 10,000 people, and half that proportion again came from the dense network of smaller cities and towns where one could live with

---

from Paul Bairoch, Jean Batou, and Pierre Chevre, *La population des villes européennes de 800 à 1850* (Geneva: Center of International Economic History, 1988). Early-modern enumerations of communities within the borders of the present-day state of Saxony can be found on the website of the Digitales Historisches Ortzsverzeichnis von Sachsen, available at: www.hov.isgv.de, last accessed January 13, 2024.

[30] Johann Jacobi von Wallhausen, *Defensio Patriae oder Landrettung. Darinnen gezeigt wird 1) Wie alle und jede in der werthen Christenheit Potentaten, Regenten, Stätte und Communen ihre und der ihrigen Unterthanen Rettung und Schützung anstellen sollen. 2) Der Modus belligerande, viel hundert Jahre bißher gefählet.* Frankfurt: Gedruckt im Verlag / Daniel und David Aubrij und Clement Schleichen, 1621, 12–18.

[31] Counting Bohemia and Moravia, but not Flanders or Reichsitalien. Heinz Schilling, *Die Stadt in der Frühen Neuzeit* (Munich: R. Oldenbourg Verlag, 2004), 3, 9.

[32] Ibid., 4.   [33] Lynn, *Giant of the Grand Siècle*, 145–150.

[34] Sella, *Crisis and Continuity*, 187, fn. 11.

decorum."[35] The disproportionately urban background of soldiers has been a constant since Corvisier.

Some Saxon soldiers came from tiny communities, like Hans and Andreas Löhlen from Schwarzenbruch in Baden, which as of the time of writing has about fifteen inhabitants. In summer and fall 1635 Hans and Andreas were infantrymen in Jacob Zader's company, whose records show a high number of sick and dead. Hans died on September 22 in Brandenburg, and Andreas two days later.[36]

These statistics do not support the idea that mercenaries were rootless. Instead, they suggest that during the 1620s and 1640s, many of the soldiers who served Electoral Saxony joined up and fought near their homes for a variety of reasons. The Saxon army was largest and therefore recruiting most strenuously during the 1630s, the same decade for which little documentation exists. However, research like Kapser's on Bavarian soldiers suggests that even in this decade, soldiers were not marginal members of civilian society.

It is also possible to determine the origins of some, but not all, members of the Mansfeld Regiment. The regimental legal books contain a list of deserters, as well as a list of soldiers in Wolfgang Winckelmann's company who had been assembled after the fabric shipment was stolen from the Swiss agents.[37] The list of deserters records cities of origin as well as names; although the Winckelmann company list does not record place of origin, seven of its names appear in recorded companies of the Saxon army in the 1620s. The origins of 102 members of the Mansfeld Regiment were also recorded in passing. These sources add up to a sample size of 343 Mansfelders whose hometowns are known. Figure 3.5 depicts their origins.

Proportionally, the Mansfeld Regiment was less Thuringian than the Saxon army. The familiar diamond shape is still there, centered as before on the cities and towns of Saxony and Thuringia; in this case the best-represented polities are Döbeln, Dresden, and Freiberg. But it is shifted, as though the shape had been pulled down and to the west. There are fewer soldiers from the north of Germany, and fewer Silesians. Comparing the entire Saxon army during the 1620s to the Mansfield Regiment, we can see that potential soldiers living in small Protestant states near Saxony would enlist for an Imperialist ally, but fighting for Spain was just a bridge too far.

From Saxony, through Bavaria, down to Lake Constance, into Switzerland, the movement of this regiment can also be tracked by the people who ended up in it; as they moved, the Mansfelders picked up

---

[35] Hanlon, *Hero of Italy*, 66, 72.   [36] SHStADr 11237 10841/3 4.
[37] SHStADr 10024 9739/6 219–232; 10024 9119/38 60–74.

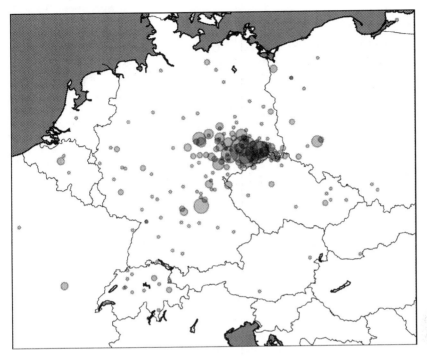

Figure 3.5 Origins of members of the Mansfeld Regiment, 1625–1627. SHStADr 10024 9119/38, 9739/6, 9539/5

recruits like beads on a string. At least seven soldiers joined them in Nuremberg: While the author of *Der Anndre Thaill Nurembergische Cronica* was recording the regiment's presence, other citizens of Nuremberg were signing up.[38] More than 3 percent of Mansfelders with known origins were Swiss, far above the percentage of Swiss in the Saxon army in any decade. The Mansfeld Regiment also had a crop of men from the Spanish Netherlands and Burgundy, who may have come in with Camargo or due in some way to his influence: One Walloon was Victoria Guarde's driver. Several Mansfeld officers were Italian. Christoph Revelheimer, the master of Ulm's city watch, called the Mansfelder cavalry "Germans, Croats, Italians, people from Trent," "Bohemians." He summed them up as "Ten companies: good and bad riders and horses, Nation: Germans, Silesians, people from Meissen, Saxons, Croats, and Austrians."[39]

---

[38] UCLA Library Special Collections MS *170/355, 348v.
[39] "Summa, der Mansfeldischen *Cavalleri*, von 10 Compagn: gute und böße Reütter und Pferdt, *Nation*, alß Teütsche, Schleßier, Meißner, Saxn, Crabanten, und Österreicher."

When left alone, soldiers may have moved around less than historians thought, but regiments could be highly mobile; if a soldier became attached to one, it could pull him right across the map. The makeup of the Mansfeld Regiment demonstrates that regiments were always recruiting. Their composition fluctuated continually as soldiers deserted, got sick, or died, and were replaced.[40] In the Mansfeld Regiment's case, we see it along the road to Lombardy itself.

Soldiers from the same place enlisted together. They may also have deserted together, as Gregory Hanlon argued. In his analysis of muster rolls counting soldiers in the service of the Duchy of Parma, Hanlon argued that groups of soldiers with similar origins were more cohesive.[41] Conversely, diverse units were more likely to disintegrate.[42]

However, we can also see friendships among men with different origins, like the Mansfeld Regiment's two lieutenant colonels of cavalry, Stach Löser and Vratislav Eusebius von Pernstein. Löser was Saxon. To the regiment he was "Stach." Nobody called him Eustachius except in the most formal documents. This garrulous young officer had been born in his familial possession of Alsdorf in the Mansfelder Lands, making him Mansfeld's feudal subject. When Saxony peeled away from the Empire and allied with Sweden six years after the Mansfeld Regiment went down to Lombardy, Löser went with it, and became a colonel in May 1631. He led a regiment at Breitenfeld and took part in a savage little action to retake Leipzig from the Imperialists after the battle of Lützen. By 1634 he was a General-Major and commandant of Zittau. Stach Löser died on October 8 that year, when he was stabbed by Duke Carl of Sachsen-Lauenburg in "a duel on horseback."[43]

Von Pernstein was the last descendant of a major Catholic Bohemian noble dynasty, which died out in the male line when he died in 1631. His grandfather had been the leader of the royal chancery of Bohemia and the confidant of Rudolph II, and his father had been the director of the Imperial artillery during the Long Turkish War (1593–1606). After his mother Marie Manrique de Lara was widowed, she remarried Wolf von Mansfeld's brother Bruno, making Mansfeld not only Vratislav Eusebius's colonel but also his step-uncle.[44]

StadtA Ulm Kriegsamtes A [5556], *Verzeichnis des Kriegsvolks zu Pferd und Fuß* by Wachmeister Christoph Revelheimer, Aufstellung der Mansfeldischen Kavallerie.
[40] Parrott, *Richelieu's Army*, 178.　[41] Hanlon, *Hero of Italy*, 65.　[42] Ibid., 109.
[43] SHStADr 11237 10831/1 *Churf. Durchl. Zu Sachsen etc Erste und Andere Kriegsverfassung Nach entstandener Unruhe im Königreich Böhmen.*
[44] Petr Vorel, *Páni z Pernštejna. Vzestup a pád rodu zubří hlavy v dějinách Čech a Moravy* (Prague: Rybka, 1999), 267–274.

These lieutenant colonels of cavalry had different backgrounds and believed in different religions. When they next met at Breitenfeld they were on opposing sides. But they were both connected to Wolf von Mansfeld through feudal and familial ties. They were also friends: In their letters they describe the times they spent with each other. These letters were written on the same paper with the same ink; Löser and von Pernstein sat together as they wrote. Networks of associations like this pervaded the Saxon army and the Mansfeld Regiment.

Of the 249 deserters in Mattheus Steiner's list, 70 (28%) were Saxon. Of the ninety-three Mansfelders whose origin is known and who did not desert, forty-two (45%) came from Saxony. Deserters were proportionally less Saxon than the soldiers mentioned in the regiment's legal documents who did not desert. But when the regiment crumbled almost everyone eventually walked off, Saxons and non-Saxons alike.

4 The Spinner-Lords of Saint Gallen
Small Group Cohesion and Military Social Networks as Seen through a Theft of Fabric

It was almost midnight when Hans Jacob Schobinger heard the officers talking about the cloth. It was Sunday, November 30, 1625: The campaigning season was over. Schobinger was a fabric trader from Switzerland, representative of *die Spindlischer-Herren von St. Gall*, the Spinner-Lords of St. Gallen. He was staying with Wolfgang Winckelmann's company in Beringen while he finalized a sale to Winckelmann for the Mansfeld Regiment. The rest of the regiment was already in Lombardy but the Winckelmann Company was still in Switzerland, practically on the shores of Lake Constance, 230 miles due north of Busto Arsizio. They had been waiting for Schobinger's shipment of twenty-one bales (*Pallen*) of fabric from St. Gallen, worth over 18,000 ducats. Now Schobinger overheard a conversation between Wolfgang Winckelmann and Alwig von Sulz, colonel of another German regiment in Spanish service. A week before, said von Sulz to Winckelmann, he talked to some of Schobinger's teamsters. They told him their wagons had arrived at Beringen on the Thursday before last, November 20.[1]

Wolfgang Winckelmann was shabby, in old black silk satin breeches, an old embroidered sword belt, old black mantle, and a little Italian cap with a long black feather.[2] By the time Schobinger overheard him and von Sulz, the shipment had been sitting in a farmyard about an hour outside Beringen for ten days.

It was dark by now, lit only by fire or tallow candles, and cold. Schobinger had been up all night. Records that specify what time things happened reveal that soldiers were up later than many others in early modern Europe. Soldiers had to wake up any time or stay up late, while officers had to handle business that might happen at any hour. Common soldiers had to stand watch at all hours: German for squad leader, *gefreiter*, meant literally that he had been "freed" from having to stand watch. "Willing service by day and night" was a common sign-off for

---
[1] SHStADr 10024 9119/38, 35–78.
[2] SHStADr 10024 9678/12, *INQUISITION Acta CONTRA Den Vorhafften Wolffen winckelmann 1631*, 185.

letters. When the Mansfeld cavalry moved out, they began their working day at 10 PM. The chronicler Friedrich Friese remembered that when he was about nine his father accepted a position as a city councilor in Magdeburg and traveled from Leipzig with his family in winter 1628 to take it. As an adult, Friese remembered passing through a checkpoint at night, how he stared at the burning match against the falling snow in the dark.[3]

Schobinger's teamsters told him they had a *salva guardia* from Mansfeld. A *salva guardia* was a letter of safe conduct which in theory protected the items mentioned in it from being looted. Colonels or captains sold them to property owners in regions controlled by armies. While this was often open extortion, Mansfeld may also have given a pass to the traders hauling this cloth so they could ship it through Switzerland without danger.[4] Winckelmann should have inspected this document when the shipment arrived, but the teamsters came "uninspected." Winckelmann also remained in Beringen, instead of receiving the fabric and giving the order to move south. "To avoid danger to the security of the farm," Schobinger walked through the dark with the teamsters to see the fabric himself.[5]

The farm was about an hour away on foot. Then Schobinger saw "a watch, with a total of four or five soldiers, all with their burning lanterns and muskets." That was probably a squad, of five soldiers. The lanterns meant readiness, since soldiers could see by lantern-light and use it to signal their lack of evil intentions to others, and musketeers relit their matches by the candles. At the farm, Schobinger's investigation was barred by the intransigent self-possession of early seventeenth-century common soldiers: "I asked [the watch] if they knew if there were any traders there and whether they were to be inspected, which they did not want to grant to me at all, it was not in the orders of the Herr Oberst-Quartermaster."[6] Unless they were ordered to do something by one of their personal superiors, these men would not go out of their way for a merchant they did not know.

Schobinger walked all the way back to where he was staying deep in the morning of Monday the first of December and told Winckelmann and von Sulz's third-in-command that the soldiers would not obey him. Winckelmann did not protest. Later that morning, he asked if there

---

[3] Friedrich Friese, "Vom Magdeburgischen Unglück, vom Oberstadtschreiber Daniel Friese," in *Die Zerstörung Magdeburgs von Otto Guericke und andere denkwürdigkeiten aus dem Dreissigjährigen Kriege*, K. Lohmann, ed. (Berlin: Gutenberg Verlag, 1913), 186–187.
[4] Fritz Redlich, *De Praeda Militari: Looting and Booty, 1500–1816* (Wiesbaden: Franz Steiner Verlag, 1956), 45.
[5] SHStADr 10024 9119/38, 39–40.   [6] SHStADr 10024 9119/38, 40.

was enough security on the place. Schobinger answered that he wanted the musketeers there to listen to him, "and so I was conscious of a certain reverence for [Winckelmann's] social status I offered him 12 ducats, he answered the 12 ducats so the soldiers could have a tip from it, which I certainly assented to."[7] In addition to tipping these soldiers for following orders, Schobinger was giving Winckelmann a cut, with the understanding that Schobinger would check on the fabric Winckelmann had contracted to purchase.

Once Schobinger promised the money, Winckelmann ordered his sergeant to get a carriage together and take Schobinger back to the farm. At least it was probably full day by this point, and Schobinger no longer had to walk, but when they got there, "we found only 18 bales, and already three entire bales, in addition to six small pieces, were gone." Schobinger loaded eight of the remaining bales into the carriage and took them back to Beringen. "Ten of the whole bales we left behind with the watch, asking them to pay very close attention to it with the promise of a tip that would come to them later." When Schobinger got back to Winckelmann's quarters he could not find him:

Night came on, and in the evening in his lordly [*Graflich*] quarters, I met the Herr Oberst Quartermaster and told him the above, and how I had brought the carriage back here, nothing more really, and because of the night I brought the remainder in here. Then the Herr Quarterm. asked me to promise to do him a favour, at which he asked for half, that is 6 ducats, of the entire that had been promised to the soldiers as a tip, and I handed it over at once, and he said that in the next day they'd get the rest according to his promise with thanks.

An officer there told von Sulz's third in command that Schobinger should go to the farm with Hieronymus Sebastian Schutze, Winckelmann's flag-bearer, and watch over it that night. The regiment needed to move out the next day.[8] That was Monday, December 1, 1625. Schobinger had eight bales of fabric. Ten were still at the farm. Three had vanished.

Tuesday, December 2. "Because of heavy rains, there was water everywhere." Night fell. "None of that could be accomplished."[9]

"In the morning, on Wednesday, very early," said Schobinger, "I myself went to that farmyard with the watch, and there we found neither watch nor any other person, the remaining ten bales had all been opened and carried away. And what we found we bundled together as best as we could and brought it back to Beringen in five bales."[10] Eight bales were

---

[7] SHStADr 10024 9119/38, 41–42.   [8] SHStADr 10024 9119/38, 42–44.
[9] SHStADr 10024 9119/38, 44.   [10] SHStADr 10024 9119/38, 44.

Table 4.1 *Total value of missing cloth as enumerated by Schobinger and Beyer, December 3, 1625*

1 Bale Cambric	In which 96 pieces	Amounting to 1,496 ducats
1 Bale Cloth (*Fazeli*)	" " 42 pieces	" " 976 d
1 Bale Fustian	" " 42 pieces	" " 770 d
1 Bale Kelsch	" " 36 p. halb ordre (half order) and ½ 50 g	" " 826 d
1½ Bales Kelsch	" " 54 p seine (his or its) Kelsch	" " 1,313.6 d
½ Bale Cloth (*Farbelet*)	" " 18 p	" " 246 d
1 Bale Fine White Linen from St. Gallen	" " 49 p	" " 863.6 d
1 Bale Cloth (*Farbelet*), except for 6 pc	Except for 6 pieces, remaining 30 p	" " 400 d
Total		6,892.12 d

safe with Schobinger himself. Five had been salvaged from the ransacked farm, for a total of thirteen.

By Wednesday December 3 the total missing fabric amounted to eight bales out of 21. It was worth 6,892.12 ducats, or 115 silver crowns (Table 4.1). This was quite a bit of money.[11]

Seventeenth-century military supply is an active area of study, and too great a topic to fit within the scope of this book.[12] Fiscal-military networks interfaced with common soldiers at the regimental or company level in the daily actions of officers like Wolfgang Winckelmann and Alwig von Sulz's third in command. Quartermasters like these interacted with their superiors, with local suppliers, and with their subordinates and the soldiers they supplied. These processes were less straightforward than a purely administrative analysis suggests.

---

[11] SHStADr 10024 9119/38, 45.
[12] Anton Ernstberger, "Hans de Witte, Finanzmann Wallensteins," *Vierteljahrdevelopments they saw schrift für Sozial- und Wirtschaftsgeschichte*, Special Edition Nr. 38 (Wiesbaden: Franz Steiner Verlag, 1954); Redlich, "De Praeda Militari;" Redlich, "German Military Enterpriser;" Perjés, "Army Provisioning;" Parker, *Army of Flanders and the Spanish Road*; Martin van Creveld, *Supplying War: Logistics from Wallenstein to Patton* (Cambridge: Cambridge University Press, 1977); Kroener, *Les Routes et les Étapes*; Pohl, "*Die Profiantirung Der Keyserlichen Armaden Ahnbelangendt*;" Lynn, *Giant of the Grand Siècle*; Derek Croxton, "A Territorial Imperative? The Military Revolution, Strategy and Peacemaking in the Thirty Years War," *War in History* 5.3 (1998), 253–279; Lund, *War for the Every Day*; Parrott, *Richelieu's Army*; Parrott, *Business of War*; Höbelt, *Von Nördlingen bis Janckau*.

Like the arms trade, the networks that fed cloth to armies spanned Europe and beyond.[13] Switzerland was a European center of textile production and trade, and St. Gallen was known for its fabrics. Cambric (*Camb. Lit.*) is a plain-weave linen. Fustian (*Parchent*) refers to a cloth woven of cotton and linen; more loosely, any cotton cloth.[14] Since the word is German, this shipment's fustian may have been produced in a German-speaking region. The cotton that went into it was grown around the Mediterranean and in Armenia, then shipped to Venice or Genoa and carted up the same Alpine passes the Mansfelders trekked down on their way to Lombardy. By the seventeenth century, low-cost fustian was produced in southern Germany using local flax or hemp for the warp and cotton for the woof.[15] The word Kelsch or Golsch (*Colschen*) meant coarse, heavy linen or hemp fabric made by peasants in Alsace; it was blue-and-white striped or plaid.[16] The word translated as "cloth" or "napkin cloth" is *fazeli* or *fazolet*, which means "cloth, neck cloth, handkerchief, or napkin" in Ladin, a group of dialects spoken in South Tyrol and the Trentino.[17] *Farbelet* may be a variant spelling by a German-speaker. These fabrics were solid and plebeian, low-cost and dull-colored, the kind of thing that was sold to a regiment by the bale. The Spinner-Lords of St. Gallen had them hauled in barrels.

In contemporary France, cloth merchants contracted directly with the monarchy for military supply, and clothing was also demanded as tribute from French cities until at least 1659. The late-seventeenth-century French army made massive demands on cloth and leather production: Sources from the turn of the seventeenth/eighteenth century mention as many as 13,000 suits of clothing or 18,000 pairs of shoes from a single contractor. These were centralized efforts, directed by the French crown. They were also largely unsuccessful. The government was usually in arrears; merchants demanded cash in hand instead of assignations on future revenue, which could take months to pay out; the soldiers went

---

[13] Julia Zunckel, *Rüstungsgeschäfte im Dreißigjährigen Krieg: Unternehmerkräfte, Militärgüter, und Marktstrategien im Handel zwischen Genua, Amsterdam, und Hamburg* (Berlin: Duncker und Humblot, 1997).

[14] Alois Kiessling and Max Matthes, *Textil-Fachwörterbuch* (Berlin: Schiele & Schön, 1993), 145; Maureen Fennell Mazzaoui, "The First European Cotton Industry: Italy and Germany, 1100–1800," in *The Spinning World: A Global History of Cotton Textiles, 120–1850*, Giorgio Riello and Prasannan Parthasarathi, eds. (Oxford: Oxford University Press, 2009), 63–87, 67.

[15] Mazzaoui, "First European Cotton Industry," 74, 88.

[16] *Deutsches Wörterbuch von Jacob Grimm und Wilhelm Grimm*, entry for "Golsch."

[17] Johannes Kramer, *Etymologisches Wörterbuch des Dolomitenladinischen*, Vol III D–H (Hamburg: Helmut Buske Verlag, 1990), 215.

barefoot in the field.[18] During the seventeenth century, France was less well supplied than its enemies.[19]

In contrast, except for his coordination with Alwig von Sulz and his third-in-command, Winckelmann appears to have been getting fabric for the Mansfeld Regiment on his own. The Imperial army retained a decentralized approach to supply in which commanders were also subcontractors. Although the Imperial *Hofkriegsrat* supervised this system, arranging support services was delegated to regimental leadership.[20] On the other side of the exchange, the Spinner-Lords of St. Gallen may have managed their end of the trade with the regiments that passed through the region as a consortium.[21]

Busto Arsizio and Gallarate produced cotton and fustian themselves.[22] The manufacture flourished during the sixteenth century in Busto Arsizio and, by the early seventeenth century was a major industry there, only second to wire-drawing.[23] Cremona was the largest center for fustian, bombasine (mixed cotton and flax), and mezzelane (a low-priced fabric mixing cotton and flax). In the early fifteenth century Cremona shipped as many as 40,000 bolts of fustian to Venice alone, and in 1565 their annual fustian output was 62,000 pieces.[24]

But although recent research on Italian finance during the Thirty Years War has emphasized Italian resilience, cloth in north Italian cities was depressed within the larger economic downturn throughout Italy, the Spanish kingdoms, and Spain's New World dominions. Fustians formed the backbone of the Cremonese economy until the late sixteenth century, but the output plummeted throughout the seventeenth century.[25] Cremona wool was "virtually obliterated" in the 1630s and 1640s, and linens and silks also fell.[26] Spanish wool shipping to Italy collapsed in 1621, not only because of wider trends but also because their war with the Netherlands had resumed and Dutch ships carried wool. Despite efforts to make it up with Basque or English shipping, exports from Spain to Italy sank to their lowest level in decades in 1623–1625, right before the Mansfeld Regiment arrived.[27] Domestic wool production "virtually disappeared" in Como and Milan. Northern Italy's old

---

[18] Lynn, *Giant of the Grand Siècle*, 169–179. [19] Kroener, *Les Routes et les Étapes*.
[20] Parrott, *Business of War*, 150, 309; Pohl, "Die Profiantirung der Keyserlichen Armaden Ahnbelangendt."
[21] Parrott, *Business of War*, 214. [22] D'Amico, *Spanish Milan*, 64–89.
[23] Sella, *Crisis and Continuity*, 19. [24] Ibid., 21. [25] Ibid., 87. [26] Ibid., 54–55.
[27] Jonathan Israel, "Spanish Wool Exports and the European Economy, 1610–40," *The Economic History Review*, New Series 33.2 (1980), 193–211, 202–204.

industrial lead on other places was evaporating.[28] Milan had been known for its silk and still was but, during the seventeenth century, the numbers of new members admitted to the silk merchants' guild and the number of silk mills in Milan both declined.[29] The number of silk looms operating in Milan fell from over 3,000 in 1606 to 600 in 1635.[30]

However, it was probably not because of the decline of fabric manufacture in these cities that Winckelmann traded with merchants from St. Gallen instead of northern Italy: He may have had prior contacts in Switzerland and southern Germany, and his lieutenant Felix Steter had fought in Bern. He may also have found local production unsuitable. The village linen production that continued in the north Italian countryside probably supplied peasants and the urban poor with daily goods coarser than "fine white linen from St Gallen."[31]

Winckelmann contracted for cloth, not uniforms. Traditionally military historians regarded the development of uniforms as one strand of the development of the modern army. John Keegan described it as a loss of individuality: Unlike the seventeenth or sixteenth-century mercenary, a uniformed soldier was dressed in livery, like a servant of the sovereign who clothed him.[32] Uniforms supposedly fostered obedience, amplifying the effects of drill. To other historians they symbolize governmental or royal control over the soldier and, therefore, over the legitimate exercise of violence. Uniforms were also beautiful: Personal accounts by common soldiers in old-regime armies recount their pride in their uniforms. Eighteenth century recruiting-sergeants picked the best-looking men for recruiting parties and dressed them in new uniforms, if possible.[33] For these soldiers, distinctive dress reinforced their belonging in what Ilya Berkovich called the military counterculture.[34]

But the development of the uniform in Europe took place over a long time and does not seem linear. Early seventeenth-century soldiers wore something more like proto-uniforms. Often the standard element was only one article of clothing rather than the entire suit, like a distinctive jacket or sash. Some late sixteenth-century Spanish holders of government contracts had to produce a thousand or more suits of clothing to the same design at one time, but the color was not specified.[35] By the late seventeenth century soldiers were often provided with basic sets of

---

[28] Sella, *Crisis and Continuity*, 81.   [29] Ibid., 87.   [30] Ibid., 54–55.   [31] Ibid., 116.
[32] John Keegan, *A History of Warfare* (New York: Random House, 1993), 342–343.
[33] Berkovich, *Motivation in War*, 140.   [34] Ibid., 187.
[35] Parker, *Army of Flanders and the Spanish Road*, 138–139.

clothing that were the same in material and pattern.[36] These not-quite-uniforms were only semi-standardized, and for different reasons from modern uniforms, like cost efficiency rather than discipline or the effacement of individuality. When the author of a French military manual of the 1620s wrote about providing soldiers with clothing, this was so they could be "well-clothed," clothed in good outfits rather than rags, not identically clothed.[37]

Seventeenth-century soldiers' clothing also displayed their membership in a distinct social group, but what was on display was freedom rather than obedience, since soldiers were exempt from sumptuary laws.[38] Complaints survive from Spanish colonels peeved at having to wear black at court.[39] The Spanish theorist Martin de Eguiluz wrote that soldiers dressed in different colors would look more dangerous than soldiers dressed "all in black, so they look like citizens or shopkeepers."[40] By the sixteenth century, dressing oneself had become a means of self-expression for urban dwellers, social elites, and soldiers.[41] Ironically, that freedom was the mark of a soldier's station in the social order.

An anonymous Spanish tract from 1610 spelled it out. "There has never been a regulation for dress and weapons in the Spanish infantry because that would remove the spirit and fire which is necessary in a soldier."[42] The feathers in their hats were also symbols of "dashing masculine courage," a bouncy visual equivalent of the zip and fire these men were supposed to display.[43] Lightweight, sprightly, and expensive – this may have been one reason why flags were revered. The brightness, briskness, energy, and vigor of feathers, flags, and brave clothing were visual reflections of the spirit admired by soldiers, who complimented one another with the words *wacker*, valiant and alert, or *frisch*, brisk. One of the ways soldiers referred to an army was the old phrase *helle haufen*, the best of the forces, the elite; the "bright band." The sartorial exuberance of a soldier who could afford to dress up was a physical manifestation of his inner fire, the same spirit that provoked the watch in the farmyard to mouth off to Schobinger and stay where they were until they had been tipped to obey him.

---

[36] Lynn, *Giant of the Grand Siècle*, 170.   [37] Ibid., 170.   [38] Ibid., 170.
[39] J. R. Hale, *War and Society in Renaissance Europe, 1450–1620* (Montreal: McGill-Queen's University Press, 1998), 127–128.
[40] Parker, *Army of Flanders and the Spanish Road*, 138.
[41] Ulinka Rublack, *Dressing Up: Cultural Identity in Renaissance Europe* (Oxford: Oxford University Press, 2011).
[42] Parker, *Army of Flanders and the Spanish Road*, 138.   [43] Rublak, *Dressing Up*, 54–55.

Saxons were ahead of the curve with proto-uniforms. As early as 1613, standard mantles were worn by members of city shooting companies in Electoral Saxony, some of which still survive.[44] Documents from 1618 survive in the Saxon State Archives stipulating uniform jackets of a different color for each new Saxon company.[45] (About thirty years later, the patent raising Melchior von Gruppach to colonel mentioned the provision of mantles for his musketeers.[46]) Unlike records relating to Saxon units in the Saxon army, no stipulations for uniform jackets or mantles for the Mansfeld Regiment survive in the Dresden archive. Its soldiers may have received standard cloth as a by-product of buying cloth in bulk; on the other hand, the red fabric may have been intended to signify Habsburg service. Once they obtained the cloth, soldiers or their family members were probably expected to cut out and sew the clothing themselves.

But more than a third of Schobinger's shipment went missing instead: The regiment's system of justice swung noisily into action. Regimental Secretary Mattheus Steiner, the regiment's first Provost Hans Wolf von Schingo, and Captain-Lieutenant Andreas Medringer opened an inquest on December 16.[47]

The eleven soldiers and officers that went to the farmyard early on the morning of December 3 testified that they had found some of the fabric barrels lying open. "Some pieces of linen were strewn around," said Andreas Melchior von Schneeberg, sergeant, "which [von Schneeberg] collected and laid together, and put them together with the other things." Then Hieronymus Sebastian Schutze "honored him" with two pieces of linen, one piece of fustian, and one piece of napkin fabric (*Tellertuch* = *fazolet?*), he said.[48] Felix Steter testified that squad leader Gregor Drescher, who had the watch over the musketeers in the farmyard, told him the goods were there. Three barrels had obviously been broken open. Earlier, Winckelmann told Steter to tell the musketeers "You should keep good watch," and Steter passed this order on while having his boy fetch nine pieces of linen "from which he cut up two pieces and sold seven pieces for seven ducats."[49] Winckelmann had ordered Schutze through Steter "to go to the farmyard and lead the watch away, and if he found any barrels with wares in them, he should bring whatever he could." Schutze obeyed "because he felt guilty, he

---

[44] Roland Sennewald, *Die Kursachsen im Dreißigjährigen Krieg: Band 1: Das kursächsische Heer im Dreißigjährigen Krieg* (Berlin: Zeughaus Verlag, 2013), 633.
[45] Ibid., 634. [46] Ibid., 637. [47] SHStADr 10024 9119/38, 47.
[48] SHStADr 10024 9119/38, 48. [49] SHStADr 10024 9119/38, 49–50.

wanted to be more obedient." It had not been so long ago he accidentally shot a man.

The guilt did not stop Schutze that evening from taking "with his own hands, roughly 13 pieces of fustian, ten pieces of small white linen, five pieces of napkin fabric (*servetel* = *fazolet*?), and some pieces of mended goods." He told the squad leader he was responsible for his men and gave him four pieces of fabric. Schutze also gave some fabric to the quartermaster, "receiving a warning," and "honored" the sergeant with some.[50]

From this cloth, soldiers and women made clothing. Hans Werner bought fustian for a pair of pants from Hieronymus Sebastian Schutze's bodyguard; Joseph Rosenhauer, "sick, received linen from the flag-bearer's bodyguard for frills." Adam Pelz may have tried to hide his involvement: He was wearing a pair of fustian pants when the company was assembled and he said "his lord the Quartermaster Lieutenant gave them to him."[51]

Wednesday afternoon was still chilly and damp from that night's rain, and cloth was scattered around the farm courtyard: Both officers and men of the watch had helped themselves to the scattered remnants of this shipment. On January 9, 1626, Camargo ordered Steiner to assemble Winckelmann's entire company. He did this on or near January 11.[52] Which soldiers who were not on watch on the morning of December 3 had taken pieces of cloth? What had they done with them? Did any of them still have any?

In their testimonies, the members of the Winckelmann Company named the people to whom they had given cloth when they divided these stolen goods. If we represent hand-overs of cloth from one man or woman to another as lines in networks, we could map relationships within the company of credit, friendship, and obligation. These networks look like those in Figure 4.1.

Most fabric in motion through Winckelmann's company proceeded from flag-bearer Hieronymus Sebastian Schutze and his household (his bodyguard; the Swabian who took care of his horse). Schutze gave fabric as gifts to numerous soldiers: Barthel Baumgartner, Hans Schreber, Jacob Tett, Christian von Heinz, Joseph Rosenhauer, Georg Seyfried ("because he helped carry everything"), Georg Lehmann, Michael Kiezel, Abraham Gottlich, Michael Ullman (Schutze's servant), Hans Tümmler, Gregor Drescher, Maz Nagel, and Sergeant Andreas

---

[50] SHStADr 10024 9119/38, 50–52. [51] SHStADr 10024 9119/38, 60–74.
[52] SHStADr 10024 9119/38, 59, 75.

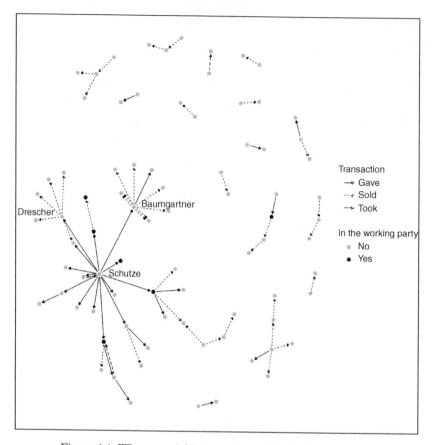

Figure 4.1 Who passed fabric to whom: Winckelmann company, Mansfeld Regiment.[53]

Melchior von Schneeberg. Winckelmann said he saw a sack full of fabric sitting in Schutze's quarters "which his people received."[54]

Schutze gave fabric to his subordinate officer and common soldiers, but the soldiers sold or bartered fabric with one another. He was their superior, while they were one another's peers. Like the inhabitants of the villages studied by Hanlon and David Sabean, they managed reciprocal obligations.[55] "David Zenischen, sick, received six ells of red linen from

---

[53] Thanks to Graham Pressey for the data visualization.
[54] SHStADr 10024 9119/38, 58.
[55] Gregory Hanlon, *Human Nature in Rural Tuscany* (New York: Palgrave Macmillan, 2007), 40–42.

Michael Melhorn, and was honored by it [*verehret bekommen*]." Peter Hagendorf used the same word to describe his comrades giving him a share of their Magdeburg booty in cash, since Hagendorf had been wounded and could not make the sack.[56] Soldiers talked about this in terms of respect paid and honor done: If one soldier gave another a piece of scavenged cloth, it was not a purely material relationship. Christoff Zisner received "blue stuff" as a gift from Michael Kiezel for a pair of hose. Gregor Kretzschmaier bought six ells of fustian from another soldier and "paid his respects to [that soldier's] wife with four ells of multicolored stuff as true payment," possibly in return for an existing debt. In this documentation, some of the links of debt and credit that veined through the regiment may have been made visible to historians for an instant.

Many of the men to whom Schutze distributed fabric had been members of the working party at the farmhouse, and Barthel Baumgartner and two of the men he gave fabric to had also been in the room when Schutze shot Hans Heinrich Tauerling in the eye. Schutze may have picked Baumgartner and his mates routinely for detached tasks, such as making noise when Schutze drank and shot his big pistols out the window, or theft. In this way, this important officer reinforced his links to men in his company, but possibly only certain men. The same men who refused to listen to Hans Jacob Schobinger received fabric from Hieronymus Sebastian Schutze's hands.

Pieces of stolen fabric are a tracking isotope: As they disseminate through the Winckelmann company, we see traces of smaller groups. Groups like these traveled together, robbed together, and backed one another up in fights. Small groups offered affection, closeness, and a squabbling, tumultuous human warmth. These were the people to whom it mattered if you were a righteous guy.

Within the field of military history, these groups have offered one explanation for why men fight. Immediately after the Second World War, influential works like S. L. A. Marshall's *Men against Fire* and Shils and Janowitz's "Cohesion and Disintegration in the Wehrmacht" cemented the place of small groups in the historiography of conflict, arguing that men fought and endured fighting for love of their primary social group.[57] Shils and Janowitz argued that the decisive fact keeping

---

[56] Hagendorf, *Ein Söldnerleben im Dreißigjährigen Krieg*, 47.
[57] S. L. A. Marshall, *Men Against Fire: The Problem of Battle Command* (New York: William Morrow and Company, 1947); E. A. Shils and Morris Janowitz, "Cohesion and Disintegration in the Wehrmacht in World War II," *The Public Opinion Quarterly* 12.2 (1948), 280–315; Samuel Stouffer, *Studies in Social Psychology in World War II: The American Soldier* (Princeton: Princeton University Press, 1949).

"the ordinary German soldier" from deserting "was that he was a member of a squad or section which maintained its structural integrity and which coincided roughly with the *social* unit which satisfied some of his major primary needs." This group comprised both soldiers and officers: A soldier "was likely to go on fighting ... as long as the group possessed leadership with which he could identify himself, and as long as he gave affection to and received affection from the other members of his squad and platoon ... as long as he felt himself to be a member of his primary group and therefore bound by the expectations and demands of its other members."[58]

In contrast, Christopher Hamner argued that there is no single reason men fight, pointing to a number of reasons including their perception of their superiors, their beliefs about the effectiveness of their equipment, ideological commitment, and the belief that fighting gives them a greater chance of survival.[59] Hamner also argued that combat motivations are historically contingent, since combat experience is historically contingent; the shoulder-to-shoulder fighting of the American Civil War is not the same as the seemingly "empty battlefield" of the Second World War. Although human affection is a powerful thing, an explanation that relies on many reasons for why people do something seems more realistic as a description of motivation than an analysis resting on one.

Marshall's and Shils and Janowitz's explanations are also somewhat rigid and literal. Marshall often stated performance in battle depends on comrades' physical presence near one another. The "touch of human nature" often literally gives men courage: What "enables an infantry soldier to keep going with his weapons is the near presence or the presumed presence of a comrade." "The other man may be almost beyond hailing or seeing distance, but he must be there somewhere within a man's consciousness."[60] Soldiers in a group must be able to see, hear, and communicate with one another.[61] It is also difficult to plug someone new into an existing group.[62] Hamner addressed the last claim when he discussed primary groups in the Wehrmacht during the Second World War. Shils and Janowitz argued that the primary social group had to maintain its structural integrity; although they did not say it was difficult to integrate new members into this group, both Marshall and Hamner seem to have believed this was the case. Shils and Janowitz also said the primary social group overlapped with the basic tactical unit, the

---

[58] Shils and Janowitz, "Cohesion and Disintegration," 284.
[59] Christopher H. Hamner, *Enduring Battle: American Soldiers in Three Wars, 1776–1945* (Lawrence: University Press of Kansas, 2011).
[60] Marshall, *Men against Fire*, 41–42. [61] Ibid., 125–127. [62] Ibid., 42, 151.

squad or section. For these reasons, Hamner argued against their contention that the cohesion of primary groups was responsible for units' tenacity, since primary groups as Shils and Janowitz describe them can disintegrate if a unit suffers massive casualties.[63] These authors imply that once a primary group's members die, they cannot be replaced.

A model of human affection that requires the literal physical presence of one's friends, and assumes that these friends are irreplaceable, seems overly restrictive. It may be more productive to think in terms of social networks, a term which connotes something larger and more flexible than primary group. As we see from Figure 4.1 and Mansfeld documents, seventeenth-century soldiers' social networks included men and women, combatants and noncombatants, officers and men. Describing the groups that met early modern soldiers' emotional needs as social networks instead of primary groups also removes the emphasis on the literal physical closeness of group members, since early modern units often operated over great distances.[64] People can enter these networks or leave them, and if some members leave or die, new members can join. Social networks need not coincide with small tactical or administrative units. The working party at the farmhouse may have been distinct from a squad; it drew from all the corporalschaffts in the company. Moreover, social networks not only contain people who give and receive affection, these groups may also contain people who feel neutral, ambivalent, or hostile to one another – or are affectionate at some times and hostile at other times. For early seventeenth-century soldiers as for ourselves, human groups comprise every shade of human interaction.

In places, Marshall makes claims that are like these descriptions, and less literal or restrictive. He writes that the soldier is unwilling to risk danger "on behalf of men with whom he has no social identity." Human beings want to be known to one another.[65] As means of obtaining, safeguarding, and redistributing resources, the social networks in Winckelmann's company are also militarized counterparts to the families in Venetian territory that Giulio Ongaro studied, who used their social positions and their internal ties to benefit financially from their dealings with the Venetian army.[66]

The discussion of small or primary groups is one element of a wider historiographical treatment of combat motivation. Most Mansfelders

---

[63] Hamner, *Enduring Battle*, 174–175.
[64] A company of Liga cavalry I analyzed in another paper maintained operational cohesion over more than ninety miles, and I believe this was routine. Staiano-Daniels, "Two Weeks in Summer."
[65] Marshall, *Men against Fire*, 153. [66] Ongaro, *Peasants and Soldiers*, chapter 6.

were more reticent than the light cavalryman who said he had become a soldier *vor rauberei*, "so I could rob people." However, although combat motivation in the early seventeenth century is outside the scope of this book, I am indebted to Ilya Berkovich's analysis of motivation among common soldiers a century later. Berkovich drew on the memoirs of eighteenth-century soldiers to argue that men enlisted for many reasons, including to attain honor, and that they then internalized the standards of the military subculture. They participated in combat for reasons including dynastic loyalty, personal loyalty, or ideology. However, like the analyses of primary group cohesion on which he rests, Berkovich argues that the main motivation of these soldiers was their friends: These men fought to not let their friends down and to obtain their good opinion.[67] The social networks visible in the Winckelmann company during the theft and circulation of this fabric may also have fought side by side.

Squad mates were recorded on the same page of Saxon muster rolls and may have eaten together, like messmates did in later armies and like squad mates did in the army of Parma. In Mansfeld sources, they sleep in the same beds.[68] In Winckelmann's company the men and women in social networks are made visible when they shared stolen fabric with one another, recorded here in their testimony and traced in Figure 4.1. With this they could make new clothing in winter, making comradeship the difference between misery and a little comfort.

But this distribution was the direct result of theft, reinforcing Hamner's insight that, instead of always supporting an army's performance, the comradeship of small groups can also produce actions that are counterproductive to it, or in opposition to the aims of the government directing it.[69] For instance, we have already seen that friends prevailed on one another to desert; Gregory Hanlon argued that soldiers who came from the same place or had similar backgrounds – and were therefore likely to be part of the same social groups – deserted together.[70] Stealing and distributing fabric was good for Hieronymus Sebastian Schutze, his household, and some people in Winckelmann's company, but it helped make that company odious to the traders with which Winckelmann did business, and it disrupted Winckelmann's quiet exercise of his prerogatives.

This raises the possibility that primary group cohesion or the influence of social networks at the micro scale were more important for the activities of seventeenth-century soldiers that did not include set-piece battle,

---

[67] Berkovich, *Motivation in War*.
[68] Hanlon, *Hero of Italy*, 65–66.
[69] Hamner, *Enduring Battle*, 176.
[70] Hanlon, *Hero of Italy*, 65.

Table 4.2 *Total value of cloth that Steiner found in Winckelmann Company, January 11, 1626, in Milanese lire*[71]

4 pc ordinary kelsch	Each 55 P		220 P
1 pc *deho soppo*	....		83
6 pc Augsburger fustian	Each 55		330
3 pc cloth (*Fazolet*) 155 M^d 16	Each 12		155
1 pc cloth 54 M^d 20	Each 16		72
1 pc cloth 50 M^d 26	Each 22		91.8
2 pc rough cloth, from which some was cut out	....		100
1 pc linen from the region	No. 19200	....	34
2 pc Dato [ditto]	No. 21220	Ea 38	76
1 pc Dato	No. 27280	....	50
1 pc Deto	No. 26270	....	48
1 pc Deto	No. 30310	....	56
1 pc linen from St. Gallen	No. 24151	....	48

like looting, scrounging, or guerrilla fighting, than to performance in battle itself.

The total monetary value of the fabric Steiner managed to track down was not high. One of the Swiss agents made a list of the fabric the soldiers of Winckelmann's company had taken for themselves or sold (Table 4.2).

This list has catalog numbers in it. Textiles have been labeled with numbers since the Middle Ages, but the practice is still understudied because of lack of documentation. These numbers categorized the prices of different grades of fabric, listed the sizes of different kinds of fabric, or denoted a textile's origin.[72] Practices varied widely by region, so exactly what the numbers in this list signify is unclear. There is an obvious difference in price among different kinds of "linen from the countryside" (*landt leinradt*), as well as between "linen from the countryside" and "linen from St. Gallen" (*galler leinwadt*). The numbers may also catalog individual bales of fabric for shipping, a kind of early-modern tracking system.

The total value of the cloth in this list amounted to only 1,363.8 Milanese pounds or 780 ducats, about a ninth of the original 6,892.12 ducat loss. The soldiers who picked through the farmyard on the

---

[71] SHStADr 10024 9119/38, 77.
[72] Christoff Jeggle, "Labeling with Numbers? Weavers, Merchants and the Valuation of Linen in Seventeenth-Century Münster," in *Concepts of Value in European Material Culture, 1500–1900*, Bert de Munck and Dries Lyna, eds. (Surrey: Ashgate, 2015), 33–56, 33.

afternoon of December 3 had just been scavenging. Three or four ells of cloth is valuable to a common soldier but compared to the kind of money a trader or a high officer handles, it is unspectacular. But, at some point before the night of November 31/December 1, three full bales of cloth went missing from Schobinger's and Beyer's shipment. The barrels had been in a farmyard near Beringen for eleven days; the theft could have happened at any time during this period. The remaining barrels were cracked open and pieces of fabric amounting to an additional five bales' worth were taken some time between Monday December 1 and the early morning of Wednesday December 3, probably on Tuesday, when most of the soldiers were indoors or trying to shelter from the winter rain.

While Schutze had been disseminating cloth through his company and other soldiers had been carrying bits of cloth off here and there, the real theft had been taking place unnoticed behind the scenes. After Schobinger and Beyer brought the original theft up in their written complaint, dated December 3, nobody mentioned it again.

After Winckelmann's company had been assembled and questioned, and the value of the cloths they had taken totaled up, Wendel Beyer wrote an irate letter (undated) demanding the refund of the entire 780 ducat sum in cash, representing both the whole pieces of cloth that Steiner had been able to track down and the cloth that the soldiers had already "turned to their own use." (In this letter the soldiers were "*Soldaten*," not "*Leute*": Those who were involved with the military community were the ones who called them "the People" and Beyer wanted to be involved as little as possible.) He demanded Winckelmann himself "give [him] satisfaction," not the regimental bailiff or anyone else.[73]

On January 13, another letter from Beyer said Mattheus Steiner gave him twenty-six pieces of cloth which he had collected himself from the soldiers of Winckelmann's company, and 1,500 Milanese pounds in cash. "For such a quittance" wrote Beyer stiffly, "in the name of the aforementioned Spinner-Lords, about all the wares broken up and taken [taken "*auser brehmen*"], I will have no more deliveries or claims upon Herr Winckelmann." He signed the letter in his capacity as the representative of the Spinner-Lords of St. Gallen.[74]

Regimental bailiff and secretary Mattheus Steiner was diligent. He wrote down all the Mansfeld Regiment's internal legal records and carried out both big investigations in the regiment: This fabric theft and

---

[73] SHStADr 10024 9119/38, 75–76. [74] SHStADr 10024 9119/38, 78.

the lieutenant colonel's murder of his wife. We see the regiment's daily activities through his actions. In his capacity as bailiff, he ordered and oversaw the torture of three common soldiers accused of theft.[75] He repaid Hans Jacob Schobinger and Wendel Beyer, but it is impossible to know if he meant them well.

The soldiers of Winckelmann's company who had already made their fabric into clothing got to keep it, perhaps those who were most in need. Hieronymus Sebastian Schutze got to assuage his guilt by obeying orders and providing for his subordinates. Only the Swiss traders came out behind: 6,892.12 ducats worth of cloth was tremendously valuable, and 1,500 lire did not come close to covering it.

A copy of a letter from Mansfeld to Winckelmann exists, written from Milan on December 16. It is brief and says little: Only that Winckelmann should reimburse the traders from St. Gallen "so they become content." The postscript is more interesting. "PS: In this and in other things you have been unsuccessful [*verfehlet*], because you need to know how to be more decisive [*dorinnen ihr bescheids bedürftig*]. Along with the Lieutenant Colonel, you should take a vacation."[76] Wolf von Mansfeld and Wolfgang Winckelmann had worked together for a while by late 1625: Winckelmann had been a cavalry trooper in Mansfeld's life company back in 1620, and he led a company in the cavalry regiment Mansfeld raised in 1623.[77] Mansfeld was an experienced commander, and he itemized the monthly bribe he paid the Imperial Commissioner of War in his budget like he had him on retainer. This instruction, and the abrupt end of the investigation once Steiner had searched the common soldiers of Winckelmann's company, seems to point – delicately – toward something more than Mansfeld wrote explicitly.

This is one of the most detailed accounts in the Mansfeld legal books. It offers a rounded view of life in the regiment: The exhausting daily effort to obtain resources, the operation of the regimental justice system, and interactions and relationships among Hieronymus Sebastian Schutze and some soldiers in his company. It also demonstrates the networks of trade and supply that joined the Mansfeld Regiment to people outside itself, and the social networks that helped govern the circulation of goods within the regiment, whether licit or illicit. Through Schutze's and his men's theft and distribution of cloth, we can track the relationships and interactions of a company-level officer, as well as the interactions of primary social groups within the company. The human connection of

---

[75] Staiano-Daniels, "Masters in the Things of War." [76] SHStADr 10024 9119/38, 46.
[77] SHStADr 11237 10839/7.

these groups did not facilitate resilience in combat, about which there is little in Mansfeld sources, but theft.

This theft was minor compared to Winckelmann's activities, and the response of the regimental staff. Mattheus Steiner went along with the coverup, although he made some effort to pay Schobinger and Beyer back. The regiment closed ranks around its own.

Wolfgang Winckelmann moved into Imperial service after he came back to Germany and kept doing what he did serving Mansfeld in Italy, but less subtly. In January 1631 he was arrested for sacking an estate near Halle that belonged to Joachim Goldstein, the chancellor of Merseburg and a feudal subordinate of the Elector of Saxony, therefore subject to his jurisdiction. It turned out Winckelmann had removed agricultural products and livestock worth 11,832.5 thaler and sent refugees streaming toward Leipzig.[78] A discreet disappearance of fabric may have been one thing, but this was crossing a line. The inquiry dragged on: By February 1632, he was kept in a room in the Rathaus in Dresden, on only "1 and a half Maß of table wine" (about three pints), "3 Maß beer" (about seven pints), and "2 [loaves] of white bread" a day.[79] Winckelmann remained jailed for years, while Saxony changed sides twice.[80] Once he and his wife paid off the costs of his upkeep during his imprisonment (the provost and other officials in Dresden and Leipzig complained about the cost of his alcohol consumption, his butter and cheese), he was ordered released on August 1, 1637, although, because he still owed a little, he remained fettered until August 5th. Then Wolfgang Winckelmann left prison.[81]

---

[78] SHStADr 10024 9678/12, 39.   [79] SHStADr 10024 9678/12, 56–58.
[80] SHStADr 10024 9678/12, 89–90.
[81] SHStADr 10024 9678/12, 114–116, 122 ff. Winckelmann's release order is p. 202.

5 The Kind of People I Know You Will Like
Social Structure in the Saxon Army and the Mansfeld Regiment

In summer 1625, Theodoro de Camargo was in Brussels brooding on the things Victoria Guarde did with Italian officers in her inner rooms every night and Wolf von Mansfeld was trying to persuade him to join his Italian expedition. He said he had already begun recruiting. "I assure you that you will find The Regiment made up of the kind of people I know you will like," he wrote in clumsy French, probably Camargo's native language.[1] When he said "people," *telles gens*, he meant what military people almost always meant when they said it, which was The People: Soldiers. He may have meant that at least some future members of this regiment were experienced. On April 27, 1626, Francisco Ocampo described it and the Sulz Regiment as "the two old regiments," although both had been recruited a year previously.[2] Early seventeenth-century military units were made up of thick networks of personal relationships, larger and more expansive versions of the networks which are visible within Winckelmann's company. Many soldiers not only stayed in the army for a long time, they did so in groups of family or friends. Within this context, soldiers gained experience slowly, through long participation in the military way of life. Training, ranks, office, and hierarchy in this environment were different from later European armies. They were also different from wider seventeenth-century society: The difference between noble and commoner was looser, and seniority may have been more important than birth. It was possible, but difficult, for common soldiers to rise socially.

Social division within companies may have been based largely on function. Early seventeenth-century military ranks are inconsistent and idiosyncratic, and muster-writers varied the way they recorded troops based on what may have been personal preference. An officer (*Offizier*)

---

[1] "Au reste ie vous asseure, que trouverer Le Regiment composé de telles gens, que ie sui certain, que vous vous entiendrez content." Letter of Mansfeld to Theorodo de Camargo, August 6, 1625, SHStADr 10024 9737/13, *Italienische und französische* Concepta *derer Schreiben Graf Wolfgangs zu Mansfeld an den Herzog von* Feria, *Spanischen bottschafter, und andere ao 1625-26*, 4–5.

[2] AST Archivio Sola Busca, Serbelloni, box 47. Letter from Francisco Ocampo, April 27, 1626.

held an office (*Officium*) in the sense of "defined task" instead of "rank." A regiment was headed by a colonel like Mansfeld. It was often led by him in combat as well, but Mansfeld spent most of the time in Leipzig, Prague, or his own estates in Schluckenau in northern Bohemia. Under him was usually one lieutenant colonel. The Mansfeld Regiment had three: Eustachius Löser and Vratislav Eusebius von Pernstein for the horse, and Theodoro de Camargo for the foot. Beneath them were the regimental staff: The third in command (Oberst Wachtmeister), quartermaster, regimental bailiff (Schultheiss), regimental secretary (Secretarius), preacher (Feldprediger), the officer in charge of provisioning (Proviantmeister), wagon master (Wagenmeister), regimental surgeon (Regiments Feldscher), legal secretary (Gerichtsschreiber), bailiff's assistant (Gerichtswebel), regimental drummer, provost and his assistants, the officer in charge of the baggage train (Hurenwebel, literally *whore sergeant*), and the executioner and his assistants. Infantry officers at company level are listed on the *prima plana*, "first page" of the infantry roll: Captain (Hauptmann), flag-bearer (Fähndrich), Lieutenant, sergeant/Feldwebel, company clerk (Muster-writer), company surgeon (Feldscher), commander (Führer), Fourier, two corporals/Gemeinwebels, one piper, and three drummers, more or less. (In some rolls sergeants and Feldwebels, or corporals and Gemeinwebels, are different ranks.)

Officers changed roles frequently: A muster-writer in one campaign could be a lieutenant in the next or vice versa. Many regimental officers also commanded companies. Sometimes individual officers doubled up: Mattheus Steiner was both the bailiff and the secretary of the Mansfeld Regiment, and Wolfgang Winckelmann was its quartermaster and its third-in-command. Senior common soldiers often became lower-level officers, lower officers sometimes dipped back down the ranks to pikeman or halberdier again. Once a company dissolved, its social ordinances were no longer obligatory. Before the war, the military theorist Johann Jacobi von Wallhausen said that as soon as "the flags have been ripped from their poles," dissolving the companies, "the least / loosest / most frivolous scoundrel can call out his captain / his lieutenant / his flag-bearer / his sergeant / his corporal / his wagon master / his quartermaster / the provost ... Yes / and say to them: Hey man / you used to be my officer / but now you aren't / now you're not a hair better than I am" and fight him one-on-one for bossing him around.[3]

---

[3] Johann Jacobi von Wallhausen, *Kriegskunst zu Fuß, zu hochnöthigstem Nutzen und Besten nicht allein allen ankommenden Soldaten, sondern auch in Abrichtung eines gemeinen Landvolcks und Ausschuß in Fürtstenthümern und Stätte* (Oppenheim: Heironymus Gallero, 1615), 20.

In the 1620s, common soldiers were divided by the function and honor of their offices. Heavily-armored cavalrymen were more honorable than lightly-armored cavalrymen, and everyone looked down on dragoons. Infantrymen were divided into pikemen, who fought with long spears, and musketeers. In the Saxon army in the 1620s, twenty men out of every company also fought with halberds. The pike was the most honorable infantry weapon. Pikemen made more than other infantrymen and were listed before them on the rolls. In battle, the flag-bearers either lined up in the center of the infantry block with the pikemen around them or, if the army fought according to Swedish drill, they stood in the center front of the infantry formation, in front of the pikes. Both pikes and flags were honorable objects, and pikes were often described as "cloaking" or "covering" the flag with their honorable presence (*bedecken*). When taking a city by storm, the place of honor was the very front, and the flag-bearer's place was there, again "cloaked" by the pikes.[4] Writers debated the pike's usefulness but agreed about its status. There was no cultural place for the brawling sword and buckler even the stout and specialized halberd, comparable to pikes: To learn something "from the pike up" is to learn by doing; "to trail a pike" is to be a soldier. If a soldier died in camp, he was borne to the grave on a stretcher made of pikes.[5] When a commander knew a battle was lost, he sometimes dismounted, grabbed a pike, and fought in the infantry's first rank with his men.[6] In contracts and muster rolls the word "weapon" (*Gewehr*) on its own with no further elaboration almost always means pike. A "short-weapon" (*Kurtzgewehr*) is a halberd.[7] A "side-weapon" (*Seitengewehr*) is literally a sidearm, a sword, another symbol of a soldier's office. Muskets were not often "weapons": A contract from 1619 specifies that the 300 soldiers it covers should be supplied "with weapons and muskets."[8] Halberdiers came second in order of precedence after pikemen, then musketeers.

---

[4] Sennewald, *Das kursächsische Heer im Dreißigjährigen Krieg*, 33.
[5] Hans Wilhelm Kirchhof, *Militaris Disciplina, Kriegs Regiments Historische und außführliche Beschreibung: Wie / und was massen / solches bey unsern löblichen Vorfahren / und der alten Mannlichen Teutschen Nation vorzeiten / innsonderheit aber bey den Großmächtigsten Keysern / Maximiliano I und Carolo V und folgendes in ublichem Gebrauch gehalten / auch nach und nach verbessert worden: in drey underschiedliche Disemß oder Bücher abgetheilet* (Frankfurt am Main: Joachim Brathering, 1602), 203.
[6] Robert Frost, *The Northern Wars: War, State and Society in Northeastern Europe, 1558–1721* (London: Routledge, 2000), 65.
[7] SHStADr 10024 9119/38, 103–115.
[8] SHStADr 11237 10798/4, *Niedereingegebene Feld-Kriegs-Und Andere Bestallungen, De Ais 1618, 19, 20, 21, 22, 23, 24, 28, 32, 35, 39*, p. 2v section 5: the soldiers should with the necessary "Wustungen, Wehren, Musqueten, und dergleichen Zugehörig aus Sr. Churf. Dr. Zeughaus bewehret gemacht."

Some of the most senior soldiers were formally labeled as squad leaders (*Gefreiter*) or senior squad leaders (*Gefreiter Corporal*), but other experienced soldiers had no written designation. In Chapter 8, I argue that in the 1620s the more experienced soldiers were visible in the rolls because they were paid more than the others, whether or not their office differed explicitly.

Historians from the middle of the twentieth century argued that soldiers in the early seventeenth century were trained by standardized drilling, delineated in printed drill manuals like Wallhausen's or Jacob de Gheyn's.[9] However, the cultural place of these manuals is complex, and there is no mention of drill in the documents that describe the daily lives of the Mansfelders. In these documents, the Mansfelders drink in The Angel and one another's quarters, they scuffle with one another, they crouch in front of the fireplace to cook rice, they chop vegetables, they go to the forest to cut wood, they help the civilians they live with get water, they sit on the stoop in front of their quarters, they play dice outside their captain's room, they fire salutes whenever a high-ranking officer leaves his quarters, they watch the civilians bring the sheep in from the meadow, and they sleep in the same bed with the two civilian brothers they stay with and the dog, but drill was not recorded. While the absence of evidence does not necessarily imply the evidence of absence, the Mansfelders gained experience gradually, and learned from one another, whether they drilled or not.

Experienced soldiers were essential for training new ones: Contemporary texts discuss how important they were and how important it was to distribute the new people among them.[10] Experienced men knew how to find food and how to sleep in the open, the little daily tasks that made up a soldier's life. They knew how to live with other soldiers with minimal friction, even people who belonged to other religions or came from other places. In battle they helped keep the block together, which is the origin of some of the French terms for old soldiers: The *chef-de-file*, "chief of the line," stood in the first rank of the formation; the *chef-de-serre-file*, "chief of the back of the line," stood in the rear; and if a regiment had enough experienced people, a *chef-de-demi-file*, "chief of halfway down the line," stood in the fourth or sixth place. The French also called experienced soldiers *anspessades*, from *Lanza Spezzata*, "broken lance."[11] Wallhausen called them "Lancepassades" and said

---

[9] M. D. Feld, "Middle Class Society and the Rise of Military Professionalism: The Dutch Army 1589–1609," *Armed Forces and Society* 1.4 (1975), 419–423; Lynn, *Giant of the Grand Siècle*, 515–518.
[10] Parrott, *Richelieu's Army*, 40–41, fn 80.   [11] Ibid., 140–141.

they should help the corporals, and hold watch only in dangerous situations.[12] Otherwise they were too good for it.

The Mansfeld Regiment's Jacob Hammer and Samuel Bernhardt were lancepassades.[13] When the Imperialist soldier Erhart Stocker was arrested by the Land Court of Schlanders in the Tyrol for killing a tavernkeeper, his captain pled for his release: Not only was it unclear whether Stocker had been responsible for the man's death when he stabbed him, but Stocker was an experienced soldier and his captain needed him to help the lower officers and train the new people (*jungen leithen*). "In favourem militiae et defensionis patriae," he asked for a pardon.[14] In 1644, Bogislav of Chemnitz described Imperial general Matthias Gallass's task force as "a beautiful old people," meaning experienced.[15] Veterans were rare, and armies needed them. Finding someone who was not a soldier and turning him into one was not the first thing that came to a recruiter's mind: Until after the 1660s, the French believed the number of potential soldiers was finite.[16]

Loose crowds of individuals with more or less formal roles accompanied armies. Common soldiers and officers had families, officers had servants and retainers. Common soldiers sometimes maintained servants. Cavalrymen had boy servants (*Jungen*) and/or cavalry servants (*Knechte*) listed under them, who probably attended to the horses, helped buckle cuirassiers into their armor, and may have accompanied the troopers into combat. Several infantry rolls count attendants (*Aufwarter*), bodyguards, and "the rabble" (*Gesindel*) attendant upon some officers. Cavalry rolls in the 1620s also sometimes record members of officers' entourages, although the actual number of hangers-on was almost certainly more than the number on the rolls. The large strings of horses that cavalry officers had may also reflect the numbers of people around them. It may be possible to see these entourages in the provisioning records. Meat was given out by the pound and in the provisioning

---

[12] Johann Jacobi von Wallhausen, *Manuale Militaire, oder Kriegs-Manual / Darinnen I, Die Fürnembste Heuteges Tages Edle Haupt Kriegß Kunste zu Landt. II, Der Griechen Lacadaemoniern / und Romanen Kriegß Disciplinen kürtzest aus dem Frantzoischen / mit schönen Kupfferstücken hergegeben werden / gemehret und gebessert. III, Ein Kriegß Nomenclatur* (Frankfurt: Paul Jacobi, 1617), 123.
[13] SHStADr 10024 9119/38, 103, 109.
[14] Martin Paul Schennach, "Lokale Obrigkeiten und Soldaten. Militärgerichtsbarkeit in Tirol in der ersten Hälfte des 17. Jahrhunderts," in *Justiz und Gerechtigkeit. Historische Beiträge (16.–19. Jahrhundert)*, Andrea Griesebner, Martin Scheutz, and Herwig Weigl, eds. (Vienna: Studienverlag, 2002), 210–211.
[15] Bogislav Philip von Chemnitz, *Königlich Schwedischen in Teutschland geführten Krieges*, Vol 4 (Stockholm: 1855), 168
[16] Rowlands, *Dynastic State*, 171.

records for some cavalry Wolf von Mansfeld led in 1624, watch-masters, Captain-Lieutenants, and cornets got more. So did members of more honorable companies in the regiment. Not only may these people have been better-fed, but more individuals may have accompanied them and, as food was passed to them, they passed it on to their entourages.[17]

The social distance between common soldiers and minor officers, and among different ranks, was smaller in the Mansfeld Regiment than it was in later armies. Because almost all members of the military community were crammed wherever there was room, officers and soldiers lived on top of one another. They socialized with one another and drank and ate together. They may have slept in the same rooms.

These close relationships were like a contemporary civilian society with few members, close quarters, and not many resources, the rural Tuscans studied by Gregory Hanlon.[18] The commoners and petty nobles in his study associated with one another and fought with one another; similarly, the comparatively relaxed social divisions in the Mansfeld Regiment may have paradoxically led to more fights between officers and common soldiers than in later armies. The chronic low-level jostling in this society could easily spin off into serious violence, not only between members of similar ranks, but sometimes between common soldiers and officers. Violence across social caste lines happened more than once in the Mansfeld Regiment.

If Busto Arsizio had more than one tavern, the Mansfelders' records do not show it. The Angel was the only tavern in Mansfelder documents, and officers and common soldiers crowded its tables. On February 12, 1626, Georg Ross, musketeer in the Life Company, walked into this tavern and accused a corporal of bounty-jumping: "you took money from the lords twice but only marched out once," he said. They ran outside with their swords out. The regimental provisions master Hans Georg Heyl decided to leave but, when Ross and the corporal were on their way back in, Ross bumped into Heyl in the doorway. This common musketeer not only shoved the provisions master away with derisive words, he also called Heyl the familiar *du*, instead of the respectful *Sie* or *Ihr* – "as though I made brotherhood with him!" complained Heyl. Heyl sent for Ross's superior, Captain-Lieutenant Andreas Medringer. Medringer was irate, not at his musketeer for snapping at a regimental officer, but at Heyl, for attempting to discipline one of Medringer's soldiers. Which

---

[17] SHStDr 11237 10940/20, *Proviant-Rechnung im Haubtt-Quartier Dölitzsch 1624*; SHStADr 11237 10831/1 *Churf. Durchl. Zu Sachsen etc Erste und Andere Kriegsverfassung Nach entstandener Unruhe im Königreich Böhmen*.
[18] Hanlon, *Human Nature in Rural Tuscany*, 87.

officer had the right to command whose men was a frequent flashpoint for fights among officers. Medringer would have attacked Heyl with a halberd he grabbed from a man on watch, had another officer not separated them. Heyl sued.

When Mattheus Steiner tracked down and listed the witnesses, it turned out that the tavernful of drinkers had segregated themselves at their tables by function, not social status or regional origin. At Heyl's table were the wagon master; the Quartermaster-Lieutenant; and Heyl himself, the provisions master: All regimental officers, all responsible for supply. At the next table were two company surgeons, two corporals, one man listed as a Gemeinwebel, and one Lancepassade: All minor officers and one experienced common soldier. Except for the surgeons, these men were responsible for directing and overseeing the common soldiers. They said they had been "too far away" from the first group to offer them a drink and a place at their table. The onlookers who thronged the tavern probably knew one another, but their seating arrangements followed their working roles. They separated themselves by rank and office. However, none of the fights followed this division. Ross's first target was a corporal, one of the lowest ranks it was possible to have and still be an officer, but once provisions master Heyl bumped into him and took the door handle out of his hand Ross lashed out, even against a regimental officer.[19] Daily life in the Mansfeld Regiment was segmented by rank but comparatively disorganized about it, and the officers were as jealous of their turf as the common soldiers.

Mansfelders jostled for personal honor even when they could do nothing to affect the formal relationship between their ranks, or sometimes their ages. Captain Ponickau's lieutenant Nicholas Korn testified that, on September 2, 1626, Michael Andreas the drummer came into his quarters and asked the piper to give him some money, because they had waited on someone together. (They were closely packed: Korn and the piper must have been together in that room.) When the piper said he had no coins and asked Andreas to be patient, Lieutenant Korn told Andreas to go home into his own quarters. He came back as angry as he was before, and when Korn told him again to go home, he answered, "What does he have to command him?" At that the lieutenant "was moved to make him tractable with a bludgeon he had in his hands." In the next room the soldiers Urban Beyer, Christoff Pfeiffer, Christoff Frederick, and Hans Werner heard Andreas scream "as though he had his arm broken in two," which Beyer could not stand, so he found a

[19] SHStADr 10024 9119/38, 103–111.

barber surgeon to see how things stood with him. Andreas went back to his room, finally tractable, but once safely out of the lieutenant's reach, he stuck his head out his window and yelled "You hit me like a rogue!" This, unlike everything else up to that point, was legally actionable: The lieutenant sued him. Michael Andreas was not only Nicholas Korn's inferior, he was probably younger, since many drummers and pipers were teens. They were also often related to officers: The unnamed piper may have been Michael Andreas's kin. Since Andreas had called the lieutenant a rogue, he was expelled like a rogue, without money or passport. Lieutenant Nicholas Korn and Drummer Michael Andreas were not equals: The striking element of this case is that Andreas fought back at all, by calling Korn a rogue in public.[20]

A Mansfeld common soldier and a lower officer fought a duel at least once. On April 12, 1626, corporal Valentin von Treutler and common soldier Jonas Eckert had a drink together in "their village" in Lombardy, meaning the village they were quartered in, like "home" was the room they were staying in at the time. As they were "walking home, very happy" (*in allen guten nach hause zugangen*), the village consul met von Treutler by chance and walked beside him. Eckert followed them both, then walked up and hit the consul once on the back of the head. "At that the peasants mobbed and threatened almost to wipe the soldiers out and smash them dead." Von Treutler reprimanded Eckert repeatedly and ordered him "to keep his sword in and be obedient to him and stay in his quarters until his captain called for him." But Eckert refused: He "became so insubordinate that he not only refused to put his sword back in the sheath but also reproached the corporal," he said that von Treutler "was taking that peasant's side [*er hielte es mit dem bauren*] and other stuff in that vein, it was improper talk. And so finally he, the corporal, after he was done exhorting him, went for his sword, and Eckert set himself against him, and received a wound." On April 16th, Eckert died.[21]

Von Treutler was giving orders and Eckert was supposed to follow them. When he did not, he was "insubordinate," "repugnant," *wiederwertig* – the same word used for mutinous soldiers. Von Treutler was acquitted because Eckert had been insubordinate. But he did not attack Eckert as a disciplinary action. A duel implies some sort of equality: The pair regarded each other as opponents. At no point did von Treutler refuse to fight Eckert because it would have lowered him. He did not call the provost's men to come discipline Eckert. Instead, he drew his sword

---

[20] SHStADr 10024 9739/6, 120–126.   [21] SHStADr 10024 9119/38, 171–177.

to fight. The two of them would not have drunk together in the first place if they had not regarded each other as equals at least on some level. The account also never referred to their difference of birth: von Treutler was a noble, and Eckert was not.

Unfortunately, there are few ways to tell how wealthy a soldier had been before he enlisted. The parents of Justus Wilhelmus Lipsius, a pikeman from Erfurt and later a lieutenant in the Mansfeld Regiment, may have known Latin, and even have been familiar with the work of his famous namesake. Whether Lipsius was deliberately named after the neo-Stoic philosopher or not, someone in his family could afford an education at one point in his or her life.[22] Soldiers' non-military jobs were not recorded, although in 1619 one cavalry trooper, Stefan Hedeler, had a note in the roll after his name reading "A *Bürger* from Köthen."[23]

But we can track the numbers of nobles and commoners in each rank, and provide a crude outline of soldiers' social mobility.[24] Tables 5.1, 5.2, and 5.3 track the classes of cavalrymen by rank and office, separated by decade. Tables 5.4, 5.5, and 5.6 do the same for infantry. The branches appear in order of their prestige. Dragoons were the least prestigious branch of service: Out of 381 counted dragoons there are only two incontrovertible nobles: Hans Wilhelm von Paudiz, common dragoon in Georg Götz's Life Company in 1645, and a Lieutenant Colonel whose last name was Haugwitz.[25] Being a dragoon was not a desirable state. When the dragoon squadron of the talented Saxon captain Andreas Masslener, nicknamed "Ungar," did exceptionally well, it was re-equipped as cavalry as a reward.[26] A few men are listed as "unknown": Some non-Germans, men listed only by initials, and soldiers or officers with obvious *noms de guerre* like von Apollo (a surname held by several soldiers and officers in the 1620s and 40s), Venus (Friedrich Venus, a captain in the 1620s), and de la Fortuna (Gideon de la Fortuna, a pikeman from 1620 to 1621).[27] Since this sorting is done by name rather

---

[22] SHStADr 11237 10840/5 1; SHStADr 10024 9739/6, 188.
[23] SHStADr 11237 10839/5 3.
[24] German nobility is listed in https://de.wikipedia.org/wiki/Liste_deutscher_Adelsgeschlechter (last accessed January 17, 2024). Bohemian nobility is listed in Adalbert Ritter Král von Dobrá Voda, *Der Adel von Böhmen, Mähren und Schlesien* (Prague: I. Taussig, 1904). English, Irish, and Scottish nobility are listed at www.burkespeerage.com/ (last accessed January 17, 2024). As of about 1600 there were few Swedish nobles, and most of them had few assets. Frost, *Northern Wars*, 119.
[25] SHStADr 11237 10841/13; SHStADr 11237 10831/1, 44.
[26] SHStADr 11237 10831/1.
[27] The von Apollos appear in SHStADr 11237 10840/3 1, 11237 10840/4 1, 11237 10839/11 5, and 11237 10841/1. Friedrich Venus appears in numerous documents, for instance SHStADr 11237 10841/6 10. Gideon de la Fortuna appears in SHStADr 11237 10840/3 10 and 11237 10840/4 6.

86   The Kind of People I Know You Will Like

Table 5.1 *Number and percentage of nobles in Saxon cavalry, 1620s*

Rank	Non-Noble	Noble	Unknown	Percent Noble	Total
Captain	5	14	0	74%	19
Cornet	6	28	0	82%	34
Lieutenant	8	15	0	65%	23
Fourier	22	0	0	0	22
Muster-writer	23	0	0	0	23
Smith	18	0	0	0	18
Saddler	1	0	0	0	1
Surgeon	27	0	0	0	27
Watch-master	1	0	0	0	1
Drummer	2	0	0	0	2
Trumpeter	98	2	0	2%	100
Corporal	24	23	1	48%	48
Noble cadet	30	64	1	67%	95
Attendant	1	4	0	80%	5
Member of entourage	6	3	0	33%	9
Ordinary cavalryman	781	331	5	30%	1,117
Jung	284	6	2	2%	292
Cavalry servant	137	1	4	.07%	142
Total					1,978

Table 5.2 *Number and percentage of nobles in Saxon cavalry, 1630s*

Rank	Non-Noble	Noble	Unknown	Percent Noble	Total
Captain	0	3	0	100%	3
Cornet	0	3	0	100%	3
Lieutenant	0	3	0	100%	3
Fourier	2	0	0	0	2
Muster-writer	1	0	1	0	2
Smith	3	0	0	0	3
Saddler	2	0	1	0	3
Armorer	1	0	0	0	1
Surgeon	2	0	0	0	2
Watch-master	2	0	0	0	2
Trumpeter	9	0	0	0	9
Corporal	4	2	0	0	6
Noble cadet	0	1	0	100%	1
Ordinary cavalryman	230	9	2	4%	241
Total					281

Table 5.3 *Number and percentage of nobles in Saxon cavalry, 1640s*

Rank	Non-Noble	Noble	Unknown	Percent Noble	Total
Captain	17	7	1	28%	25
Cornet	9	3	0	25%	12
Lieutenant	6	4	0	40%	10
Fourier	11	0	0	0	11
Muster-writer	11	0	0	0	11
Smith	11	0	0	0	11
Saddler	3	0	0	0	3
Surgeon	9	0	0	0	9
Watch-master	10	1	0	9%	11
Trumpeter	14	0	0	0	14
Corporal	22	0	2	0	24
Noble cadet	2	1	0	33%	3
Ordinary cavalryman	643	13	1	2%	657
Cavalry servant	117	0	0	0	117
Total					**918**

Table 5.4 *Number and percentage of nobles in Saxon infantry, 1620s*

Rank	Non-Noble	Noble	Unknown	Percent Noble	Total
Captain	10	29	1	71%	41
Flag-bearer	10	41	0	80%	51
Lieutenant	40	9	0	18%	49
Sergeant (Feldwebel)	47	0	0	0	47
Muster-writer	35	0	0	0	35
Surgeon	40	0	0	0	40
Commander	46	0	0	0	46
Fourier	46	0	0	0	46
Corporal (Gemeinwebel)	100	1	0	1%	101
Piper	40	0	0	0	40
Drummer	96	0	0	0	96
Attendant	5	3	1	33%	9
Cadet (Adelsbursch)	25	10	0	29%	35
Squad leader	124	18	2	13%	144
Bodyguard	8	0	0	0	8
Pikeman	2,921	211	15	7%	3,147
Halberdier	729	7	2	9%	738
Musketeer	6,745	37	9	0.5%	6,791
Total					**11,464**

Table 5.5 *Number and percentage of nobles in Saxon infantry, 1630s*

Rank	Non-Noble	Noble	Unknown	Percent Noble	Total
Captain	3	2	0	40%	5
Flag-bearer	4	1	0	20%	5
Lieutenant	5	0	0	0	5
Sergeant (Feldwebel)	5	1	0	17%	6
Muster-writer	6	0	0	0	6
Surgeon	5	0	0	0	5
Commander	6	0	0	0	6
Fourier	6	0	0	0	6
Corporal (Gemeinwebel)	8	0	0	0	8
Sergeant (Chargant)	4	0	0	0	4
Corporal (Corporal)	20	0	0	0	20
Piper	2	0	0	0	2
Drummer	21	0	0	0	21
Squad leader	125	0	0	0	125
Musketeer	249	0	0	0	249
Unspecified	870	3	1	0.3%	874
Total					**1,347**

Table 5.6 *Number and percentage of nobles in Saxon infantry, 1640s*

Rank	Non-Noble	Noble	Unknown	Percent Noble	Total
Captain	17	12	1	40%	30
Flag-bearer	16	1	0	6%	17
Lieutenant	15	1	0	6%	16
Sergeant (Feldwebel)	17	0	0	0	17
Muster-writer	18	0	0	0	18
Surgeon	16	0	1	0	17
Commander	18	0	0	0	18
Fourier	17	1	0	6%	18
Corporal (Gemeinwebel)	10	0	0	0	10
Sergeant (Chargant)	24	0	0	0	24
Corporal (Corporal)	63	0	0	0	63
Piper	15	0	0	0	15
Drummer	58	1	1	2%	60
Attendant	8	2	0	20%	10
Bodyguard	28	0	1	0	29
Squad leader	469	9	1	2%	479
Musketeer	131	0	0	0	131
Unspecified	1,669	7	3	0.4%	1,679
Gesindel	6	0	0	0	6
Total					**2,657**

than place of origin, the data also includes soldiers whose origins were not recorded or impossible to pin down.

Tables 5.1, 5.2, and 5.3 detail the raw numbers and percentage of noble and non-noble cavalrymen by rank and office for each decade of the Thirty Years War. Ranks are all company-level. These tables list the officer ranks of captain, cornet/infantry flag-bearer, lieutenant, fourier, surgeon, muster-writer, watch-master, drummer and trumpeter, as well as smiths, saddlers, and from the 1630s, armorer (all the 1630 cavalry rolls were from cuirassier companies). They then list corporals and common cavalrymen.

There are more nobles in the top cavalry posts than there are in the other officer ranks or the non-officer positions. Seventy-four percent of cavalry captains were noble in the 1620s, 82 percent of flag-bearers or cornets, and 65 percent of lieutenants. Nobles are also well-represented among non-officers: In the 1620s, 48 percent of corporals, 67 percent of "noble cadets" (*Fahnenjunker*), and 30 percent of regular cavalrymen were noble. So were four out of five attendants and one third of those listed as belonging to someone's entourage. Cavalry servants and boys were rarely noble: Those few nobles who did fill these roles almost all served officers. One was a prince, "Stoffel, Prince von Schlauendorff."[28] Below the top three company officer posts, captain, flag-bearer, and lieutenant, there are no nobles in any cavalry officer position except trumpeter and corporal. The positions which required a specific technical skill, like literacy or playing the massive cavalry kettledrums, were occupied almost entirely by common-born cavalrymen. While many common troopers shared names with the Saxon noble families that fill the lists of colonels and members of the court, the people who kept a cavalry company going day to day by finding and arranging forage, crafting saddles and tack, or repairing armor, were common born. Nobles filled the ranks of the common cavalrymen because the cavalry was prestigious, but one of these noble troopers could have found himself being led by his social inferior in battle.

As the war continued, the proportion of nobles even in higher company-level cavalry ranks collapsed. The 1630s are problematic because of the limited number of surviving records: Only three cavalry rolls survive from the entire decade. These companies may exhibit a high proportion of nobility because they were cuirassiers, a more honorable position than arquebusiers. But a fall in the percentage of nobility is visible from the 1620s to the 1640s: The percentage of noble cavalry

---

[28] SHStADr 11237 10839/11 2.

captains fell from 74 to 28 percent, noble flag-bearers from 82 to 25 percent, and noble lieutenants from 65 to 40 percent. There were no noble corporals in cavalry documents from the 1640s. There were fewer noble non-officers in this decade as well: 30 percent of noble cadets in the 1640s were noble, and only 2 percent of ordinary cavalry troopers.

A similar development took place in the infantry.

Tables 5.4, 5.5, and 5.6 detail the raw numbers and percentages of noble and non-noble infantry officers and common soldiers by rank and office for each decade of the Thirty Years War. No regimental staff or officers are included.

The distance between noble and common was neither small nor easily crossed, but it was less great than among non-soldiers. By the eighteenth century, nobles in the military were concentrated in the cavalry. In the early seventeenth century, things were more complicated. In the 1620s, 71 percent of infantry captains were noble, compared to 74 percent of the equivalent cavalry rank; and 80 percent of infantry flag-bearers were noble, compared to 82 percent of cavalry cornets. The largest discrepancy is among the lieutenants: 65 percent of cavalry lieutenants were noble in this decade, but only 18 percent of infantry lieutenants. As was the case for cavalry officers in this decade, no nobles are attested in the remaining infantry officer ranks.

In the 1630s, the percentage of nobles in most infantry officer ranks fell to 40 percent of infantry Hauptleute, 20 percent of flag-bearers, and no lieutenants. Although these percentages are far below the 100 percent noble background of the three top company-level ranks for cavalry in this decade, one sergeant out of the six attested for the 1630s was also a noble, slightly less than 17 percent: In contrast, no lower officers in the cavalry during this decade were noble. However, by the 1640s, while the percentage of nobles among the flag-bearers fell precipitously to 6 percent, that of noble Hauptleute remained steady at 40 percent. Proportionally, more infantry captains in this decade came from a noble background than cavalry captains. Meanwhile, the percentage of noble infantry lieutenants rose, to slightly over 6 percent.

In general, the proportion of nobles among infantry officers declined during the war, like the proportion of noble cavalry officers. By the second generation of this war, the Saxon nobility may have been running out of men.

The proportion of noble flag-bearers in the 1620s was high because of the symbolic importance of the company flag: According to Wallhausen, the flag-bearer was supposed to be of a higher social standing than both the captain and the lieutenant. Hieronymus Sebastian Schutze was a flag-bearer but he was not a noble. In the 1630s and 1640s the position of the flag-bearer fell from second in the company to third, and so did the proportion of nobles in the position.

Regular infantrymen from noble backgrounds are mentioned rarely in secondary sources. In English-language historiography these are called "gentlemen volunteers," and they are associated more with the sixteenth century than the seventeenth.[29] They are especially well-attested in Spanish sources.[30] Noble pikemen, sword-and-buckler men, and squad leaders show up in Hungary.[31] Although noble infantrymen are not numerous, they appear in Saxon muster rolls as well, where they made more money. Like noble officers, the greatest proportion of noble infantrymen is seen in the 1620s. The proportion of nobles in a position increased with the honor of the role: 0.5 percent of musketeers in this decade were noble-born, 0.9 percent of halberdiers, 7 percent of pikemen, and 12.5 percent of squad leaders.

Some of the noble pikemen and squad leaders may have been young men placed into these positions to prepare for a career literally "from the pike up." Adam Adrian von Wallnitz was a pikeman in Löser's free company in 1619. He was absent for at least two musterings – whether he left with permission or deserted is unrecorded – but returned to the Saxon army next year as a flag-bearer in the von Schlieben Regiment. By February 1621, he was the captain of a company of his own, a position he held until his regiment was dismissed in October 1622.[32]

Noble halberdiers and musketeers are more interesting, since no secondary source mentions people like them. Although they were rarer in later decades and their role was often not specified, noble common soldiers appear in documents from the 1630s and 1640s. Nobles comprised 0.3 percent of common soldiers during the 1630s and 0.4 percent during the 1640s, only slightly less than the proportion of nobles in the musketeers in the 1620s. Only 2 percent of squad leaders were nobles during the 1640s, a significant decline from twenty years earlier. Like the proportion of noble lieutenants, the proportion of common soldiers and squad leaders who were of noble background ticked up in the 1640s from the previous decade.

The proportion of nobles was greater in higher ranks of both the infantry and the cavalry, but there appears to have been no military rank

---

[29] Hale, *War and Society in Renaissance Europe*, 138–139.
[30] Parker, *Army of Flanders and the Spanish Road*, 33–34.
[31] Zoltán Péter Bagi, "Life of Soldiers," 387–388.
[32] SHStADr 11237 10840/1-1, 11237 10840/3 9, 11237 10840/4 10, 11237 10840/5 3. For when Saxon regiments were raised and dismissed, see SHStADr 11237 10831/1.

or office at the company level that was closed to commoners. Neither do more humble positions appear to have been closed to nobles. (These points hold especially true for dragoons. There were only two noble dragoons listed in all records, and one was an enlisted man.) Although roles with more social prestige often contained more nobles – pikemen as opposed to musketeers, cavalry as opposed to infantry or dragoons – this was not always the case. There is no indication in these brief entries of whether these nobles were born noble or became ennobled after service. Some soldiers may have taken it upon themselves to claim noble status, especially officers like the cavalry corporal Hans Harold von Bauer who was listed in the Life Regiment in 1645; the name literally means "von Peasant."[33]

To a limited extent, it was possible to "make yourself" as a soldier. If they were talented, if they lived long enough, and if they were very lucky, early seventeenth-century armies seem to have offered common-born soldiers the opportunity for upward social mobility and the chance to attain a position of respect within their own society. In some cases, we can track this as it happens.

Surviving muster rolls from the 1620s in the Saxon State Archives in Dresden are so numerous that they cover the same companies through multiple musterings. Each gives a snapshot of a company at a particular moment. Collating this data, soldiers can be tracked from roll to roll over a period, like a flipbook generating the illusion of movement. The company in which one of the fastest social advancements is visible is the eighth company in the von Schlieben Regiment, captained first by Christian von Brandstein and then by Joachim von Zeutzsch. This was Mattheus Steiner's old company, four years before the Mansfeld Regiment went to Lombardy.[34] He first appears in these records in 1620 as a common pikeman, at 10 gulden a month.[35] By 1621, Steiner had moved to another company in the same regiment and he made 14 gulden a month, which means he may either have been promoted to squad leader, or had some position of authority that was informal or not recorded on paper.[36] His pay was above-average but not elite. I do not know how he made the jump from pikeman to regimental bailiff and secretary.

---

[33] SHStADr 11237 10841/20 10.
[34] Three rolls survive from this company: SHStADr 11237 10840/3 8, 11237 10840/4 8, and 11237 10840/5 8.
[35] SHStADr 11237 10840/3 8. For Gottfried Reichbrodt, see SHStADr 11237 10840/3 6, 11237 10840/4 4, and 11237 10840/57.
[36] SHStADr 11237 10840/4 1.

One of the soldiers in Steiner's old company, Hans Leopold from Ziegenrück in Saxony, was listed as a musketeer in February 1620; he became the company muster-writer on January 10, 1621. Most ascents in this company were not as steep. The musketeer Baltzer Lipman made 7 gulden a month in February 1620 and 8 gulden a month by April 1621, which is not startling or unusual. Heinrich Rabner made it from musketeer to pikeman, with a corresponding raise of 3 gulden a month. Advancements over time were common. The elite pikemen – the pikemen who were listed at the top of the roll, and who made the most – fed steadily into the ranks of the lower officers. Andreas Eisfeld went from elite pikeman to commander, and Hans Georg Vogel became a corporal. In another company, Hans Sparr from Torgau was brought in to replace an elite pikeman and eventually became the company surgeon.[37]

Soldiers could stay in their units, or the Saxon army, for a long time. The surviving muster rolls that span the longest period belong to a set of free companies of infantry which began their service under Colonel Dietrich von Starschedel the Elder. The best-documented of these companies, with four rolls surviving, is the fourth, which began under Eustachius Löser in summer 1619 and was taken over by Hans von Taube when Löser left to become the Lieutenant Colonel of another regiment.[38] Of the 290 common soldiers in this company mustered in on 7 August 1619, 149 (51%) remained on March 12, 1624 when the company was dismissed. (One or two of them were deserters who later returned to the same company.) Fifty-six percent of musketeers and 46 percent of pikemen remained in the company for the entire four years and seven months it was in being; only 24 percent of halberdiers served this entire time. Pikemen and halberdiers may have had higher mortality rates than musketeers; they often covered retreats.

This turnover is relatively low. If Hamner is correct that primary group motivations for combat do not pertain when the primary group falls apart, this would be an argument that primary group cohesion was powerful in the Electoral Saxon army in the 1620s, which was also the period when they were most consistently victorious. On the other hand, this series covers the period before the Saxon army's really crippling losses, at the battle of Wittstock (October 4, 1636) and in Matthias Gallas's campaign in Pomerania (1637–1640). Research on early-modern Hungary found many experienced soldiers on the Military Border between Hapsburg and Ottoman territories, some who were soldiers for up to twenty-five or thirty years.[39] The dead in a mass grave

---

[37] Friedrich Venus's company, 1621–1622, SHStADr 11237 10841/8 no 10.
[38] SHStADr 11237 10831/1. [39] Bagi, "Life of Soldiers," 391.

from the battlefield at Lützen showed numerous healed injuries, also suggesting long-term service.[40]

Although data from the 1630s and 1640s are not as extensive as data from the 1620s, it is possible to determine that some men remained in the Saxon army for multiple decades. Christoff Rauchhaupt from Gaschwitz was a pikeman from 1620 to 1622 in Andreas von Eberleben's company; in 1644 he was a corporal in Wolf Christoff von Arnim's Life Company.[41] A musketeer with the distinctive name of Hans Catherine or Katherinus served in Ernst von Günterrode's free company from 1619 to 1620, and may also be attested in Daniel von Schlieben's company in the same unit from 1623 to 1625. (The two entries have different hometowns listed: Either one muster-writer made a mistake, or these are different men.[42]) Twelve years later, he was on a military tribunal for a murder trial in Wittenberg.[43] Experienced common soldiers like Catherine may have been sought out for legal proceedings.

Relatives went to war together, like the pair of troopers in Moritz Herman von Oynhausen's company of cuirassiers in 1631, Franz von Nossitz the elder and Franz von Nossitz the younger. "These troopers still have no horses," comments the marginal note; "Franz von Nossitz the younger died at Eger."[44]

Noble military dynasties like the Piccolomini or Montecuccoli produced high officers, and the ranks of Saxon colonels and captains are full of representatives of families like the von Arnims. In contrast, the Metzsches are a military family of ordinary individuals. Heinrich Bernard Metzsch was an arquebusier in Caspar Pflugk's cavalry company in November 1618.[45] By 1620 Heinrich Bernard was gone, but Friedrich, Heinrich, Bernard, and Hans Caspar Metzsch were attested in the same company; the first three were listed in one entry, as "Friedrich, Heinrich, and Bernard Metzsch, 6 horses."[46] Hans Adam Metzsch was a trooper in Hans Marschall's company in the same regiment until 1622.[47] From 1620 to 1621, Hans Wilhelm Metzsch was a pikeman in the von Schlieben Regiment, a rare foray into the infantry for a member of this family.[48] From 1623 to 1624, Heinrich Bernard

---

[40] Nicole Nicklisch, Frank Ramsthaler, Harald Meller, Susanne Friederich, and Kurt W. Alt, "The Face of War: Trauma Analysis of a Mass Grave from the Battle of Lützen (1632)," PLoS One 12.5 (2017), available at: http://journals.plos.org/plosone/article?id=10.1371/journal.pone.0178252 (last accessed January 17, 2024).
[41] SHStADr 11237 10841/6 18 doc 5, 11237 1041/1, 11237 10841/8 8, 11237 10841/13.
[42] SHStADr 11237 10839/6, 11237 10840 /12.   [43] SHStADr 11237 10796.
[44] SHStADr 11237 10841/2 1.   [45] SHStADr 11237 10840/3 1, 11237 10831/2.
[46] SHStADr 11237 10839/27 2.   [47] SHStADr 11237 10839/27 3, 11237 10839/8 7.
[48] SHStADr 11237 10840/4 1.

appears again, this time as the captain of his own cavalry company under Wolf von Mansfeld.[49] Heinrich Sebastian Metzsch was a member of the Saxon court company in early spring 1624.[50] Martin Metzsch was a cuirassier in 1631.[51] Finally, in August 1645, Hans Georg Metzsch left Fischer's company of cavalry and joined the enemy.[52] To say "desertion" in this context is imprecise: Each of these men may have been in an individual company only briefly, but the Metzsch family as a group had a relationship with the cavalry, whether Saxon or otherwise, that spanned decades.[53]

The family with one of the longest sustained commitments to Saxon arms is the von Breitenbachs. Julius Caesar von Breitenbach was in the room when Hieronymus Sebastian Schutze shot Hans Heinrich Tauerling in 1625.[54] Centurius or Century von Breitenbach, named after the Roman military unit, was a corporal in Caspar Christoff von Nossitz's infantry company in 1681.[55] That makes at least fifty-six years of Saxon military service and at least twenty more of exuberant ill-informed love for classical Rome, since Julius Caesar von Breitenbach was at least a young man when he saw Tauerling get shot and he was presumably given his name at birth.

The life sketch of Melchior Gruppach is not only a steep social ascent, but also an illustration of the long commitments some people had to the profession of arms. Melchior came from Gruppach, a ghost town southeast of Delitzsch in Saxony. In 1621, he was a pikeman in the Löser/von Taube free company. He was already relatively highly paid for a pikeman at 13 gulden a month, which means he probably occupied a position of some responsibility and may already have had military experience.[56] At some point after June 1621 he left, but he was back in the same company by May 1622, the top halberdier on the list this time, making the good sum of 20 gulden a month.[57] He left a second time and, when he returned by March 1623, he was listed as making only 17 gulden a month, a pikeman again.[58] Then he drops out of the record. By the early

---

[49] SHStADr 11237 10839/11 6. [50] SHStADr 11237 10840/11 doc 2, 7–62.
[51] SHStADr 11237 10841/2 1. [52] SHStADr 11237 10841/13.
[53] Luciano Pezzolo, "Professione militare e famiglia in Italia tra tardo medioevo e prima età moderna," in *La Justice des familles: Autour de la transmission des biens, des savoirs et des pouvoirs*, Anna Bellavitis and Isabelle Chabot, eds. (Rome: École française de Rome, 2011), 341–366; Hanlon, *Hero of Italy*, 213.
[54] SHStADr 10024 9119/38, 27–39.
[55] *Rolla über des Hauptmanns Casper Christophen von Nosstitz Zum Churfürstl: Sachß: Leib Regiment gehorige Compagnie Zu Fuß*, in the large bound collection of late seventeenth-century muster rolls, SHStADr 11237 11241.
[56] SHStADr 11237 10840/1 2. [57] SHStADr 11237 10840/9.
[58] SHStADr 11237 10840/11 1.

1630s, Gruppach was the third in command of the Electoral Field Life Guard, aka the Life Regiment, and therefore probably the captain of its third-most-prestigious company. He was promoted to lieutenant colonel of this regiment on April 26, 1632, then received absolute command of it in 1639 when his colonel died.[59] In 1641 he and his troops occupied Zittau where he came to the attention of the Saxon chronicler Johann Benedict Carpzov:

> After the city of Görlitz was taken both armies broke off toward Silesia on the 13 Octobr., but the lieutenant colonel Melchior von Gruppach lodged near Zittau with eight companies of the Life Regiment to occupy it. This *Commandante* organized the watch daily with flags flying, and each time he had them appear on the city square in front of his quarters, while he held a prayer service der the regimental chaplain, which deserves to be mentioned as something unusually appropriate.[60]

Gruppach received a formal commission as a full colonel in July 1643. In 1651, exactly thirty years after he first appeared in the historical record, the Life Regiment was dismissed and Colonel Melchior von Gruppach, former pikeman and habitual deserter, was granted the position of senior administrative officer (*Ampthauptmann*) for Delitzsch, Bitterfeld, and Zörbig.[61]

Like Mansfeld promised Camargo, many members of his regiment seem to have been experienced before they left for Italy. Many officers already had careers, like Dam Vitzthum von Eckstedt and his brother August, or Eustachius Löser. Wolfgang Winckelmann had already served under von Mansfeld more than once. Some soldiers in the Mansfeld documents can also be found in other Saxon military documents and cross-referenced: Soldiers who served in earlier Saxon units are securely attested.

It might be argued that a sample that rests so heavily on a list of deserters could be problematic as a source for finding veterans. (343 Mansfelders have a known place of origin, and of those 249 are in Mattheus Steiner's list of deserters. 229 Mansfelders from Wolfgang

---

[59] SHStADr 10831/1.
[60] "Nach Eroberung der Stadt Görlitz brachten den 13 Octobr. die Armeen alle beyde nach Schlesien auf, nacher Zittau aber, waren der Obrist Lieutnant Melchior von Gruppach mit 8. Compagnien vom Leib-Regiment zur Besatzung eingeleget. Dieser *Commandante* ließ täglich die Wache mit fliegender Fahne aufziehen, und alle Zeit zuvor auf den Platz vor seinem Quartier durch den Feldprediger, Bethstunde halten, welcheß als etwas seltsames billig verdienet angemerket zu werden." Johann Benedict Carpzov, *Analecta fastorum Zittaviensium, oder historischer Schauplatz der löblichen alten Sechs-Stadt des Marggraffthums Ober-Lausitz* (Zittau, 1716), 241.
[61] SHStADr 11237 10831/1.

Winckelmann's company were listed but their hometowns were not recorded, making them difficult to find in other documents.) Deserters could be more likely to be newer soldiers, either because they would eventually realize they hated soldiering or because they had no social network yet within the military community. Yet this is not the case: Experienced soldiers also deserted from this regiment, like Brosius Dürring, documented in several Saxon units in 1620 and 1625.[62] This supports the argument that desertion was a casual act.

Many soldiers in both the Mansfeld Regiment and the Saxon army served for years, whether part time or full time, which was how they learned the art of war. They served in groups of friends or family and would have been loyal not only to their flags or superiors but to people they knew. These networks of friendships or relationships not only spanned different companies or regiments, but different armies entirely: Hans Georg Metzsch was not the only Saxon soldier who casually joined the enemy, just one of the ones who were recorded when they did. (Peter Hagendorf fitted solidly into the Swedish army when he was taken prisoner and impressed into it.) Although remaining in any individual army could be a casual thing, soldiers were attached to one another.

---

[62] SHStADr 11237 10841 6/18 doc 9; 11237 10840/12.

6 Elizabeth Sanner and the Dead Men
Mansfeld Interactions with Their Surroundings

At 8 AM on January 8, 1626, Wolfgang Winckelmann's Musterschreiber Heinrich Teichmeyer called Mattheus Steiner into his quarters with Albrecht Wehen of the staff and Michael Hevel the flag-bearer, to take his testament and watch him die. Teichmeyer was sitting on his bed.

"In the fear of God," Teichmeyer said, "I can see that humanity shall have neither certain nor eternal happiness in the misery of this fleeting world." Instead, we have been shaped by God "so that a human being must sojourn in the present exhausting life and be certain of nothing." Teichmeyer was leaving this exhausting life and the challenges of the military, and he was on the brink of the "step of death" which his Savior would "demand of him," the separation of body and soul. Therefore, freely and with good will, he made his testament "according to order, Spiritual and Temporal Military Law." He commended his soul to almighty God, asked to be buried "according to Christian order and military custom," and thanked God for his earthly goods; then he left his property to his wife and children, and the cash he had on him to Wolfgang Winckelmann.[1]

Heinrich Teichmeyer died like a soldier. Although the preambles to last testaments are often generic texts, and what was written down may not have matched what he spoke aloud, he also may have died like a Calvinist, since his testament said he was going to the "home-like joy that has been ordered for all the elect."[2] But most members of the Mansfeld Regiment did not talk overtly about denominationally precise subjects, an important silence in a religiously fraught theater of war.[3] When they mentioned religious topics, Mansfelders usually echoed their own

---

[1] SHStADr 10024 9119/38, 86–90.   [2] SHStADr 10024 9119/38, 86–90.
[3] Debates about the importance of religion for early modern wars are long-standing. A central example of the cultural approach to the history of religious conflict is Natalie Zemon Davis, "The Rites of Violence: Religious Riot in Sixteenth-Century France," *Past & Present* 59 (1973), 51–91. For France, see Mack Holt, "Putting Religion Back into the Wars of Religion," *French Historical Studies* 18.2 (1993), 524–551; Henry Heller, "Putting History Back into the Religious Wars: A Reply to Mack P. Holt," *French Historical Studies* 19.3 (1996), 853–861; Mack Holt, "Religion, Historical Method, and Historical Forces: A Rejoinder," *French Historical Studies* 19.3 (1996), 863–873; Wilson, *Europe's Tragedy*, 9–10; Peter Wilson, "On the Role of Religion in the Thirty Years War," *Institute for Historical Research* 30 (2008), 473–514; Cornel Zweierlein, "The Thirty Years War:

Articles of War and stuck to general phrases that could have been spoken by members of any denomination: "God have mercy on Victoria Guarde's soul," said Michael Steiner, after she was dead. The "on-the-job" neutrality about religion in this regiment looks less striking to us than to contemporary observers.

Armies were multi-denominational, but Saxon soldiers' religion is difficult to track, since Saxon muster rolls do not list denomination. Sometimes it is clearer than others, like the men in Dietrich von Taube's life company in 1634 who gave their origin by their Catholic parishes rather than their native cities. They were listed in a solid block, their names almost uninterrupted. These soldiers came from "Hofkirchenpfarr" in the bishopric of Passau; "Wolfsegger pfarr" (Wolfsegg, Bavaria); "Buerbacherpfarr," the little town of Puerbach in northern Austria; and "Waizenkirchen pfarr," right next to Puerbach, thirteen Catholics, all southerners, standing close together in the middle of a Saxon company.[4]

Some men in Saxon service may have been Jewish. Jonathan Israel claimed that armies were less antisemitic than the rest of central Europe during the Thirty Years War, but this subject needs more research.[5] Barbara Tlusty found evidence of numerous Jewish soldiers during the war.[6] Entire companies of Jews fought in the army of Poland–Lithuania.[7] In this context, the recorded surname of Martin Jude, a common soldier in Dam Vitzthum von Eckstedt's company in 1635, is interesting.[8] He appears in the roll right next to a man named Barthel Bernhold, which means they may have stood together during the mustering: Bernhold came from the small community of Gleicherwiesen in Thuringia, which was about one-third Jewish.[9]

A Religious War? Religion and Machiavellianism at the Turning Point of 1635," in Olaf Asbach and Peter Schröder, eds., *The Ashgate Research Companion to the Thirty Years War* (London: Routledge, 2014), 240–242. Peter Wilson has been criticized for downplaying the religious aspect of this war. See Mark Charles Fissel, "Review of *Europe's Tragedy*," *Journal of World History* 22.4 (2011), 873–877.

[4] SHStADr 11237 10841/12.
[5] Jonathan Israel, "Central European Jewry during the Thirty Years War," *Central European History* 16.1 (1983), 3–30, 5.
[6] Barbara Tlusty, *The Martial Ethic in Early Modern Germany: Civil Duty and the Right of Arms* (New York: Palgrave Macmillan, 2011), 182.
[7] Frost, *Northern Wars*, 191, fn 71.   [8] SHStADr 11237 10841/3 doc 1.
[9] SHStADr 11237 10841/3 doc 1; Thüringer Verband der Verfolgten des Naziregimes – Bund der Antifaschisten und Studienkreis deutscher Widerstand, ed., *Heimatgeschichtlicher Wegweiser zu Stätten des Widerstandes und der Verfolgung 1933–45, Reihe: Heimatgeschichtliche Wegweiser Band 8: Thüringen* (Erfurt: Thüringer Verband der Verfolgten des Naziregimes – Bund der Antifaschisten und Studienkreis deutscher Widerstand, 2003), 124.

The Mansfelders were more southern than the Saxon army as a whole, more Belgian, more Swiss, and probably more Catholic. They also had to live in crowded rooms with one another for years no matter who believed what. In a regiment that roiled with interpersonal conflict of many kinds, I noted someone use a denominational insult only once: Sergeant Hans Ritter claimed that because he had spread the rumors that Michael the Surgeon told him about Lieutenant Wolf Heinrich von Dransdorf, someone called him a "Catholic dog." He did not say who.[10] Theodoro de Camargo, Vratislav von Pernstein, and probably Felix Steter were also Catholic. (Mansfeld himself converted in 1629.) So, possibly, was Mattheus Steiner, here as elsewhere apparent more by his silence than what he wrote explicitly.

The Mansfeld infantryman Michael Kleiben, who roamed around with his untrustworthy friends threatening civilians, also made a pact with the devil. On February 24, 1626, Kleiben and his countryman, both very drunk, came into the quarters they shared with at least three other soldiers. Tobias Krause said someone had taken three Zicks out of his breeches, stashed under the bed. "I haven't left this room – one of you must have done it." A fight broke out. Kleiben was sitting next to the fire. The fight angered him: "The devil should come and knock them from one wall to the other," he said, "so that their brains would stick to the wall." The other soldiers told him not to talk about the devil. He answered that "he had made a pact with the devil, [who] could do nothing to him, and when Georg Schneider begged him to be silent from such talk and instead far more to think about our Lord God, he let the following words leave his mouth: God's hundred thousand sacraments – I shit on them."[11] This was the macho posturing one historian said motivated the little magic of soldiers, their art of making yourself bulletproof: Endangering your immortal soul proves you are a hard man.[12] Hans Devil the cavalryman was probably not born with that name.

Kleiben was fettered for fourteen days and lost his rank.[13] Compared with his possible fate in a civilian court he got off lightly: Mattheus Steiner might have been so scandalized by what Kleiben said he refused to write it all down, but executing him for diabolism and blasphemy was probably less important than retaining a willing soldier.

---

[10] SHStADr 10024 9739/6, 170.   [11] SHStADr 10024 9119/38, 117–119.
[12] Barbara Tlusty, "Bravado, Military Culture, and the Performance of Masculine Magic in Early Modern Germany," in the panel *Masculinity and Military Culture*. 8th Annual FNI Conference, *Rethinking Europe: War and Peace in the Early Modern German Lands*, March 9, 2018.
[13] SHStADr 10024 9119/38, 119.

If this was Steiner's opinion, the Inquisition did not share it. Despite the Spanish Monarchy's connection to Saxony, religious officials in Milan thought non-Catholic German soldiers were heretics and dangerous foreigners who should have been supervised.[14] Inquisitorial control over seventeenth-century armies in Italy has scarcely been studied. Between 1622 and 1630, thirty-eight soldiers appear in Inquisitorial legal records from Crema, a Venetian exclave lodged inside Spanish Lombardy.[15] In contrast to the religious neutrality in Mansfeld documents, these records display soldiers who are irreverent but interested in religion, who discuss it with their messmates, listen to preaching, or attempt to convert others. Some Venetian soldiers did convert: Baptismal records survive of formerly Jewish or Muslim soldiers in Venetian service.[16]

This probably does not mean that Venetian soldiers were religious but their enemies in the Mansfeld Regiment were not. Instead, each set of documents examines what caught the eyes of those who prepared them. The Inquisition in Crema tried to police Catholics and bring heretics back to the Church, while the House of Catechumens in Venice recorded its converts. Like the ecclesiastical response to Protestant soldiers in the eighteenth-century Piedmontese army, the Catholic Church in early seventeenth-century Venice worried about cultural or religious contagion from foreign soldiers.[17] On the other hand, Mattheus Steiner, the legal authority of a working regiment, did not record its soldiers' religions as long as they kept the peace.

But a regiment made up of both Protestants and Catholics in Milanese territory was a problem for devout Catholics who were not involved in military life. "A great part of the German infantry and cavalry regiments are repulsively marked by abominable heresy, and one regiment in particular," possibly Mansfeld, "is almost all Lutheran, so that after the loss of property, and of honor, there is no lack of danger to the soul itself," reported ambassador Cesare Visconti in 1627.[18] In June that year, the

---

[14] D'Amico, *Spanish Milan*, 119.
[15] Susanna Peyronel, "Frontiere religiose e soldati in antico regime: il caso di Crema nel Seicento," in Claudio Donati, ed., *Alle frontiere della Lombardia: politica, guerra e religione nell'età moderna* (Milan: FrancoAngeli, 2006), 19–40.
[16] Daphne Lappa, "Religious Conversions within the Venetian Military Milieu (17th and 18th Centuries)," *Studi Veneziani* LXVII (2013), 4.
[17] Sabina Loriga, *Soldats: Un laboratoire disciplinaire: l'armée piémontaise au XVIII siècle* (Paris: Les Belles Lettres, 2007).
[18] "Dei reggimenti d'infanteria, et cavalleria alemana gran parte di abominevole heresia è bruttamente machiata, et un regimento in particolare è quasi tutto luterano, in modo che dopo la perdita della robba della vita, et dell'honore non mancano ancora pericoli all'anima istessa …" Cesare Visconti to the court of Philip IV, 1627. Angiolo

Inquisitor of Milan said that German soldiers were tolerated because of the wars and he did not fear them as long as they avoided scandal, but when they got drunk in taverns they insulted the pope and the Catholic religion. Some locals said that they tolerated the heretical or scandalous actions of non-Catholic soldiers to avoid violent reprisal.[19]

Other locals were prepared to attack or threaten the Mansfelders whether or not they had done anything. The Cremonese memoirist Giuseppe Bresciani wrote that when the Mansfelders entered Cremona in "4 companies of German cavalry" on January 30, 1626, "the entire city took to arms because the greater part of their people were heretics and insolent, and 2 corps of the city guard mobilized, and the next day there came another 3 companies, so in all there were seven, all of which were quartered in barracks, which aroused spite in them."[20] Antonio Rasini, chronicler and local notable in Gallarate, described an armed standoff in January 1626 between two companies of Mansfeld cavalry and local youths: The soldiers put out two detachments overlooking the piazza, where the youth of Gallarate formed up with muskets and pikes behind a barricade of carts. This bellicose display lasted "as long as the transit of such enemies of Catholics."[21] Unlike later armies, these Mansfelders may not have been able to take superiority in weapons over civilians for granted: Everyone possessed muskets and edged weapons and I do not know whether this regiment possessed any artillery, although small cannon were called "Mansfelders" in northern Italy until; at least the 1640s.

In contrast to these external sources, Mansfeld documents themselves barely mention religious divisions. If Mansfelders were scuffling with the locals over religion, Steiner may not have thought it was worth recording.

Heinrich Teichmeyer wanted to be buried "according to Christian order and military custom" but, although he may have been carried to the grave on a stretcher made of pikes, if he had been Lutheran or Calvinist, canon law in Milan prohibited burying a heretic within city

---

Salomoni, *Memorie storico-diplomatiche degli ambasciatori, incaritati d'affari, corrispondenti, e delegati, che la città di Milano inviò a diversi suoi principi dal 1500 al 1796* (Milan: Pulini al Bocchetto, 1806), 298–305.

[19] Irene Fosi, *Inquisition, Conversion, and Foreigners in Baroque Rome* (Leiden: Brill, 2011), 124–125.

[20] "Venne in Cremona 4 compagni de cavalli todeschi, dove si pose in arme tutta la citta per essere la maggior parte gente heretiche et insolenti, et si pose 2 corpi di guardia, et il giorno seguente ne venne altre 3 compagnie, che in tutto furono sette, quali alloggiorono tutti in case erme al loro dispetto." Giuseppi Bresciani, *Memorie delle cose occorse me vivente nella città di Cremona quivi descritte d'anno in anno*, ed., Emanuela Zanesi (Cremona: Lions Club, 2019), 14.

[21] Antonio Rasini, "Alloggi militari."

Lucian Staiano-Daniels

Table 6.1 *Infantry strength, Mansfeld Regiment, September 1626–July 1627*

Date	Nov 2, 1625	Sep 2, 1626	Feb 23, 1627	Jul 5, 1627
Mansfeld Company		279	276 (Feb 3)	261
Camargo		271	260	214
D Vitzthum von Eckstedt		280	265	237
A Vitzthum von Eckstedt		277	264	251
Von Arnswald	242	221	186	175
Von Körbitz	286	236	172	153
Von Ponickau	271	251	182	180 (May 31)
Winckelmann		275	263	236
Medringer	261	232	223	205
Richter	275	223	213 (Feb 27)	172
Total Infantry	Incomplete	2,545	2,304	2,084

Source: SHStADr 10024 9239/2, 54r-82.

walls. Winckelmann's company probably buried Teichmeyer anonymously outside Gallarate, under ice and rain.

The Mansfeld Regiment dwindled from fall 1625. Although most of their deaths were not recorded by the civilians where they were quartered, soldiers both died at a substantial rate and affected the death rate and other demographic indices of local communities. Analysis of these records provides a quantitative supplement to the individual stories of personal interactions between Mansfelders and the people around them.

I determined attrition rates for the infantry from the musters compiled by Dam Vitzthum von Eckstedt when he tried to bill Milan for their bread in summer 1627 (Table 6.1).[22] Because Vitzthum von Eckstedt prepared this list, he and his brother August are on it as the captains of the third and fourth most honorable companies in the regiment and Wolfgang Winckelmann is listed almost last; in documents by everyone else, Winckelmann comes third. Andreas Medringer is on this list as a captain: He must have been promoted since winter 1626, when he stood over Victoria Guarde's body next to Mattheus Steiner in the dark.

Cavalry strength in horse early in the Mansfeld Regiment's lifespan is taken from the record produced in Ulm during its stopover in August 1625, although most numbers are suspiciously round: These data may have come directly from the captain of the Ulm city watch, rather than a military source.[23] Cavalry records, as always, count the mounts but not the troopers themselves (Table 6.2).

[22] SHStADr 10024 9239/2, 54r-82.
[23] StadtA Ulm Kriegsamtes A [5556], *Verzeichnis des Kriegsvolks zu Pferd und Fuß* by Wachmeister Christoph Revelheimer, Aufstellung der Mansfeldischen Kavallerie.

Table 6.2 *Cavalry strength in horses, Mansfeld Regiment, August 1625*

Date	Aug 1, 1625	Aug 10, 1625	Aug 1625
Ulleben Company			40
Marquese Mandoce			110
Picke	80	80+36	116
Mansfeld Life Coy of Horse			130
Pernstein Company	80	120	120
Löser			80
Goldacker			100
Kettel	120	113	113
Schönfelßer			100
Löbel			70
Total Cavalry (Horse)			979[24]

Source: StadtA Ulm Kriegsamtes A [5556].

The big killer was probably sickness. Malaria cut down the Mansfelders' French enemies in sheaves, and Pappenheim directed his little mountain campaign on his back.

Shortly after Teichmeyer died, on or about January 11, 1626, Mattheus Steiner assembled Winckelmann's company to ask them about the fabric they had taken from the Swiss traders, and he took the roll.[25] On that date this company numbered 235 soldiers on paper, not counting the *prima plana*, forty soldiers fewer than the company count eventually climbed to that September. Armies were always recruiting as well as always dwindling.[26] Twenty-four or twenty-five soldiers out of 235 were sick that day: A *k* or *kr* was written next to their names for *krank*, sick. (The writing in one entry is unclear.) A few were so sick they could not understand what Steiner said to them. For example, Jacob Fritzsch *hat kein verstandt mehr gewesen*, he could no longer understand anything.[27] Seven soldiers out of 235 had died; some just then, like Paul Scheckner and Elias Kerdenmit, next to whose names the *k* was scribbled out and the cross for "dead" was written, as Steiner corrected himself abruptly.[28] Michael Melhorn gave six ells of red linen to David Zenischen and both were later recorded as sick, which may depict contagion within one group of close contacts.

---

[24] The recorded total number for the Mansfelder cavalry in StadtA Ulm Kriegsamtes A [5556] is 986 horses, but at least six horses or cavalrymen in Kettel's company, and the company scribe, died in the fire on the night of August 10/11.
[25] SHStADr 10024 9119/38, 59, 75.   [26] SHStADr 10024 9119/38, 60–74.
[27] SHStADr 10024 9119/38, 61.   [28] SHStADr 10024 9119/38, 71.

I do not know when the roll to which Steiner compared this list was produced; it is not listed in Dam Vitzthum von Eckstedt's records for November 2, 1625. If it had been made in early November like the company records in Vitzthum von Eckstedt's list, these numbers in January mean that almost 3 percent of Wolfgang Winckelmann's infantry company died within three months, and more than 10 percent of the living were unfit for duty.

Like the Mansfelders' religious actions and interactions, their dismal health cannot be studied in isolation, since the members of this regiment also affected the health of the people around them, as well as their more general wellbeing.

Locals reported military abuses to the Spanish military authorities in Milan, and the Duke of Feria printed numerous edicts attempting to check them.[29] The Mansfeld Regiment was no exception: The Montferratese chronicler Gioanni Domenico Bremio said that "the count of Mansfeld with his soldiers" acted "according to the custom of the other northerners" when his cavalry encamped in the territory of Casale on November 9, 1625, ransacked the wine cellars for wine, and destroyed and scattered all the things they found.[30] On May 28, 1627 the Commissario General issued an edict that the Estado was not obliged to house, pay, or feed soldiers who changed quarters on their own initiative or deserted, and specified that this order should be observed in the territories of the Milanesado, "especially in Vergante," a territory in Novara, "by the person of the count of Mansfelt."[31] Antonio Rasini wrote that the rich as well as the poor in Gallarate were ruined by the great quantity of wine and goods the Mansfelders used up. Everyone in the territory sent all their linens and their best goods away, like Rasini and his father. "Between me and mine," Antonio and his family had eight Mansfelders in their house.[32]

---

[29] AST Archivio Sola Busca, Serbelloni, box 47, 1625 and 1626.
[30] "Alli 9 de Novembre entrò nello Stato di Montferrat il Conte di Mansfelt con li suoi soldati et alloggiarono nelle Terre vicine a Casale et parte nelle cascine della Piana, et fecero ancor loro alla usanza degli altri oltremontani molti danni lasciando persino andare per li cantine il vino et dissipando tuttte le robe che trovando." Bremio, *Cronaca monferrina*, 78.
[31] "Le Terre del Ducato osserveranno il sudetto ordine per quello ad essi spetta, & in particolare nel Vergante per la persona del Sig. Colonello il Conte di Mansfeld." AS-Cr, Miscellenia alloggiamenti, Tomus 23, 273, *Ordinario del Sig. Commissario Gen. per li absenti, & quelli che non risi edono per essecutione dell'antecedente Reale lettera de S.M.*
[32] "... tra me e mio del quale ne avevamo in casa otto, ai quali si dava da mangiare et bere; del quale alloggiavano tanto gli ricchi, quanto gli poveri restarono ruinati per la grande quantità della robba et vino che giornalmente si consumava in casa di ciaschuno ... ciaschuno della terra, per tema che non saccheggiassero la tera haveva fatto menare via tutta la biancheria, et il miglior di casa, come feci anch'io e mio padre, nell qual anno si

To investigate the statistical effect of interactions between Mansfelders and local populations, I collected demographic data on these populations from parish records where the regiment was quartered. The following charts and tables track baptisms, marriages, and funerals for communities, with available data occupied by the regiment's infantry and cavalry. The entire decade from 1620 to 1629 establishes a baseline for comparison. Since Cremona was a large city, Busto Arsizio and Legnano were large, well-organized towns, and Pontestura was a very small town, this analysis compares the effects of the Mansfelders on communities of different sizes. It also compares the effects of infantry to cavalry, and of soldiers who were barracked (Cremona) to those of soldiers who were not (all infantry; Pontestura).

The events that chronicles or the regiment's sources describe were striking but also anecdotal: The personal struggles that produced the legal documents forming the bulk of the regiment's internal record, or the kind of events a chronicler remembers. Statistical evidence from these towns themselves is more ambiguous.

The towns in which Mansfeld infantry were quartered for which I have obtained data are Busto Arsizio and Legnano. According to Rasini, the largest single group of Mansfeld infantry – 1,050, almost half their infantry complement, as well as most of the regimental officers – was quartered in Gallarate.[33] However, the local clergy did not allow me to obtain records from this town. Records from Samarate were destroyed in a flood in 1800.

Not every church was a *pieve*, which handled and registered baptisms, marriages, and funerals. Busto Arsizio had two *pievi*: San Michele, the records of which are not complete, and San Giovanni Battista. Their figures are totaled in Figure 6.1, but separated in Table 6.3. The years the Mansfeld Regiment spent in northern Italy are shaded. Records from Legnano are delineated in Figure 6.2.

Busto Arsizio seems to have been lightly affected by the Mansfelders' presence statistically, but the data for funerals may be even more fragmentary than they appear. Legnano was obviously badly hit (Figure 6.2). Baptisms slumped and funerals rose while the Mansfelders were there; in 1625 funerals were relatively few early in the year and ramped up during the fall. Yet both towns were also in a bad situation throughout the decade. Baptisms declined from 1620 to 1629, and the worst years for funerals were before the Mansfelders arrived: 1623 in Legnano, and

---

haveva alloggiato grande quantita di fanteria Alemana." Rasini, "Alloggi militari," 132–133.
[33] Ibid., 132.

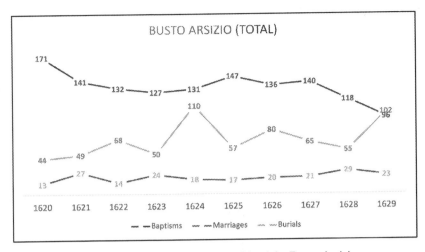

Figure 6.1 Baptisms, marriages, and burials, Busto Arsizio, 1620–1629.
ASGBu and ASMBu (combined)

1624 in Busto Arsizio. In these towns, the Mansfeld Regiment was one negative influence in a decade full of them.

South of Milan, seven companies of Mansfeld cavalry were quartered in Cremona and three in Pontestura, ninety miles apart. Cremona is a major city; baptism, marriage, and funeral data for the 1620s survive from twenty-four churches. Records in St. Agatha's, Pontestura's only church, remain unordered in a single cupboard.

Pontestura is situated on the south bank of the Po and controlled an important crossing. The Mantuan diplomat and spy Giovanni Battista Sannazaro reported to his superiors that this location was heavily fought over during summer 1625 and served as a staging-point for multiple military units; at one point Pontestura had 4,600 infantry quartered in it.[34]

Pontestura's baptism rate was steady until 1624, and the drop that year had nothing to do with the fighting, which began in midsummer 1625, months before the Mansfelders arrived in fall 1625 (Figure 6.3). Baptisms in 1625 seem to revert to the previous average, but these numbers by themselves are misleading: In late fall, the number of babies baptized at home or by the midwife "ad necessitas causa" increased substantially. In 1626, fewer children were baptized per month; summer is often leaner for baptisms, but in Pontestura none were recorded

[34] AS-M Archivio Gonzaga, E. XLIX. 3. 1758, Gio. Battista Sannazaro I 1625, 292. Letter from Giovanni Battista Sannazaro, August 29, 1625.

Table 6.3 *Baptisms, marriages, and burials, Busto Arsizio, 1620–1629*

Year	1620	1621	1622	1623	1624	1625	1626	1627	1628	1629
San Giovanni										
Baptisms	112	97	88	92	72	110	91	88	74	56
Marriages	7	18	8	13	9	8	14	14	11	12
Burials	44	49	68	50	110	57	80	65	55	102
San Michele										
Baptisms	59	44	44	35	59	37	45	52	44	40
Marriages	6	9	6	11	9	9	6	7	18	11
Burials										

Source: ASGBu and ASMBu, 1620–1629.

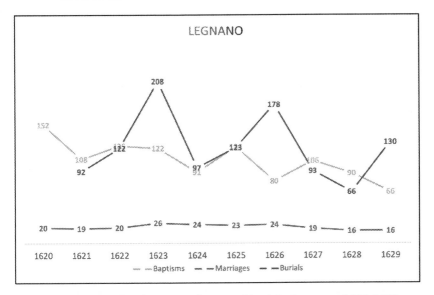

Figure 6.2 Baptisms, marriages, and burials, Legnano, 1620–1629.
ASML

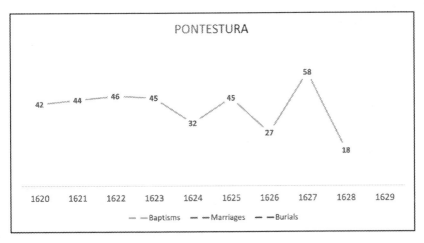

Figure 6.3 Baptisms, Pontestura, 1620–1628.
CSA

between March and July 1626. Baptisms in 1626 and 1627 were sometimes irregular, such as one godparent instead of two, or two godparents of the same sex. Baptisms increased sharply in 1627 but plummeted in 1628.

There are several possible explanations for these data. One is that repeated quartering and combat in and near Pontestura ruined the locals' health, including women's fertility, the viability of their pregnancies, and the health of their newborn infants. Evidence in support of this theory includes the increase in baptisms at home and the gap in baptisms six to ten months after the Mansfelders arrived. In this explanation the arrival of hostilities was a sudden shock in mid-1625, leading to fear, stress, poor health, and miscarriages for women in Pontestura. Lack of food and an increase in contagious diseases would have compounded these effects. Not only would no infants have been born between March and July 1626, but infants born in late 1625 would have been frailer, and midwives would have baptized them as quickly as possible.

Another explanation is that the Mansfelders and the other units in the area disrupted the locals' ability to live normally, including conceiving or baptizing children and recording baptisms. For instance, the priest or many parishioners may have fled for safety. Evidence in support of this theory includes the gap in baptisms, the increase in incomplete records, and the increase in irregular baptisms. In this explanation, the gap in baptisms in mid-1626 is because of instability at that time; children would have been born in this scenario, but not recorded. This explanation also makes sense of an increased tendency for multiple baptisms to take place on the same day: The inhabitants of Pontestura may have been leaving their homes less often, possibly in groups for safety. In this scenario, the substantial increase in the number of baptisms in 1627 may be due to parents whose children were born in 1626 making up for the lost year, or the return of refugees.

Whether soldiers in the area affected the residents' physical health, their ability to lead normal lives, or both, Pontestura, the smallest settlement in this analysis, is the one in which the most extreme statistical effects are visible. This is not only the result of statistical skewing; Pontestura's size probably contributed to these effects, since in the larger towns I examined, massive fights between Mansfelders and locals eventually drew the attention of the authorities in Milan. In contrast, Sannazaro reported that soldiers committed repeated crimes "under the name of foraging" near this unimportant village.[35] The demographic effects in Pontestura, such as are visible, may be due to soldiers with little oversight at all.

In this context, Cremona serves as a massive control group, since the Mansfelders there were housed in barracks until the regiment returned north. Records left by Cremonese churches survive in varying degrees of completeness, reproduced in Table 6.4.

---

[35] AS-M Archivio Gonzaga, E. XLIX. 3. 1758, Gio. Battista Sannazaro I 1625, 321. Letter from Giovanni Battista Sannazaro, October 22, 1625.

Year	1620	1621	1622	1623	1624	1625	1626	1627	1628	1629
1. San't Andrea										
Baptisms	10	21	13	17	19	22	15	18	23	8
Marriages					8	1	9	8	4	
Burials										
2. San Antonio										
Baptisms	7	3	8	5	10	9	7	7	9	7
Marriages	1	0	2	0	1	1	2			
Burials	1	4	2	2	2	0	4	4		
3. San Bartolomeo										
Baptisms	11	14	9	17	18	6	14	11	11	19
Marriages					3	6	1	4	4	3
Burials				25	34	32	33	34	35	73
4. Cathedral										
Baptisms	82	93	83	89	63	58	74	59	37	100
Marriages	9	14	9	20	15	12	17	21	16	22
Burials	12	35	56	64	28	39	34	27	26	105
5. Santi Carlo e Donino										
Baptisms			4			4	6	8	1	8
Marriages		1	4	1	1		2	2		3
Burials			5				1	5	1	8
6. Santa Cecilia										
Baptisms									5	7
Marriages									1	2
Burials									3	5
7. San Donato										
Baptisms	15	20	7	17	9	15	12	7	19	5
Marriages	4	7	3	7	5	4	6	5	2	4
Burials	6	9	16	14	8	4	7	15	9	31
8. Santa Elena										
Baptisms	14	16	14	15	17	19	14	16	18	12
Marriages										
Burials										

Table 6.4 (cont.)

Year	1620	1621	1622	1623	1624	1625	1626	1627	1628	1629
9. San Erasmo										
Baptisms										32
Marriages	1		2	11	7	6	6	9	7	7
Burials	43	41	36	33	16	25	22	10	13	57
10. Santi Faustino e Giovita										
Baptisms	4	3	1	2	3	5	5	5	3	4
Marriages	0	2	1	2	0	0	0	2	2	0
Burials	2	4	2	3	8	6	0	0	7	4
11. San Giorgio										
Baptisms	22	12	17	15	9	10	17	13	14	18
Marriages						4	9	5	3	6
Burials	19	17	10	8	14	13	17	9	9	50
12. Santi Imerio e Clemente										
Baptisms	27	28	28	26	20	21	13	32	23	8
Marriages	10	7	7	9	7	12	16	7	7	8
Burials		10	22	18						
13. San Leonardo										
Baptisms	23	37	21	28	25	22	28	24	21	24
Marriages	6	8	4	6	3	6	7	2	0	0
Burials	10	24	23	12	17	11	14	10	13	34
14. Santa Lucia										
Baptisms	44	42	32	39	39	33	31	26	25	26
Marriages										
Burials	24	27	18	29	40	28	21	18	22	42
15. Santa Maria in Betlem										
Baptisms	81	58	67	66	55	67	60	42	65	53
Marriages	8	15	13	10	17	17	7	16	15	6
Burials										
16. San Nicolo										
Baptisms	17	12	11	13	7	12	11	20	11	14
Marriages	4	2	3	4	5	4	5	2	0	
Burials	12	15	9	20	5	10	14	8	9	18

112

17. Santi Omobono e Egidio										
Baptisms	27	27	26	27	14	18	21	24	20	20
Marriages	10	16	7	5	3	4	6	9	4	1
Burials										
18. San Pantaleone										
Baptisms										
Marriages	6	2	3	12	4	15	3	4	1	
Burials	8	6	28	14	16	17	29	16	7	
19. San Paolo										
Baptisms	39	59	52	70	39	19	40	47		
Marriages										
Burials	20	35	34	38	31	37	28	44	41	68
20. San Pietro										
Baptisms	39	45	54	31	28	49	47	39	40	30
Marriages	9	15	11	14	12	6				
Burials	47	59	71	59	76	55	44			
21. San Prospero										
Baptisms	13	19	18	21	12	10	14	4	29	8
Marriages	5	2	4	1	2	0	5	2	4	4
Burials	4	7	3	10	11	6	5	6	3	7
22. San Salvatore										
Baptisms	29	37	30	24	23	27	26	17	23	16
Marriages	3	4	6	11	4	7	7	6	5	5
Burials	35	32	34	36	7	24	32	19	18	48
23. Santa Sofia										
Baptisms	12	13	13	11	16	8	11	6	11	7
Marriages										
Burials	3	3	8	1	1					
24. Santi Vito e Modesto										
Baptisms	5	3	9	4	1	4	5	6	6	7
Marriages	2	0	0	3	0	1	6	2	1	1
Burials	1	3	4	7	5	3	6	6	6	12

Source: ASDCr.

Cremonese demographics fluctuated throughout this decade, and do not appear to have been directly affected by the Mansfeld cavalry in particular. But the Mansfeld Regiment was not the only military unit in northern Italy in the 1620s. Like Busto Arsizio and Legnano, Cremona may have been impacted by this decade's problems more generally.

In the case of Cremona's cathedral, we can see that this included troop movements. Unlike most Cremonese churches, the cathedral tracked the burials of prisoners, residents of dormitories and soldiers, including Germans. In 1629, the same year most churches in Cremona as well as Busto Arsizio and Legnano recorded an increase in burials, these men began to die. Some obviously were killed by violence; those who were not included a German soldier on January 6, a Neapolitan on January 10, another German on January 20, and a Spaniard on January 29. Two men died on March 3: One in prison, another in the bell tower. Another died in prison some time later and a Spanish flag-bearer on March 14, and the priest who wrote the record buried him in the church of St. Francis with the permission of his captain. Two weeks later, four soldiers died in one day: Two Spanish, one German and one in the service of the Duke of Gonzaga; another Neapolitan soldier died on March 30. Two German soldiers and one man in prison died in April. May was catastrophic: Sixteen soldiers, prisoners and men in dormitories died that month, including Benedict the Rat, soldier of a German tercio in the service of Genoa. Two more prisoners died that June.[36] These men may have died of the plague, the first tremors of a great epidemiological shaking. Right before the epidemic of 1630, the plague in Cremona may have been a disease of men, because it was a disease of soldiers, transients, and prisoners, and many were buried in the field.

Unlike this striking pattern in Cremona, diocesan records from Casale Montferrato show regular burials of soldiers between 1625 and 1627. Most were soldiers of Casale quartered in the Arce, the smaller of Casale's two forts. (The larger had its own priest.) These troops were largely Italians. But some in these documents were not Casale troops: These men were from central Europe or were unknown and could have been Mansfeld cavalrymen.

Two of these men were buried in late October and early November 1625, after the Mansfeld cavalry had sacked the estates of Mantella and Roberti but before they took quarters in Cremona and Pontestura; one was buried in December and may have been from the Mansfeld cavalry or another unit of the King of Spain's army.

---

[36] ASDCr Cattedrale IV-1, *Libro de Morti dall anno 1606 sino l'anno 1706*, 38r–47r.

"24 October, 1625. Some soldier who was determined to have been a northerner, age 25 years," body found "outside the new gate of the City of Casale. He returned his soul to God in the field. May he retain the crown he found, even in his lime," alluding to the quicklime poured over the dead; "his body was buried in the Cathedral for free, for mercy's sake." "6 November, 1625. Anthony Crow, a German soldier, age unknown, of the parish of the Cathedral, gave up his soul to God after having taken communion at St. Martin's Church. His body was buried for free at the same church, because he is destitute." Like Benedict the Rat, a man called Anthony Crow who may not have known his own age could have been a lifelong soldier. "4 December 1625. A young man was found dead outside the new gate of the City of Casale, his name and fatherland were unknown, he was of the King of Spain's army under Verrua." His soul went "with a crown to heaven," but "his body was buried for free in the Cathedral because he was destitute."[37]

In contrast, the German soldiers buried in fall 1627 in Casale are city troops; although it is impossible to tell, these men, like the German soldiers who died in Cremona in 1629, may have been ex-Mansfelders who were left behind when the regiment fell apart. In this case, they may have joined the army of Casale Montferrato. These men are less abject: They belonged to parishes in the city, they were known to the people who took care of them while they died, and they left behind enough to pay for their own burials.[38] They died in homes, not the fields outside Casale's gates.

Unlike these funeral records, in which soldiers' bodies are treated compassionately but more or less as outsiders, in 1625 and 1627

---

[37] "1625 8bris 24. Quidam miles iudicatus ultramontanes etatis annos 25 ex et propre portam novam Civitatis Casali in agro animam Dei reddidit et cum inventa sit corona in eius calcis eius ideo corpus sepultum fuit in Cathdr gratis ex misericordia." "1625 9bris 6: Antonius Corvus Germanos miles etatis annos innota parrochiam Cathedram Casali animam Deo reddidit in communione st Martins ecclesiae eius corpus sepultum fuit in idem ecclesia gratis quia miserabilis." "1625 Xbris 4: Quidam iuvenis inventus fuit mortuus ex et propre portam Novam Civitatis Casalensis, eius nomen et patria ignoratur erat ex exercitu Regis Hispanensis sub verruam erat cum corona ad Coelum eius corpus sepultum fuit in Cathedram gratis quia miserabilis." ASDCC *Sacristae et Defunctorum 1620 ad 1628.*

[38] "1627 7bris 24: Laurentius Pratis Alemannus etatis annus 21 miles in Arce in da. Par. In Com. S. M. Ecc. Animus Deo redido cuius Corpus in Cathedral sepultus est." "1627 8bris 2: Johannes Borogonus Alemannus miles in Arce annos 30 ecc in dar Par in Commune Soll. Eccl. Anima Deo reddidit Corpus iuius in Cathed sepultus est." "1627 8bris 13: Johannes Michaelis Alemannus etatis annos 25 Miles in Arce, in eiusdem Parroch, In Commne. S. M. Ecclesia Animam Deo reddidit iuius Corpus in Cath die uq sep est." ASDCC *Sacristae et Defunctorum 1620 ad 1628.*

churches in Busto Arsizio and Legnano recorded the baptisms of Mansfeld infantrymen's children. Some Catholic Mansfelders were baptizing their children in local churches, which indicates some integration with the local social world. However, since both mothers and fathers are recorded in these records, we can also tell that these central European soldiers were married to central European women, and also that Mansfelders were the godparents for these baptisms, often officers like Stach Krakow and Theodoro de Camargo, godfathers for Ro Rotte's child.[39] This implies that at least some central European soldiers in northern Italy and their families formed a separate caste, similar to the Spanish soldiers and their families in the Milanese Castello.

In this way, the Mansfeld Regiment was moving within a bubble: Of some kinds of socialization but not others. Dead soldiers in Cremona were treated similarly to other marginal men. The Catholic Mansfelders in Busto Arsizio and Legnano worshipped with local Catholics, but they were less likely to marry them; and, when they died, they were not buried with them.

Written evidence of Mattheus Steiner's family may also exist in these records of his interaction with their Italian surroundings, but not from Steiner's diligent record-keeping itself. Elizabeth Weraer was born on February 1, 1627 to Christoffer and Rebecca Weraer and baptized on the ninth in San Giovanni in Busto Arsizio; her godparents were Ivan Frederich and a woman whose name was recorded as Elizabeth Sanner, "wife of the noble Signor Auditor [*Auditore*] of Colonel Mansfeld."[40] If "auditor" is the same office as *Regimentsschultheiss und Secretarius*, then Mattheus Steiner was not only married, and went to Lombardy with his wife, but his wife and probably he as well were Catholic.

Interactions between soldiers and other people not only took the form of interactions between the central European, multi-religious Mansfelders and the Italian Catholics surrounding them, in the early seventeenth century they also entailed continual interactions among combatant soldiers and the women, children, and servants who went to war alongside them. If Elizabeth and Mattheus were in fact married, if Sanner and Steiner meant the same name, Mattheus wrote about none of this, nor any reflection cast onto other parts of his life by his duties. The Mansfeld Regiment's bailiff and secretary not only rarely recorded

---

[39] ASML, *Liber Batizatora Eclesie Eslep Santi Magni Bargi Legnani*, baptism of Giovanni Massimo Rotte, November 28, 1625.

[40] ASGBu *Anagrafe*, reg Nati, 1595–1641. Franco Bertolli and Umberto Colombo, *La Peste del 1630 a Busto Arsizio: rilezione commentata della "Storia" di Giovanni Battista Lupi* (Busto Arsizio: Bramante Editrice, 1990), 396.

denominational conflict or even denominational differences; he may have practiced a different denomination from most members of his regiment and said nothing about it. Similarly, although he played a pivotal role in the Mansfeld Regiment's largest single legal investigation, Theodoro de Camargo's murder of his wife Victoria Guarde, in which the interactions between men and women that are largely implicit in the rest of the Mansfelders' story come brutally to the foreground, Mattheus Steiner was almost entirely opaque during it.

7   To Be Happy Doing What You Want
The Death of Victoria Guarde and the Life of Theodoro de Camargo

Mattheus Steiner found Victoria Guarde on her back in the middle of "a vaulted room" in Theodoro de Camargo's quarters in Gallarate, hands drawn up over her body. Her dress was purple brown and the bodice was gone: Above the waist her big linen shift was torn open, one breast exposed. Steiner had been a soldier for at least six years, but he wrote that when he found her Victoria lay in "a welter of blood" (*ein großen gebluth*). Dam Vitzthum von Eckstedt had ordered Steiner to Camargo's quarters. He and eight other witnesses stood looking at the body. Captain-Lieutenant Andreas Medringer; Andreas Weigel, who was now a flag-bearer but who became Mansfeld's master of horse three years later; Heinrich Muller, corporal; Hans Fleck, squad leader; the legally sworn common soldiers Abraham Sonnewald, Ulrich Braunert, and David Henning; and Peter Kirchner, regimental surgeon. "God have mercy on her soul," Steiner wrote. It was Sunday, March 1, 1626.[1]

Steiner and Peter Kirchner lifted her up.

And enjoined by the Regiment's aforementioned surgeon, to lift her up and inspect what kind of wounds she had on her body, which at my command he did, and the dead body of the aforementioned Victoria Guarde was found with the aforementioned wounds, thus: five stab wounds on the left breast, one through the left shoulder, two on the left side, one over the belly button, one under the left arm, one more or less [*unngleichen einen*] above the left hand on the arm, and one through the right breast, in all twelve stab wounds.

One of her earrings was broken, the links of its chain were split.[2] Had they carried the body outside, stripped and washed it and cut it open in sunlight, or did Kirchner and Steiner kneel in clotted gore in indoor half-light and stick their fingers in the wounds to make their examination? The room had been recently stripped of all belongings and furniture, and it would have stunk of blood and a corpse about half a day dead. Except for the defensive wound, any one of these wounds could have been fatal on its own: The assailant had known what he was doing.

---

[1] SHStADr 10024 9119/38, 120–164.   [2] SHStADr 10024 9119/38, 122.

Victoria and her entourage had been returning from a nearby town on the evening of February 28. Antonio Rasini recounted: "And as she was dismounting from the carriage ... the aforementioned Lieutenant Colonel shot at her twice with an arquebus" and missed. In a society whose members routinely shot loaded pistols out their windows for fun, Camargo was able to persuade Victoria it had been an accident. She and the gentlemen with her, and her sister and sister-in-law, went into his quarters, and that night "he put his hand on a stiletto" and killed her.[3]

When Mattheus Steiner questioned him, Camargo recounted his past with Victoria from the beginning. Victoria Guarde or Giavarda was a noble of Cremona. Because of her "evil beginnings," she was "walled up by her parents," sent to a convent. Then Camargo went to Germany in the service of the King of Spain: Probably in 1619, with a force recruited out of Naples that went up through the Brenner Pass that summer under Carlo Spinelli and Guillermo Verdugo.[4] By the early 1620s, he was on General Verdugo's staff.[5] He left Guarde with her parents "because he wanted her to be safer," but after he went to war she fought with her parents again and told him she refused to stay with them. He allowed her to move into a cloister near Milan.

From 1622 to 1623 Camargo was a captain in a regiment belonging to Ott Fugger, one of the most active generals in Bavarian service during the Thirty Years War.[6] At some point Camargo was wounded. Guarde got the news in her cloister and wrote "It grieves me to hear that you have been hurt, but even more that you did not die" (*Es wehre ihr laidt der Beschädigung halben, aber noch mehr, daß er nicht gar todt bliebenn seye*). Then "without his foreknowledge or permission" Victoria got herself out of the cloister, "and never did she have the will or intention to do him any good." From then on, "she began to live an unseemly life."[7]

---

[3] "Alli 28 sud.o alle due hore di notte in c.a venendo la domenica il sud.o Tenente Colonello diede due archibugiate alla S.a Victoria Giavarda, cremonese, sua moglie, non molti giorni avanti, con grande pompa et applauso menata a Gallarate, quale da due mesi inanzi era venuta da Fiandra; nel'atto che smontava dalla carocia, che erano stati a Lonate Pozzolo a destinare et a festa, et non havendo ferita, stimando che fosse stato caso accidentale, entrati in casa alla presenza di tutti li Gentilhomini che seco haveva, et d'una sorella et cognata di detta signora, messo mano ad un stiletto, gli diede sedici stilettate, dalli quale se ne morì ..." Rasini, "Alloggi militari," 134.

[4] Henry Kamen, *Spain's Road to Empire: The Making of a World Power 1492–1763* (London: Allen Lane, 2002), 316.

[5] Kouřil, *Documenta Bohemica*, No. 140, 66.

[6] Stephanie Haberer, *Ott Heinrich Fugger (1592–1644): Biographische Analyze typologischer Handlungsfelder in der Epoche des Dreißigjährigen Krieges* (Augsburg: Wißner-Verlag, 2004), 256.

[7] SHStADr 10024 9119/38, 125–126.

Ambrogio Spinola besieged Breda in summer 1624, and Camargo followed when Gonzalo de Córdoba sent him there. Spinola's confessor Herman Hugo recorded him.[8] Camargo was pleased to leave Germany and return to his homeland, but when he sent his personal servant to Milan with orders to bring Victoria back, she put him off for thirteen months. She wanted to stay with her lechery, Camargo said. Finally, she left Milan and went to Villette, in Vaud; one of the men she was sleeping with had been ordered to Tafers (*Taverna*, wrote Steiner), in nearby Fribourg. "He left with such a good title," sniped Camargo.

In Switzerland, Victoria had a surgical abortion because she got pregnant and needed to hide the evidence. As Camargo put it, she would have carried her boyfriend's fetus (*ihres bulers cannterfert* – literally "counterfeit," "forgery," or "image" in Italian or French) "with her at all times, except in Switzerland she went to Faci again, and scraped it out with an itty-bitty knife." This was a thing, he said in imperfect German, "that mens aren't supposed to know about."[9] Surgical abortion was widespread and common in early seventeenth-century Italy.[10] Tertullian describes the tools for it, and so does Ovid.[11]

Camargo's description of this tumultuous past cycled back repeatedly to money and rich objects. When he and Victoria married, her dowry had not been given to him. He said it was a mistake, and also only "some hellers or pennies' worth." Nevertheless, he treated her well "according to his estate, at all times, without any lack or defect ... which many witnesses would testify to."[12] Before Camargo left for the Netherlands, he made a will in which "6,000 crowns went to her (in case he didn't come back)." He told his agent, "everything she wanted should be toted up in a receipt, and he would follow it," and buy those things for her.[13] When Guarde followed him to the Netherlands, Camargo settled her in Brussels with a friend of his. She asked for "her own house, in which she could have her free will" and he gave it to her, as well as "4,000 crowns, cash in hand," for a carriage and servants.[14] Camargo's money enabled

---

[8] Herman Hugo, "The Siege of Breda by the Armes of Philip, 1627," in D. M. Rogers, ed., *English Recusant Literature 1558–1640*, vol. 261 (London: The Scholar Press Ltd., nd), 141–142.

[9] "doch in Schweizerlandt zu Faci wieder hier fürgezogenn, unndt mit einem kleinen messerleinn ausgekrazet, daß manns nicht kennen sollen." SHStADr 10024 9119/38, 129.

[10] Research of John Christopoulos, available at: www.history.ac.uk/events/abortion-early-modern-italy (last accessed January 25, 2024).

[11] Tertullian, *De Anima* 25.5–6. Julian Barr, *Tertullian and the Unborn Child: Christian and Pagan Attitudes in Historical Perspective* (New York: Routledge, 2017), 157.

[12] SHStADr 10024 9119/38, 123. [13] SHStADr 10024 9119/38, 124–125.

[14] SHStADr 10024 9119/38, 125–127.

his pursuit of honor, as he financed his own military ventures. If he also viewed his marriage as transactional, Victoria had not held up her end of the bargain. Camargo supported her according to his estate, he said, he spent money on her carriage, her wall hangings, her furniture. Unlike Wolfgang Winckelmann, his immediate inferior, Camargo and Guarde were surrounded by opulent objects. Immediately after he killed her, he loaded these rich things up and rode away. "He left with all the furniture, tapestries, and silver, accompanied by more than forty horsemen, which all met at his house in the middle of the night. Therefore people think this was because she did not conduct herself honorably with that Signor Lieutenant, her husband."[15]

Soldiers were conscious of themselves as men: A popular form of respectful address in letters was for the writer to call the recipient "stern and manly," *Streng und Mannlich*. To some contemporary observers, soldiers were prototypically masculine.[16] But, although relationships among masculinity, warfare, and violence have been well-theorized, they have been less well explored outside the "conventional warfare" between around 1700 and around 1990.[17] Discussing soldiers' interactions within the gender order of early-modern Europe is complex. For instance, although it would not be inaccurate to say soldiers helped uphold the domination of men over women, in a society in which military men were not valorized as heroes but despised as criminals and threats to non-soldiers, it would also be somewhat simplistic. Most Mansfelders did not occupy socially hegemonic positions, and within Italy they were disruptive outsiders. They lived with the women accompanying them in ways non-soldiers interpreted as licentious. They were a religiously mixed group. As the incidents in Gallarate and Cremona show, the Mansfelders catalyzed flashpoints of conflict with local men. One theorist has argued that masculinity is most visible, least apparently natural, when it is acted out by those who are not socially dominant.[18] Common soldiers were not only hyper masculine and socially marginal, they were

---

[15] "... et esso alle cinque hore di detta notte, parti con tutta mobilita, tapezeria et argenteria, accompagnato da più de quaranta cavalli, quali tutti alla med.na hora si ritrovarono alla sua casa, ce perciò si stima fosse caso pensato, perchè essa non si portasse honoratamente con detto S.r Tenente suo marito." Rasini, "Alloggi militari," 134.

[16] Merry Wiesener, "Manhood, Patriarchy, and Gender in Early Modern History," in Amy E. Leonard and Karen L. Nelson, eds., *Masculinities, Childhood, Violence: Attending to Early Modern Women – and Men* (Newark, NJ: University of Delaware Press, 2011), 81.

[17] David Duriesmith, *Masculinity and New War: The Gendered Dynamics of Contemporary Armed Conflict* (Abingdon: Routledge, 2017).

[18] Jack Halberstam, *Female Masculinity* (Durham: Duke University Press, 1998), 2.

also "on display" to one another and to non-soldiers most of the time, in extremely close proximity.

This chapter supplements the work in Gregory Hanlon's *Italy 1636*, an analysis of the same northern Italian theater of the war in which the Mansfelders fought, ten years later. In this book, Hanlon explains soldiers' actions with a "neo-Darwinian" approach in which he states that there is a human male tendency to violence, universal and biological.[19] For Hanlon, military masculinity is the result of biological sex. The virtue of this approach is that it argues that the emotional lives of early seventeenth-century common soldiers and our own share some things that are universal – fear, catastrophe, crisis – and that we can empathize with these men and the women with them despite social and cultural differences. However, it runs the risk of effacing the great differences among experience in different armies into the simple proposition that men can be violent. The social interactions among small groups of people within the military society of early seventeenth-century central Europe remain interesting whether the "ultimate" reasons for the course they take are biological, cultural, or a mix of both. In this chapter, I discuss the ways men and women interacted within the Mansfeld Regiment and other seventeenth-century military units, but I reserve judgment about these interactions' ultimate cause.

The way Camargo talked about his past shows that his conception of honor as a man and as an officer included the ability to make money, the willingness to put his money on the line for others, and – like the men under his command who exchanged stolen fabric – the expectation that debts be met with obligations. Camargo also expected to be able to control his wife. This was not necessarily about sexual continence. Soldiers pimped their women out to other soldiers; women in the neighborhood of the Castello to Milan's northwest, where the Spanish garrison and their families lived in their own enclosed society, sometimes paid its captain protection money to host gambling and prostitution in their homes.[20] The point was that Victoria should have been obeying his orders.

But Camargo had not been able to keep order within his own household: He told Steiner that Guarde had been sleeping with other officers more-or-less behind his back for years. He was angry but does not appear

---

[19] Hanlon, *Italy 1636*, 141. See also Hanlon, *Hero of Italy*.
[20] D'Amico, *Spanish Milan*, 138. For the Spanish garrison in Milan, Luis Antonio Ribot Garcia, "Soldados españoles en Italia. El Castillo de Milán a finales del siglo XVI," in Enrique Garcia Hernan and Davide Maffi, eds., *Guerra y sociedad en la monarquía hispánica: política, estrategia y cultura en la Europa Moderna, 1500–1700, Volume 1* (Madrid: Laberinto, 2006), 401–444.

to have been ashamed. She cavorted with different cavaliers in her room, he said. She slutted around with them on the road and in Milan.

As soon as he turned his back on the house she went whoring around to her boyfriends (because [Camargo] wasn't present to go to her) ... And there was also a nobleman from her homeland visiting him, in [Camargo's] absence, once when she was lying in bed, he came to her ... she gave him to grab her breast and then her whole body. And she had allowed him as much as to sleep by her, but however out of fear of [Camargo] ... he left, and told five captains about this magnificent deed of his wife's.[21]

Camargo had this story from the servants. He said that Victoria planned to kill him, that she told someone that "if she knew somebody who would poison him or bring news that he had died, she would honor him with a pair of gloves worth 1,000 pistoles."[22] Camargo said Victoria's maid begged her weeping on bended knee to reconcile with him because he was "a valiant cavalier" who "not only loves you greatly but has also willingly done everything your heart desires."[23]

Camargo claimed that Guarde was confined by her parents before he met her because of "her evil beginnings," and that she fought with them so often she would rather live in a convent than in Cremona. However, other events in his testimony and the chronicler Rasini's account are consistent with a family that was close to Victoria and opposed to Camargo. Victoria's sister helped her cuckold him and carried messages between her and her boyfriends.[24] According to Rasini, Victoria's sister and sister-in-law had been part of her entourage the night she was killed. Some of "the gentlemen" who entered Gallarate with Victoria that evening may have been her male kin; Camargo may have left town with Victoria's goods immediately after he killed her to keep them from her relatives. According to Camargo, Victoria spent at least a month with her father in Cremona.[25] Camargo's father even went to Brussels to visit Victoria, his daughter-in-law, and met her on the road to Ghent.[26] Moreover, the citizens of Gallarate seemed to view Victoria ambiguously: Rasini wrote that she did not live honorably with her husband, but also that she entered Gallarate "with applause and great pomp."[27]

As Theodoro de Camargo finished his testimony, he said that he could not let his wife's adultery stand, and that he was afraid that "if he pardoned her" she would poison him. He "judged her himself with a stiletto, because of her great evil deeds; for others it should be an

---

[21] SHStADr 10024 9119/38, 127–132.   [22] SHStADr 10024 9119/38, 130–131.
[23] SHStADr 10024 9119/38, 128–129.   [24] SHStADr 10024 9119/38, 130.
[25] SHStADr 10024 9119/38, 144.   [26] SHStADr 10024 9119/38, 138.
[27] Rasini, "Alloggi militari," 134.

abhorrent example and to her a well-earned punishment."[28] These words were common parlance when a death verdict was reached in a capital case. In Camargo's office as the lieutenant colonel of the Mansfeld Regiment he said them himself, and I have seen them written at the end of legal files. He did not explicitly compare his domestic authority as the head of his household to the legal authority of a colonel or the presiding officer of a tribunal, but he framed himself as an agent of the law, as a political authority writ small. This rhetoric contrasted with his actions immediately after the murder; within three days, Camargo had apparently recovered his sangfroid.

Victoria Guarde was buried the day after she died, "with much funeral pomp, and all the soldiery in arms, she was carried to the sepulcher and the exequies were done with great ceremony, and she was put in the sepulcher in the Palazzi of the Chapel of Corpus Domini, then they fired a great salute of muskets."[29] Victoria was buried as an elite member of the regiment, however uncomfortably she had lived within it. She also seems to have been given at least some respect by the citizens of Gallarate.

The locals' reaction to her killing is not known. According to Philippa Maddern, violence within early modern households was understood within a "moral economy of violence" within which those in charge had the moral authority to discipline those beneath them with force.[30] But this assault was bloody and uncontrolled; Camargo was also a soldier, a non-Italian, and an outsider. This splendid funeral makes it appear that Gallarate may not have approved of him. We cannot know if this was more than respect for Guarde's rank and station – if Theodoro Camargo had been her family's enemy, or if he and locally important Italians had been in conflict before or as a result of Victoria's death. Rasini or other Galleratese might have regarded her murder as a provocation.

Mattheus Steiner agreed to act as Camargo's representative and collect evidence in his defense. He went down to Milan with some officers from the Schaumburg Regiment and questioned the family's servants. Victoria had not wanted to go to the Netherlands, and the men she associated with there were all other Italians. Her page, fifteen-year-old Wilhem Stum from Brussels, told Steiner it was well-known that when she lived

---

[28] SHStADr 10024 9119/38, 132.
[29] "Il lundei poi seguente con assai pompa funerale, et sendo tutta la soldatesca in armi, fu portava alla sepoltura et fattegli le esequie con grande cera, et fu messa nella sepoltura dei Palazzi nella Capella del Corpus Domini, poi si fece una grande sparata di moschette ..." Rasini, "Alloggi militari," 134.
[30] Philippa Maddern, *Violence and Social Order: East Anglia, 1422–42* (Oxford: Clarendon Press, 1992), 98–110.

in Brussels "different Italian lords" visited her. They stayed until the middle of the night, regaled her with food and other presents. Wilhelm looked in and saw for himself an Italian officer sitting on the bed with Victoria playing cards.[31] She joined up with a Count Rosario on the two days' travel into Milan, "and they were happy with each other."[32] She held banquets with her boyfriends and made merry, eating and drinking and enjoying the pleasures of the body. Was this in the Spanish military district near the squat brutal walls of the Castello, in a garden villa in the cool grassy expanse between Milan's medieval walls and the new Spanish bastions?[33]

Steiner knew Italian, but not well enough to examine a witness, so a Milanese lord questioned Victoria's maid Margarita Pellegrini in Italian while Steiner simultaneously translated their dialogue into German and wrote it down.[34] Not all Italians applauded Victoria: Margarita said she had not been happy with her mistress's adultery. She said she quit because "this could not remain hidden for long," and other households refused to hire her since they knew where she had been a maid. Margarita may have also been where Camargo got the idea Victoria was planning to poison him, since she said one of Victoria's boyfriends gave her poison to kill Camargo. Victoria was hanging around officers with a bad reputation, said Margarita Pellegrini.[35] Another maid, Anna Luisa Ségers from Maastricht, said Victoria went around with another officer even though Camargo was a better-looking man.

Victoria and her women knew she was in danger. Anna Luisa said that once she realized what was going on, she begged Victoria "many times by God's will to leave off from the thing because the Herr Lieutenant Colonel would learn about it and he would take such an evil exit." She said Victoria said "she wanted to be happy doing what she liked, because it was the kind of thing she did" (*sie wolle ihres gefallens lustig sein, dann es also der brauch*).[36] In the context of the early seventeenth century, this desire for happiness was deeply suspicious: Victoria was attempting to attain happiness not only on earth instead of in heaven, but as a subversion of her socially ordained subordinate role. Yet this may have been an early manifestation of a coming change in attitudes toward personal feeling which occurred more than a century after her death: During the Enlightenment, happiness shifted from an attribute of the blessed or unusually fortunate to something human beings could aspire to in this

---

[31] SHStADr 10024 9119/38, 137–138. [32] SHStADr 10024 9119/38, 139.
[33] D'Amico, *Spanish Milan*, 14–15. [34] SHStADr 10024 9119/38, 151.
[35] SHStADr 10024 9119/38, 153–155. [36] SHStADr 10024 9119/38, 156–157.

life.[37] Victoria's statement is strikingly individualistic, which was also dangerous. Frances Dolan argues that if early modern people were becoming individuals in the modern sense but marriage made husband and wife "one flesh," one individual had to be suppressed, implying that marital conflicts necessitated violence.[38]

Victoria's flesh and the rich goods and fabrics surrounding it were objects of fascination to the men in this case. Michael de Labey looked into her room at night and saw her give Count Rosario a sash in *Leibfarbe*, silk the color of flesh.[39] She played cards and ate with her Italian noblemen sitting on her bed surrounded with hangings; when Camargo killed her, he took all these goods back within hours. She died in a dress Steiner described as purple brown and was buried in a dress Rasini described as *rosso*. Was it the same garment? The disjected, filthy dress Steiner described is transfigured in Rasini's account: The color red appears, but no blood. Victoria's lacerated flesh is no longer covered in gore. When she was buried, "this lady was in an outfit red and beautiful, she really seemed to feel and not be dead, and she was most beautiful in appearance and body."[40] While in Victoria's own words as reported by another woman, she is an active person, even in Rasini's ambiguously sympathetic account she is both living and unliving, as much a beautiful possession as the goods in which Camargo smothered her.

The trial took place on April 16, 1626 in Alessandria. In light of the "collected information," especially "the great honor, love, loyalty, and" – of course – "monetary assets" that Victoria had received from "her lord," the verdict was that Camargo had been "moved to wrath ... in order to save his honor and reputation, he was advised and forced by necessity to this extremity of life and body."[41] This tribunal regarded the "wrath" (*Zorn, ira*) to which Camargo was moved as a legitimate justification for homicide. Aristotle described this emotion as the impulse of a superior to seek revenge against a slight by someone of lower rank.[42] Camargo was moved to the same emotion when his flag-bearer deserted a year later.[43] The angry person is angry because of his superior rank; from the *Summa*

---

[37] Darrin M. McMahon, *Happiness: A History* (New York: Atlantic, 2006).
[38] Frances Dolan, *Marriage and Violence: The Early Modern Legacy* (Philadelphia: University of Pennsylvania Press, 2008).
[39] SHStADr 10024 9119/38, 143.
[40] "qual signora era in modo rossa et bella, che veramente pareva havesse li sentimenti, et non fosse morta, et era d'aspetto bellissima et di corpo." Rasini, "Alloggi militari," 134.
[41] SHStADr 10024 9119/38, 160–161.
[42] Karl A. E. Enenkel and Anita Traninger, "Introduction: Discourses of Anger in the Early Modern Period," in Karl A. E. Enenkel and Anita Traninger, eds., *Discourses of Anger in the Early Modern Period* (Leiden: Brill, 2015), 2.
[43] SHStADr 10024 9739/6, 148.

to Locke the desire for revenge is a part of wrath.[44] The social understanding of anger stemming from a relationship between unequal parties held from the classical period until after the seventeenth century: It was only in the late eighteenth century that the desire for revenge upon a subordinate was discarded as a motive for anger.[45] Theodoro was Victoria's "lord." Within the social networks of the upper levels of Italian/Spanish/Imperial military society, he believed that her license was a threat to his manhood.[46] Male honor in Italy, Germany, and the Low Countries, in military and civilian society, depended on a man's willingness to fight, but soldiers may have been more comfortable with anger as a motivation. The military community may also have been slower to criminalize homicide, if done to protect the killer's honor.[47] Camargo was acquitted.[48]

In Leipzig, Mansfeld had known that Camargo murdered his wife since at least April 1: "I cannot express with what travail and amazement I have received the news of the incident that took place between my Lieutenant Colonel Camargo and his wife," he wrote the Duke of Feria. The regiment must "administer justice to the one who was accused," and "considering my absence and in order to flee every cause of suspicion, I would prefer it if his cause were judged by a judicial inquiry made up of other regiments of the German nation, with neither love nor hatred." Nevertheless, he continued smoothly, "I recommend his person to the clemency of Your Excellency, under the shadow of which I can hope for nothing from you save grace and favour and mainly because ~~I desire greatly that he be with the regiment as soon as possible~~ the prosperity of my Regiment ... requires his presence as soon as possible."[49]

The verdict had been determined from the beginning. The tribunal was made up largely of officers and soldiers who were not Mansfelders and, as in Wolfgang Winckelmann's fabric theft, nobody said a thing. The citizens of Gallarate might mutter, but the regiment was preserved

---

[44] Johannes F. Lehmann, "Feeling Rage: The Transformation of the Concept of Anger in the Eighteenth Century," in Karl A. E. Enenkel and Anita Traninger, eds., *Discourses of Anger in the Early Modern Period* (Leiden: Brill, 2015), 17–18.
[45] Johannes F. Lehmann, *In Abgrund der Wut: Zur Kultur und Literaturgeschichte des Zorns* (Freiburg im Breisgau: Rombach Verlag, 2012).
[46] Christopher Black, *Early Modern Italy: A Social History* (London: Routledge, 2001), 118.
[47] Pieter Spierenburg, "Men Fighting Men: Europe from a Global Perspective," *The Cambridge World History of Violence Vol III, 1500–1800* (Cambridge: Cambridge University Press, 2020), 300.
[48] SHStADr 10024 9119/38, 161.
[49] SHStADr 10024 9737/13, *Italienische und franzosische* Concepta *derer Schreiben Graf Wolffgangs Zu Mansfeld an den Herzog zu* Feria, *Spanische Bottschafter, und andere Ao 1625–26*, 76–77: Rough draft of letter from Wolf von Mansfeld to the Duke of Feria, undated but filed with papers dated April 1, 1626.

for another day. After Steiner wrote "the Herr Lieutenant Colonel, as an honorable and prominent cavalier and high officer ... had been moved to wrath," he continued, "(although nobody should be the judge in his own case)."[50] Steiner recorded many deaths, but only for Victoria had he written, "God have mercy on her soul."

Before the eighteenth century, women went on campaign in large numbers, especially in central European armies.[51] In contrast to the magnetic and disturbing sexual images that Mattheus Steiner, Antonio Rasini, and Michael de Labey associated with Victoria Guarde's body, these women's lives were quotidian. They filled support roles: Preparing food, sewing, washing, taking care of the sick, digging and construction, hauling the big guns into place or emplacing them. Sometimes these women show up in legal records. Soldiers did not carry, it was demeaning, so on their backs women carried "knapsacks, cloaks, shawls, pots, kettles, pans, brooms, small bags, roosters, all kinds of trash."[52] They carried straw. Wood was not issued so they picked up branches on the way and carried them. Their backpacks were great wicker baskets, wood-framed and fastened over their shoulders with ropes or leather straps. They carried fresh-dug earth for fortifications, and they dug it. They carried water jugs, canteens, their men's clothing, their own clothing and their children's clothing, collars and stockings, sheets and blankets, tents and the poles for tents. They carried food.[53] A diary from 1612 says these women walked with little dogs on ropes; when the weather was bad, when the horses struggled up to the hocks in mud, they carried the dogs in their arms.[54]

They carried children. One eyewitness saw military women carrying tiny children in bundles on their heads to leave their hands free for the

---

[50] SHStADr 10024 9119/38, 160–161.

[51] For women and armies in the sixteenth and seventeenth centuries, see Barton C. Hacker, "Women and Military Institutions in Early Modern Europe: A Reconnaissance," *Signs* 6.4 (1981), 643–671; Lynn, *Women, Armies, and Warfare*; and Mary Ailes, *Courage and Grief: Women and Sweden's Thirty Years War* (Lincoln: University of Nebraska Press, 2018). For military masculinity and the diminished but still interesting place of women in armies in the eighteenth century, see Jennie Hurl-Eamon, *Marriage and the British Army in the Long Eighteenth Century: "The Girl I Left Behind Me"* (Oxford: Oxford University Press, 2014). Only after military supply grew more modernized and women were no longer needed were authorities able to act on their disapproval and restrict their presence. Ailes, *Courage and Grief*, 8–9.

[52] Kirchhof, *Militaris Disciplina*, cited in Wilhelm Haberling, "Army Prostitution and its Control: An Historical Study," in Victor Robinson, ed., *Morals in Wartime; Including General Survey from Ancient Times; Morals in the First World War and Morals in the Second World War* (New York: Publishers Foundation, 1943), 33–34.

[53] Lynn, *Women, Armies, and Warfare*, 160–163.

[54] Hans Delbrück, *The Dawn of Modern Warfare: History of the Art of War Vol IV* (Lincoln: University of Nebraska Press, 1990), 66.

rest of their baggage.[55] The lives of children in early seventeenth-century armies have scarcely been explored.[56] Hans Jacob von Grimmelshausen, the writer of the famous Thirty Years War novel *Simplicissimus*, was kidnapped as a teenager and forced to serve in the Imperial army, and he married a soldier's daughter.[57] The daughters of officers and common soldiers stayed part of the military community when they grew up, and often married soldiers.[58] The men and women of the Spanish Army of Flanders intermarried routinely, producing a distinctive Spanish–Netherlandish military society.[59] The boys and servants listed in cavalry rolls were probably teens. Some grew up to become cavalrymen. Some died, like the fourteen-to-seventeen-year olds buried in the camp in Latdorf where a Swedish army spent fall and winter 1644. Their bones were marked by hard physical labor.[60]

It is difficult to produce hard statistics for military children during this conflict: Although Saxon muster rolls from the 1680s recorded how many children went along with each soldier, earlier Saxon field army records did not. The children in the Saxon fortress of Königstein were counted on the orders of the Elector of Saxony at least twice. One count happened on May 3, 1670. The other is undated, but may have taken place during the 1620s.[61] Königstein contained more children proportionally than field armies in the 1680s: More than four per family instead of the one or two for soldiers in field companies, both the "bodily children" of the soldiers they lived with and "of their household." Members of more mobile units may have sent their children to stay with either civilian relatives or to relatives in forts or garrisons like Königstein when they were on the move. If the civilian relatives of the soldiers in that great fortress had to travel, they may also have sent their children there.

---

[55] Anonymous, "Kriegstagebücher aus dem ligistischen Hauptquartier 1620," *Abhandlungen des Phil.-Hist. Klasse der Bayerischen Akademie der Wissenschaften* 23 (1906), 77–210, 171.
[56] Peter-Michael Hahn, "Kriegserfahrungen im Zeitalter des Dreißigjährigen Krieges," in Dittmar Dahlman, ed., *Kinder und Jugendliche in Krieg und Revolution: vom Dreißigjährigen Krieg bis zu den Kindersoldaten Afrikas* (Paderborn: Schönigh, 2000), 1–16.
[57] Wilson, *Europe's Tragedy*, 818.   [58] Ailes, *Courage and Grief*, 55–56.
[59] Parker, *Army of Flanders and the Spanish Road*, 175.
[60] J. Fahr and P. Pacak, "Das schwedische Feldlager Latdorf," in Susanne Friederich and Harald Meller, eds., *Archäologie am Kalkteich 22 in Latdorf. Die Chemie stimmt! Arch. Sachsen-Anhalt* (Halle: Landesamt für Denkmalpflege und Archäologie Sachsen-Anhalt, 2008), 105–114.
[61] SHStADr 11237 10803/8, *Die Garnison des Berg Vestung Königstein de Ao 1623 biß 80*; #1, #141.

Fatherhood was as important as motherhood, but less visible. Glimpses of the relationships between fathers and children appear in baptismal records, in muster rolls, or the counts of children in Königstein. Simon Funcke of Königstein, who had served for a total of nineteen years, was recorded as having "two little daughters, one over ten" and "a very small little son" (*Ein gar klein Söhnlein*).[62] Peter Hagendorf spent the sack of Magdeburg in his shack outside the city recovering from wounds; he was also tending his three-year-old daughter Elizabeth, since his wife had gone into the city to plunder. He and Elizabeth watched Magdeburg burn together.[63] When his son Melchert Christoff turned five, Peter paid ten gulden a year plus the cost of clothing to send him to school.[64] This was his first child to live past toddlerhood, but education was also important to this future judge, who kept a diary and who had bought a book half in German and half in Swiss on his way up the military road from Italy. Melchert Christoff eventually became a lawyer; he died in 1721 at sixty-seven.[65] Camargo had at least one child, a son also named Theodoro.[66]

First-hand accounts of seventeenth-century military life are full of military women and children, and some are by the women themselves, like the Styrian Maria Cordula Freiin von Pranckh. She wrote her experiences in a family book which she began for her female relatives in 1673 and worked on until her death, a military version of the family books or memorial books familiar from other social groups. Although this account is far later than the Mansfeld Regiment's time in service, its rarity as a first-person documentation of seventeenth-century military life by a woman makes it a valuable source to illuminate not only the lives of these women, but also the social networks of women in seventeenth-century armies, which are harder to track in quantitative sources. Maria Cordula's oldest half-brother and first husband were captains and her second husband was a colonel.[67] Military manuals described women's

---

[62] SHStADr 11237 10803/8; #1.
[63] Hagendorf, *Ein Söldnerleben im Dreißigjährigen Krieg*, 47. [64] Ibid., 123.
[65] Medick, *Der Dreißigjährige Krieg*, 115–122.
[66] This Theodoro de Camargo eventually moved to the Netherlands and married a woman named Marie l'Hermite (1622–1661), who remarried after his death. Like the Camargos, the second family l'Hermite married into, the Snouckaerts, engaged in military and financial service to the Habsburgs. Ernstberger, "Hans de Witte," 24. Papers relating to the Camargos and the Snouckaerts are in the Snouckaerts' family papers in the Dutch National Archive. Inventoried in W. D. Post, *Inventaris van het archief van de familie Snouckaert van Schauburg, 1487–1986* (Den Haag: Nationaal Archief, 1986).
[67] Maria Cordula von Pranckh, "Gedenkbuch der Frau Maria Cordula, Freiin von Pranck, verwitwete Hacke, geb. Radhaupt, 1595–1700 (1707)," *Steiermärkische Geschichtsblätter* 2.1 (1881), 9–29, 9.

activities, like Hans Wilhelm Kirchhof's account of a baptism in camp which specified that the nearest church should be used only if it was safe to walk to. Like other military rituals, such as von Gruppach's prayer sessions or camp funerals, a baptism required at least one piper and drummer.[68] One diarist said that after a big battle, there were weddings in camp. He said the soldiers felt safe then but the couples had probably also been waiting, since, if a fight was victorious, they could pay for the weddings from plunder.[69]

Hard statistics are rarer. Saxon muster rolls from the 1680s and the eighteenth century recorded whether soldiers were married but rolls from the Thirty Years War do not. Strength returns are large sheets of paper, sometimes used to wrap stacks of muster rolls, which summarize data in tabular form. These returns contained more information than muster rolls alone, sometimes including the number of women in a regiment: One big table summing up the effectives in three cavalry companies at Luckau at some point in the 1640s recorded twenty women and nine children for eighty-nine officers and men.[70] Along with fifty-seven men, a 1633 list of Imperialist prisoners in Leipzig lists twenty women, the widows of dead Imperialist soldiers. A male prisoner had two children and a maidservant mentioned in a marginal note but not counted in the list; it is unclear exactly how many women were there who were not recorded.[71] Even in the eighteenth century, scarcely half the individuals in an army were men.[72]

The relationships military women created formed networks now almost invisible: Partnerships, long or short-term (as Kirchhof noted about "this People," "those who today join their hands together / tomorrow walk away from each other with their feet"[73]); family relationships between soldiers on the female side, which passed down no name. Peter Hagendorf went around with men in his second wife's family, his close male kin by marriage.[74] The godparents of Maria Cordula von Pranckh's

---

[68] Kirchhof, *Militaris Disciplina*, 147–148. Military funerals are on p. 203.
[69] Mortimer, *Eyewitness Accounts*, 38.
[70] SHStADr 11237 10841/13, *Eingegebene Muster Rollen und Extracte von Ihro Chur Furstl: Durchl: zu Sachßen Regimentern zu Roß und Fuß von Anno 1630 bis Anno 1640, 9 Convol.*
[71] SHStADr 11237 108351-1, *Extract der in Leipzig zuruckgebliebenen und verwunderten Offiziere und Knechte von der Kaiserl. Armee 1633.*
[72] Stefan Kroll, *Soldaten im 18. Jahrhundert zwischen Friedensalltag und Kriegserfahrung: Lebenswelten und Kultur in der kursächsischen Armee 1728–1796* (Paderborn: Schöningh Paderborn, 2006), 49.
[73] "Wie auch etliche heut mit den Händen zusamen gehen warden / so lauffen sie morgen mit den Füssen wider von einander." Kirchhof, *Militaris Disciplina*, 147.
[74] Mortimer, *Eyewitness Accounts*, 34.

children were members of the military community, while between 1646 and 1700 she was the godmother to seventy-eight children.[75] Officers and their wives were often patrons or creditors, and often godparents, like Camargo or the woman who may have been Mattheus Steiner's wife. In 1595, the godmother of the baby who grew up to become Maria Cordula's father had been the wife of a Colonel-and-master-of-horse: Maria Cordula's book records a series of substantially female relationships of marriage and godparentage among the military elite which spanned more than 100 years.[76]

After the Mansfeld Regiment returned to Germany, Camargo transferred into Imperial service and was promoted to colonel. In October 1632, "when the soldiers were placed" in Mühlhausen in Saxony, on the way to Lützen, Camargo "had a tailor's apprentice, who had served under him earlier and had deserted, and whom he received again while he was putting out a fire, hanged off a tree in the Spittelsgrab near the city pond (at St. Margaret's hospital, in the garden)."[77] On another occasion he attempted to forbid officers under his command from engaging in single combat during a melee; although he threatened to have them hanged, they ignored him, and were supported in this by the other commander on the scene.[78] In a societal context within which men went to war alongside members of their households, there is little distinction between the "public" violence of combat or military discipline and "private" violence within the household. Both took place within and as expressions of, and helped shape, hierarchies of gender, status, rank or office, and age. As Cynthia Cockburn argued in another context, in early modern central Europe military violence existed on the same continuum as interpersonal violence: "gender relations are like a linking thread, a kind of fuse, along which violence runs."[79]

But Camargo's social interactions also depended on his personal characteristics. He could not command obedience or affection from his

---

[75] Von Pranckh, "Gedenkbuch," 19–28.   [76] Ibid., 9.
[77] "Als die Soldaten hier lagen, ließ der Oberst Camario einen Schneidergesellen, der früher unter ihm gedient hatte und desertirt war, den er bei diesem Feuerlöschen wieder bekam, im Spittelsgraben am Burgteiche (zu St. Margarethen-Hospital im Garten) an einen Baum hängen." Reinhard Jordan, *Chronik der Stadt Mühlhausen in Thüringen*, Vol. 3 (Mühlhausen: Dannischer Buchhandlerei, 1905), 63.
[78] Augustin von Fritsch, *Tagebuch des Augustin von Fritsch: Taten und Schicksal im Dreißigjährigen Krieg. Obrist und Kommandant von Parkstein und der Stadt Weiden*, ed. Hans J. Rudnik (Merching: Forum Verlag, 2012), 123–124.
[79] Cynthia Cockburn, "The Continuum of Violence: A Gender Perspective on War and Peace," in Wenona Giles and Jennifer Hyndman, eds., *Sites of Violence: Gender and Conflict Zones* (Berkeley: University of California Press, 2004), 44.

subordinates and, when they disobeyed him, he lashed out with lethal anger. Like his wife, Camargo seemed to chafe within his brutal, demanding society. Their story is one area in which change over time may be visible in the interactions and feelings of members of the military community in the early seventeenth century. If so, it is not toward greater discipline but greater individuality, even the pursuit of happiness. But, for both Victoria and Theodoro, attempts to be happy, or respected, were skewed and self-destructive: Neither could "be happy doing what they wanted."

On November 16, 1632, Theodoro de Camargo led the Camargo-Reinach Regiment at the van of the Imperialist left at Lützen and was severely wounded. He died on the withdrawal, when the Imperialists stopped in Chemnitz.[80]

On February 11, 1627, Camargo notified Mattheus Steiner that his flag-bearer, Juan Gammert from 's-Hertogenbosch, had "the audacity to treat his servant very evilly with blows without any cause." Juan Gammert's parents may have been members of the Spanish–Netherlandish military community mentioned by Geoffrey Parker. The multiethnic character of the Spanish monarchy and its armies is visible in his name: He signed it Juan, but Steiner and the Germans in Gammert's company called him Johann.

Before Gammert could be arrested for abusing his subordinate, which Camargo did not tolerate in others, he packed, had his horse new-shod, and ran on a forged passport. He made it to a Franciscan cloister near Milan but someone caught him and brought him back.[81] Gammert tried to explain that he had never served in a German regiment before and was not familiar with German military legal norms, but Camargo had none of it. Gammert had left his flag, he had set himself against the praiseworthy war law, and "like an honor-and-oath-forgetting impudent rogue, thief, and scoundrel," when he ran, he "stole gold and pay from the purse of the King of Spain, our most gracious lord." Camargo sentenced him to hang from a withered tree, but ordered Steiner to review the case.[82]

Steiner collected Gammert's brother officers, Lieutenant Johann van Velle and Fourier Matthias Laiber, and Laiber told him Gammert had tried to persuade them to leave with him because "he wanted to be able to share everything with him." "They could well find another lord" together; "I don't trust the Lieutenant Colonel [Camargo]." Laiber

---

[80] Christian Lehmann, *Die Kriegschronik: Sachsen mit Erzgebirge*, ed. Hendrik Heidler (Norderstedt: Books on Demand, 2009), 55.
[81] SHStADr 10024 9739/6, 138–161.   [82] SHStADr 10024 9739/6, 156.

refused. "No, it's completely unethical [*ganz Unrecht*]. I want to stay and handle the situation like an upright soldier." Laiber was *redlich*, not *rechtschaffen*: When Gammert left, Laiber informed on him.[83]

Despite Camargo's wishes, Steiner wrote that Gammert should be freed, saving his life: Gammert was released on July 7, 1627.[84]

---

[83] SHStADr 10024 9739/6, 146–147.   [84] SHStADr 10024 9739/6, 161.

Scene II Hieronymus Sebastian Schutze, Felix Steter, and Wolfgang Winkelmann

Felix Steter was the lieutenant in Wolfgang Winckelmann's infantry company; he came from Wiener Neustadt, just south of Vienna. He had been a corporal in Dam Vitzthum von Eckstedt's company from 1620 to 1621, in the same regiment that Mattheus Steiner had served in when he was a pikeman.[1] Steter was the direct subordinate of Wolfgang Winckelmann's flag-bearer Hieronymus Sebastian Schutze, who killed Hans Heinrich Tauerling by accident and reappropriated some of the cloth delivered to the Winckelmann Regiment. Within the Mansfeld Regiment's comparatively loose organization, Steter struggled against Schutze for precedence.

On May 1, 1626, Schutze and some other officers and soldiers got drunk together in The Angel after midday, then went to a friend's lodgings to keep drinking with Steter. Schutze was "completely hammered": He left the room and came back leading his horse. He mounted it, rode it into the room, and jumped over the table, but it didn't make the jump cleanly and fell with Schutze on its back. The horse's hind leg hit Felix Steter in the chest so that he "sank to the earth and lay before death." Bystanders managed to revive him. Schutze asked him how he was doing. "The horse gave me a good one," Steter said.

Schutze followed him down the street. He tried to set Steter on his horse, and then tried to get Steter to come back to his own quarters with him. He wanted, however ineptly, to make amends. Steter objected: "The officers who drank with me can get me home. Let me go, I have my own horse, if I want to ride I can fetch her but I'd rather not."[2] Versions of what happened next diverge.

On May 7, Felix Steter complained that when he did not accept Schutze's help, Schutze grabbed Steter's rod of office out of his hands and broke it in two. Schutze then supposedly insulted Steter in German, Italian, and possibly Spanish or French: "*Du schinder, du hundt, Caion, du Bestia*": "you skinner, you dog, testicle, you beast."[3] For Schutze to insult Steter on the street in front of other soldiers was bad enough,

---

[1] SHStADr 11237 10840/4 9.   [2] SHStADr 10024 9739/6, 14–16.
[3] SHStADr 10024 9739/6, 16.

but to call him a *schinder*, a knacker or skinner, would have been a tremendously damaging insult. Skinners made their living handling the bodies and skins of dead animals and human corpses, and German society regarded all contact with these objects, especially skins, as polluting, except in the performance of magic. Skinners and executioners were the worst of the "dishonorable trades," excluded from almost all normal life.[4] If this exchange had occurred as Steter claimed, if Schutze and Steter had been common soldiers instead of officers in the third most honorable company in the regiment, they would have drawn swords on the spot. Instead Steter sued: This was a high injury, he could not bear such dishonor because of his office, he said. Uphold the praiseworthy war law, cite Hieronymus Sebastian Schutze, restore my honor to me and punish him, make him distasteful before others.

Steter insisted his colleagues would back him up: "Many officers and soldiers, especially officers from my company, who had drunk with me, whom I hereby offer as witnesses, will not withhold [evidence of] this, or suffer it." But, while witnesses remembered the horse jumping the table, and a scuffle between the flag-bearer and the Lieutenant, nobody who was interrogated remembered hearing Schutze insult Steter. The company muster-writer Heinrich Teichmeyer had had nothing against Schutze, but he did have something against the Lieutenant. Sergeant Andreas Melhorn, whom Steter had mentioned as a character witness against Schutze, confirmed that some time ago in Bern he and Schutze quarreled, but he said he had never complained about Schutze and the problems between them had been patched up. In fact, it was Steter he was still angry at. (If Steter, Schutze, and Melhorn had been in Bern together, it implies that although Steter was probably Catholic he may have fought for Bern, which was Protestant.[5]) Felix Steter had a history of disputes with other officers. Moreover, when the witnesses were questioned, squad leader Mattheus Pohl said that he heard "the Lieutenant, after the insults he had poured out against the flag-bearer," say that, after the incident with the horse, "he had good justification to take the flag for himself, and have him arrested."[6]

The company flag was a potent focus of loyalty, culturally and practically. Infantry flags were big and square, up to nine feet by nine feet, nailed to the pole with short brass big-headed nails. Schutze's job was to carry one. Although they carried side-weapons like a sword or Schutze's pair of pistols, flag-bearers were supposed to carry no other weapons, and were

---

[4] Kathy Stuart, *Defiled Trades and Social Outcasts: Honor and Ritual Pollution in Early Modern Germany* (Cambridge: Cambridge University Press, 2006), 2–3.
[5] SHStADr 10024 9739/6, 24   [6] SHStADr 10024 9739/6, 23–26.

not required to fight. Instead, they were to tend their massive flags and present them in battle. When a flag-bearer was carrying the flag, he was to bow to nobody but the colonel.[7] The pole was short enough to be lifted with one hand, leather-wrapped handle protruding a few feet beyond the bottom of the flag, and flag-bearers propped them on their shoulders.

Kirchhof said the flag of the colonel's personal company, which was either white or had mainly white in its design, was "larger and more beautiful" than the other flags in the regiment. He thought the employer's arms should be "in gold and silver most luminously painted and finished" on it.[8] Beauty was associated with light since before the Middle Ages: Thomas Aquinas drew on Dionysius the Areopagite when he said beauty requires proportion, integrity, and *claritas*, clarity and luminosity.[9] Claritas was manifest in white, highly colored clothing, precious metals, and precious stones; in rich shining things. One flag cost an average of forty to fifty gulden, five to seven times the monthly pay of a common musketeer.[10]

Flags were translucent and shining. They were light and crisp, and they made a sharp snapping noise in the wind, or when waved quickly. Brilliant red and gold-shot scarlet; dark green or acid seafoam; deep, clear blue: When an army was encamped, each company's flagpole was driven into the earth before that company's row of shacks. According to Wallhausen, each company's assembly-place should be before the flag-bearer's lodgings.[11] When the company was quartered the flag was kept in the flag-bearer's room. Kirchhof, who had been a mercenary before he wrote military manuals, said flag-bearers hung the flags out their windows "so everyone can find his quarters better."[12] This was a symbol you could grab and touch.

When Moser's Company in the Mansfeld Regiment mutinied, the flag-bearer ordered Commander Christoff Hendel to take the flag, present it to the mutineers, and talk them down. They formed a ring around him and told him "Get out of here with the flag or we will shoot you dead." He yelled back "This flag is mine and entrusted to me, I will live and die by it and then I will be wrapped in it" (*das fendel wehre sein unnd ihme vertrauet, er wolte dabey leben und sterben auch sich darauf ein*

---

[7] Wallhausen, *Manuale Militaire*, 128. [8] Kirchhof, *Militaris Disciplina*, 85.
[9] Umberto Eco, *On Beauty: History of a Western Idea* (London: Martin Secker and Warburg, 2004), 99.
[10] Roland Sennewald, *Die Kursachsen im Dreißigjährigen Krieg: Band II: Die Kursächsischen Feldzeichen im Dreißigjährigen Krieg 1618–1648* (Berlin: Zeughaus Verlag, 2013), 19.
[11] Wallhausen, *Manuale Militaire*, 128.
[12] "Jeglicher Fähnrich stecket sein Fähnlein an seinem Losament zum Fenster hinaus / kan männiglich sein Quartier desto besser finden." Kirchhof, *Militaris Disciplina*, 123.

daßelbe gewickelt).[13] This echoed the words military manuals said were spoken when the flags of a newly-raised company were nailed to their poles and handed to the flag-bearers amid the assembled men. The words are so similar they may have been a ritual formula: Whether Hendel had ever read a military manual or could even read, the same phrase shows up in two different manuals nineteen years apart.[14] Hendel's willingness to live and die by his flag eclipsed his relationship to the King of Spain, whom he never mentioned.

Taking flags in combat was a mark of victory and counting the number of flags you had taken versus the number of flags your enemy had taken from you was one of the ways commanders ascertained victory or defeat. The flags of defeated enemies were presented to commanders and displayed in public places. An honorable capitulation granted a defeated army permission to march away from the field or fallen strong place with their drums beating and music playing, a bullet in each musketeer's mouth and their matches lit, and "flags flying," uncased and unfurled: *I can still fight you if I want, I simply choose not to*. If an army did not get those terms, they had to extinguish their matches and the torches they used to light them, and furl their flags; the commander might have to dismount and walk away on foot.[15]

The presence or absence of a company's flag had legal force. Contracts specified that the companies they ordered were to be paid "as long as the flags fly on their poles."[16] This was a literal statement: When a company

---

[13] SHStADr 10024 9119/38, 95.

[14] "Vnd da jr vom feindt die eine handt verlieren / sollet jhr das fähnlein in die ander handt fassen. Da euch dieselbige auch (gott wöls verhüten) abgeschossen oder geschlagen wurde: / sollet ihr mit den zähnen dreyn fallen / es so lang ewer leib und leben wehret / mit tretten / reissen / und wie euch menschlich und müglich / vertheydigen. Auch ehe jhr es willig den feinden vberliesset / euch dareyn winden und wickeln / und also lebens oder todts erwarten." Kirchhof, *Militaris Disciplina*, 74. "Nach diesem gibt man dem Fähnrich das Fähnlein in die Handt / errinert ihn / daß ihm solcher Gestalt dasselbige gegeben und vertrauet werde / daß er dasselbige soll zu Feldt führen fliegendt und eingewunden / wann und was Zeit und stundt ihm solches anbefohlen würdt / bey demselbigen zu leben und zu sterben / Auch ehe er es verlassen solte / sich in dasselbig einzuwickeln und darinnen erwurgen zu lassen / und gleichsamb sein Todenlade seyn: So er das bejahet so läst man ihne auch ein Eyd drauff schweren." Johann Jacobi von Wallhausen, *Defensio patriae oder Landrettung. Darinnen gezeigt wird 1) Wie alle und jede in der werthen Christenheit Potentaten, Regenten, Stätte und Communen ihre und der ihrigen Unterthanen Rettung und Schützung anstellen sollen. 2) Der Modus belligerande, viel hundert Jahre bißher gefählet* (Frankfurt am Main: Gedruckt im Verlag / Daniel und David Aubrij und Clement Schleichen 1621), 69.

[15] Jane Finucane, "Before the Storm: Civilians under Siege during the Thirty Years War," in Alex Dowdall and John Horne, eds., *Civilians under Siege from Sarajevo to Troy* (London: Palgrave Macmillan, 2017), 137–162, 144.

[16] Sennewald, *Die Kursächsischen Feldzeichen im Dreissigjährigen Krieg*, 28; SHStADr 11237 10798.

was dismissed, the flag was ripped off its pole.[17] The significance of this act, and how it feels to break up your company, was clear to Stach Löser: "when the dismissal publicly takes place the cornets in the presence the riders ripped from their poles not only the riders but also the captains gets sad in large part and so everyone count in his purse and then have to deal with his affairs."[18] Conversely, when a company ripped its flag off its pole, it dissolved. As the Mansfeld Regiment fell apart, the members of stricken companies removed the flags from their poles as their last act before leaving. When the remnants of the Mansfeld Regiment reached Wangen and Memmingen, several companies "ripped the flags from their poles themselves, handed them over to the flag-bearers, and walked away." So it was "that no more than the officers" of the dissolved companies "and two flying flags, which were Daniel von Schlieben's and Carol von Komnitz's" – that is to say, only von Schlieben's and von Komnitz's companies were still complete and loyal – "arrived at Frankfurt am Main."[19]

It is this light-bearing, honorable object that Felix Steter said he wanted to take from Hieronymus Sebastian Schutze. Did he want Schutze's job? Both men were common-born, which was rare for a flag-bearer and a lieutenant in the 1620s. This may be why they struggled so viciously against each other.

Mattheus Steiner and the rest of the tribunal did not respond until May 20, when Steter reappeared before them and repeated his complaints. Their verdict seemed balanced between him and Schutze. They stated that flag-bearer Hieronymus Sebastian Schutze had attacked Lieutenant Felix Steter with "unseemly words," and Steter was now declared honorable. But they continued: "Because also however Lieutenant Steter sent after his witnesses the next morning and consulted with them about this incident, it is probable that he must have been no less drunk than the flag-bearer," and according to the praiseworthy articles of war, everyone must "hold themselves apart from drunkenness ... both officers and common soldiers must present the best

---

[17] Sennewald, *Die Kursächsischen Feldzeichen im Dreissigjährigen Krieg*, 28–29. Destroying a company's flag was a punishment in Imperial armies but according to Sennewald, this was not the case in Saxon units.

[18] "wan aber die abdanckungk öffendlich gesehen die cornet in *presntz* die Reutter von der Stangen gerissen wirdt der mundt niht allein den Reuttern sondern auch den Ritmestern zum guthen theil fallen unt sih also ein jchliche nach seinem beuttel rechten unt seine sache darnach anstellen mushen." SHStADr 10024 9239/2, 32v.

[19] "Wievol nun von den ubrigen acht fendlein, etzliche *compagnien* solchen auch nachgehen wollen, so haben sie sich doch noch so weitt weißen laßen, daß sie die fendlein an stangen gelaßen, und biß uff reichs bordem in ordnung verblieben." SHStADr 10024 9239/2, 51r–52r.

example." Therefore, it was up to Lieutenant Colonel Camargo's discretion whether both Schutze and Steter should be arrested at once.[20]

The tribunal knew that everyone in the regiment got drunk and nobody cared, but they could not openly call Felix Steter a liar: Slandering an honorable man would open them up to a lawsuit. The implication was that the tribunal knew that Steter had not conferred with his witnesses because he had been drunk, he had been trying to get them to lie for him. If he tried to pursue the matter further, he would be punished.

*****

Hieronymus Sebastian Schutze and Felix Steter quarrelled so often they got into a fight coming back to their quarters from an earlier court date. On Wednesday, May 20, 1626, Steter appeared before the military tribunal in Legnano to testify regarding his complaint against Schutze from May 1. Now Schutze and Steter were returning: They and their retinues were mounted, accompanied by at least six musketeers on foot. It was about an hour from Legnano to Busto Arsizio; the Winckelmann Company's flag-bearer and Lieutenant did not travel outside the regiment's home base without an armed escort. "About a musket shot before the city," the two officers fought again.[21]

Steter said Schutze rode in front of him and waited for him next to the footpath. "Herr Lieutenant, the flag-bearer halts there and the bodyguard does not want to go on, but I have spoken to him, go gently now, do you think he'll do anything to us," said Steter's bodyguard, allegedly. Steter said he rode between Schutze and his companion, the steward Christian Hubrich; Schutze spurred his horse and galloped toward him and rode around him. "Finally, he grabbed onto my horse, onto the saddle, and spoke with these words," said Steter:

"you dog, I want to give it to you right now [*du hundt ich wolte dirs bald machen*]," and he laid his hand on his pistol. At which I said, "Do you want to attack me on the street [*wilt du mich den auf der straßen angreifen*]? I'll ride back and file suit against you in the regiment for a street-robber and a rogue." But he barred the way to me with his horse and would not let me ride on, but I rode out with violence.

Then the little convoy rode toward Busto Arsizio.[22]

In Steter's testimony, Schutze is savagely and deliberately violent. The counter-complaints and the eyewitness reports of some of the watching musketeers tell a different story.

---

[20] SHStADr 10024 9739/6, 27–28.   [21] SHStADr 10024 9739/6, 43.
[22] SHStADr 10024 9739/6, 43–44.

According to Hieronymus Sebastian Schutze and Christof Hubrich, Schutze did go off the main path – into some bushes, which knocked his hat off. He turned onto the footpath "to ride away from the lieutenant's gaze," but Felix Steter followed him, calling him a robber and a rogue "in a loud voice."[23] When he was sober, Hieronymus Sebastian Schutze was a nervous, self-conscious man, and somewhat clumsy. Steter may have sniffed him out as a convenient target because he perceived these traits as weakness. Flag-bearers in sixteenth and seventeenth-century visual art rest their hands on their hips or on the pommels of their swords, sticking their elbows out in a swaggering, macho display. If the picture is of a group of soldiers, the flag-bearer is at the center, dominating space with his body, the easy beauty of a man.[24] Did Schutze swagger like this? Was he clothed as magnificently as they? They sometimes performed gymnastic-like exercises while twirling and flourishing the flag, like spinning it or passing it under one leg.[25] Wallhausen thought this was a beautiful display: The flag-bearer is "shut up right in the middle of a battalion / and there he has nothing more to do / than hold his flag / swing it / and put heart into the soldiers" (*den Soldaten ein gut Hertz zusprechen*).[26] Schutze's office required him to act in a physically assertive, flamboyant way that is out of keeping from much of his everyday actions. It is difficult to imagine him carrying these duties out sober. But he could also be a decisive leader: He handled most of the stolen fabric that made its way through his company, and distributed it to his men.

"Throughout my life I behaved conscientiously," Schutze said about the fight on the path, "with all uprightness and virtue, so that nobody had any cause against me," which is why this stung so badly.[27] He had to answer such an injury he said, because "He is no rogue nor highway robber but an honorable soldier," and he rode back to Busto Arsizio. Lieutenant Steter rode after him, galloping through the watch. Steter yelled to Hubrich, who had halted in a courtyard, that he was a rogue and a highway robber exactly like the flag-bearer.[28]

The mounted men pulled up. Felix Steter called out to a musketeer squad leader named David Schmidt, who had seen and heard everything, "if he had been there, and would testify to the real truth." The squad leader knew that Steter wanted him to lie. He answered, "He would, if he

---

[23] SHStADr 10024 9739/6, 54.
[24] Joneath Spicer, "The Renaissance Elbow," in Jan Bremmer and Hermann Roodenburg, eds., *A Cultural History of Gesture: From Antiquity to the Present Day* (Cambridge: Polity Press, 1991), 90, 101.
[25] Sennewald, *Die Kursächsischen Feldzeichen im Dreissigjährigen Krieg*, 34–35.
[26] Wallhausen, *Kriegskunst zu Fuß*, 27.   [27] SHStADr 10024 9739/6, 47.
[28] SHStADr 10024 9739/6, 54–55.

should be asked, and give witness in the matter which was due an honorable soldier." Schutze may have been unusually circumspect in his interactions with other officers, but his role as a distributor of stolen fabric may be evidence that he was a centrally important figure to the Winckelmann company's ordinary soldiers, and essential to their well-being. Was this also why the musketeers in this regiment shot their muskets out the window when Schutze exercised his pistols? Certainly, this soldier refused to lie on Steter's behalf to damage Schutze's reputation. At once, "the aforementioned Lieutenant cursed all the sacraments to the squad leader, and on the way and when they stopped often wanted to beat him." Another witness said, "the Lieutenant lifted [his rod of office] and said I want to beat you and cursed all the sacraments before him."[29]

The entire watch "saw this and heard this," although accounts differed as to whether Schmidt refused to lie for Steter because of his apprehension of his own honor, or because he thought Schutze was an honorable officer and did not deserve to be slandered.[30] He may also have been conscious of Steter's value as a distributor of resources throughout the company. In any case he had enough pride to stand up to his Lieutenant in the face of physical threats.

Hieronymus Sebastian Schutze, Felix Steter, and Christoff Hubrich clattered into Busto Arsizio and rushed to the authorities: Steter to Lieutenant Colonel Theodoro de Camargo, and Schutze to Mattheus Steiner. Some factionalism may be on display here: Camargo and Steter may have liked each other. They acted similarly, each according to his own estate. Hubrich filed his own suit against Steter at the same time Schutze and Steter sued each other. The three barely stopped to dismount.[31]

While the case was pending, Schutze's honor was in doubt and, after he started his legal process, someone went into his room and removed his flag. He was no longer allowed to carry it. It remained confiscated while he and Steter were in court. Schutze complained to Camargo: "at your grace's order for a time until now I was confined to the Herr Hauptmann's and the regimental provost's, Hanns Wolff von Schingo, and after that other flag-bearers' quarters, during which the flag was taken out of my lodgings ... and given to another to unfurl." This "despairs me greatly" said Schutze; "*mir zu höchsten despert.*" As long as his honor was in question due to the accusations that Steter had leveled against him, Schutze could not perform his office, and may not even have been allowed to touch the company flag. In his complaint against Steter, Schutze requested that "his" flag, "which was taken away unjustly, once

---

[29] SHStADr 10024 9739/6, 63–64.   [30] SHStADr 10024 9739/6, 56, 62–63.
[31] SHStADr 10024 9739/6, 44, 78–79.

again be delivered to my hand and ... be allowed to remain with me."[32] He delivered this letter to Camargo by hand.[33] This attempt was clumsy, and it failed. When Camargo objected to Schutze's complaint, Schutze "excused himself most strenuously:" "He had not known that it was on His Grace's orders that the flag was taken from him, but completely thought that Lieutenant Steter had done it on his own account."[34]

Felix Steter lost his case for dishonoring Hieronymus Sebastian Schutze and lying. He was made to swear an oath that he knew only good things about Schutze. But Schutze was also sanctioned. He had been told to remain under house arrest until the case was concluded, and he had not.

*****

That was the last time Hieronymus Sebastian Schutze appeared in Mansfeld Regiment documents. Felix Steter appeared once more, when he picked a fight with his captain, Wolfgang Winckelmann.[35]

On the night of January 24, 1627, Winckelmann invited his flag-bearer, by now no longer Hieronymus Sebastian Schutze but a man named David von Bernleben; Captain Moser's flag-bearer; "and, as usual, my collected officers, to join me at table." What this meant even for the third in command of the regiment was that he and these officers sat together on the bed in front of the table (*welches in seinem camin bey seinem bette uber der tafel beschen*).[36] "And I had a great time with them [*mich auch mit ihnen lustig erzeiget*]."

As the party was winding down, "when most of the officers were drunk and left, Lieutenant Felix Steter came into my room, where my flag was [*alldar mein Fendl*], walked toward me, and said, Herr Hauptmann, how can you tolerate the muster-writer, who is such a lightminded rogue and thief, among your company?"[37] The muster-writer is not named in this account; Winckelmann's former muster-writer Heinrich Teichmeyer was dead. Unless the muster-writer was Hieronymus Sebastian Schutze in a new office, Steter appears to have gotten tired of harassing Schutze and moved to another target. Where honor was backed by potentially lethal

---

[32] "mich eine zeit hero uf eur gnade bewelich inn deß herren haubtmann unnd regiments profosen, hanns wolff von schingo, unndt hernach anderer Fähndriche quartier enthaltten, unnter deß das fendtlein aus meinenn *losament* (mir zu höchsten despert) nehmen und ein anderen enwerffen zu laßen." SHStADr 10024 9739/6, 47–48.
[33] SHStADr 10024 9739/6, 90.   [34] SHStADr 10024 9739/6, 88.
[35] SHStADr 10024 9119/38, 184–219.   [36] SHStADr 10024 9119/38, 204.
[37] SHStADr 10024 9119/38, 185.

violence, this was a dangerous pastime. Winckelmann reported he told Steter to

> consider whether he could back up his claims, because the muster-writer was an officer as much as another, and such a [dishonorable] person would not have been suffered at my table. If he knew something about him, he should remain quiet today because there was no time to talk about things like that this evening, therefore he should get a drink down him [*eins austrinken*] and be happy.[38]

For Steter to dishonor his captain's muster-writer was to dishonor his captain himself, which was serious business, especially in front of the company flag.

Steter drank Winckelmann's wine, but he refused to calm down and refused to leave. He cursed and insulted the muster-writer. "For God's sake, go away and sleep and let me rest," begged Winckelmann, joined by both flag-bearers and Christian Hubrich. "So I went out of my room to the door to the hall so he would leave," reported Winckelmann, "and he said that he had drunk too much wine at my place."

After the officers led him out of the room Steter came back repeatedly, the last time with a stiletto in his hand. Winckelmann "took his sword from the wall" off the nail where it had been hanging, "drew it, and threw the sheath on the bed." In the struggle, Winckelmann was stabbed twice.[39] David von Bernleben blocked Steter's stiletto by throwing a carpet over Steter's hand; he did not know Winckelmann had been wounded until he opened his jacket to show him. Von Bernleben and the senior squad leader in the room were wounded. "Am I going to command you," yelled Winckelmann to Steter, "or are you going to command me?"[40]

When Steter started losing, he ran across the street into a big white "Italian house" to save himself (*einem welsch hauß salviret*), possibly a building where soldiers were not quartered.[41] Winckelmann yelled for the watch, and a drummer to beat the alarm.[42] Then he ran outside after Steter, onto the stairs outside the front door. He stood there bleeding while the drum hammered, a pistol in his hand loaded and wound, yelling into the night. On his orders a group of soldiers followed Steter and manhandled him back. They beat him up and they beat his wife up. When they hauled Steter to the foot of the stairs where Winckelmann was standing, Winckelmann almost shot him. He shouted, "that nobody [should] talk to me or have anything to do with me," complained

---

[38] SHStADr 10024 9119/38, 185–186.   [39] SHStADr 10024 9119/38, 213.
[40] SHStADr 10024 9119/38, 205.   [41] SHStADr 10024 9119/38, 187–188.
[42] SHStADr 10024 9119/38, 205.

Steter. "The Hauptmann said he wanted to give 200 Zicks to [anyone who would] lay my head in front of his ass."[43]

Winckelmann brought a simple case against his lieutenant, and the verdict hinged on who had drawn his weapon first, since the other would have been acting in self-defense. Witnesses said they did not know whether Steter had drawn his weapon before he ran toward Winckelmann, or after Winckelmann had drawn his. Some of them had not seen what had happened, like Christof the Drummer, gambling in the hall outside Winckelmann's room.[44] Winckelmann said Steter had drawn first, "secretly" – the witnesses just couldn't see it.[45] He was an experienced officer and deeply corrupt, but a clumsy liar. Steter walked: Although he had "behaved himself indecently" and insubordinately, Winckelmann could not prove that he had been acting in self-defense. The case was left to Camargo's discretion and tabled. The last trial took place just a few days before the regiment went north, so it came to nothing.

Felix Steter said later that "he didn't anticipate" that Wolfgang Winckelmann "would use such violence against him, and thus fall upon him with murderous resistance."[46] Steter chafed against his fellows. Hieronymus Sebastian Schutze had let Steter bully him for a year and took legal action but nothing more. He avoided Steter's gaze, he rode into some bushes and knocked his own hat off. Winckelmann was fully prepared to retaliate physically against a challenge to his authority and a threat to his life.

Wolfgang Winckelmann was the quartermaster of the Mansfeld Regiment and the captain of its third-most-honorable company, violent and self-assured. He was willing to sue his lieutenant, but he was also willing to kill him.

---

[43] SHStADr 10024 9119/38, 210–211.   [44] SHStADr 10024 9119/38, 208.
[45] SHStADr 10024 9119/38, 187.   [46] SHStADr 10024 9119/38, 216.

8   Making It in This Thing
Money and Payment within Saxon Regiments in the 1620s*

The Fourier who wrote a letter to Stach Krakow before deserting expressed the moral economy of the mercenary in eloquent words, although he never left his name. When he described his service in his own terms, monetary and moral considerations were intertwined. His complaint continued after the excerpt I quoted in Chapter 3: After he described the great effort he had gone to, he wrote, "To make it in this thing you've really got to be young, and you've got to look at others with your fists."[1] In German he said *Zurechnen*, to apportion, attribute, or calculate, count cash, or make money. To "make it." The Winckelmann Company's muster-writer Heinrich Teichmeyer said something like this while he was dying five months later.

This chapter discusses how soldiers "made it," analyzing common soldiers' pay primarily during the 1620s, for which the most data exist. Since pay seems to have been based on complex unrecorded social interactions within companies, it can also be used to track soldiers' social status relative to other soldiers, which is often invisible elsewhere.

Seventy-two known infantry muster rolls in the Saxon State Archives from the 1620s and late teens list pay, as well as three cavalry payrolls from 1624. Contracts to order troops (*Bestallungen*) also specify pay. The rolls with pay are from the 1620s only. Pay for this decade is well-documented but pay is not listed in Saxon muster rolls from the 1630s, only in contracts (*Bestallungen*). I found no pay data of any kind from the 1640s. Therefore, This chapter primarily handles Electoral Saxon practice during the 1620s.

Pay varied widely, and these contracts only give a vague and general picture of what was going on. Soldiers haggled: In Joachim von Zeutzsch's company, when Cilian Hildebrand entered Hans Adam Birckner's vacant spot, since Birckner had made more than Hildebrand

---

* Thanks to Zhou Fang for assistance with this chapter.
[1] "Ich hette zwar vermainet, in dieser sache besser gelegenheit zuhaben undt mein *officium* verheißener sach Zubedienen, weil ich aber sehe, daß ich nur den bloßen nahmen führen, undt ein dießer sache Zurechnen, nur Iunge sein muß und anderen ein die fäuste sehen." SHStADr 10024 9119/38, 15–16.

Table 8.1 *Infantry officers' pay, 1619–1625*

Rank	Pay (gulden/month)
Captain	360
Flag-bearer	70
Lieutenant	50
Sergeant	36
Commander	24
Fourier	24
Surgeon	24
Muster-writer	20
Corporal	20
Drummer	12
Piper	12

had, Hildebrand asked for more money per month, and got it. This kind of raise was recorded for four soldiers in this company.[2] Although written evidence exists only in this roll and a few others, haggling may have been common.[3] Mercenary soldiers were also subcontractors in their own right.[4]

The pay for company-level infantry officers was standard and did not change throughout the 1620s (Table 8.1). Although some officers were highly paid, the money was not intended for their own use only: Just as Hieronymus Sebastian Schutze distributed cloth through his company, officers also rewarded soldiers with cash.

Wages for common infantrymen varied considerably. Soldiers' wages from 1619 to 1625 are broken down in Table 8.2, which produces the graph in Figure 8.1. These wages are taken from muster rolls as well as from soldiers mentioned in sample trial documents.

Figure 8.1 depicts the information in Table 8.2 visually. This graph and table are produced from 20,002 separate entries (5,422 for pikemen, 1,338 for halberdiers, and 13,242 for musketeers). This is more than the number of infantrymen in the surviving muster rolls for this decade: Unlike the maps tracking soldiers by place of origin, these data contain repeat entries. Since the relevant data is amount of money made per month rather than number of men, if the same man shows up multiple times, he is counted multiple times. These graphs do not include men

---

[2] SHStADr 11237 10840/4 8. [3] SHStADr 11237 10481/1.
[4] John Lynn, "Comments on Mercenary Military Service in Early Modern Europe," IISH Conference in March 2010, 7; quoted in Frank Tallett, "Soldiers in Western Europe, c. 1500–1790," in Erik-Jan Zürcher, ed., *Fighting for a Living: A Comparative Study of Military Labor 1500–2000* (Amsterdam: Amsterdam University Press, 2010), 152.

Table 8.2 *Common infantry pay in gulden (R)/month by specialization, 1619–1625*

Pikemen
Number	511	2,133	525	482	140	495	173	365	146	196	30	84	10	108	5	2	8	2	2	4	1
%	10	40	10	9	3	9	3	7	3	7	0.6	2	0.2	2	0.1	0.04	0.15	0.04	0.04	0.07	0.02
R/month	7	8	9	10	11	12	13	14	15	16	17	18	19	20	24	25	30	32	36	40	48

Total: 5422

Halberdiers
Number	108	480	252	149	58	102	60	25	16	33	22	20	12	1
%	8	36	19	11	4	8	4	2	2	2	2	2	1	0.07
R/month	7	8	9	10	11	12	13	14	15	16	17	18	20	24

Total: 1,338

Musketeers
No	963	9,470	2,089	440	215	18	37	9	1
%	8	71	16	3	2	0.1	0.3	0.07	0.007
R/mo	6	7	8	9	10	11	12	14	15

Total: 13,242

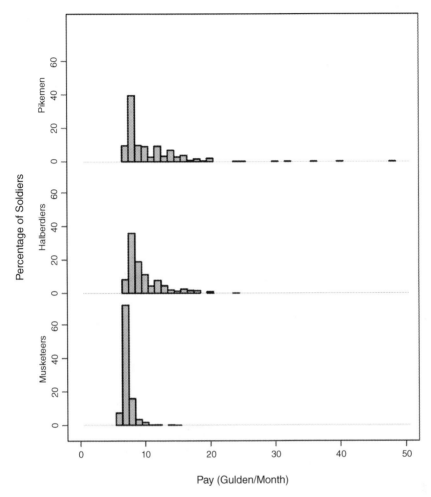

Figure 8.1 Common infantry pay in gulden/month by specialization, 1619–1625.

listed only as squad leaders since those could be either pikemen or halberdiers, nor do they include the members of one company who were listed with the unhelpful designation "Mercenaries paid more including squad leaders" (*Doppelsöldner sambt die gefreyter*). All individuals labeled as "reformed officers" were removed: To "reform" a company was to dissolve it, after which its officers could be placed on another company's roll as pikemen and paid more than usual until someone figured out where to place them.

The old word "double mercenary" (*Doppelsöldner*) for pikeman, still used alongside *piquenier*, is a simple word for a complicated situation. In total, 2,133 pikemen made eight gulden a month: 40 percent of all pikemen in the sample. Thirty-six percent of halberdiers (480 men) also made eight gulden a month. A larger percentage of musketeers made seven gulden a month – about 70 percent. Most pikemen and halberdiers seem to have made only a little more than most musketeers. But pikemen's and halberdiers' wages varied more than that of musketeers. Some made far more than other infantrymen and even most company-level officers: They form the right side of this graph, the pikemen's and halberdiers' long tail. Pay clusters around numbers that are easy to divide in your head. There were more very highly-paid pikemen than very highly-paid halberdiers, and they could also make more: Four pikemen made forty gulden per month while only one halberdier made twenty-four, already as much as a fourier or a company surgeon. The highest-paid pikeman in any document – Heinrich Philip from Steinsdorf – was paid forty-eight gulden a month. The previous incumbent of his spot on the roll, Wolf Heinrich von Grünthal, had been both a reformed flag-bearer and a noble: Philip may have managed to persuade his regimental authorities to pay him the same wages as his predecessor.[5] These extremely-highly-paid men, whom I have found only in passing, may have been experienced soldiers, comparable to senior noncommissioned officers in later armies but with no formal written designation.

I now sort infantry by social origin as well as pay. Table 8.3 sorts the pay of noble and common-born infantrymen by specialty, and this information is represented visually in Figure 8.2. (The total number of infantrymen in Table 8.3 is 19,889. It does not add up to the total in Table 8.2 because soldiers of unknown class origin are not counted in Table 8.3.)

In all three weapons specializations, common-born infantrymen cluster at the more usual rates of pay; the pay rate with the highest percentage of common-born pikemen and halberdiers is eight gulden a month, and for musketeers seven. Noble pay was both higher and more variable. Either they were paid better, or they were more likely to be promoted. One word for "squad leader," in Hauboldt von Schleinitz's company in the early 1620s, may have been *Pigknir von Adelsburch*, "noble pikeman."[6] It was probably harder for common-born soldiers to advance, although they were not barred from higher-paying positions. But, unlike

---

[5] SHStADr 11237 10840/5 no 9.
[6] Despite the literal meaning of this phrase, not all of them were of noble birth. It may be another term for squad leader. SHStADr 11237 10840/3 7 and 11237 10840/4 3.

Table 8.3 *Noble and common infantry pay in gulden/month by specialization and social background, 1619–1625*

Noble Pikemen																				
Number	11	4	8	9	50	18	85	34	48	6	31	54	2	2	1	1	2			
%	3	1	2	2	14	5	23	9	13	2	8	15	0.5	0.5	0.25	0.25	0.5			
R/month	8	9	10	11	12	13	14	15	16	17	18	20	24	25	30	32	40			
Total: 366																				
Common-Born Pikemen																				
Number	510	2122	528	474	129	430	148	276	106	140	24	53	10	49	2	7	1	2	2	1
%	11	43	11	9	3	9	3	6	2	3	0.5	1	0.2	1	0.04	0.1	0.02	0.04	0.04	0.02
R/month	7	8	9	10	11	12	13	14	15	16	17	18	19	20	24	30	32	36	40	48
Total: 5,004																				
Noble Halberdiers																				
Number	3	2	3	1	1	2			1	1										
%	21	14	21	7	7	14			7	7										
R/month	8	9	10	11	12	13			16	17										
Total: 14																				
Common-Born Halberdiers																				
Number	108	477	250	145	57	99	58	25	16	32	21	20	12	1						
%	8	36	19	11	4	7	4	2	1	2	2	2	1	0.08						
R/month	7	8	9	10	11	12	13	14	15	16	17	18	20	24						
Total: 1,321																				
Noble Musketeers																				
Number	20	9	7	8		16		4												
%	31	14	11	13		25		6												
R/month	7	8	9	10		12		14												
Total: 64																				
Common-Born Musketeers																				
No	961	9,418	2064	430	205	16	20		5	1										
%	9	72	20	4	2	0.2	0.2		0.04	0.009										
R/mo	6	7	8	9	10	11	12		14	15										
Total: 13,120																				

151

Making It in This Thing

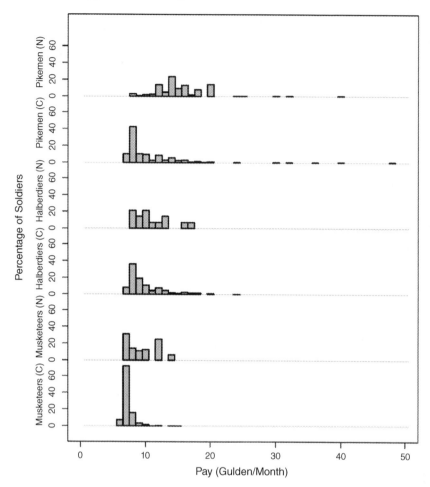

Figure 8.2 Noble and common infantry pay in gulden/month by specialization and social background, 1619–1625.
Abbreviations: N, nobles; C, commoners.

the highly-paid pikemen, the extremely highly-paid halberdiers were all common-born.

The social position of different weapons is also visible: Pay slopes upward gently from common-born musketeers to noble halberdiers and common-born pikemen, and then jumps upward to noble pikemen, the top earners. It is unfortunate that soldiers' ages were not listed in early-seventeenth-century Saxon rolls, since some of these high-earning noble pikemen were probably young future officers, placed in the ranks to learn the art of war.

It may seem plausible for soldiers from Saxony to have made more than non-Saxons, but this is not the case. Saxon soldiers made very slightly less than soldiers from elsewhere: Given two infantrymen of equal social background with the same weapon, the soldier from Electoral Saxony got about a twelfth of a gulden less per month. If you do not control for social background, the difference is more pronounced; then, the Saxon soldier got slightly more than a third of a gulden less on average. More non-Saxon soldiers were nobles. Nobles traveled more widely to enter Saxon military service, but even common-born non-Saxons made more. More widely-traveled soldiers were also more experienced.

In these ways, the amount infantrymen made per month, which we can see, is a proxy for the complex social organization inside an early-seventeenth-century infantry company, which we cannot see. Infantrymen's pay and status depended on their prior experience, their class, whether they were good at haggling, and the weapon they fought with, as well as talent, personal charisma, whom they knew, where they were from, and the other factors that regulate human interaction in small communities. When the pike was dropped at the beginning of the next century, an entire way of life must have gone with it.

The cavalry payrolls I found are from the Saxon Hoffahne, the "Court Company," an elite unit connected to the Elector of Saxony and based in Dresden.[7] They cover three and a half consecutive months in the spring of 1624. (Unlike infantry in the same decade, cavalry may have kept their records of pay in separate documents from records of troop strength.) In addition to pay this document also notes "*Vertheil*," "money to distribute," for many officers. In addition to giving out rewards, many soldiers, especially officers and nobles, had their own retinues that were either not on the books or only appeared on the books indirectly, such as in provisions records. These people also had to be given money and fed.[8]

Pay for cavalry officers is listed in Table 8.4.

Although cavalry officers usually made more than infantry officers, the cavalry captains made far less than infantry captains, possibly because this data comes from the Hoffahne: An elevated position in this Dresden-based company might have been intended as a sinecure or bonus for someone whose major source of income was elsewhere.

Unlike infantrymen, the troopers in the Hoffahne records made a standard amount: They were paid by the horse, at fifteen gulden a horse. The troopers with one horse apiece made fifteen gulden per month, while

---

[7] SHStADr 11237 10840/11 doc 2.
[8] The distribution of money to servants and retinues appears in some Imperial records. Pohl, *Die Profiantirung Der Keyserlichen Armaden Ahnbelangendt*, 66.

Table 8.4 *Cavalry officers' pay, Hoffahne rolls, 1624*

Rank	Pay (gulden/month)
Colonel	150
Captain	150
Lieutenant	150 or 90
General-Surgeon	150
Flag-bearer	120
Quartermaster	90
Watch-master	75
Corporal	60 or 45
Muster-writer	45
Fourier	30
Wagon-master	30
Preacher	20
Kettledrummer	15
Trumpeter	15

common troopers with two horses, like Abraham Paritzsch, nicknamed "Tartar," made thirty gulden per month. Higher positions like Fahnenjunckers made anywhere from fifteen to sixty gulden a month, depending on how many horses they had in their string. Fifteen gulden a month per horse was comfortably above most infantrymen's pay, but a cavalryman was expected to buy his horse's fodder himself. According to the Saxon Hoffahne, oats for one horse cost four gulden and twelve groschen a month; a common cavalryman's monthly take-home was closer to ten gulden. From this, he probably also paid a groom.

Cavalry companies were probably also subdivided by complex informal social divisions: Both the number of horses a cavalryman had and the amount he made were probably dependent on his social position in the company. Both pay and social status in these units were highly variable. In the 1620s, every position in a muster roll was treated independently. For instance, if the tenth pikeman in the list died, the muster-writer would not write that they needed one more pikeman, but that the tenth slot had become vacant. Since a soldier's position on the roll may have reflected where he stood in line during the mustering, the social hierarchy of the company would have been visible without ever seeing a copy of the roll yourself.

These wages seem high, and they are higher than the wages Burschel identified for soldiers in southern Germany, four Rhenish gulden a month.[9] Economic historians often use building trades as their

---

[9] Burschel, *Söldner in Nordwestdeutschland*.

benchmark for civilian wages, since the data is good.[10] Although laborers were paid by the day and soldiers by the month, most common soldiers made about as much as some craftsmen. In 1622 Munich, a master mason made the equivalent of ten gulden a month, a journeyman seven and a half, and an apprentice six and a half.[11] But, during the depths of the *Kipper- und Wipperzeit* a coin maker in Saxony could make seven gulden eighteen groschen a week, and a smith working in a mint making debased money took home eleven gulden eighteen groschen a week. That was very high, but it was in bad money.[12]

Highly paid infantrymen or cavalrymen made much more than many unskilled workers, comparable to skilled artisans or some of the seasonal jobs. It took years to learn how to wield a pike or halberd, or how to manage your horse, but pay did not correspond only to the amount of effort and skill an individual's position required: The lower officers did not make all that much. An infantry muster-writer or corporal made about as much as a reaper in Munich during harvest (the equivalent of twenty-one gulden a month between 1578 and 1608[13]), and a trumpeter or drummer noticeably less.

However, many non-military laborers were only paid on days they worked, and the work did not last the whole year.[14] Many were also paid differently at different times of year. In Augsburg between 1600 and 1640, rakers made the equivalent of five and a quarter gulden a month from the end of September to June and seven gulden a month from July to the middle of August. In contrast, soldiers were theoretically paid whether they were fighting or not, and they were paid the same amount year-round. This may have contributed to the popular image of soldiers as lazy.

On paper, soldiers in the 1620s could make more than workers, but there were complications and limitations to this. In the Saxon army, only soldiers received pay, not their female partners.[15] If a soldier had a female companion they required twice as much food and clothing, if they had children even more. When supplies got short in Peter Hagendorf's regiment and a pound of tobacco went for three thalers and a pair of

---

[10] Fernand Braudel and Frank Spooner, "Prices in Europe from 1450 to 1750," in E. E. Rich and C. H. Wilson, eds., *The Cambridge Economic History of Europe Vol 4, The Economy of Expanding Europe in the 16th and 17th Centuries* (Cambridge: Cambridge University Press, 1967), 426; M. J. Elsas, *Umriss einer Geschichte der Preise und Löhne in Deutschland*, Vol. 1 (Leiden: AW Sijthoff, 1936), 57.
[11] Tables, Elsas, *Umriss*, 64–67. [12] Wuttke, "Kipper- und Wipperzeit," 143–144.
[13] Ibid., 143–144. [14] Ibid., 58.
[15] At least sometimes in the Imperial army under Gallas, soldiers' dependents received some money for food. Pohl, *Die Profiantirung Der Keyserlichen Armaden Ahnbelangendt*, 64.

boots for six, he and his second wife Anna Maria made a little mill out of two whetstones, dug a hole and baked bread in the hole, and sold the bread.[16] David Sabean argued that the peasant household was not the economic unit of traditional German historiography, but a site of alliances between husband and wife.[17] A soldier and his female partner formed the "family economy" of the soldier, but each was also an economic actor in his or her own right, and they maintained an implicit contract between themselves.[18] The sexual interactions of soldiers and military women were inextricable from their forms of labor, which were flexible and precarious. Both were highly mobile. Each soldier could fight; each woman could sew and carry, sell goods or sell sex, dig a trench or shove a cannon into place. Contemporary observers noted that soldiers and their partners joined and separated in a way that seemed casual to them; even so, military theorists recognized at the time that soldiers who were partnered had an easier life.[19] The roll recording Bernhard Miltirz's company from October 1621 to October 1622 noted when corporal Christoff Tiel became a widower.[20] Except for elites – nobles and officers like the miserable Theodoro de Camargo and Victoria Guarde – the relationships of most soldiers and military women to the control of property and its transfer to legitimate offspring over generations may have been different from most civilian groups, which deserves further study.

From 1619 to 1623, the years surviving muster rolls were begun, the average pay on paper of common infantrymen rose, but not by much: By slightly over one-quarter gulden per year, each year (correcting for position and social status), which is fifteen Kreutzer. This gradual paper wage increase, probably not even perceptible, may have occurred because long-term soldiers were gaining experience during this time, becoming worthy of being paid more.

However, real wages in this "iron century" had been falling in Europe since the mid-1500s, and by 1625 were at their lowest point in most German cities.[21] Economic historians calculate price levels by monitoring the price of wheat or rye, wine and bricks; these prices moved in vast

---

[16] Hagendorf, *Ein Söldnerleben im Dreißigjährigen Krieg*, 94.
[17] David Warren Sabean, *Property, Production, and Family in Neckarhausen, 1700–1870* (Cambridge: Cambridge University Press, 1990), 97–98.
[18] Lynn, "Comments;" quoted in Tallett, "Soldiers," 152.
[19] James Turner, *Pallas Armata, Military Essayes of the Ancient Grecian, Roman, and Modern Art of War Vvritten in the Years 1670 and 1671* (London: Richard Chiswell, 1683), 277.
[20] SHStADr 11237 10840/5 no 6.
[21] Ulrich Pfister, "Consumer Prices and Wages in Germany, 1500–1850," Westfälische Wilhelms-Universität Münster Historisches Seminar, March 2010, 17, 22.

cycles beneath the ephemera of events.[22] In the 1620s, prices were at the end of a great swing upward.[23] Per capita civilian consumption of meat fell.[24] The gentle rise in soldiers' pay on paper was not enough to make up for the rise in the cost of goods in many areas of Germany.[25] Hostilities also caused regional increases in the cost of food and supplies: During war years, the prices of grain, lard, and salt spiked in Munich.[26] Severe monetary debasement from 1619 to 1623 made fixed incomes difficult. Some Saxon communities, especially in the Erzgebirge, held public contributions to support ministers and teachers.[27]

The same period that a Saxon army was first in being during the Thirty Years War was also when the monetary debasement and disturbances of the late sixteenth and early seventeenth centuries were most severe. The same pay on paper in 1620, during the *Kipper- und Wipperzeit*, and 1625, after Saxon officials had made substantial efforts to withdraw bad money from circulation, might mean different things. Although sources often specify that the soldiers were paid in "good money," on November 22, 1623, lightened coins of the face value of 6,935 gulden were withdrawn from the *Soldatenkasse* and re-coined into 863 full-value gulden.[28]

Whether or not the money held the value it should have, Saxon soldiers in the Saxon army were paid on time between 1619 and 1625. Signatures on muster rolls from the 1620s indicate regular payment of about four times a year; the Saxon commissioner of war oversaw this process and signed off on it. Not coincidentally, during this time the Saxon army was also consistently at paper strength.[29]

Saxon wage data from the 1630s are sketchier, and none seem to have survived from the 1640s. A mercenary contract from 1631 indicates nominal wages, which are itemized in Table 8.5.

The muster-writer has moved up in the *prima plana*; the lieutenant is now the second-highest ranking company officer, a position lieutenants had from then until the present day.

Except for lieutenants, officers' pay fell substantially by 1631 from their position in the 1620s. For the majority of ordinary pikemen and musketeers, wages did not fall: According to this contract, squad leaders were supposed to make the equivalent of ten and a half gulden a month, pikemen nine gulden a month, and musketeers seven and a half gulden a

---

[22] Braudel and Spooner, "Prices in Europe." [23] de Vries, "Economic Crisis," 157.
[24] Jan van Zanden, "Wages and the Standard of Living in Europe, 1500–1800," *European Review of Economic History* 3.2 (1999), 175–197, 190–191.
[25] Pfister, "Consumer Prices and Wages," 11, table. [26] Elsas, *Umriss*, 52–53.
[27] Wuttke, "Kipper- und Wipperzeit," 149. [28] Ibid., 149.
[29] Staiano-Daniels, "Determining Early Modern Army Strength."

158   Making It in This Thing

Table 8.5 *Infantry officers' pay, 1631*[30]

Rank	Pay (equivalent in gulden/month)	% change from 1620s
Captain	255	−29
Lieutenant	67.5	+35
Fähndrich	52.5	−25
Sergeant	27	−25
Muster-writer	16.5	−17.5
Commander	16.5	−31
Fourier	16.5	−31
Surgeon	15	−37.5
Corporal	15	−25
Drummer	10.5	−12.5
Piper	10.5	−12.5

month.[31] However, in this contract there is no recorded difference between usual infantrymen and others, which may mean that pay fell precipitously for experienced and elite soldiers.

Pay for common cavalrymen seems to have remained constant into the 1630s, although not cavalry officers. On November 24, 1632, the contract for Franz Albrecht von Sachsen's regiment of arquebusiers specified the rates of pay shown in Table 8.6.

Most of the officers on this list saw deep cuts in pay on paper, which might have been ameliorated if this was in full-value currency. The major exception is the captain, who was finally making something comparable to an infantry captain's pay, supporting my hypothesis that pay for the higher officers in the Hoffahne was intended as a bonus to someone with an existing means of support. On the other hand, common arquebusiers were still supposed to receive the equivalent of fifteen gulden a month per horse.

There are some caveats. The Hoffahne was an elite organization so it is possible their numbers are unusual: The data from Albrecht von Sachsen's regiment may be closer to usual cavalry pay. Moreover, these sources for cavalry pay refer to arquebusiers specifically. I did not find pay data for cuirassiers, and the Saxon army did not field lancers.

At first glance, the limited data for cavalry and infantry for the 1630s does not demonstrate that bad a situation: Officers' wages fell sharply or fluctuated and very highly-paid soldiers are no longer attested at all but, for most common soldiers, pay on paper either remained constant from

[30] SHStADr 11237 10798/4. Wages given in thalers; one thaler is one and a half gulden.
[31] SHStADr 11237 10798/4. Wages given in thalers; one thaler is one and a half gulden.

Table 8.6 *Cavalry officers' pay, Franz Albrecht von Sachsen's regiment, 1632*[32]

Rank	Pay (equivalent in gulden/month)	% change from 1624
Captain	255	+70
Lieutenant	75	−50 or −17
Cornet	60	–
Fourier	15	−50
Corporal	18	−60 or −70
Muster-writer	15	−66
Surgeon	15	–
Smith	15	–
Saddler	15	–
Trumpeter	15	–

the 1620s or rose slightly. However, during the war, real wages for civilians rose by 40 percent.[33] The 1630s also saw a subsistence crisis in Germany as well as repeated outbreaks of plague, which would have made living on their pay even harder for soldiers.[34] If soldiers' official wages remained static or fell in the 1630s while everyone else's wages went up, military service would have been a less attractive option for a potential soldier had it not given him the opportunity to loot or steal. However, if these figures are in solid currency, that would represent a more comfortable situation after the disturbances of the early 1620s.

From the 1630s, the sources I have found are contracts. They specify what soldiers should receive, as opposed to pay records that record what each soldier did receive. Most muster rolls from the 1620s were countersigned by the Saxon commissioner of war every time soldiers were paid. Later documents do not show when or if payment was received.

Contracts do not preserve traces of company social organization like the results of haggling, or a paymaster's opinion of a prospective soldier's skill. Most records from the 1630s and 1640s do not even label soldiers by weapon: They do not show when Saxony stopped fielding halberdiers or sword-and-buckler men. The social distinctions among the infantry regarding different weapons, different roles, and different individuals, and the constant negotiations over money and social status, visible only as traces in documents from the 1620s, now disappear entirely. They may have collapsed. Within its informal organization, the Saxon army of

---

[32] SHStADr 11237 10798/4 52r–54r. Wages given in thalers; one thaler is one and a half gulden.
[33] Pfister, "Consumer Prices and Wages," 23.   [34] Ibid., 10.

the 1630s and 1640s may have been a more egalitarian institution than the army of the 1620s. Surviving rolls from these decades are more disorganized in general, more casually-written: It is also possible that the countless little gradations among the soldiers, amid the untenable situation for Imperialist-aligned forces after the Peace of Prague, were now too much trouble to write down.

The Saxon army was paid on time and surprisingly well during the 1620s, but the Electorate could not support this outlay in the long run. During the 1620s, the Saxon Estates granted new taxes to support the Elector's debts, which included spiraling war expenses. In 1628, the Diet announced that debts had more than doubled over the past six years, but Johann Georg I refused to tell the Estates what had happened to the earlier funding. Nevertheless, the Estates took over some of the debt and granted new taxes.[35] Ogilvie describes Saxony as an "early-developing" state that modernized its finances during the war and "grew huge bureaucratic and financial structures."[36] This should not be taken too far; Saxony also raised revenue by increasing customary methods such as taxes on commodities like meat or activities like the milling of grain.[37] The bureaucratic organizations that handled war finance, whether they were launched during the war or before it, were not exceptionally sophisticated structures; the *Obersteuerkollegium* was instituted in 1570 to service the Elector's personal debts and revenues and was made up of four noble tax receivers and four princely councilors.[38]

Saxon finances collapsed in the 1640s, by which soldiers were supporting themselves directly off the land. Nevertheless, the new tax instituted for the army in 1646 became regular and was collected every quarter; in this case, we can see the development of new fiscal–military structures.[39] However, these developments did not increase Johann Georg I's successors' power compared to the Estates. Instead, the Electoral war debts made Johann Georg III "rely not less, but more, on the financial support of the Estates." In contrast to the Electorate of Brandenburg, in Saxony the army did not increase the power of the centralized state but, during the seventeenth century, vitiated it.[40]

It is hard to imagine the Electoral treasuries in the 1640s being able to spare the kind of money demanded by some elite pikemen in the 1620s.

---

[35] Carsten, *Princes and Parliaments*, 229–230.
[36] Sheilagh Ogilvie, "Germany and the Seventeenth-Century Crisis," in Geoffrey Parker and Lesley Smith, eds., *The General Crisis of the Seventeenth Century*, 2nd ed. (New York: Routledge, 2005), 68.
[37] Uwe Schirmer, *Kursächsische Staatsfinanzen (1456–1656): Structuren – Verfassung – Functioneliten* (Stuttgart: Franz Steiner Verlag, 2006), 805–810.
[38] Carsten, *Princes and Parliaments*, 223–224. [39] Ibid., 232. [40] Ibid., 239–240.

If what was written down in contracts really was what the common soldiers made, some of the losers during the war's endgame would have been the elite pikemen and halberdiers, the infantry battalion's erstwhile aristocracy of labor. But, during the war, the ratio of men with some kind of supervisory position, like sergeants or corporals, to common soldiers may have increased. I do not know whether this increase was actual or only on paper; or whether the highly-paid, top-listed pikemen and halberdiers filled a similar role before the proliferation of formally-designated noncommissioned officers.

This chapter implies that the Thirty Years War can be divided into several parts for Saxony, not only in terms of political acts and allegiances but also in terms of socioeconomic factors and therefore structure and living strategies of the army. The Saxon army of the 1610s and 1620s – small, infantry-heavy, at paper strength constantly – is not the same as the Saxon army of the 1630s, which peaked at 36,000, at or near Saxony's carrying capacity, fought at Wittstock and in Pomerania as one half of a joint Imperialist-Saxon venture, and died in Pomerania almost to the man. Neither was the same as the Saxon army of the 1640s, which was very small, far under paper strength at every time measured, equal parts infantry men and cavalry horses, possibly not paid by the state, able to sustain itself indefinitely, and which only dissipated when formally disbanded. But the same men peopled all three.

We can now compare pay in the Mansfeld Regiment to that of soldiers in Saxon units in the Saxon army during the 1620s. The Mansfeld Regiment's cavalry made the same as the cavalry in all other records: Fifteen gulden a horse.[41] The amount Mansfeld gave his cavalrymen to support themselves on the way to Lombardy was less generous. On September 17, 1625, Mansfeld wrote in a letter to the Duke of Feria that he was giving his cavalrymen four batzen a day to maintain them. He said he had "employed great expense" and "done more than obligation carried," but this works out only to eight gulden a month.[42] If it cost four gulden and twelve groschen a month to buy fodder for a single horse in Dresden, these cavalrymen would have found it difficult or impossible to obtain food for themselves and their mounts on their delivery money alone. But the infantry was also in a miserable state.

On the night of July 7, 1626, Georg Schmaliner and Lucas Paz came at the head of some other "lads" (*pursche*) to the quarters their commander shared with at least two other officers. They called the commander

---

[41] SHStADr 10024 9235/6, 90r.
[42] SHStADr 10024 9737/13, 24. Rough draft of a letter from Wolf von Mansfeld to the Duke of Feria, September 17, 1625.

outside to face the crowd. They said that the recruiting agent (*Impresarius*) who had signed them up "had said that they would be given 13 Sold a day," three soldi more than the two batzen/day they said was the usual rate, "but they are now receiving only 10, and would therefore like to know where the other 3 Sold went and why it should not be coming to them." This was part of a wider pay dispute in this company: "Herr Commander, because the corporals and squad leaders are now asking for what's theirs, it's no more than equitable that we also further what's ours," Paz said in front of the roaring crowd.[43]

The money Schmaliner and Paz thought was the going rate, what they ended up receiving, works out to four gulden a month. This is half what most pikemen in Saxony made. They had been promised five and four-fifths gulden a month, three batzen less than the lowest amount recorded for common musketeers in Saxony. For these wages Schmaliner and Paz agitated, for demanding these wages they were condemned to death. Paz was pardoned and Schmaliner was hanged.[44]

The regiment's authorities presented an iron front in public but Dam Vitzthum von Eckstedt was livid when he wrote to Gonzalo de Córdoba a year later in September 1627. The recruiting agent had not lied to Paz and Schmaliner. An extra three soldi per soldier per day had been promised to the Mansfeld Regiment's authorities by the governor of Milan. This money, wrote Vitzthum von Eckstedt, "which the Duke of Feria ordained to give daily on top of each ration, over and above the other support, and not to have it charged, he promised with princely words, but now such princely words and promises about the set-down and aforementioned 3 soldi have been entirely annulled." The total amount Córdoba owed the regiment for this breach came to 31,753 scudi.[45] This was a fraction of what the Governor of Milan owed the regiment and its officers in total.

Lucas Paz and Georg Schmaliner's pay dispute and Schmaliner's death were the results of the cascading series of financial failures within Spanish northern Italy's administration of their regiment, which I analyzed in Chapter 2. While he was attempting to secure the loan of 300,000 scudi that had been intended to fund the Mansfelders, Giovanni Castone wrote "I think that while the soldiers are in the field, they will want to spare them (? *parcerli* = Latin *parcer*, to spare?) this way, but when

---

[43] SHStADr 10024 9739/6, 30–35. [44] SHStADr 10024 9739/6, 30–35.
[45] "Die durey solt, welche der *Duca de feria* aff iewdem *Racion*, Vber den andern *socors*, deglige Zu geben *ordiniret*, Vndt solche nicht *Cargiren* zu laßen, mitt furstl. worten zugesagett, itzo aber solche furstl. wort Vndtt zusage an dan gesetzett Vndt gedacht 3 Solt gentzligen abgeZagen worden, beluffen sich Aff – 31753." SHStADr 10024 9239/5, 63.

they are withdrawing, they will want to appear (?*parcerli* = Spanish *parecer*, to appear?) at our backs."[46] These failures took place at the level of the political and financial decisions of important people, but their results impacted the lives of ordinary soldiers.

Neither Georg Schmaliner nor Lucas Paz shows up on surviving Saxon muster rolls: They may not have been experienced enough to tell that what they had been offered was lower than what most soldiers made in Saxony. On the other hand, although infantry wages in this regiment were low, when this dispute took place food was issued to the soldiers. Food plus pay may have worked out to decent support: If it took about six gulden a month for one soldier to feed himself, issuing food to him plus four gulden cash is the equivalent of about ten gulden a month. This too is less than the face value of what many Saxon infantrymen got in Saxony. When they did not receive food the Mansfeld Regiment's infantrymen got only fifteen soldi a day, six gulden a month.[47] This was just enough for a single soldier to buy food. It is hard to see how some Mansfelders survived on pay alone.[48]

The Mansfeld Regiment's funding problems were insuperable. The war they had come to Lombardy to fight was short, and the great cities of Spanish northern Italy did not raise the money to pay them while it lasted. Once this conflict ended in March 1626, the government in Alessandria may have forgotten them. By this point, Mansfeld and his officers did not have enough money to dismiss their men, since soldiers' back pay had to be settled in full upon dismissal. They lingered around Milan and Cremona for more than a year. In summer 1627, the Mansfeld Regiment collapsed.

---

[46] "Tengo che mentre li soldatti saranno in campagna voranno parcerli in questa maniera, ma puoi ritiratti che saranno voranno parcerli alle nre spalle." AS-AL Serie II, *Lettere de 1625 del Sig. Grat. Castone, Tomus 50*, 308. Letter from G. Castone, November 6, 1625. This passage is extremely obscure.

[47] SHStADr 10024 9239/5, 61r.

[48] Buchner and Hoffman-Rehnitz, "Irregular Economic Practices," 10; Beverly Lemire, *Global Trade and the Transformation of Consumer Cultures: The Material World Remade, c. 1500–1820* (Cambridge: Cambridge University Press, 2018), chapter 4.

9 And to My Son the Breaking Wheel
The Mansfeld Regiment Falls Apart

On February 2, 1627, Lieutenant Wolf Heinrich von Dransdorf, with his friends Commander Hans Reinhardt Kochstetter and Fourier Barthel Golzer, took a walk for pleasure. Sergeant Georg Lauren followed. These were officers in the company of August Vitzthumb von Eckstedt, Dam's younger brother.

"Now the Lieutenant had on him that day no more than one ducat, and thus no more than I" Golzer said, "and he wondered to me where he could get some clothing. I had brought a fine penny out of my own country" – Arnswald in Pomerania, now Choszczno – "and I just can't give him anything from it [if] I [wanted to] be able to cover my own body" (*kan doch nichts er übergenn daruon ich wie etwz an leib schaffen köntte*).[1] By early 1627 things were so bad these officers were budgeting pennies for new clothing. Lice probably clotted in their long hair. The skulls of seventeenth-century soldiers in multiple mass graves bear traces of inflammation caused by an unusually large number of lice. The immune reaction ate into the bone.[2] These officers may have been wearing cotton or cotton-blend, like the fabric Winckelmann had contracted for, and these fabrics do not insulate when wet. Wool gets heavier the wetter it gets, but cotton clothing gets cold. Linen in Habsburg red, lined in cotton fustian of heavy blue and white: Working their fingers under damp rags, bundled against the gray Milan winter, von Dransdorf, Kochstetter, and Golzer would have scratched their grimy skin with grimy nails until they bled.

Up came the sergeant behind them. "Oh, the Lieutenant's a big noble," he sneered: "*O der Leuttenantt ist izundt hierinnen ein großer vonn Adel.* But if he had no lord, there's no other way he could help himself than by going from one fair to another with his wife and cutting purses."

---

[1] SHStADr 10024 9739/6, 162.
[2] Bettina Jungklaus and B. Prehn, "Ein Soldatenmassengrab vom Friedländer Tor in Neubrandenburg aus dem Jahre 1631 und dessen anthropologische Untersuchung," in *Heimatgeschichtliches Jahrbuch des Regionalmuseums Neubrandenburg* 35 (Neubrandenburg: Regionalmuseum Neubrandenburg, 2011), 10–33; Markus Plum, "Archäologische Zeugnisse des Dreißigjährigen Krieges in Bayern: Die Erstürmung von Höchstadt an der Aisch 1633 und die Schlacht bei Nördlingen 1634," 2011, available at: academia.edu/1235094, last accessed March 11, 2024.

Lauren continued: He knew von Dransdorf's wife's former man had been hanged. She was pregnant then. As they led this man to the gallows hill [*richtstadt*] he turned to her and said: If you have a daughter, I want to bequeath her the rod of correction with which the hangman should beat her back; if you have a son I'd leave him the breaking wheel.[3] Three weeks later she was whipped out of that city by the hangman: *ausgestäupet und gestrichen*, the same fate her man advocated for their unborn child.[4]

Wolf Heinrich von Dransdorf was a noble, whose family had provided officers to the Saxon army for generations. A relative of his named Christof von Dransdorf had custody of a collection of Imperialist prisoners, probably Lützen veterans, in Leipzig in 1633.[5] August Adolf von Dransdorf was the flag-bearer of the fortress of Pleißenburg just outside Leipzig when he put on a fireworks show in honor of Elector Johann Georg II on July 8, 1667.[6] But Wolf Heinrich's wife was a criminal, like her dead man. Like Wolf Heinrich himself could become, said Lauren, if he had no lord.

I do not believe Lauren's comments were insulting because he said an officer's wife was involved with criminals; the insult was that she had suffered rituals of punishment. Halfway to the gallows – halfway up the ladder, in one witness's account – her man allegedly looked back at her and said her future child deserved to be whipped out of the city or broken on the wheel. This was a dishonoring thing: Any contact with the executioner, even saying that someone should have such contact.[7] Von Dransdorf's wife had also been dishonored when her man was hanged. Even if she had not been scourged out of the city and he had kept his mouth shut, she would have been shamed because her lover had been shamed.[8] Georg Lauren attempted to insult Wolf Heinrich von Dransdorf through his wife, assuming that if she and her child had been dishonored, von Dransdorf would be too, when Lauren spread the story around.

---

[3] SHStADr 10024 9739/6, 162, 168.   [4] SHStADr 10024 9739/6, 163.
[5] SHStADr 11237 108351-1, *Extract der in Leipzig zuruckgebliebenen und verwunderten Offiziere und Knechte von der Kaiserl. Armee 1633.*
[6] August Adolf von Drandorff, *Augenschein und Positur Derer Feuer-Wercks Stücken/ Welche Der ... Churfürst zu Sachsen Hertzog Johann Georg der Andere in Gegenwart ... Hertzogen Augusti zu Sachßen ... Hertzogen Mauritii zu Sachßen ... Hertzogen Johann Adolphen/ zu Holstein ... jenseit der Pleiße bey der Vestung Pleißenburgk den 8. Julii Anno 1667. ... angeordnet An statt Einer Feuerwercks-Probe...abgeleget und gehorsamst verrichtet worden durch Augustum Adolphum von Drandorff/ der Zeit bestalten Fähndrich bey der Vestung Pleißenburgk von Leipzigk.* Digitized by the Universitäts- und Landesbibliothek Sachsen-Anhalt, 2008.
[7] Stuart, *Defiled Trades and Social Outcasts.*
[8] Susanne Pohl-Zucker, *Making Manslaughter: Process, Punishment and Restitution in Württemberg and Zürich, 1376–1700* (Leiden: Brill, 2017), 98, fn 19.

I do not know where this happened, or what von Dransdorf's wife and her earlier partner had done. I do not know why Georg Lauren was angry at Wolf Heinrich von Dransdorf. The person who did have a reason to be angry at him was the surgeon of Mansfeld's personal company, Michael Meder. On Pentecost 1626 his wife and Wolf Heinrich von Dransdorf's wife got into a fight, and Meder's wife was "injured in her honor" by von Dransdorf's wife. "Know that my wife is better in one finger than the lieutenant's wife is in her entire body," Meder said. But when von Dransdorf's wife's previous lover was hanged, "[Meder's wife's] sister was beaten out with rods, [and] the same sister's man was broken on the wheel." Meder's brother, "who was led into it by [von Dransdorf's wife's man]," was executed with the rest. This was the original cause of the fight: Michael Meder blamed von Dransdorf's wife's dead lover for the deaths of his brother and brother-in-law, as well as the dishonor of multiple family members; his wife blamed von Dransdorf's wife.[9] Georg Lauren attacked von Dransdorf on Michael Meder's behalf.

These officers and women were bound together by murky ties of blood, marriage/sexual association, and friendship. Michael Meder and Georg Lauren called each other "gaffer," *Gevatter,* an affectionate term for an old man or someone in charge of a group.[10] Otherwise Michael the Surgeon was respectfully addressed as "Master" (*Meister*). Von Dransdorf's wife's earlier partner was Meder's brother's accomplice, possibly also a relative. When Michael Meder's wife and Wolf Heinrich von Dransdorf's wife brawled in Lauren's quarters, Meder "became enraged and called the Lieutenant's wife a tremendous whore … at which [Lauren] answered, should my Lieutenant have a wife like that?"[11] Like honor and dishonor, blame traveled from relative to relative, and friend to friend. Michael Meder and Georg Lauren had planned to get revenge on von Dransdorf's wife and her child, and on von Dransdorf for being married to her. Lauren said "Now my heart is healthy, since if I have taken one I also get the other": When they dishonored von Dransdorf's wife, they also dishonored von Dransdorf.[12] The Mansfeld Regiment was crawling with hidden conflicts. Wolf Heinrich von Dransdorf married into this thicket of old associations when he married into this group of officers – associations which predated this regiment and would probably postdate it.

Meder and Lauren spread slander around their companies together. ("The Surgeon asked me another time," said Lauren, "saying: Gevatter sergeant, didn't you know that I wanted to say more to you, can you stay

---

[9] SHStADr 10024 9739/6, 168–170.   [10] SHStADr 10024 9739/6, 168.
[11] SHStADr 10024 9739/6, 168.   [12] SHStADr 10024 9739/6, 175.

quiet about it when you get drunk? At which I said, when it doesn't touch me I can well be silent."[13]) When you look for von Dransdorf you'll find the horn they said, he was a cuckold. Lauren sent Meder a note by two musketeers describing what happened on the gallows hill, but Meder said himself he "could not read, much less write." He gave it to the senior squad leader to read to him.[14] The musketeers heard him say in the doorway that Lieutenant von Dransdorf's wife was a whore and should have accompanied her previous man to the gallows.[15] Eventually von Dransdorf took it to court. Georg Lauren was forced to swear that his words had only been "lightminded talk" and that he had slandered von Dransdorf, and to beg the latter for Christian forgiveness.[16] The truth of any of these claims was less important to Mattheus Steiner than good relations among these squabbling officers.

That was February and March 1627, but the case was only decided in June. By 1627, cases were progressing more slowly: Mattheus Steiner was the legal record-keeper as well as the bailiff and he was overwhelmed with work. Probably this was for the same reason Wolf Heinrich von Dransdorf and Barthel Golzer had no money for clothes: The regiment's funding almost certainly ran out in early March.

As the analyses of historians like David Parrott demonstrate, the public–private networks of finance by which early modern armies were raised, funded, and supplied had many strengths. Raising troops by private contract was flexible. Armies could be raised quickly. Taken as a whole, the numerous military enterprisers in central Europe formed a resilient network with no single point of failure. But each individual army or regiment was fragile. In the Mansfeld Regiment's case, private military enterprise and its cooperation with the ramifying networks of the state failed.

In October 1625, while Mansfeld cavalrymen were dying unknown outside the New Gate in Casale, the Spanish and French signed a six-month truce. On March 5, 1626, the two great powers concluded the Treaty of Monzón. This suspended the fighting between French and Spanish forces, as well as between the Duke of Savoy and the Republic of Genoa.[17] Although the treaty largely restored the pre-1617 situation, it also officially recognized the Valtelline as Catholic.[18] This victory was not mentioned in the Mansfeld Regiment's surviving written documents.

---

[13] SHStADr 10024 9739/6, 169.   [14] SHStADr 10024 9739/6, 173.
[15] SHStADr 10024 9739/6, 175–176.   [16] SHStADr 10024 9739/6, 180–181.
[17] Thomas Allison Kirk, *Genoa and the Sea: Policy and Power in an Early Modern Maritime Republic 1559–1682* (Baltimore: The Johns Hopkins University Press, 2005), 100–102.
[18] Wilson, *Europe's Tragedy*, 383.

Its officers' concerns were not political or strategic. They were worried about whether the regiment was going to survive or disband.

On June 18, 1626, Don Gonzalo de Córdoba wrote that the Mansfeld Regiment's arrears should be paid in full, as the Duke of Feria had promised.[19] Although this was essential to dismiss the soldiers without a mutiny or a riot, nobody had the money to do it.

Mansfeld and his lieutenant-colonels and captains avidly followed the progress that other German regiments in northern Italy made getting their troops out of the area.[20] "Successfully leaving" the theater of war meant a colonel managing to dismiss his troops or lead them north without an incident. By July 17, Wolf von Mansfeld wrote a letter saying he was disbanding his troops and had it distributed to all his officers: "Therefore we don't feel that there is any danger, yes everyone here is confident that the dismissal in Italy should succeed."[21] The troops would be dismissed and paid off in Italy. Mansfeld himself remained on his estate in Schluckenau.

On September 23, 1626, Lieutenant Colonel Vratislav Eusebius von Pernstein wrote Mansfeld that a courier had come to him four days previously with orders to dismiss the troops, but nobody knew what was going on. The cavalry's activities are infrequently mentioned in Mansfeld sources compared to the infantry, especially because the cavalry's legal book is fragmentary. But its interactions with the surrounding world, and therefore the effects of the regiment's financial problems on the common soldiers, are more well-documented.

The infantry held a muster just before von Pernstein wrote to Mansfeld, but according to him the cavalry had not started settling their accounts since they did not have the money to pay off the men. They were not interested in Milan's explanations: "What the Duke of Feria has promised, nobody wants to know now" (*will man Itzt nichts davon wißen*). "We have nothing to console ourselves with except good poor comrades remaining on hand now" (*gute arme gesellen bei dem Itzigen handt zubleiben*); "It's heartbreaking to see the cavalry now, and how they hoped to be, sick, tattered, miserable, the change is indescribable." They were short of food. "Many of them have been forced by need to hock their

---

[19] AST Archivio Sola Busca, Serbelloni, Box 47. Letter from Don Gonzalo de Córdoba to Ferrante Caimo, June 18, 1626.
[20] SHStADr 10024 9239/2, 49v; SHStADr 10024 9239/5, 62r.
[21] "So haben wir doch nicht für Unrath befinden, da ia uber alles Verhoffen undt Zuversicht die Abdankung in Italien erfolgen sollte." SHStADr 10024 9239/2, *Die Beiden in Italien Stehenden Regimenter des Grafen Wolfgang von Mansfeld: Schreiben Desselben an die Unterbefehlshaber, des Rechnungswerk, die Abdankung u.a.bet. 1626–28*, 2–3r. Letter from Wolf von Mansfeld to his officers, July 17/27, 1626.

pistols, cloaks, and everything they have. Winter is before the door, but the cavalrymen are very poorly clothed." He had supported them out of his own pocket ever since they were mustered in, "for the maintenance and reputation of the regiment."[22] On September 23, von Pernstein sent a provisional order to prepare to deduct the small amount of a half batzen (eight pennies) from each cavalryman's wages per day; he hoped he would not have to, but this would stretch his funds. "Except that a battle has just taken place" he wrote, hoping for plunder. "So the account settlement should be good."[23]

By September 30, von Pernstein learned that the regimental officials at Cremona "have not paid, and cannot, and do not know anything about payment." Stach Löser told him everything would work out all right (*dieselbe sachen auch köcte zur richtigkeit gebracht warden*). Von Pernstein began deducting money from his cavalrymen's pay.[24] He and Löser spent time together in fall 1626. They talked about the horse that Löser had taken as plunder: Turkish breed, outfitted with a saddle and a pair of pistols, everything chased in worked silver. Horse and tack together cost 200 Thalers. "I don't want the horse," said von Pernstein: "I'll let him sell everything and hand it over."[25] A letter arrived, from Colonel Mansfeld in Saxony: It was not a line of credit, it was not instructions for how to salvage the situation, or advice; Mansfeld was asking about the Majolica pottery he had ordered in Italy. It was supposed to have been shipped to Leipzig but it never arrived, had it been sent somewhere else by mistake?[26]

Meanwhile, Milan was attempting to swindle the Mansfeld officers on the exchange-rate between the money they used and the money available in northern Italy. The Governor of Milan told Dam Vitzthum von Eckstedt he would exchange gulden for soldi at a rate of sixty-three soldi and four denarii per gulden. When the Mansfeld Regiment was mustered in on November 2, 1625, the *Viador General* had promised that the Milanese authorities would reckon the exchange rate at sixty-six soldi per gulden. Per soldier per day, the cumulative difference between what was promised and what was eventually supplied worked out to 13,818

---

[22] SHStADr 10024 9239/2, 4v–15v.
[23] "Sonderlich weiln es ein schlacht anstehen hat, das die abrechnung, gut sell warden." SHStADr 10024 9239/2, 4r–4v. Letter from Vratislav Eusebius von Pernstein to Wolf von Mansfeld, September 23, 1626.
[24] SHStADr 10024 9239/2, 6r–9v. Letter from Vratislav Eusebius von Pernstein to Wolf von Mansfeld, September 30, 1626.
[25] SHStADr 10024 9239/2, 8v. Letter from Vratislav Eusebius von Pernstein to Wolf von Mansfeld, October 7, 1626.
[26] SHStADr 10024 9239/2, 17r. Letter from Wolf von Mansfeld to unknown recipient, undated.

scudi, about 22 percent of the over 63,000 scudi Milan failed to pay the regiment.[27] This kind of manipulation of exchange-rates was one way local authorities made money off a unit, and one reason why some commanders hauled the massive amounts of silver necessary to pay their troops with them rather than rely on bills of exchange.[28]

After not writing about the Mansfeld Regiment for almost a year, the notables of Alessandria and Milan decided on October 17 to raise 24,000 scudi at 6 percent to pay the "Swiss and Germans" to disband. They considered paying them the excess from monetary exchange, even up to 36,000 scudi.[29] Even this higher amount was about a tenth of the funding that should have gone to the regiment one year previously. Mansfeld sources do not mention receiving any money from government sources during this period.

Wolf von Mansfeld wrote to Camargo from Dresden on October 24. The Elector of Saxony had written to him in secret and wanted to talk to both Córdoba and the Spanish Ambassador. But the Swiss were making so much difficulty that Mansfeld did not believe the regiment would make it out of Italy until at least the following spring.[30] We'll have to winter over he told von Pernstein, thanking him for his efforts: "I ask you to do your best again."[31] Von Pernstein stayed with the regiment only a little longer: In early January the general and financier Albrecht Wallenstein offered him a regiment of horse if he would come up north to join him, and von Pernstein agreed. He would have left immediately if Don Gonzales had not told him to stay in northern Italy to help handle the dismissal. Tactlessly, von Pernstein wrote to Mansfeld to ask him to tell Don Gonzales to give him permission to leave the regiment. "People are speaking very strongly about this dismissal and there is no hope of [the regiment] coming back to Germany," he justified himself: "I no longer have the financial means to remain like this, the will is indeed good but the abilities are weak."[32] By March 1627, he was leaving.[33]

That fall and winter the officers cast around through the people they knew for someone to bail them out. Von Pernstein wrote on

---

[27] SHStADr 10024 9239/5, 63r heading #3.   [28] Parrott, *Richelieu's Army*, 245.
[29] AS-AL Serie II, *Lettere de 1626 del Sig. Grat. Castone, Tomuss 51*, 294–295. Letter from G. Castone, October 17, 1626.
[30] SHStADr 10024 9239/2. 11r–12r. Letter from Wolf von Mansfeld to Theodoro de Camargo, October 14/24, 1626.
[31] SHStADr 10024 9239/2, 13r. Letter from Wolf von Mansfeld to Vratislav Eusebius von Pernstein, October 16/26, 1626.
[32] SHStADr 10024 9239/2, 48r–49v. Letter from Vratislav Eusebius von Pernstein to Wolf von Mansfeld, undated.
[33] SHStADr 10024 9239/2, 16v, Letter from Wolf von Mansfeld to Theodoro de Camargo, March 1, 1627.

November 11 that the seven cavalry companies at Cremona were "very badly accommodated."[34] Camargo put out feelers to Ambrogio Spinola's oldest son Don Philip Spinola but they went nowhere.[35] Mansfeld wanted to "remain in the service of the most praiseworthy House of Austria."[36] Giovanni Battista Castone still expected 200,000 scudi to aid the Mansfelders' departure as of April 6, 1627, this time from Spain.[37] At some point Mansfeld made contact with Albrecht Wallenstein, Generalissimo of the Imperial army.

For most of the regiment's stay in northern Italy, high politics took place in the background. Most Mansfelders probably had little conception of the wider sociopolitical context around them, or at best a garbled one: When the rumor went around that everyone would be sent to Spain, it was probably because Theodoro de Camargo had just arrived from the Spanish Netherlands. But Wolf von Mansfeld and Wallenstein had hated each other for a while.[38] Wallenstein was then near the height of his fame, and in summer 1627 was mopping up the Danish army. ("Wallenstein's going to completely destroy" the King of Denmark and his allies, Mansfeld told Camargo in October 1626.[39]) As Peter Wilson says, Mansfeld's operations in Italy gave him a patronage base outside Wallenstein's influence.[40] His relationship to Saxony and its Elector was also one step removed from Imperial networks of power. But, as Mansfeld looked around for funding in early 1627, Wallenstein offered to bail him out if the Mansfeld Regiment entered Imperial service.[41] On March 10, the Emperor decided to take "the Regiment of Foot as well as two or three companies of the best cavalry."[42]

Mansfeld's instructions to Eustachius Löser for negotiations with Wallenstein are dated July 10, 1627. "We ... present ourselves before

---

[34] SHStADr 10024 9239/2, 15r, Vratislav Eusebius von Pernstein to Wolf von Mansfeld, November 11, 1626.
[35] SHStADr 10024 9239/2, 41r.   [36] SHStADr 10024 9239/2, 45r.
[37] AS-AL Serie II, *Lettere de 1627 del Sig. Grat. Castone, Tomus 52*, 106–107. Letter from G. Castone, April 6, 1627.
[38] Golo Mann, *Wallenstein: Sein Leben Erzählt* (Frankfurt am Main: S. Fischer Verlag, 1986), 221–222.
[39] SHStADr 10024 9239/2, 11r. Letter from Wolf von Mansfeld to Theodoro de Camargo, October 14/24, 1626.
[40] Wilson, *Europe's Tragedy*, 398.
[41] A number of the letters tracking the detente between Wallenstein and Mansfeld are in SHStADr 10024 9235/6, which is mislabeled as *Rescript Von Kaiser Ferdinand II an graf Mansfelden, angleichen verschiedenen Schreiben des general Wallensteins und andern angedachten Grafen Wolfgang zu Mannsfeld 1628*. Despite the title, there are many letters from 1627 in this file as well. According to SHStADr 10024 9235/6, 54, the switch into Imperial service was Wallenstein's idea.
[42] SHStADr 10024 9235/6, 53.

Your Noble Grace with deserved respect and obedience and ask that [you] remember our need," Mansfeld began, ingratiatingly. (This was in stark contrast to the catty way he talked about Wallenstein behind his back – there, whereas Tilly "has been favoured by happy success" which covers his enterprises with "immortal glory," Wallenstein "has only responded with presumptions, mentioning which has worked to his disadvantage."[43]) Mansfeld and Löser should try to nail Wallenstein down on when exactly they had to "shove on up to Your Grace with this People" (*Wan wir mit diesemm Volck Zu Ihr stoßen müsten*),[44] ask for written instructions about how the officers were to be remunerated, and ask him to send documents to the colonels in the places where the Mansfeld Regiment was heading. Nobody other than Wallenstein himself should command the regiment, none of Wallenstein's people.

This set of instructions contains three collections of notes, which are different layers of rough drafts. Each is less emotionally guarded than the previous one. "I will uncover my feelings to the Lieutenant Colonel, namely that I cannot give way to the General Lieutenant and Field Marshal." Make clear to Wallenstein that the Mansfeld Regiment's top officers should still be appointed by Mansfeld himself, these letters urged. Stress that Mansfeld would under no circumstances give up his Life Company of Horse.[45] Finally, in Mansfeld's own hand: "Remember, in order to further my high name, to be conscious of the title and authority with which I command."[46] As he faced the prospect of losing control over his regiment, Mansfeld clung more fiercely to the baroque displays of power that were his titles, his "high name," and his Life Company of Horse. Von Pernstein acted for similar reasons when he pumped his own money into the cavalry to maintain the regiment's "reputation."

While Stach was negotiating, the regiment ground north. The letter from the Imperial war council to Mansfeld stating the regiment's Imperial service shall date "from the day when they shall be paid in Italy and might be dispatched" was written on May 21, 1627.[47] So was his Imperial patent.[48] On July 5, the regiment was assembled: They were mustered out by Philip IV's war commissioner and immediately mustered into Imperial service.[49] Wallenstein wanted them to join his

---

[43] SHStADr 10024 9239/2, 11r–12r. Letter from Wolf von Mansfeld to Theodoro de Camargo, October 14/24, 1626.
[44] The rough draft of this point probably sounded more like Mansfeld actually talked: "da man midt den *exercitu* Zu Sam steßen soldt ..." SHStADr 10024 9235/6, 60v.
[45] SHStADr 10024 9235/6, 58r–59r.   [46] SHStADr 10024 9235/6, 60r.
[47] SHStADr 10024 9186/2, *Akten von Wolfgang von Mansfeld, 1619–1630*, 58.
[48] SHStADr 10024 9186/2, 59.   [49] SHStADr 10024 9239/2, 51r.

own forces in Alsace and the Palatinate.[50] The regiment's officers would pay for the passage up through Switzerland and be reimbursed later.[51] It headed north and northeast through the Valtelline, swinging wide around Bern and other Protestant territories. Some companies and officers stayed in northern Italy, including Mattheus Steiner. He followed the regiment north to Ulm later, and was still copying Mansfeld Regiment records in 1628.

On July 11, while the regiment was heading through the Grisons, Hans von Ponickau's company mutinied. They were joined by those of Camargo, Arnswald, and August Vitzthum von Eckstedt. The men ripped their flags off their poles, forced passports and money from their officers, and "in summa, were guilty of all the insolence and crime that it was possible to think of."[52] They also "partly sold and partly gave away their weapons, the cost for which they had still been two-thirds indebted"; as usual, the regiment's officers had expected the common soldiers to pay them back for the cost of their weapons.[53] Lively trade in second-hand military goods existed to take advantage of opportunities like this.[54]

The rest of the Mansfelders struggled north. In Lindau, six companies almost mutinied "from the instigation of the city folk and the mob," but they were given cash so they vowed to follow the flags as long as they flew in Imperial service.[55] In Memmingen and Ulm, again incited by local civilians, most of the remaining companies mutinied and walked away.[56] It was polite: Mansfeld later wrote "Our regiment that was mustered out in Italy mostly made a friendly mutiny on the way and left."[57]

In August, when they reached Sachsenhausen on the Main, the exhausted soldiers requested "either their dismissal or money, and wanted to go no further." A flag-bearer "with great affirmations persuaded them that when they came over the Main they would find good

---

[50] SHStADr 10024 9235/6, 27, letter from Albrecht von Wallenstein to Wolf von Mansfeld, May 11, 1627.
[51] SHStADr 10024 9239/2, 51r.   [52] SHStADr 10024 9239/2, 51r–51v.
[53] SHStADr 10024 9239/2, 51r–52r.
[54] Brian Sandberg, "The Magazine of All Their Pillaging: Armies as Sites of Second-Hand Exchange during the French Wars of Religion," in Laurence Fontaine, ed., *Alternative Exchanges: Second-Hand Circulation from the Sixteenth Century to the Present* (New York: Berghahn Books, 2008), 76–96, 78.
[55] SHStADr 10024 9239/2, 51v.   [56] SHStADr 10024 9239/2, 51v.
[57] "Welcher gestalt Unser in *Italia* abgedanckten Regiment meistlich unter Wegens freundlicher Weiße *meutiniret* und ais gerißen." SHStADr 10024 9239/5, *Allerhand Schriften, das aus Italien Zurückgekehrten Regiment zu Fuß des Kais-Generals Grafen Wolfgang Mansfeld, dessen übler Zustand, aufenthalt zu Frantfurt a.m. samt u.d.a.*, 83r.

quarters and money, and that Frankfurt would give them some thousands of Reichsthalers."[58] According to military manuals, the flag-bearers were supposed to treat the common soldiers well so that if they became mutinous and were refusing to negotiate with the other officers, the flag-bearer could plead for loyalty.[59] They were supposed to make themselves beloved by the soldiers so the soldiers would follow them, and stay with them in times of danger.[60] It was a desperate and pathetic lie, but this flag-bearer enticed the regiment the last few miles across the river. About six hundred men, without food, without decent clothing, and without weapons, came to rest just outside Frankfurt.[61]

Surviving information about summer and fall 1627 and early 1628 comes from local archives as well as repeated clashes between Mansfeld officers and local authorities on the way. South to north, the regiment passed through Sigmaringen, villages and a monastery near Ulm, Darmstadt, the Electorate of Mainz, and Frankfurt am Main.

Many Mansfeld sources for late 1627 were written by Dam Vitzthum von Eckstedt: In contrast to documents composed by other Mansfelders, in these documents Vitzthum von Eckstedt presents himself as the regimental third-in-command. Although he had assumed a leading position among the remaining officers by this point, I do not know whether he actually held this office by fall 1627 or whether Wolfgang Winckelmann still occupied his accustomed place. Even now the Mansfeld officers were jostling for position.

A document specifying that the remnants of the Mansfeld Regiment were supposed to be given quarters and food had been written by the Emperor and copies had been sent out ahead to places along the regiment's potential path, not only to Frankfurt but to Nuremberg, Cologne, and the latter city's Elector.[62] Frankfurt refused, and was able to make its refusal stick.[63] This city was still surrounded by its broad moat and great fourteenth-century curtain walls. It was beginning to build modern thick-walled low defensive works: Construction on the northeastern Friedberger Gate bastion began in 1626 and the Mansfelders might have seen it in progress as they crossed the Main from the south. Although the modernization of Frankfurt's defenses did not begin in earnest until the

---

[58] SHStADr 10024 9239/5, 30v–31r.
[59] Lorenz von Trouptzen, *Kriegs Kunst Nach Königlicher Schwedischer Manier Eine Compagny zu richten / in Regiment / Zug: und Schlacht-Ordnungen zu bringen / Zum Ernst anzuführen / zu gebrauchen / und in esse würcklich / zu unterhalten* (Frankfurt: Mattheus Merian, 1633), 6.
[60] Wallhausen, *Manuale Militaire*, 127–128.   [61] SHStADr 10024 9239/2, 51v.
[62] SHStADr 10024 9239/5, 3.   [63] SHStADr 10024 9239/5, 5v.

1630s, there was still no way for 600 exhausted and hungry soldiers to force their way in.[64]

Frankfurt did not let them remain before its gates.[65] At some point before August 10 the last Mansfelders scattered into nearby villages. "They had to support themselves and were almost entirely ruined and dispersed," wrote the Mansfeld officers. "That's a measure that's easy to measure," they said: "without quarters and provision from the officers their companies and troops broke up because of hunger, and the officers had to start letting them go, it had become impossible to hold them together for long."[66] They concluded: "Before God and the world, we the assembled captains and officers want to be exonerated of the destruction of the Imperial Count Mansfeld Regiment, which happened because we were in no way paid off."[67] These officers stayed with their people north through Switzerland and into Germany, and paid for everyone's food and passage until they had no money left. If they were still alive, Felix Steter and Hieronymus Sebastian Schutze were there too.

Some officers, led by Dam Vitzthum von Eckstedt and Wolfgang Winckelmann, lobbied Frankfurt am Main and the Elector of Mainz for food and quarters. The Electorate of Mainz was the most senior political entity in the Empire. Its Elector was the *primas Germaniae*, the Pope's vicar north of the Alps, and arch-chancellor of the Empire.[68] In contrast to its formal and ritual preeminence, this polity was not large, with discontinuous territories along the Main, on both sides of the Rhine, and in Thuringia. From late summer 1627, the Elector was Archbishop Georg Friedrich von Greiffenklau. His immediate predecessor, Johann Schweikhard von Kronberg, had been politically moderate, favoring compromise and dialogue with moderate Protestant powers like

---

[64] Emil Padjera, "Die bastionäre Befestigung von Frankfurt aM," *Archiv für Frankfurts Geschichte und Kunst, Band 31* (Frankfurt am Main: Selbstverlag des Vereines für Geschichte und Alterthumskunde, 1920). See also the Merian engraving of the city from 1628.
[65] SHStADr 10024 9239/5, 26r.
[66] SHStADr 10024 9239/5, 5v, "biß auf ein we[...]ges so noch alhier zu befinden, undt biß anhero umb das ihrigen Zehren müßen, fast ganz Zurgangen *ruiniret* und vorstrunet worden, Maßen dan leicht zu ermeßen, daß ohne Quartier und proviant den Hauptleuten ihre *Compagnie*n undt Troppen, welche hungers halben sich trennen, undt die Hauptleute umb erlaßung anlangen müßen, in die lenge Zu erhalben Unmüglich gefallen."
[67] SHStADr 10024 9239/5, 6r, they are writing "alß wollen wier hiermit die anwehsender Hauptleute undt Befehlshaver, Vor Gott Undt der Weldt, an dieser deß Keyserl. Graff. Mansfeldisch. Regiments beschener Zerrittung, welches aber weil wier keineswegs abgedancket ..."
[68] This was a formal post, but policy was made by the vice-chancellor, appointed by the Emperor. Wilson, *Europe's Tragedy*, 17, 350.

Saxony.[69] Schweikhard died in September 1626; von Greiffenklau was more extreme. He was a stalwart supporter of the Emperor's opinions, and his influence helped shape the Edict of Restitution.[70]

On August 11, the Mansfeld officers wrote to von Greiffenklau: They wanted to follow the Emperor's patent and remain unstained ("non-infamous," *unbeschweret*), and they begged him not to ignore their requests for quartering like Frankfurt had. They wanted to pull the regiment back together and lead it out against the Emperor's enemies. They had led their soldiers up through Switzerland at their own expense for ten days, they said: They kept coming back to this in the middle of unrelated sentences. They reminded him that the Emperor had signed their patent with his own hand.[71]

Von Greiffenklau responded on August 24 with a firm "no." Their Imperial patent required those who read it to provide the regiment with food and shelter, but the documents referred to "a regiment." Since the Mansfelders had dissolved their companies when they ripped their flags off the poles, they were no longer legally "a regiment" and, until it was reconstituted, the soldiers could not stay in his territories.[72] This threaded the needle of legal pedantry with some precision, ignoring that, in addition to an Imperial patent to demand supplies for the remnants of his regiment, Mansfeld also had a patent to recruit a new one. Von Greiffenklau may have been this intransigent because many of the Mansfeld Regiment's officers were Protestants. But these officers probably never had the opportunity to meet him let alone discuss their beliefs: von Greiffenklau wrote that letter from Aschaffenburg, twenty-five miles southeast of Frankfurt. He had gone there on August 15 for his episcopal consecration.[73] It is more likely that von Greiffenklau just did not want soldiers in his dominions. Villages in Mainz had already faced "total ruin" when troops came through two years earlier.[74] The Elector's agents harassed Mansfeld's officers and, on September 17, Mansfeld's emissary Bernard Lauerwald described the Elector of Mainz as "insubordinate." "Yesterday evening I was returning from Darmstadt and I was asked for my written commission by His Grace, who then discarded it."[75]

---

[69] Ibid., 226, 245, 227.
[70] Anton Philipp Brück, "Georg Friedrich v. Greiffenclau zu Vollrads," in Historische Kommission bei der Bayerischen Akademie des Wissenschaften, ed., *Neue Deutsche Biographie*, Band 6 (Berlin: Duncker & Humblot, 1964), 219.
[71] SHStADr 10024 9239/5, 10r–12v.   [72] SHStADr 10024 9239/5, 33r.
[73] Ferdinand Sender, *Georg Friedrich Greiffenclau von Vollrads 1573–1629. Ein Prälat aus der mittelrheinischen Ritterschaft. Aufstieg und Regierungsantritt in Mainz* (Mainz: Gesellschaft für Mittelrheinische Kirchengeschichte, 1977), 146.
[74] Wilson, *Europe's Tragedy*, 402.   [75] SHStADr 10024 9239/5, 52v.

From August to September, the Mansfeld officers tried to get food and quarters for their men from the Frankfurt city council. They failed despite their letters from the Emperor and the Council of War. "Your Grace would not believe," wrote Dam Vitzthum von Eckstedt to Mansfeld, "how offensive the inhabitants (*leitte*) here are, and when I'm looking for something or other, or I have someone else look for something for me, I'm made fun of."[76] Mansfeld officers frequently used the word "insubordinate' or "offensive" to describe civilians around them who did not want to do as they were told. These officers may have had few words to describe those who were not soldiers, neither their superiors nor inferiors.

These officers knew that the remnants of their regiment were extorting food, supplies, places to sleep, and sex from the inhabitants of those villages. They brought it up in their negotiations: "The evil and destroyed condition of these places and the surrounding area is well known by the lords."[77] The city council of Frankfurt still refused to quarter soldiers, and only gave out bread and beer once, and a little money.[78]

The regiment's final collapse was not the first time its members had severely mistreated other people, or the worst; Mansfelders had caused a serious incident two years previously. In late fall 1625, early in the morning on November 1, 700 Mansfeld cavalrymen had raided two estates near Alessandria.[79] After interrogating some of the common soldiers and cavalry servants involved, Vratislav Eusebius von Pernstein recorded one of these incidents in the legal books. He did not mention and may not have known either place's name: They were the estates of Mantella and Roberti, on the road from Verrua to Alessandria. These were large farms with multiple connected structures around a courtyard, typical of Lombardy. Italian sources call them *cassine* or *cascine* and the houses inside "the village of the cassina."

The Mansfeld cavalry had had a rough introduction to Lombardy and Montferrat and had been forced to change quarters several times already. Four thousand Montferratese, likely peasant militia, nearly all armed with muskets – if this improbable number is accurate, almost double the Mansfeld infantry's real strength and far outnumbering the cavalry –

---

[76] SHStADr 10024 9239/5, 24v: "EG können nicht glauben wie wiederwurtig leitten eß alhie hatt, Undt wan ich einß oder daß anders suche oder suchen laßen, Wurde ich noch höhnisch darzu geholten."
[77] SHStASr 10024 9239/5, 30r: "Bey den herrn der Uble unndt verderbte Zustanndt dieser orten unndt der Nachbarschafft wohl bekannt ..."
[78] SHStADr 10024 9239/5, 55r–55v.
[79] AS-M Archivio Gonzaga, E. XLIX. 3. 1758, Gio. Battista Sannazaro I 1625, 343. Letter from Giovanni Battista Sannazaro, November 5, 1625.

had ambushed them earlier, as they were passing through Casteletto and San Salvadore.[80] Both the Alessandrian official Giovanni Battista Castone and the Mantuan diplomat and spy Giovanni Battista Sannazaro mentioned that "the German cavalry" had taken a "serious blow" that would take a lot of money to repair: "peasants in great number did a lot of damage to their vanguard."[81] The Mansfelders withdrew and took lodging in and near the Borgoglio (northern) quarter of Alessandria, from which base they sacked Mantella and Roberti.[82]

Less than an hour after daybreak the horsemen stormed the estate.[83] The cavalryman that Mattheus Altman served woke him up and berated him for not getting up and fetching something like everyone else.[84] Jobst Meyßer said he didn't know who began sacking the place, except his lord the cavalryman he served said everyone was getting something so he should go to the estate too.[85] Georg Caner saw someone from his company whose name was Marx beat a window open and climb inside.[86] Christof Heschler heard trumpet blasts as he ran down toward the estate.[87] Marcus Wagner was there two hours after daybreak: He said he saw a full 700 horsemen in and around the estate.[88]

"Were priests, children, women, and old people killed? How many and by whom?" asked the interrogating officer.[89] Hans Ernst Grosch saw three dead men; "whether they were murdered though, he doesn't

---

[80] "Essendo in questo mentre arriuato d'Alemana nello Stato di Milano il Conte Carlo di Mansfelt con quatro mila fante, e mille Caualli, passò alli vene'vno di Ottobre per Alessandria; & havendo nel medesimo giorno condotta la sudeta gente, à Felizzano, ivi fece alto sino alli due del seguente mese, nel qual tempo ritorno in questa Citta, ma i Môferatesi in numero di quattro mila in circa, quasi tutti armati di moscheto, si misero in agguato per affarlirla, douendo ella passare per Casteletto, e San Saluadore, ende quelli Alemanni, per nō mettersi ad euidente pericolo con gente poco meno che disperata, s'appigliarono a sauia risolutione di ceder per all'hora, è tornar addietro, come fecero, è pigliarono alloggiamento nel confine di Alessandria verso Borgoglio, done, & in particolarie nel Villaggio, delle Cassine de'Mantelli, & in questo de'Roberti fecero molti danni, è saccheggiarono tutte quelle Case, Finalmente alli quattro de Novembre, giorno festiuo di San Carlo, abbandonarono li sudeti quartieri, e lasciate da vna parte le Territorio del Monteferate, andarono di lungo a Pontestura." Ghilini, *Annali di Alessandria*, 208.

[81] AS-AL Serie II, *Lettere de 1625 del Sig. Grat. Castone, Tomus 50*, 249. Letter from G. Castone, September 28, 1625. AS-M Archivio Gonzaga, E. XLIX. 3. 1758, Gio. Battista Sannazaro I 1625, 358. Letter from Giovanni Battista Sannazaro, November 18, 1625.

[82] Ghilini, *Annali di Alessandria*, 208. [83] SHStADr 10024 9739/5, 28.
[84] SHStADr 10024 9739/5, 29. [85] SHStADr 10024 9739/5, 32.
[86] SHStADr 10024 9739/5, 40. [87] SHStADr 10024 9739/5, 39.
[88] SHStADr 10024 9739/5, 41.
[89] SHStADr 10024 9739/5, 25–26; H. E. J. Cowdrey, "The Peace and the Truce of God in the Eleventh Century," *Past & Present* 46 (1970), 42–67.

know."[90] Jobst Meyßer said he didn't see more than one dead person.[91] Lorenz Pfeiffer saw "an old man and an old woman, but they were fresh and healthy."[92] "Were any women dishonored?" Trumpeter Heinrich Lehnfeldt "had well seen that a woman was raped, she screamed piteously, who it was [who did it] however he doesn't know, because he wasn't known to him."[93] Christof Heschler also saw a rape.[94] Hans Ernst Grosch saw two women going into a room, then he saw nothing else.[95]

Historians of the early-modern period and contemporary observers recognize that rape was common in early-modern war.[96] Not all mercenaries were rapists, but there would have been plenty of men like Lehnfeldt and Heschler, or women, who knew what was happening but did nothing. It is hard to tell the extent to which a unique military subculture contributed to rape because it is hard to tell how common sexual violence was in non-military society in comparison. Laws varied between jurisdictions; rape was probably underreported; and some sexual crimes appeared to be isolated to a few locations.[97] However, the material conditions of sixteenth- and seventeenth-century war made sexual assault extremely likely. There were no "battle lines" which distinguished a safe place from a hostile area. Soldiers took what they wanted from others whether they were "friendly" or "hostile," making other violent acts likely. Soldiers were more likely to commit exceptionally violent rape and to do it in gangs.[98] A historian of the twentieth century has noted an "astonishingly high level" of gang rapes committed by American soldiers in Western Europe in the last days of the Second World War.[99] The small-group cohesion of soldiers was not only for mutual defense, bands of friends could also egg one another on to attack. Early-modern soldiers and officers may have believed they had a right to rape civilian women and some soldiers were accustomed to it.[100] The descriptions of Victoria Guarde's dead body as violated and alluring may

---

[90] SHStADr 10024 9739/5, 34.
[91] SHStADr 10024 9739/5, 21.
[92] SHStADr 10024 9739/5, 31.
[93] SHStADr 10024 9739/5, 36.
[94] SHStADr 10024 9739/5, 39.
[95] SHStADr 10024 9739/5, 34.
[96] Lynn, *Women, Armies, and Warfare*, 153.
[97] Garthine Walker, "Sexual Violence and Rape in Europe, 1500–1750," in Sarah Toulalan and Kate Fisher, eds., *The Routledge History of Sex and the Body: 1500 to the Present* (New York: Routledge, 2015), 431–432.
[98] Karin Jansson, "Soldaten und Vergewaltigung in Schweden des 17. Jahrhunderts," in Benigna von Krusenstjern and Hans Medick, eds., *Zwischen Alltag und Katastrophe – Der Dreißigjährige Krieg aus der Nähe* (Göttingen: Vandenhoeck & Ruprecht, 2001), 195–225.
[99] R. M. Douglas, "Neither Apathetic nor Empathetic: Investigating and Prosecuting the Rape of German Civilians by US Servicemen in 1945," *The Journal of Military History* 87 (2023), 404–437, 415.
[100] Ailes, *Courage and Grief*, 29.

have been examples not only of an attitude toward sexualized violence in early-modern European military society but also conceptions by non-soldiers of military society as violent in a sexualized way.

Finally, the interrogating officer asked what the cavalrymen got. One witness saw the cavalry's third in command ordering people away from the estate, but a single officer was not enough to keep 700 men from looting the place. His attempts to enforce the law of war were selective: Several of the cavalrymen who had been questioned reported giving up some of their haul to him or seeing someone else do it, because it was church property.[101] Noc Münch, who robbed a civilian on the road near Alessandria, "saw nothing but rice and wheat mixed together, of that he only got a little for his prize."[102] Lorenz Pfeiffer and Hans Kreiss got some beans, Jobst Meyßer some wheat.[103] Marcus Wagner got a little jacket (*röckel*) worth about a ducat, and fodder for his horse.[104] Heinrich Lehnfeldt went home by himself.[105] Hans Altman fetched a bundle of hay. After he tied it together, he left, and nobody ordered him away.[106]

Sannazaro reported that the Mansfeld cavalry had been receiving bread and wine from Mantella and Roberti when they attempted to enter them by force, against an agreement made with Don Gonzalo de Córdoba. "A company, they say it was de Blacche [possibly Picke], came to the plain of Casale, and stole many cattle and [carried out] other robberies, and it was still necessary to provide for these despicable fugitives." The Milanese authorities ordered soldiers not to "enter the countryside" under threat of death. Sannazaro seems to have thought the Saxons who had done this were Polish; this was before Saxony's connection with Italy, and it may have been the first time this Mantuan diplomat encountered people from the German lands who were not from strongly Catholic places like the Hereditary Lands or Bavaria.[107]

---

[101] SHStADr 10024 9739/5, 40, 42.   [102] SHStADr 10024 9739/5, 27.
[103] SHStADr 10024 9739/5, 30–32, 37.   [104] SHStADr 10024 9739/5, 41.
[105] SHStADr 10024 9739/5, 36.   [106] SHStADr 10024 9739/5, 29.
[107] "Si quarla che la soldatesca di Mansfelt aloggiata in questi Cassinale, doppo d'havere havuta dalla sudetta Comunita pane, vino, et altre repeschi, pretendeva per forza entrave nella terra, et che questo era contro il concertatio col Sig Gonzale di Cordova ... la soldatesca restate nelli Cassinale conforme al stabilito, soggiongendole che hieri venne una compagnia dicono de Blacche sopra questa piana di Casale, che rubboino molti bessiame, et altro robbe et che a questo ancora era necessario il provedesse per sfugine questi sconerti che fossere per nascone ... havra mandato ordine espresso a Capi della soldatesca che si trova nelli Cassinale ... che non debbino procurare d'entrare nella terra sotto pena della vita et che peri Consoli non le dattero cosa alcuna senza il pagamento ... Crea al rubatto fatto hieri da Polache, mi dice che questo Signore Ministri procurino di sapere di che compagnie fossero ..." AS-M Archivio Gonzaga, E. XLIX. 3. 1758, Gio. Battista Sannazaro I 1625, 353. Letter from Giovanni Battista Sannazaro, November 14, 1625.

These estates belonged to the diocese of Casale Montferrato. Because burial records from the Cathedral of Casale do not specify the settlement in which people "from the countryside" lived, it is impossible to determine if some of the people buried in Casale in October and November 1625 had been inhabitants of Mantella or Roberti. Sannazaro said that when the Mansfelders entered them by force, with "cruel great sacking and killing," they killed, "they say," eighteen peasants.[108]

Vratislav von Pernstein closed the case without comment: "The thing is passed over in silence, and will not be gone into further."[109] German-speaking commanders called looting, rape, murder, and torture by common soldiers "inconvenience" (*Ungelegenheit*), and military authorities like von Pernstein often tacitly let inconveniences go. But this raid sparked heated discussion in Milan. The Duke of Feria wanted to withdraw from Verrua only if his main force were covered, and hopefully without any further damage to the locals: Giovanni Battista Sannazaro replied that the quartering of Mansfeld troops had caused much damage, and that Montferrat "is completely ruined for the service of His Catholic Majesty." Bickering with the Duke of Feria and other Milanese officials, he tried to promise that the Mansfelders would only remain in their quarters for a brief period. However, "seeing that they remain so long it seems to me that this should be called a formal quartering, because I do not see how the lord ministers can give them other accommodations."[110] According to Sannazaro, the German soldiers did not even have forgiveness from the church for causing the deaths of subjects of the Duke of Mantua.[111] He believed this violence would excite local feeling against Germans.[112] On November 4, 1625, the feast of San Carlo, the Mansfeld

---

[108] AS-M Archivio Gonzaga, E. XLIX. 3. 1758, Gio. Battista Sannazaro I 1625, 362. Letter from Giovanni Battista Sannazaro, November 20, 1625.

[109] SHStADr 10024 9739/5, 42.

[110] "Io l'ho risposto che dove ha aloggiato la soldatesca regia, ha cagionato grandissimi danni et che il Monferrato per servire a Sua Maesta Cattolica e tutto in rovina, et che S E et Don Gonzalo mi promittero che di passaggi sarebbero state solo che per due o quatro giorne, et che videndoli hora andar tanto in longo, mi pareva ce si dovessoro chiamare aloggi formali, che percio non sapero come gli signori Ministri puotranno dale altre aloggio."AS-M Archivio Gonzaga, E. XLIX. 3. 1758, Gio. Battista Sannazaro I 1625, 358. Letter from Giovanni Battista Sannazaro, November 18, 1625.

[111] "Dovra V.A. ma sapere che hieri l'altro andorono da millecinquecento fra Cavalli et fanti Alemanni sotto nome di foraggio alla terra di Cardona Cantone di Villadeati e barbaricmente la sacheggiorno gelta dovia il vino che non poterano condare via, non havendo ne ancho perdonato alla Chiesa con morte di alquanti sudditi di V.A." AS-M Archivio Gonzaga, E. XLIX. 3. 1758, Gio. Battista Sannazaro I 1625, 321. Letter from Giovanni Battista Sannazaro, October 22, 1625.

[112] AS-M Archivio Gonzaga, E. XLIX. 3. 1758, Gio. Battista Sannazaro I 1625, 343. Letter from Giovanni Battista Sannazaro, November 5, 1625.

cavalry abandoned their quarters and returned to Pontestura, where they stayed for a long time.[113]

Many accounts of the Thirty Years War portray its violence as a field of undifferentiated horror. Nineteenth- or early twentieth-century accounts often make this war a morality tale, depicting either the righteousness of a particular side or specific denomination, or sadistic soldiers and victimized civilians. But cruel acts in war happen at specific places and times, for specific reasons. The cruelty of sixteenth- and seventeenth-century warfare was the result of the complex interaction of many factors. Heads of state had the money to raise armies but not regularly to pay the soldiers, as the 300,000 scudi which should have gone toward the Mansfeld Regiment demonstrate. This may have contributed to attitudes according to which regiments could be forgotten after the initial flurry of effort to raise them. Financial systems were inefficient and easily corrupted by people like Wolfgang Winckelmann, while seventeenth-century armies faced massive logistical challenges getting food, supplies, and money to the field.[114] Soldiers tried to secure food, clothing, sex, and places to sleep by threatening or harming others. The Mansfelders were chronically ill-supplied and physically wretched. They were accustomed to violence among themselves and against others. Some did not speak Italian and it was difficult for them to communicate in Lombardy.[115]

Civilians could negotiate, live with soldiers, flee, or fight. They could profit by taking advantage of the violence around them. Some cooperated with soldiers, in what could be ambiguous relationships. Bartolomeo Gattone, called "The Bag" (*il Saccha*), was a translator for one of the Mansfeld companies in Gallarate. When his dog bit a soldier's boy on October 25, 1625, the boy went to the Bag's house accompanied by soldiers and killed all the hens, then went to the slaughterhouse and cut into pieces an ox that the Bag had ordered killed for himself. He beat everyone he found, threw stones, and fired a musket off in the piazza. The populace gathered with their firearms, and many soldiers and the Bag were wounded in the riot. "I was there too," wrote Antonio Rasini, "with my wheellock arquebus."[116]

---

[113] Ghilini, *Annali di Alessandria*, 208.
[114] Lauro Martines, *Furies: War in Europe, 1450–1700* (New York: Bloomsbury Press, 2013), xii–xiii.
[115] Wilson, *Europe's Tragedy*, 834.
[116] "Die Jovis decimo sexto hora vicesima tertia ... sendo stato morduto nelle Beccherie un ragazzo d'un soldato della compagnia d'Allemani che alloggiavano in questo borgo d'un cane di Bartolomeo Gattone do. il Saccha, l'interprete d'essa compagnia, accompagnato da molti soldati, andato alla casa di do. Saccha percosse chi trovò in d. a casa, amazando tutte le galline, poi andò alle beccherie del med.no et taglò in pezzi un bove che ivi amazato del medesimo Saccha percuottendo chi andò a vedere ett chi vi si

Like the peasants who might have beaten the missing Saxon soldier Jobst Steinnetze to death in 1635, civilians' actions could be terrible.[117] Rasini's account of an incident in Legnano earlier in October describes the danger civilians posed to troops, and the ratchet effect of action, retaliation, and paranoia. On October 18, 1625, some Mansfelders went to a local's house demanding money. In the ensuing tumult, one of the soldiers was killed and another was wounded. Before the soldiers could retaliate, the local notables led the citizens of Legnano to arm themselves, and "according to what people say twenty-five soldiers were left dead, and their bodies were never found." This armed civilian force barred access to the countryside for fear of the soldiers; they posted guards at the gates, locked some soldiers inside a large tavern, and placed sentries beneath the bell tower of Sant Erasmo so the bell could be rung every time they saw more than two people on the street together. This went on for four days. The notables who instigated this massacre and lockdown rode through the town on horseback, with armed footmen at their heels. The civilian violence only stopped when the Captain of Justice in Milan arrived with an infantry escort, but "they say only two dead soldiers were found."[118] This episode left little to no trace in the Legnano death records, which did not track soldiers' deaths. By the end of October,

---

trovò presente, tirando anche delli sassi, arrivando anche sulla piazza del Pasquè ove a molti fu tirato, et anco sparato una terzetta, di modo che non potendo alcuna persona stare in piazza, fu forzato il popolo gridare che si sonasse campana martello, il che fu fatto, et concorso il popolo armato, fra quali v'ero anch'io con archibugiro di ruota, furono feriti molti soldati et d.o interprete, et per assicurarsi, sendo andato la maggior fuori dalla terra, si fece un corpo de guardia nella Piazza de S.to Pietro al lungo solito, si misero la guardia s.a. il campanile et quindici personi armate at ogni ponte, qual durò sino alle dodici hore del giorno seguente, et havendo il capitano d'essa compagnia trattato con il S Vicario del Seprio che non sarebbe seguito altro, fu levata la guardia havendo però prima dato parte del tutto al Castellano del Milano vice governatore." Rasini, "Alloggi militari," 132.

[117] Wilson, *Europe's Tragedy*, 837. SHStADr 11237 10841/3 3. Jobst Steinnetze, new soldier, recruited in Stolberg in 1635: "nach hause gehen Wollen, aber nichtt dahin kommen, ob er in Feindes haende kommen oder Von bauern erschlagen sey, Weiss niemandt."

[118] "18 Ottobre 1625. A di sud.o. gli soldati che alloggiano nel borgo di Legnano sendo andati a casa d'un particolare per certi danari che pretendevano, seguì tumulto et restò morto uno della terra et un altro ferito, per il che sonatosi la campana, fu in arme tutta la gente guidati dalli Gentilhuomini di detto borgo, ove, per quanto se dice, restarono morti da venticinque soldati i corpi dei quali non si sono trovati, si sbarrarono tutte le contade per tema che li soldati che alloggiavano ivi intorno insieme non assaltassero detta terra sendo la compagnia del Tenente colonello, si fece la guardia a tutte le porte, gli soldati che restarono nella terra furono serrati nell'hostaria grande, havendogli levate l'armi, si misero le sentinelle sopra il campanile della Chiesa de S. Erasmo et in terra, sonandosi la campana quando si vedeva più di due persone; il che durò per quatro giorni continui tando tutto il giorno li sud.i. Gentilhuomeni a cavallo con un pedone per ciascuno armato, al qual borgo vi andò il Vicario del Seprio et di poi il Sr Capitano di

when the Mansfeld cavalry sacked Mantella and Roberti, violent clashes between the infantry and the locals in Legnano, several days' walk from the cavalry near Casale, had been continuing for a month.

The Mansfeld cavalry had also been fighting locals on the way to Italy for months. The Ulm housing document lists companies of Mansfeld cavalry by town of quartering on the way to Italy in summer 1625: Some companies spent as many as ten or eleven days in a single village, but one troop under Captain Ulleben could not. In Asselfingen this company "had taken quarters without the knowledge of my heart, and resided there 2 nights and 1 day, [I] had driven them out," wrote the city master of the watch. They moved to Rammingen, a mile and a half away: "in the same they spent 4 days, from which I also drove them out *per forza.*" Harried south they retreated to Dornstadt, almost fourteen miles away, and lodged there for one night, when the next day the master of the Ulm city watch drove them out again toward Donauwörth.[119] The Mansfeld cavalry moved quarters repeatedly in Lombardy as well, such as when they entered Cremona.

October 1625 was catastrophic for both branches of the regiment, and the most miserable burial records for German soldiers in Casale were also recorded that autumn. Even before they raided Mantella and Roberti, the cavalry was operating within a context that made atrocity more likely, what Robert Lifton called "an atrocity producing situation," "one so structured, psychologically and militarily, that ordinary people, men or women – no better or worse than you or I, can commit atrocities."[120] Von Pernstein said his cavalrymen were so poor they had to pawn their cloaks and pistols. They had recently been mauled from ambush and may have feared all Italians were their secret enemies. Lifton cited the assumed presence of "invisible adversaries" as a trigger for American atrocities in Vietnam.[121] One reason German troops killed unarmed civilians as they entered Belgium in 1914 was that they were panicked by the fear of irregular civilian violence like the ambush that had

---

Giustizia di Milano con una cavalcata de fanti et se dice che si è trovato solamente il conto di due soldati morti ..." Rasini, "Alloggi militari," 132.

[119] StadtA Ulm Kriegsamtes A [5556], *Verzeichnis des Kriegsvolks zu Pferd und Fuß* by Wachmeister Christoph Revelheimer, Aufstellung der Mansfeldischen Kavallerie.

[120] Robert Jay Lifton, "Haditha: In an 'Atrocity-Producing Situation' – Who Is to Blame?" *Editor & Publisher*, 2006; Robert Jay Lifton, *Home from the War: Learning from Vietnam Veterans* (New York: Simon and Schuster, 1973).

[121] On vengeance and grief as a motivation for atrocities, see Neta Crawford, *Accountability for Killing: Moral Responsibility for Collateral Damage in America's Post 9/11 Wars* (Oxford: Oxford University Press, 2013), 244. Howard Jones, *My Lai: Vietnam, 1968, and the Descent into Darkness* (Oxford: Oxford University Press, 2017), 41.

met the Mansfeld cavalry.[122] The cavalrymen who raided Mantella and Roberti may have been afraid of the road between Verrua and Casale, or consumed with grief, or they may have perceived plunder and murder as revenge. They would have feared not only death from the locals who surrounded them, but death that was invisible, followed by utter disappearance: When civilians in Legnano trapped and killed Mansfeld soldiers, most of the bodies were never found. These civilians themselves may have massacred soldiers because they feared reprisal after a soldier was killed. Both soldiers and civilians were hungry in northern Italy in the 1620s but, in Mantella and Roberti, the soldiers were the ones in control.

But it was not because they had to eat that the infantrymen Barthel Meylig and Hans Kley menaced non-soldiers, or Meylig almost killed Kley. These two and the men they hung out with, including Michael Kleiben, who had made a pact with the devil, were written up repeatedly on the trip south in summer 1625. The members of this little group may have known one another before they joined up; Kley was from Radburg but the rest were all from Torgau.

Petrus Naubrandt, priest in a small town in Switzerland or southern Germany, testified that the wife of Hans Wather, peasant, told him Meylig and Kleiben were quartered on her family. They promised to shove a sword through her husband. "Take heed – do you feel safe here now?" they whispered to him (*"ob er nun wehl sich versichert gewust"*). "Watch that you do not give the soldiers cause to do it." Hans Wather ran to the priest's house and closed the window: He told the maid that if anything comes from soldiers, give them no answer. Barthel Meylig followed him running, naked sword in his hand. He jumped to the door and pounded on it.

Anna, the wife of Michael Kletterlaus, another peasant, said that, on August 8, 1625, in the evening when the sheep were coming in and she was going into her own courtyard, Michael Kleiben as well as Barthel Meylig and Hans Pönisch came by, and Meylig pulled his sword out and stabbed a sheep. Martin Drey said that Hans Pönisch beat his window in. Hans Noll said that Hans Kley came drunk into his quarters and demanded a quart of wine from him, which he gave him. But when Noll had left the house for his evening farm chores, Kley called Meylig, Kleiben, and Pönisch to the house, and they came. They forced Noll's wife to pour out three more quarts of wine. Meylig and the other two brought Noll's wife into the room, opened a pillow, and pulled out three pieces of linen, each thirteen ells. They took one piece, and when what they had done was over, the place was also missing two pieces of linen,

---

[122] John Horne and Alan Kramer, *German Atrocities 1914: A History of Denial* (New Haven: Yale University Press, 2001).

two tablecloths, one pair of scissors, one big peasants' knife (*Beimesser* – peasants wore them on their belts like swords), and one old pair of hose. The enigmatic gap in the account of this incident is taken from the report itself. On the same day Kley, Meylig, Kleiben, and Pönisch were clapped in irons and their infraction was recorded in the regimental legal books.[123]

Meylig and Kley show up in a report on May 8, 1626, in which Meylig, perhaps the ringleader, also turned on his comrade. The two had bought a basin of fish and they had a tankard of wine to go with it, "they had drunk three or four" rounds. When they were finished with the wine Meyling asked Kley to go to the tavern known as The Angel with him for another one. Meylig "took the drink like *that*" ("he chugged it," "*erschnellet*"), and at the end of the evening he fell off the bench. Kley held him and asked him to go back with him into quarters, which Meylig said he could do himself; he didn't need help. But Kley left his hat lying on the table and turned back for it and went out again, and "Meylig pulled leather on me," he drew his sword, hitting Kley on the head. Kley lived. He "forgave the pain and the associated wound," but the provost brought suit because the regiment "forgives nothing in this matter." Because he had not shortened Kley's life Meyling was not punished with his life; he was sentenced to stand watch for eight days, each watch of six hours, wearing six suits of armor. He was also required to pay Kley's medical bills.[124]

Meyling, Kley, Kleiben, and their gang were not ordinary men: When they threatened people, they whispered. Kleiben's testimony in another trial that he had made a pact with the devil may have been the usual soldiers' bravado, but it may reflect a state of mind that was more vicious or more sinister. On the other hand, like other soldiers they were drunk most of the time. Meyling himself testified that he drank so much the night he attacked Kley that he did not know how or why he did it.[125] The provost's commitment to prosecuting Meyling for assaulting Kley despite Kley's non-cooperation may reflect official disapproval of these men, who might have been poisonous individuals in any society. But the regimental authorities could also have been grateful for men who were willing to fight: Their names do not appear on the list of deserters.[126]

One ambassadorial complaint may mention the Mansfeld Regiment: While describing a German regiment that was "almost all Lutheran," Cesare Visconti wrote that he "saw no exemplary punishment against delinquents and wrongdoers, although the crimes counted for legitimate

---

[123] SHStADr 10024 9119/38, 11–14. [124] SHStADr 10024 9739/6, 185–188.
[125] SHStADr 10024 9739/6, 186. [126] SHStADr 10024 9739/6, 219–232.

trials."[127] Seventeenth-century mercenaries were deeply conscious of law, and military units operated according to a legal code. As part of his assiduous execution of his duties, Mattheus Steiner tried and convicted soldiers who harassed locals, including one major case where he had some tortured, probably to find out how many soldiers and officers were in on a conspiracy to steal sheep.[128] But his priority was to keep the regiment together and functioning. To see justice done may have come second, as may religion, even his own possible Catholic faith, of which he wrote nothing.

At least one person in this regiment may have realized the nature of his position, but the evidence is unusual. On May 20 or 21, 1627, the Emperor wrote an edict which described how Mansfeld was to lead his regiment from the service of the King of Spain into Germany. There are two copies of this text in the regiment's records. One is dated May and filed with other documents from the spring.[129] The other one, identical in content, is dated August 7, while the regiment was falling apart.[130] The second copy is not in Mattheus Steiner's handwriting. Whoever wrote it down recopied the Emperor's promises after they had been proven hollow. The soldiers will be given passage. They will be given food. There are references to those they were not supposed to prey on: The "poor subjects" (*Arme Untherthanen*), "the guiltless poor common man" (*desß armenn gemeinenn mannß*).[131] This copy is spotted with drops of liquid front and back which hit the paper when the ink was still wet, as though the scribe had been working outside and been dashed with sudden rain.

Wolf von Mansfeld's emissary Bernard Lauerwald and some of his officers spent early fall 1627 shuttling back and forth between Frankfurt and other places in Germany, delivering letters from Mansfeld, asking for money. Lauerwald himself was so hard up he was in debt to the civilians in whose houses he stayed.[132] On September 13, Dam Vitzthum von Eckstedt recommended his adjutant Daniel Daumer and his flag-bearer Schörteln to raise companies of their own, which might help bring the regiment up to twelve full companies again while advancing these young officers' careers. He also hoped for "luck health and all prosperity, And

---

[127] October 31, 1627. "... dal che si vede, che da nemici appena poteva lo Stato ricevere maggior percossa, desolatione; et ruina, non essendosi per li ricorsi fatti ottenuta alcuna sufficiente provisione, ne visto alcun esemplar castigo contro i deliquenti, et malfattori, benché dei misfatti contasse per legitimi processi ..." Salomoni, *Memorie storico-diplomatiche degli ambasciatori*, 303.
[128] Staiano-Daniels, "Masters in the Things of War."   [129] SHStADr 10024 9239/5, 2r.
[130] SHStADr 10024 9239/5, 67r–68r.   [131] SHStADr 10024 9239/5 67v.
[132] SHStADr 10024 9239/5, 53r.

that Your Grace with happy artifice and good contentment with God's help will remain fresh and healthy in the same, and might gain [the regiment] again, from the heart I wish it."[133]

Mansfeld spent summer and fall 1627 on his estates in Schluckenau. Early in September he wrote that he would head to Prague and from there take the post coach to Vienna. He would be better able to discuss matters at the Imperial court in person.[134] Several days later, Dam Vitzthum von Eckstedt reported that Jacob Binder had written to Lauerwald and told him that Mansfeld could not make it to Vienna yet because of "bodily weakness."[135] This was a common reason for letting soldiers or officers go: Communicating within the networks adumbrated in the daily actions of military units required tremendous physical effort. Unless they expected an attack or were planning a battle, big units spread out so the soldiers could supply themselves. Once dispersed, armies could not easily be concentrated again.[136] At the end of August some members of the regiment were scattered as far away as Darmstadt.[137] The frequent exchange of messages as the Mansfeld Regiment responded to a crisis, or during its daily operations, entailed almost constant travel from one part of the scattered regiment to others. Writers passed information on. Pappenheim's regiment was dismissed successfully in Italy in mid-September. An entire company of horse was surprised by peasants and scattered on the march to Lorraine, where they had been heading in search of quarters.[138]

On August 14, Mansfeld in Schluckenau had wanted to know the strength of the officers and common soldiers and reported he had a lead on 6,000 men's worth of "good Dutch weapons" (*Gewehr*, probably pikes) from Jobst from Brussels, a businessman he met in Prague.[139] On the same date, Dam Vitzthum von Eckstedt and some of the other officers in Frankfurt decided they had to start dismissing the remaining soldiers. The officers no longer had the means to live in Frankfurt with honor. Mansfeld got the news on September 4.[140] A day earlier they had still thought Frankfurt would be the muster place for a reconstituted Mansfeld

---

[133] SHStADr 10024 9239/5, 36r, "glick heil undt alle *prosperitet*, Auch daß E.G. mitt glichligern Vorrichtung undt gudem *Contento* mitt Gotteß hilff frisch undt gesunt in deroselben haffetatt, wiederumb erlangen mag, von hertzen wunschen tun."
[134] SHStADr 10024 9239/5, 43r.   [135] SHStADr 10024 9239/5, 61v.
[136] Denis Showalter and William J. Astore, *Soldiers' Lives through History: The Early Modern World* (Westport, CT: Greenwood, 2007), 15.
[137] SHStADr 10024 9239/5, 77v; GLA 98, Nr. 1265; GLA 98, Nr. 7676 and 7677; HStAD E 8 A Nr. 64/2 and 67/1.
[138] SHStADr 10024 9239/5, 61v–62r.
[139] SHStADr 10024 9239/5, 18v. This may have been the same Jobst von Brüssel, colleague of Jan de Witte, who served Ferdinand II. Ernstberger, "Hans de Witte," 22.
[140] SHStADr 10024 9239/5, 49r–49v.

Regiment, and wrote a letter to the mayor and city council stating the captains would pay for the quartering in the hosts' houses themselves.[141] I do not know where the money was supposed to come from for this, although Dam Vitzthum von Eckstedt wrote to Mansfeld that he was expecting money on the twenty-seventh.[142] The captains lingered in Frankfurt. Dam Vitzthum von Eckstedt and the other officers quarreled.[143] It rained.

Gradually Mansfeld stopped using the word "reconstitute" (*recolligiren*) to refer to the fragments of the regiment. Instead, he wrote about raising new units. By February and March 1628 he was quartered in Memmingen and taking an administrative role over Imperialist units near Ulm, leading at least one new regiment of horses.[144]

The captains remaining in Frankfurt spent late 1627 attempting to settle the debts they had racked up during their stay. Some young officers could not leave because they lacked the money to travel in a manner befitting their honor and estate. On September 11, Bernard Lauerwald made it to a tavern in Frankfurt, after heavy rain. "I was prevented from travelling because of the rain and the bad roads stemming from that, and the great storms, this last Saturday was the 11th, and with good luck, praise God, I arrived here, and found in the tavern" Dam Vitzthum, his brother August Vitzthum, Captain Answald, the adjutant Daniel Daumer, flag-bearer Schörteln, the provost, and other Mansfeld officers. Daumer and Schörteln depended on Dam Vitzthum von Eckstedt for future promotion; they were not about to leave. Wolfgang Winckelmann and some other officers had left eight days previously. Lauerwald gave the officers who remained a copy of a letter from Mansfeld letting them go.[145] "I brought Your Grace's writing as well as the verbal testimony that was necessary up to the council here," he wrote to Mansfeld on September 23. "They wondered that people were still bothering them with this thing."[146]

Nobody expected that Spain and France would go to war again over the same territory in less than a year. "I heard that the Duke of Mantua is dead," wrote Mansfeld to Camargo on November 28, 1626. This was Ferdinando Gonzaga, who died on October 29 and left the duchies of Mantua and Montferrat to his younger brother Vincenzo II. "Please God it's true, since it'd stop this thing for all time," said Mansfeld. If Vincenzo

---

[141] SHStADr 10024 9239/5, 37r.   [142] SHStADr 10024 9239/5, 58r.
[143] SHStADr 10024 9239/5, 51r.
[144] GLA Best. 98, Nr. 1265, *Kloster Salem: Einquartierung hauptsächlich der Mansfelder bei Schennerberg und Ehingen. Requisitionen. Korrespondenz mit den Pfleger zu Schemmerberg, Johann Ernst von Pflaumern, ua die Beschickung des Kreistages zu Memmingen*; GLA Best. 4, Nr. 7676 + 7677, *Schutzbrief des Grafen Wolfgang von Mansfeld vom 16. März 1628 für das Kloster Salem.*
[145] SHStADr 10024 9239/5, 88r.   [146] SHStADr 10024 9239/5, 88v.

II lived, the succession crisis that Mansfeld feared would never happen. There might be peace in northern Italy.[147] In early December the Count-Duke of Olivares wrote that the Spanish Monarchy had little to fear from France: Richelieu's domestic position was ambivalent and his attempt to invade Genoa and the Valtelline had failed.[148]

Vincenzo II Gonzaga died on Christmas Day, 1627. The conflict over the Mantuan succession eventually sucked Spain and France into open war, a parallel Thirty Years War that lasted from 1635 to 1659.[149] Philip IV said later that if he had ever erred in his life, it was when he began that war.[150] He said 1629 was the year his monarchy began to decline.[151] It was a punishment from God. The war devastated northern Italy.[152] In fall 1629, a crop failure aggravated by the trade disturbances of war led to a disastrous famine and the Martinmas revolt in Milan.[153] Recorded funerals rose in Busto Arsizio, Legnano, and Cremona; that year in Cremona, soldiers and men in prison started dying, and their burials were recorded at the cathedral.

What I can see of the Mansfeld Regiment is a sliver cut into a large complex of wars. Its stay in the State of Milan took place during a brief window of relative calm between the famine and economic collapse of the 1590s and the war, famines, economic collapse, and epidemic of the late 1620s into the 1640s. Compared to the catastrophes that followed, the war that brought the Mansfeld Regiment down to Milan was not very important. It is now almost entirely forgotten.[154] The only people whose lives the Mansfelders ruined when they went down to Italy were some civilians, and themselves.

---

[147] SHStADr 10024 9239/2, 22v.
[148] "Parecer del Conde Duque de San Lúcar sobre el estado de las cosas en todas partes. En Madrid a cinco de diziembre de 1627," quoted in R. A. Stradling, *Spain's Struggle for Europe, 1598–1668* (London: The Hambeldon Press, 1994), 99, 138.
[149] Stradling, *Spain's Struggle for Europe*; Graham Darby, *Spain in the Seventeenth Century* (London: Longman, 1995); David Parrott, "France's War against the Habsburgs, 1624–1659: The Politics of Military Failure," in Enrique García Hernán and Davide Maffi, eds., *Guerra y Sociedad en La Monarquía Hispánica: Política, Estrategia y Cultura en la Europa Moderna (1500–1700)*, Vol. 1 (Madrid: Laberinto, 2006), 31–49.
[150] Elliott, *Count-Duke of Olivares*, 310.   [151] Stradling, *Spain's Struggle for Europe*, 51.
[152] Hanlon, *Hero of Italy*; Hanlon, *Italy 1636*.   [153] Sella, *Crisis and Continuity*, 51, 144.
[154] D'Amico's description of the military situation in Lombardy in the 1620s is typical in glossing over the comparatively unimportant period from 1625 to 1627: "The strategic and military importance of Milan increased exponentially in the seventeenth century with the first war of Mantuan succession (1613–18), the beginning of the Thirty Years War in 1618, and the reopening of the conflict with the Netherlands after the 12-year truce in 1621. In 1628, at the start of the second war of Mantuan succession and the descent of the French army into northern Italy, the State of Milan found itself the effective center of military operations. After the Treaty of Cherasco in 1631, Milan enjoyed only a few years of peace. By 1635, the war with France had recommenced." D'Amico, *Spanish Milan*, 141.

Conclusion
A Beautiful Regiment

Colonel Alwig von Sulz was dying. He had led a regiment through Switzerland and northern Italy for the king of Spain in the same expedition that brought the Mansfeld Regiment there: In spring and summer 1625 his people were quartered in the possessions of a monastery near Ulm on their way south, and paid out of contributions it made.[1] After the 1625–1626 expedition he disbanded his troops without incident, and most of them went north.[2] He raised another regiment but, by fall 1627, something was wrong.

Sulz fetched up in or near Hanau, where his new regiment lingered without being mustered in.[3] From there, he wrote to the Emperor. His letters were in another's hand, possibly his adjutant Johann Beck. Below the words his signature skitters shakily around the bottom of the page. Sulz could barely hold a pen. He had led a regiment to Milan in the service of His Majesty in Spain, he said, but unfortunately with "bad satisfaction": The expedition had not been economically rewarding for him.[4] If so, this would have been despite the grifting: A report sent to Gian Paolo Mazza dated July 18, 1626 specified that when Milanese authorities made a final inspection it turned out Sulz had been given 40,000 scudi more than necessary for his men's wages.[5]

After his people were dismissed, Sulz heard more were being enrolled for the suppression of the same rebels who had begun the unrest in Bohemia, under "His Majesty the Duke of Friedland" (sic).[6] Sulz

---

[1] The quartering agreement stipulated March 29 to the beginning of May but they were still there on June 8. GLA Best. 98 Nr. 1262, *Kloster Salem: Einquartierung des Fußvolks des Obersten Grafen von Sulz*.
[2] AST Archivio Solo Busca, Serbelloni, Box 47. Letter from Juan de Prado Verde, 21 Aug 1626. Letter from Don Gonzales de Còrdova, July 29, 1626.
[3] SHStADr 10024 9235/4, *Entreffende das Sulzische Regiment Zu Fuß, Mansfeldischen 1627*, 9. Letter from unknown writer to Ferdinand II.
[4] SHStADr 10024 9235/4, 10r. Letter from Alwig von Sulz to Ferdinand II, September 26, 1627.
[5] "... ne si lascia di dire, che nella remata de Conti fatta del primo Reggimento del Conte de Suls si trova esso haver ricosso quaranta mile Scuti piu di quello importino de sue paghe conforme alle dette gride et ordini." Salomoni, *Memorie storico-diplomatiche degli ambasciatori*, 292.
[6] SHStADr 10024 9235/4, 10r.

accepted that the war was against an illegitimate rebellion, so he decided "along with other cavaliers, to set down and add my body, my goods, and my blood against the same enemy again."[7] Like Mansfeld, Sulz was forced to dismiss his previous regiment without paying them or settling his accounts. They still owed him 1,000 gulden for their weapons. When he raised the new regiment, he footed the bill himself. Then he appointed the captains and officers "so that I could bring it complete and onto its feet in the good springtime." The regiment went out to Wissembourg in April 1627: It was "happy and strong" then.[8]

Wissembourg did not give them quarters or lodging. This "pulled some of the newly enlisted soldiers lamentably into exile" (they deserted). To his shame some of them "sought their opportunities elsewhere" (they enlisted with other commanders).[9] The Imperial *Kriegscommissarius* Wolf Rudolf von Ossa zu Dehla assigned them mustering places: Four companies and their staffs were supposed to live among the Imperial knights of lower Alsace; five in Strasbourg, thirty-eight miles south of Wissembourg; and Sulz and his own company in the County of Hanau, a hundred miles northeast. From Alsace to Hanau, the future regiment was spread out over more than 150 miles. There was no way Hanau could support those people but, since Wissembourg rejected them, there was little Sulz could do.[10] Once Sulz got to Hanau he made the mistake of selling the Count of Hanau a *salva guardia*.[11] The count immediately used this letter of safe conduct to demand Sulz move the soldiers out of his territory, since other regiments had traveled through in 1621 and 1622, the land was "quite empty, without peasants," and Wallenstein was demanding 6,000 gulden a week.[12] Since Sulz got no order to leave, either from the Emperor or from Wallenstein, he stayed there.

Then something happened to him. His soldiers started walking off. According to Sulz's secretary, it was only through Sulz's personal financial intervention that another thousand did not leave.[13] Sulz "begged and

---

[7] SHStADr 10024 9235/4, 10r.
[8] SHStADr 10024 9235/4, 10v. Letter from Alwig von Sulz to Ferdinand II, September 26, 1627.
[9] SHStADr 10024 9235/4, 10v.
[10] SHStADr 10024 9235/4, 20v. Letter from Alwig von Sulz to unknown recipient, October 30, 1627.
[11] SHStADr 10024 9235/4, 11r. Letter from Alwig von Sulz to Ferdinand II, September 26, 1627.
[12] SHStADr 10024 9235/4, 3r–3v. Letter from Count of Hanau to Albrecht von Wallenstein, August 22, 1627.
[13] SHStADr 10024 9235/4, 12r–12v. Letter from Sulz's secretary Jacob Brizzer to Wolf von Mansfeld, undated.

cried" to the Emperor to force Hanau and Strasbourg to pay him and his regiment, "me and mine."[14] He said he had raised one regiment for service in Italy and another on the Rhine; he remembered when the second was "happy and strong." Sulz summed up his life, his efforts, and his obligations, and said he wanted his soldiers to be paid "so they can be content with me."[15]

On October 6, 1627, Wallenstein heard Alwig von Sulz was dead. "Now I have wanted to offer his vacated regiment to you," he jotted to Mansfeld later the same day.[16] Mansfeld was still in Prague. He got the news on the tenth. "We would have well seen, we would have liked it," he wrote emolliently to Sulz's Lieutenant Colonel the next day, "if God the almighty could have led this young man to a longer life, and longer in His Imperial Majesty's service, but because it fell otherwise to him, we must submit ourselves to His gracious will."[17] Mansfeld took command of Sulz's regiment.

But letters from Alwig von Sulz appear again on October 27 and 30, 1627. His signature is still shaky, pale as new beer, but Sulz was alive. He got a letter on October 26, delivered by Mansfeld's cavalry captain Krakow, informing him Mansfeld had been nominated as a general over the people in the Empire. Krakow himself may have been promoted after he got the letter from his friend the deserter in 1625. Sulz wished him much dignity, much luck, every prosperity of body and soul, and a victorious hand against the Estates who were rebellious against the Emperor. "I will work hard for you," he said.[18] But he took little part in the activity teeming around him: The ultimate authority over Sulz's regiment was still Wolf von Mansfeld.[19] Mansfeld left Prague and went to Schluckenau again; he had only taken the job against his will.[20] *Kriegscommissarius* Ossa headed west to handle things in person.[21]

---

[14] SHStADr 10024 9235/4, 11r. Letter from Alwig von Sulz to Ferdinand II, September 26, 1627.
[15] SHStADr 10024 9235/4, 10r. Letter from Alwig von Sulz to Ferdinand II, September 26, 1627.
[16] SHStADr 10024 9235/4, 7r. Letter from Albrecht von Wallenstein to Wolf von Mansfeld, October 6, 1627.
[17] SHStADr 10024 9235/4, 8r–8v. Letter from Wolf von Mansfeld to Lieutenant Colonel Johann Beck, October 1/11, 1627.
[18] SHStADr 10024 9235/4, 37r–38r. Letters from Alwig von Sulz to Wolf von Mansfeld, October 30, 1627 and October 27, 1627.
[19] SHStADr 10024 9235/4, 17r. Letter from Ferdinand II to Wolf Rudolf von Ossa zu Dehla, October 23, 1627.
[20] SHStADr 10024 9235/4, 86r–86v. Letter from Wolf von Mansfeld to Ferdinand II, December 1, 1627.
[21] SHStADr 10024 9235/4, 42v. Letter from Wolf Rudolf von Ossa zu Dehla to Wolf von Mansfeld, November 13/23, 1627.

Conclusion

Almost nobody in the Mansfeld Regiment let alone its high command had mentioned the religion of individual soldiers or civilians, but Wolf Rudolf von Ossa zu Dehla knew every city, town, and village near the Sulz Regiment and kept a list of their confessional affiliations in his head so he could punish the Protestants by directing soldiers toward them. "The Herrschaft of Barr ... has that place because this city was ... with the horrible *Union*," the Protestant Union, and therefore must quarter troops.

I see Württemberg and Rappolstein [Ribeaupierre], as well as Fürstenberg, as real servants of the Catholic League, [but] they need to take the People because they will not have more than three villages, which they will be able to do, especially Colmar, Schlettstadt [Sélestat], Kaysersburg, Turckheim, and Münster im Gregoriental, since they have suffered nothing at all in this war. They have set themselves hard against His Highness my gracious lord.[22]

He listed each polity in the region down to the villages and marked the religion for each.[23] As a Commissioner of War, Ossa was responsible for directing the allocation of quarters. He must have had either a written map or a phenomenal memory of a time when he walked that ground himself, because his knowledge of the region around Alsace was so granular that he made sure the villages to which he assigned the Sulz People were at most three miles from one another, more usually one or two.[24]

Yet the date for the Sulz Regiment's mustering-in kept getting pushed back.[25] They were originally supposed to have been mustered in in June. On November 13, Ossa assumed they would muster in on the twentieth. Then he would see "what sort of people [the Sulz Regiment] was."[26] On November 29, he thought they would be mustered in on December 21.[27] This was well into the off-season. By this point remnants of the Mansfeld Regiment were being mentioned too: The plan may have been to muster them in with the Sulz people. Ossa knew about them since at least early November, when he noted "Wissembourg is Lutheran, has

---

[22] SHStADr 10024 9235/4, 44v. Letter from Wolf Rudolf von Ossa zu Dehla to Wolf von Mansfeld, November 12, 1627.
[23] SHStADr 10024 9235/4, 57r–58r. Undated copy of report with no author given, probably Wolf Rudolf von Ossa zu Dehla, probably early November.
[24] SHStADr 10024 9235/4, 69r. Letter from Wolf Rudolf von Ossa zu Dehla to Wolf von Mansfeld, November 19/29, 1627.
[25] This happened frequently: Whether it was deliberate or not, the locals experienced it as a form of tax increase. Bagi, "Life of Soldiers," 398.
[26] SHStADr 10024 9235/4, 42v. Letter from Wolf Rudolf von Ossa zu Dehla to Wolf von Mansfeld, November 13/23, 1627.
[27] SHStADr 10024 9235/4, 69v. Letter to Wolf Mansfeld from Wolf Rudolf von Ossa zu Dehla, November 19/29, 1627.

about 800 citizens and a little village, was in the [Catholic] League, and Mansfeld also has a company there [*auch hatt Mannsveldt ein Compagni mitterhalten*]. Landau is Lutheran, has about 1,000 citizens and 2 villages, was also in the Union, and paid Mansfeld for one company of infantry [*ein Fendel Knecht*]."[28] Leopold of Further Austria wrote that, except for Colmar and Sélestat, his territories on the Rhine were devastated by "the Mansfeld Regiment's onslaught" and "forced payment with threats of fire;" they were "entirely ruined" right up to the border with Lorraine.[29] This may mean that Mansfeld's Life Company of Horse was still extant. It is also possible that some of Mansfeld's cavalry made it out of Italy by late November, or the new cavalry regiment he possessed by early spring 1628 was already assembling.

After Wolf Rudolf von Ossa saw Sulz's people, he wrote "It would be a shame for such a beautiful regiment to scatter for lack of support, or be compelled to live at home, which they would have to do only with great outrages and destruction of the land."[30] The Mansfelders saw both horrible things and visual splendor, but they did not use the word "beautiful" often: For white on a flag or gold and silver, and a fighting regiment. This was how officers described regiments of which they approved. I do not expect the reader to approve of the war people. But I hope he or she can think about what *Kriegscommissarius* Ossa might have seen when he sized Sulz's people up that late November day, bright flags snapping in the waning sun.

The Mansfeld Regiment's social organization and material contexts shaped the way it was formed, the path it took from Dresden to Lombardy, and the way it disintegrated. I have tried to avoid demonizing or romanticizing these soldiers and women, but instead to analyze their social lives from the evidence I could track. Some assumptions about early seventeenth-century military life may have to be reexamined in the light of their interactions with one another and local Italian communities, and the statistical data I obtained for the Saxon army, especially in the first third of the Thirty Years War.

The concepts of the fiscal-military state and the military revolution are intertwined. Nascent states attempted to extract resources and provision

---

[28] SHStADr 10024 9235/4, 57v. Undated copy of report with no author given, probably Wolf Rudolf von Ossa zu Dehla, probably early November.
[29] SHStADr 10024 9235/4, 81r. Letter from Leopold of Further Austria to Ferdinand II, November 16, 1627.
[30] "Es were schad, dz ein solch schön Regiment, Auß mangel underhalt, solte Zer lauffen, oder daheim gennötigt warden, daß sie mit großen *exorbidanzien*, undt Landts verderben, leben mußten." SHStADr 10024 9235/4, 70r, Letter to Mansfeld from Wolf Rudolf von Ossa zu Dehla, November 19/29, 1627.

armies through cooperation with local authorities or elites. The growth of the fiscal-military state took place within the knitting-together of states in other contexts and is not separate from this broader trend. This development was slow, halting, and not teleological. But whether state agents succeeded in carrying out their aims or not, the belief that the state should underwrite these endeavors at all already represents a change in kind in the idea of the state.[31]

But the Mansfeld Regiment was deeply shaped not only by these developments in military finance, but also by its weaknesses: This regiment was upheld by a multitude of relationships, but its margin of error was slim. Although the most important single cause of this regiment's collapse was an accident, the conditions for this accident had been laid by structural weakness.

Moreover, I did not see the changes in behavior, social interaction, and practice among common soldiers in this regiment that some historians believe accompanied these economic and political developments. When the officers and soldiers of the Mansfeld Regiment describe their lives, drill is not mentioned. Other sources describe experienced soldiers training new recruits on an informal basis. The only Justus Lipsius in this book is not the author of famous neo-Stoic works that enjoined his readers to discipline themselves, but Justus Wilhelmus Lipsius, pikeman from Erfurt, eventual lieutenant in the Mansfeld Regiment.[32] The most strikingly modern emotional development in this account is not an increase of social disciplining within the army, but Victoria Guarde's ungoverned pursuit of happiness, which led to her death. Considering the relatively small proportion of officers and the profound challenges of conducting mobile operations over huge distances without modern communications technology, it seems likely that mercenaries were motivated by their own values and the belief they could get something out of soldiering, as well as or more than by pressure from above.

The common soldiers in the Mansfeld Regiment were assertive, and energy and dash were part of their idea of themselves. They used the words *wacker*, valiant and alert, or *frisch*, brisk, to compliment one another. Objects that were lightweight, shining, lofting, or mobile like a flag or a feather in your cap expressed the zip and dash a soldier should display. Most soldiers and their women could not afford luxuries: Wolfgang Winckelmann embezzled with diligence but owned three pairs of breeches and held a party with his officers sitting on his bed. For those who could afford it, conspicuous consumption was a manifestation of a

---

[31] Ongaro, *Peasants and Soldiers*, 207–208.
[32] Oestrich, *Neostoicism and the Early Modern State*.

soldier's inner fire. So was mouthing off to anyone who tried to tell you what to do.

The Mansfeld Regiment was in being during the mid-1620s, and it would be interesting to compare these findings to a similarly well-documented unit from the 1630s or 1640s. This would allow a researcher to test the belief that the war was more savage in its later years empirically. The Saxon army during the 1640s was small, cavalry-heavy, supplied itself almost fully off the land, and operated in the eastern part of central Europe. Its members interpenetrated frequently with their Swedish enemies. The daily social interactions of the men and women in an army like this might have been very different from the Mansfelders, who spent two years in a densely populated area that was culturally, linguistically, and religiously foreign to many of them. On the other hand, I believe my observation that early modern armies were made up of social networks of families and friends, and that these men and women remained in them for intangible reasons as well as tangible ones, will turn out to hold true throughout the war.

Mercenaries may have been uprooted by circumstance, but the mercenaries I observed were not rootless. The Saxon army in the 1620s was a thick network of more or less long-term soldiers surrounded by looser crowds of people who came and went. Soldiers were united by ties of blood and friendship which crisscrossed individual companies as well as extending from one company to another. Where records are dense enough, individual soldiers can be traced over multiple years, or different members of the same family can be traced through the army over multiple generations. Even in the war's later years the men of the Metzsch family provided cavalrymen to Electoral Saxony or to Sweden. The odds were slim, but the early seventeenth-century military community offered the low-born a chance to attain money, position, and respect.

The experience of these mercenaries is one facet of the human condition in the early seventeenth century. The fragility coexisted with the swagger. After Jonas Eckert was wounded in his duel with Valentin von Treutler, he lingered for four days. When he was about to die, someone called von Treutler into Eckert's quarters. Von Treutler ordered a small crowd of other officers and soldiers from their company to come too, most from the Saxon town of Döbeln. He bent over the dying man's bed: "How now?" he said. "What are you doing?" Eckert looked up. "I'm thinking hard about getting better," he said: *er heffte der beßerungk*. "If you had not hit that peasant, this calamity would not have broken out," said von Treutler. Eckert was "stunned" at first, then agreed. The common soldier Barthel Grinzelman asked Eckert if he forgave the corporal but Eckert was so weak the witnesses could barely hear him. They clasped hands, and Eckert died.[33] To stare the superior officer who mortally wounded you in the eye and tell him a joke about your own death takes some nerve.

We see the wear and tear of military operations day to day not only in the efforts of the big decision-makers like Italian politicians or financiers but also in the lives of the Mansfelders. The common soldiers killed one another over real or imagined slights; the officers sued. The officers mistreated the men under their command and the men fought back. A lot of them were in it for the money or the license to hurt others. Everyone drank too much. Many, like Wolf Heinrich von Dransdorf's relatives by marriage, or Wolfgang Winckelmann himself, were criminals. They were capable of selflessness and great loyalty. On the way up through Switzerland and southern Germany, a desperate dedication remained: The Mansfelders who deserted did so according to the social and legal norms they knew. Even in the sordid conditions outside Frankfurt am Main, some soldiers never left.

On November 27, 1627, Alwig von Sulz wrote to the Emperor in his own hand. His writing was dark and steady: His hand no longer shook. He was taking an active role in his regiment's affairs again. The mustering place was in Strasbourg, where Ossa had led seven of Sulz's companies himself, and in the nearby Duchy of Barr.[34] As he prepared to head out again in his Emperor's service, Sulz wrote that Barr was a terrible place for his people to be quartered in: Not only did it have few villages, but "partly through hail and a bad year, partly through careless quartering and troop movements," those villages were "entirely destroyed, chewed up [ausgemegelt], and impoverished, so most of the subjects have left house and home, their nourishment, much less what a soldier needs, little of the maintenance of life" [sic].[35] Alwig von Sulz was experienced, having led an army through the Lower Engadine in August 1622.[36] He was conscious of his duty and good to his people, he tried his best to provide for them from what he thought would be his

---

[33] SHStADr 10024 9119/38, 171–177.
[34] SHStADr 10024 9235/4, 90r. Letter from Alwig von Sulz to Ferdinand II, November 27, 1627.
[35] SHStADr 10024 9235/4, 90r–90v. Letter from Alwig von Sulz to Ferdinand II, November 27, 1627.
[36] Friedrich Pieth, "Der Dreibündengeneral Rudolf v. Salis und ein österreichischer Bericht über den Einfall des Grafen Alwig v. Sulz in Graubünder 1622," in *Bündnerisches Monatsblatt: Zeitschrift für bündnerische Geschichte, Landes- und Volkskunde* 4 (1915), 113–115, 114; Friedrich Pieth, "Der Dreibündengeneral Rudolf v. Salis und ein österreichischer Bericht über den Einfall des Grafen Alwig v. Sulz in Graubünder 1622: Fortsetzung und Schluß," in *Bündnerisches Monatsblatt: Zeitschrift für bündnerische Geschichte, Landes- und Volkskunde* 5 (1915), 158.

deathbed, and when he complained about the devastation around him it was without a hint of guilt, or consciousness that he might have had something to do with it. Before his regiment mustered in, he hoped the Emperor would send him money and do what was necessary "for the conservation of this my fresh and brave regiment [*frisch und dapfer*], reported without fame."[37]

On December 1, 1627, Wolf von Mansfeld wrote to Sulz from his estate in Schluckenau: He just heard Ossa had mustered the Sulz Regiment.[38] Former members of Mansfeld's old regiment may have been among them. They would take the field in spring.

---

[37] SHStADr 10024 9235/4, 91r. Letter from Alwig von Sulz to Ferdinand II, November 27, 1627.
[38] SHStADr 10024 9235/4, 71r. Letter from Wolf von Mansfeld to Alwig von Sulz, December 1, 1627.

Bibliography

Primary Sources: Archival

AS-AL	Archivio di Stato Alessandria
AS-Cr	Archivio di Stato Cremona (antico archivio del Comune di Cremona)
AS-M	Archivio di Stato Mantova
ASDCC	Archivio Storico Diocesano di Casale Montferrato
ASDCr	Archivio Storico Diocesano di Cremona
ASGBu	Archivio Storico della chiesa collegiata de San Giovanni Battista in Busto Arsizio
ASMBu	Archivio Storico della chiesa San Michele in Busto Arsizio
ASML	Archivio Storico della chiesa San Magno in Legnano
AST	Archivio Storico Civico e Biblioteca La Trivulziana, Milan
CSA	Chiesa de Sant'Agatha, Pontestura
GLA	Landesarchiv Baden-Württemberg, Generallandesarchiv Karlsruhe
HStAD	Hessisches Staatsarchiv Darmstadt
SHStADr	Sächsisches Hauptstaatsarchiv Dresden, primarily documents from 10024, the Geheimer Rat (Geheimes Archiv) 11237, the Geheimes Kriegsratskollegium
StAWu	Staatsarchiv Würzburg
StadtA Ulm	Stadtarchiv Ulm
UCLA Library Special Collections MS *170/355	Der Anndre Thaill Nurembergische Cronica

In particular, the Mansfeld Regiment legal books:

Book 1   SHStADr 10024 9119/38, *Protocoll aller gerichtlichen sachen, so sich unter des herrn Wolfgang Graf von Mansfeld ... Regiment Zu Fuß ereignet und vorgegangen, Mit sonderne fleiß aufgezeichnet und beschrieben, durch mich: Mattheum Steinern, Regiments Schultheissenn und Secretarien uber das Regiment. Pars I 1625–1626.*

Book 2   SHStADr 10024 9739/6, *Protocoll aller gerichtlichen sachen, so sich unter des herrn Wolfgang Graf von Mansfeld ... Regiment Zu Fuß ereignet und vorgegangen, Mit sonderne fleiß aufgezeichnet und beschrieben, durch mich:*

Mattheum Steinern, Regiments Schultheissenn und Secretarien uber das Regiment. Pars II.

Book 3   SHStADr 10024 9539/5, *Protocoll aller gerichtlichen sachen, so sich unter des herrn Wolfgang Graf von Mansfeld ... Regiment Zu Pferd ereignet und vorgegangen, Mit sonderin fleiß aufgezeichnet und beschrieben, durch mich: Mattheum Steinern, Regiments Schultheissen solches Regiments. Pars I.*

Primary Sources: Published

Anonymous. "Kriegstagebücher aus dem ligistischen Hauptquartier 1620," *Abhandlungen des Phil.-Hist. Klasse der Bayerischen Akademie der Wissenschaften* 23 (1906), 77–210.

Bremio, Gioanni Domenico. *Cronaca monferrina (1613–1661) di Gioanni Domenico Bremio speciaro di Casale Monferrato*, ed. Giuseppe Giorcelli. Alessandria: Societa poligrafica, 1911.

Bresciani, Giuseppe. *Memorie delle cose occorse me vivente nella città di Cremona quivi descritte d'anno in anno*, ed. Emanuela Zanesi. Cremona: Lions Club, 2019.

Carpzov, Johann Benedict. *Analecta fastorum Zittaviensium, oder historischer Schauplatz der löblichen alten Sechs-Stadt des Marggraffthums Ober-Lausitz Zittau*. Leipzig: Johann Jacob Schöps, 1716.

von Chemnitz, Bogislav Philip. *Königlich Schwedischen in Teutschland geführten Krieges*. Original 1644. Stockholm: George Rethen, 1855.

Dilich, Wilhelm. *Geograph. und Histor. Kriegsbuch / darin die Alte und Neue Militia eigentlich beschrieben un alle Krigßneulinge / Bau und Buchsenmeistern / zu nutz und guter anleitug in Druck geben und verfertigt*. Casel: Wilhelm Wessel, 1607.

von Drandorff, August Adolf. "Augenschein und Positur Derer Feuer-Wercks Stücken/ Welche Der ... Churfürst zu Sachsen Hertzog Johann Georg der Andere in Gegenwart ... Hertzogen Augusti zu Sachßen ... Hertzogen Mauritii zu Sachßen ... Hertzogen Johann Adolphen/ zu Holstein ... jenseit der Pleiße bey der Vestung Pleißenburgk den 8. Julii Anno 1667. ... angeordnet An statt Einer Feuerwercks-Probe...abgeleget und geborsamst verrichtet worden durch Augustum Adolphum von Drandorff/ der Zeit bestalten Fähndrich bey der Vestung Pleißenburgk von Leipzigk," 1667.

von Fleming, Johann Friedrich. *Der vollkommene teutsche Soldat, welcher die gantze Kriegs-Wissenschafft, insonderheit was bey der Infanterie vorkommt, ordentlich und deutlich vorträgt, und in sechs besondern Theilen die einem Soldaten nöthige Vorbereitungs-Wissenschafften, Künste und Exercitia, die Chargen und Verrichtungen aller Kriegs-Bedienten, von dem Mousquetier an bis auf den General; ... nebst einem Anhange von gelehrten Soldaten, Adel und Ritter-Stande, von Duellen, Turnier- und Ritter-Spielen, auch Ritter-Orden ec...* Leipzig: Martini, 1726.

Fossati, Giovanni Francesco. *Memorie historiche de delle guerre d'Italia del secolo presente*. Milan: Filippo Ghisolfi, 1639.

Friese, Friedrich. "Vom Magdeburgischen Unglück, vom Oberstadtschreiber Daniel Friese," in K. Lohmann, ed., *Die Zerstörung Magdeburgs von Otto*

Bibliography

Guericke und andere denkwürdigkeiten aus dem Dreissigjährigen Kriege. Berlin: Gutenberg Verlag, 1913.

von Fritsch, Augustin. *Tagebuch des Augustin von Fritsch: Taten und Schicksal im Dreißigjährigen Krieg. Obrist und Kommandant von Parkstein und der Stadt Weiden*, ed. Hans J. Rudnik. Merching: Forum Verlag, 2012.

Ghilini, Girolamo. *Annali di Alessandria, overo Le Cose Accadvte in esta Città: Nel suo, el Circonvincino Territorio dall'Anno dell'Origine Sua Sino al M.DC.LIX*. Milan: Gioseffo Marelli, 1666.

Grimm, Jacob and Wilhelm Grimm. *Deutsches Wörterbuch von Jacob Grimm und Wilhelm Grimm*. Trier center for Digital Humanities/Kompetenzzentrum für elektronische Erschließungs-und Publikationsverfahren in den Geisteswissenschaften an der Universität Trier 1998–2011, available at: http://woerterbuchnetz.de/cgi-bin/WBNetz/wbgui_py?sigle=DWB, last accessed January 13, 2024.

Hagendorf, Peter. *Ein Söldnerleben im Dreißigjährigen Krieg: Eine Quelle zur Sozialgeschichte*, ed. Jan Peters. Berlin: Akademie Verlag, 1993.

Hartmann, Johann Ludwig. *Neue Teuffels-Stucklein: Passauer-Kunst, Vest-machen, Schies- und Buchsen-Kunst, Feuer-loschung, Granaten- und Kugel-dampffen, Unsichtbar machen, Noth-Hembd, Waffen-Salb, Aus-seegnen etc. Nach Ihrer Mannigfaltigkeit, Abscheuligkeit, und Abstellungs-Nothwedigkeit betrachtet, Und Zu praeservirung der Jugend bey jetzigen Krieges-Laufften heraus gegeben*. Frankfurt: Zunner, 1678.

Hugo, Herman. *Obsidio Bredana armis Philippi IIII auspiciis Isabellae ductu Ambr. Spinolae perfecta*. Antwerp: Ex Officina Plantiniana, 1626.

trans. Sir Henry Gage, *The Siege of Breda by the Armes of Philip, 1627, English Recusant Literature 1558–1640*, vol. 261, ed. D. M. Rogers. London: Scolar Press Ltd., nd.

Kirchhof, Hans Wilhelm. *Militaris Disciplina, Kriegs Regiments Historische und außführliche Beschreibung: Wie / und was massen / solches bey unsern löblichen Vorfahren / und der alten Mannlichen Teutschen Nation vorzeiten / innsonderheit aber bey den Großmächtigsten Keysern / Maximiliano I und Carolo V und folgendes in ublichem Gebrauch gehalten / auch nach und nach verbessert worden: in drey underschiedliche Disemß oder Bücher abgetheilet*. Frankfurt: Joachim Brathering, 1602.

van den Leene, Joseph. *Le theatre de la noblesse du Brabant, representant les erections des terres, seigneuries, & noms des personnes, & des familles titrées, les creations des chevaleries, & octroys des marques d'honneurs & de noblesse: Accordez par les princes souverains ducs de Brabant, jusques au roy Philippe v. a present regnant. Divisé en trois parties, enrichies des genealogies, alliances, quartiers, epitaphes, & d'autres recherches anciennes & modernes*. Liege: J. F. Broncaert, 1705.

Pomey, François. *Le Grand Dictionnaire Royal*. Cologne and Frankfurt: Jean Melchior Bencard, 1709.

von Pranckh, Maria Cordula. "Gedenkbuch der Frau Maria Cordula, Freiin von Pranck, verwitwete Hacke, geb. Radhaupt, 1595–1700 (1707)," *Steiermärkische Geschichtsblätter* 2.1 (1881), 9–29.

Rasini, Antonio. "Alloggi militari, carestia, e peste nelle due notai galleratsi 1," *Rassegna Gallarattese di Storia e d'Artve* XXXI.4(118) (1972), 131–140.

Salomoni, Angiolo. *Memorie storico-diplomatiche degli ambasciatori, incaritati d'affari, corrispondenti, e delegati, che la città di Milano inviò a diversi suoi principi dal 1500 al 1796*. Milan: Pulini al Bocchetto, 1806, 298–305.

Tadino, Alessandro. *Raguaglio dell'origine et giornali successi della gran peste contagiosa, venefica, & malefica seguita nella Città di Milano, & suo Ducato dall'anno 1629. sino all'anno 1632.* Milan: Filippo Ghisolti, 1648.

von Trouptzen, Lorenz. *Kriegs Kunst Nach Königlicher Schwedischer Manier Eine Compagny zu richten / in Regiment / Zug: und Schlacht-Ordnungen zu bringen / Zum Ernst anzuführen / zu gebrauchen / und in esse würcklich / zu unterhalten.* Frankfurt: Mattheus Merian, 1633.

Turner, James. *Pallas Armata, Military essayes of the ancient Grecian, Roman, and modern art of war vvritten in the years 1670 and 1671.* London: Richard Chiswell, 1683.

von Wallhausen, Johann Jacobi. *Defensio Patriae oder Landrettung. Darinnen gezeigt wird 1) Wie alle und jede in der werthen Christenheit Potentaten, Regenten, Stätte und Communen ihre und der ihrigen Unterthanen Rettung und Schützung anstellen sollen. 2) Der Modus belligerande, viel hundert Jahre bißher gefählet.* Frankfurt: Gedruckt im Verlag / Daniel und David Aubrij und Clement Schleichen, 1621.

Kriegskunst zu Fuß, zu hochnöthigstem Nutzen und Besten nicht allein allen ankommenden Soldaten, sondern auch in Abrichtung eines gemeinen Landvolcks und Ausschuß in Fürstenthümern und Stätte. Oppenheim: Heironymus Gallero, 1615.

Manuale Militaire, oder Kriegs-Manual / Darinnen I, Die Fürnembste Heuteges Tages Edle Haupt Kriegß Kunste zu Landt. II, Der Griechen Lacadaemoniern / und Romanen Kriegß Disciplinen kürtzest aus dem Frantzoischen / mit schönen Kupfferstücken hergegeben werden / gemehret und gebessert. III, Ein Kriegß Nomenclatur. Frankfurt: Paul Jacobi, 1617.

Zedler, Johann Heinrich, ed. *Grosses vollständiges Universal Lexicon Aller Wissenschafften und Künste, Welche bißhero durch menschlichen Verstand und Witz erfunden und verbesert worden.* Halle/Leipzig: Johann Heinrich Zedler, 1735.

Secondary Sources

Ailes, Mary. *Courage and Grief: Women and Sweden's Thirty Years War.* Lincoln: University of Nebraska Press, 2018.

Ambüh, Rémy. *Prisoners of War in the Hundred Years War: Ransom Culture in the Late Middle Ages.* Cambridge: Cambridge University Press, 2013.

Anderson, M. S. *War and Society in Europe of the Old Regime, 1618–1780.* Leicester: Leicester University Press, 1988.

Bagi, Zoltán Péter. "The Life of Soldiers during the Long Turkish War (1593–1606)," *The Hungarian Historical Review* 4.2 (2015), 384–417.

Bairoch, Paul, Jean Batou and Pierre Chevre. *La population des villes européennes de 800 à 1850.* Geneva: Center of International Economic History, 1988.

Banks, Stephen. *A Polite Exchange of Bullets: The Duel and the English Gentleman, 1750–1850.* Suffolk: Boydell and Brewer, 2010.

Barr, Julian. *Tertullian and the Unborn Child: Christian and Pagan Attitudes in Historical Perspective.* New York: Routledge, 2017.

Baumann, Reinhard. "Protest und Verweigerung in der Zeit der klassischen Söldnerheere," in Ulrich Bröckling and Michael Sikora, eds., *Armeen und ihre Deserteure. Vernachlässigte Kapitel einer Militärgeschichte der Neuzeit*. Göttingen: Vandenhoeck und Ruprecht, 1998, 16–49.

Bean, Richard. "War and the Birth of the Nation State," *Journal of Economic History* 33 (1973), 203–221.

Berkovich, Ilya. *Motivation in War: The Experience of Common Soldiers in Old-Regime Europe*. Cambridge: Cambridge University Press, 2017.

Bertolli, Franco and Umberto Colombo. *La Peste del 1630 a Busto Arsizio: Riedizione commentata della "Storia" di Giovanni Battista Lupi*. Busto Arsizio: Bramante Editrice, 1990.

Black, Christopher. *Early Modern Italy: A Social History*. London: Routledge, 2001.

Blanning, T. C. W. *The Culture of Power and the Power of Culture: Old Regime Europe 1660–1789*. Oxford: Oxford University Press, 2002.

Boehm, Christopher. *Hierarchy in the Forest: The Evolution of Egalitarian Behavior*. Cambridge, MA: Harvard University Press, 1999.

Bognetti, Giuseppe and Giuseppe de Luca. "From Taxation to Indebtedness: The Urban System of Milan during the Austrias' Domination (1535–1706)," in Michael Limberger and José Ignacio Andrés Ucendo, eds., *Taxation and Debt in the Early Modern City*. New York: Routledge, 2016, 13–28.

Brandenburgisches Landesamt für Denkmalpflege und Archäologisches Landesmuseum Brandenburg. *1636 – ihre letzte Schlacht: Leben im Dreißigjährigen Krieg*. Stuttgart: Konrad Theiss Verlag, 2012.

Braudel, Fernand and Frank Spooner. "Prices in Europe from 1450 to 1750," in E. E. Rich and C. H. Wilson, eds., *The Cambridge Economic History of Europe Vol 4, The Economy of Expanding Europe in the 16th and 17th Centuries*. Cambridge: Cambridge University Press, 1967, 378–486.

Brewer, John. "Microhistory and the Histories of Everyday Life," *Cultural and Social History* 7.1 (2010), 87–109.

The Sinews of Power: War and the English State, 1688–1783. London: Unwin Hyman, 1989.

Brück, Anton Philipp. "Anselm Casimir Wamboldt v. Umbstadt," in Historische Kommission bei der Bayerischen Akademie des Wissenschaften, ed., *Neue Deutsche Biographie*. Vol. 1. Berlin: Duncker & Humblot, 1953, 310.

"Georg Friedrich v. Greiffenclau zu Vollrads," in Historische Kommission bei der Bayerischen Akademie des Wissenschaften, ed., *Neue Deutsche Biographie*, Vol. 6. Berlin: Duncker & Humblot, 1964, 219.

Brumwell, Stephen. *Redcoats: The British Soldier and War in the Americas, 1755–1763*. Cambridge: Cambridge University Press, 2006.

Buchner, Thomas and Philip R. Hoffman-Rehnitz. "Irregular Economic Practices as a Topic of Modern (Urban) History: Problems and Possibilities," in Thomas Buchner and Philip R. Hoffmann-Rehnitz, eds., *Shadow Economies and Irregular Work in Urban Europe: 16th to Early 20th Centuries*. Münster: LIT Verlag, 2011, 3–36.

Buono, Alessandro. *Esercito, istituzioni, territorio: Alloggiamenti militari e "case herme" nello Stato de Milano (secoli XVI e XVII)*. Florence: Firenze University Press, 2009.

Burschel, Peter. "Himmelreich und Hölle: Ein Söldner, sein Tagebuch, und die Ordnung des Krieges," in Benigna von Krusenstjern and Hans Medick, eds., *Zwischen Alltag und Katastrophe: Der Dreißigjährige Krieg aus der Nähe.* Göttingen: Max-Planck-Institut für Geschichte, 1999, 181-194.

Söldner in Nordwestdeutschland des 16. und 17. Jahrhunderts. Göttingen: Vandenhoeck & Ruprecht, 1994.

Calabria, Antonio. *The Cost of Empire: The Finances of the Kingdom of Naples in the Time of Spanish Rule.* Cambridge: Cambridge University Press, 1991.

Carsten, F. L. *Princes and Parliaments in Germany from the Fifteenth to the Eighteenth Century.* Oxford: Oxford University Press, 1959.

Chagnon, Napoleon. *Yanomano: The Fierce People.* New York: Holt, Rinehart, and Winston, 1968.

Christman, Robert J. *Doctrinal Controversy and Lay Religiosity in Late Reformation Germany.* Leiden: Brill Publishers, 2011.

Cipolla, Carlo. *Mouvements monétaires dans l'Etat de Milan (1580-1700).* Paris: Librairie Armand Colin, 1952.

Cockburn, Cynthia. "The Continuum of Violence: A Gender Perspective on War and Peace," in Wenona Giles and Jennifer Hyndman, eds., *Sites of Violence: Gender and Conflict Zones.* Berkeley: University of California Press, 2004, 24-44.

Colombo, Emanuele. *Giochi di Luoghi: Il territorio lombardo dei Seicento.* Milan: FrancoAngeli, 2008.

Corvisier, Andre. *L'armée françise de la fin du XVIIe siècle au ministère de Choiseul: Le soldat.* Paris, Presses Universitaires de France, 1964.

Costa, Dora and Matthew Kahn. *Heroes and Cowards: The Social Face of War.* Princeton: Princeton University Press, 2008.

Cowdrey, H. E. J. "The Peace and the Truce of God in the Eleventh Century," *Past & Present* 46 (1970), 42-67.

Cramer, Kevin. *The Thirty Years War and German Memory in the Nineteenth Century.* Lincoln: University of Nebraska Press.

Crawford, Neta. *Accountability for Killing: Moral Responsibility for Collateral Damage in America's Post 9/11 Wars.* Oxford: Oxford University Press, 2013.

van Creveld, Martin. *Supplying War: Logistics from Wallenstein to Patton.* Cambridge: Cambridge University Press, 1977.

Croxton, Derek. "A Territorial Imperative? The Military Revolution, Strategy and Peacemaking in the Thirty Years War," *War in History* 5.3 (1998), 253-279.

D'Amico, Stefano. *Spanish Milan: A City within the Empire, 1535-1706.* London: Palgrave Macmillan, 2012.

Darby, Graham. *Spain in the Seventeenth Century.* London: Longman, 1995.

Dattero, Alessandra. "Towards a New Social Category: The Military," in Andrea Gamberini, ed., *A Companion to Late Medieval and Early Modern Milan: The Distinctive Features of an Italian State.* Leiden: Brill, 2015, 454-476.

Davis, Natalie Zemon. "The Rites of Violence: Religious Riot in Sixteenth-Century France," *Past & Present* 59 (1973), 51-91.

Delbrück, Hans. *The Dawn of Modern Warfare: History of the Art of War Vol IV.* Lincoln, NE: University of Nebraska Press, 1990.

Dermineur, Elise, ed. *Women and Credit in Pre-Industrial Europe*. Turnhout: Brepolis Publishers, 2018.

Dolan, Frances. *Dangerous Familiars: Representations of Domestic Crime in England, 1550–1700*. Cornell: Cornell University Press, 1994.

Marriage and Violence: The Early Modern Legacy. Philadelphia: University of Pennsylvania Press, 2008.

Döring, Eduard. *Handbuch der Münz-, Wechsel-, Mass- und Gewichtskunde*. Koblenz: J. Hölscher, 1854.

Douglas, R. M. "Neither Apathetic nor Empathetic: Investigating and Prosecuting the Rape of German Civilians by US Servicemen in 1945," *The Journal of Military History* 87 (2023), 404–437.

Downing, Brian. *The Military Revolution and Political Change: Origins of Democracy and Autocracy in Early Modern Europe*. Princeton: Princeton University Press, 1992.

Duffy, Christopher. *The Army of Maria Theresa: The Armed Forces of Imperial Austria, 1740–1780*. New York: Hippocrene Books, 1977.

Duffy, Michael, ed. *The Military Revolution and the State, 1500–1800*. Exeter: University of Exeter Press, 1980.

Duriesmith, David. *Masculinity and New War: The Gendered Dynamics of Contemporary Armed Conflict*. Abingdon: Routledge, 2017.

Eco, Umberto. *On Beauty: History of a Western Idea*. London: Martin Secker and Warburg, 2004.

Edelmayer, Friedrich. *Söldner und Pensionäre: Das Netzwerk Philipps II im Heiligen Römischen Reich*. Vienna: R. Oldenbourg Verlag, 2002.

El-Hage, Fadi. *Vendôme: La gloire ou l'imposture*. Paris: Belin, 2016.

Elliott, John H. *The Count-Duke of Olivares: The Statesman in an Age of Decline*. New Haven: Yale University Press, 1986.

Elsas, M. J. *Umriss einer Geschichte der Preise und Löhne in Deutschland*, Vol. 1. Leiden: A. W. Sijthoff, 1936.

Enenkel, Karl A. E. and Anita Traninger. "Introduction: Discourses of Anger in the Early Modern Period," in Karl A. E. Enenkel and Anita Traninger, eds., *Discourses of Anger in the Early Modern Period*. Leiden: Brill, 2015, 1–15.

Ernstberger, Anton. "Hans de Witte: Finanzmann Wallensteins," *Vierteljahrschrift für Sozial- und Wirtschaftsgeschichte* Special Edition 38 (1954).

Ertman, Thomas. *Birth of the Leviathan: Building States and Regimes in Medieval and Early Modern Europe*. Cambridge: Cambridge University Press, 1997.

Fahr, J. and P. Pacak. "Das schwedische Feldlager Latdorf," in Susanne Friederich and Harald Meller, eds., *Archäologie am Kalkteich 22 in Latdorf. Die Chemie stimmt! Arch. Sachsen-Anhalt*. Halle: Landesamt für Denkmalpflege und Archäologie Sachsen-Anhalt, 2008, 105–114.

Fahr, J., P. Pacak, Nicole Nicklisch, A. Grothe, H. J. Döhle and S. Friederich. "Herbst 1644 – Das schwedische Feldlager bei Latdorf," in Harald Meller and M. Schefzik, eds., *Krieg. Eine Archäologische Spurensuche*. Halle: Theiss Verlag, 2015, 433–440.

Fallon, James A. "Scottish Mercenaries in the Service of Denmark and Sweden, 1626–1632." PhD dissertation, University of Glasgow, 1972.

Färber, Silvio. "Bündner Wirren," *Historisches Lexicon der Schweiz/Dictionaire Historique de la Suisse/Dizionario Storico della Svizzera*. Basel: Schwabe Verlag, 2001.
Farge, Arlette. *The Allure of the Archives*. New Haven: Yale University Press, 2013.
Fragile Lives: Violence, Power, and Solidarity in Eighteenth-Century Paris. Cambridge, MA: Harvard University Press, 1993.
Farge, Arlette and Michael Foucault. *Disorderly Families: Infamous Letters from the Bastille Archives*. Minneapolis: University of Minnesota Press, 2016.
Feld, M. D. "Middle Class Society and the Rise of Military Professionalism: The Dutch Army 1589–1609," *Armed Forces and Society* 1.4 (1975), 419–423.
Finer, Samuel. "State and Nation-building in Europe: The Role of the Military," in Charles Tilly, ed., *The Formation of National States in Western Europe*. Princeton: Princeton University Press, 1975, 84–163.
Finucane, Jane. "Before the Storm: Civilians under Siege during the Thirty Years War," in Alex Dowdall and John Horne, eds., *Civilians under Siege from Sarajevo to Troy*. London: Palgrave Macmillan, 2017, 137–162.
Fischer, David Hackett. *The Great Wave: Price Revolutions and the Rhythm of History*. Oxford: Oxford University Press, 1996.
Fissel, Mark Charles. "Review of Europe's Tragedy," *Journal of World History* 22.4 (2011), 873–877.
Fontaine, Laurence. *The Moral Economy: Poverty, Credit, and Trust in Early Modern Europe*. Cambridge: Cambridge University Press, 2014.
Fosi, Irene, trans. Giuseppe Bruno-Chomin, *Inquisition, Conversion, and Foreigners in Baroque Rome*. Leiden: Brill, 2011.
Frevert, Ute. *Men of Honor: A Social and Cultural History of the Duel*. London: Polity Press, 1995.
Frost, Robert. *The Northern Wars: War, State and Society in Northeastern Europe, 1558–1721*. London: Routledge, 2000.
Frühsorge, Gotthardt. "Die Begründung der 'väterlichen Gesellschaft' in der europäischen oeconomia christiana. Zur Rolle des Vaters in der 'Hausväterliteratur' des 16. bis 18. Jahrhunderts in Deutschland," in Hubertus Tellenbach, ed., *Das Vaterbild im Abendland*, vol. 1. Stuttgart: Kohlhammer, 1978, 110–123.
Fullbrook, Mary and Ulinka Rublack. "In Relation: The 'Social Self' and Ego-Documents," *German History* 28.3 (2010), 263–272.
Gehrmann, Rolf. "German Census-Taking before 1871," working paper for the Max Planck Institute for Demographic Research WP 2009-023, August 2009.
Gianna, Luca. "Frammenti di luoghi. Le valli Belbo e Bormida di Spigno nel Piemonte dell'età moderna," in Renato Bordone, Paola Guglielmotti, Sandro Lombardini and Angelo Torre, eds., *Lo spazio politico locale in età medievale, moderna e contemporanea. Atti del Convegno internazionale di studi*. Alessandria: Edizioni dell'Orso, 2007, 177–190.
Giavini, Luigi. *Dizionario della lingua bustocca*, 3 vols. Busto Arsizio: Pianezza Editore, 1983.
Gilje, Paul A. *Liberty on the Waterfront: American Maritime Culture in the Age of Revolution*. Philadelphia: University of Pennsylvania Press, 2004.

Glete, Jan. *War and the State in Early Modern Europe: Spain, the Dutch Republic, and Sweden as Fiscal-Military States.* New York: Routledge, 2001.

Gotthard, Axel. "'Politice seint wir bäpstisch'. Kursachsen und der deutsche Protestantismus im frühen 17. Jahrhundert," *Zeitschrift für Historische Forschung* 20 (1993), 275–319.

Greene, Ann Norton. *Horses at Work: Harnessing Power in Industrial America.* Cambridge, MA: Harvard University Press, 2008.

Greene, Graham. *The Quiet American.* London: William Heinemann Ltd., 1955.

von Greyerz, Kaspar. "Observation on the Historiographical Status of Research on Self-Writing," in Claudia Ulbrich, Lorenz Heiligensetzer and Kaspar von Greyerz, eds., *Mapping the "I": Research on Self-Narratives in Germany and Switzerland.* Leiden: Brill, 2015, 34–57.

Guthrie, William P. *Battles of the Thirty Years War: From White Mountain to Nördlingen, 1618–1635.* Westport: Greenwood Publishing Group, 2001.

The Later Thirty Years War: From the Battle of Wittstock to the Treaty of Westphalia. Westport: Greenwood Publishing Group, 2003.

Gutman, Myron. *War and Rural Life in the Early Modern Low Countries.* Princeton: Princeton University Press, 1980.

Haberer, Stephanie. *Ott Heinrich Fugger (1592–1644): Biographische Analyze typologischer Handlungsfelder in der Epoche des Dreißigjährigen Krieges.* Augsburg: Wißner-Verlag, 2004.

Haberling, Wilhelm. "Army Prostitution and its Control: An Historical Study," in Victor Robinson, ed., *Morals in Wartime; Including General Survey from Ancient Times; Morals in the First World War and Morals in the Second World War.* New York: Publishers Foundation, 1943, 33–34.

Hacker, Barton C. "Women and Military Institutions in Early Modern Europe: A Reconnaissance," *Signs* 6.4 (1981), 643–671.

Hahn, Peter-Michael. "Kriegserfahrungen im Zeitalter des Dreißigjährigen Krieges," in Dittmar Dahlman, ed., *Kinder und Jugendliche in Krieg und Revolution: vom Dreißigjährigen Krieg bis zu den Kindersoldaten Afrikas.* Paderborn: Schönigh, 2000, 1–16.

Halberstam, Jack. *Female Masculinity.* Durham: Duke University Press, 1998.

Hale, J. R. *War and Society in Renaissance Europe, 1450–1620.* Montreal: McGill-Queen's University Press, 1998.

Hamner, Christopher H. *Enduring Battle: American Soldiers in Three Wars, 1776–1945.* Lawrence: University Press of Kansas, 2011.

Hanlon, Gregory. *The Hero of Italy: The Duke of Parma and the Thirty Years War.* Oxford: Oxford University Press, 2014.

Human Nature in Rural Tuscany. New York: Palgrave Macmillan, 2007.

Italy 1636: Cemetery of Armies. Oxford: Oxford University Press, 2016.

The Twilight of a Military Tradition: Italian Aristocrats and European Conflicts, 1560–800. London: Routledge, 2014, original printing 1998.

Harari, Yuval. *Renaissance Military Memoirs: War, History, and Identity 1450–1600.* Woodbridge: The Boydell Press, 2004.

The Ultimate Experience: Battlefield Revelations and the Making of Modern War Culture 1450–2000. Basingstoke: Palgrave Macmillan, 2008.

Heiligensetzer, Lorenz. "Swiss-German Self-Narratives: The Archival Project as a Rich Vein of Research," in Claudia Ulbrich, Lorenz Heiligensetzer and Kaspar von Greyerz, eds., *Mapping the "I": Research on Self-Narratives in Germany and Switzerland*. Leiden: Brill, 2015, 58–75.

Heller, Henry. "Putting History Back into the Religious Wars: A Reply to Mack P. Holt," *French Historical Studies* 19.3 (1996), 853–861.

Hintze, Otto. "Military Organization and the Organization of the State," in *The Historical Essays of Otto Hintze*, trans. F. Gilbert. Oxford: Oxford University Press, 1975, 178–215.

Hitchcock, Tim. "A New History from Below," *History Workshop Journal* 57 (2004), 294–298.

Hitchcock, Tim, Peter King and Pamela Sharpe, eds. *Chronicling Poverty: The Voices and Strategies of the English Poor, 1640–1840*. Basingstoke: Macmillan, 1997.

Höbelt, Lothar. *Von Nördlingen bis Janckau: Kaiserliche Strategie und Kriegführung 1634–1645*. Vienna: Heeresgeschichtliches Museum, 2016.

Hochedlinger, Michael. "The Habsburg Monarchy: From 'Military-Fiscal State' to 'Militarization'," in Christopher Storrs, ed., *The Fiscal-Military State in Eighteenth-Century Europe: Essays in Honor of P. G. M. Dickinson*. Surrey: Ashgate, 2009, 55–94.

Hochmuth, Christian. "What Is Tobacco? Illicit Trade with Overseas Commodities in Early Modern Dresden," in Thomas Buchner and Philip R. Hoffmann-Rehnitz, eds., *Shadow Economies and Irregular Work in Urban Europe: 16th to Early 20th Centuries*. Münster: LIT Verlag, 2011, 107–126.

Holt, Mack. "Putting Religion Back into the Wars of Religion," *French Historical Studies* 18.2 (1993), 524–551.

"Religion, Historical Method, and Historical Forces: A Rejoinder," *French Historical Studies* 19.3 (1996), 863–873.

Horne, John and Alan Kramer. *German Atrocities 1914: A History of Denial*. New Haven: Yale University Press, 2001.

Hrncirik, Pavel. *Spanier auf dem Albuch: Ein Beitrag zur Geschichte der Schlacht bei Nördlingen im Jahre 1634*. Maastricht: Shaker, 2007.

Hughes, Steven C. *Politics of the Sword: Dueling, Honor, and Masculinity in Modern Italy*. Columbus: Ohio State University Press, 2007.

Hugo, Herman. "The Siege of Breda by the Armes of Philip, 1627," in D. M. Rogers, ed., *English Recusant Literature 1558–1640*, vol. 261. London: The Scolar Press Ltd., nd, 141–142.

Humbert, Jacques. "En Valtelline avec le Marquis de Coeuvres," *Revue Historique de l'Armeé* 14 (1958), 47–67.

Huntebrinker, Jan Willem. *"Fromme Knechte" und "Garteteufel:" Söldner als soziale Gruppe im 16. und 17. Jahrhundert*. Konstanz: Universitätsverlag Konstanz, 2010.

Hurl-Eamon, Jennie. *Marriage and the British Army in the Long Eighteenth Century: "The Girl I Left behind Me"*. Oxford: Oxford University Press, 2014.

Iggers, Georg. "From Macro- to Microhistory: The History of Everyday Life," in Georg Iggers, ed., *Historiography in the Twentieth Century: From Scientific Objectivity to the Postmodern Challenge*. Hanover: Wesleyan Press, 1997, 101–117.

Israel, Jonathan. "Central European Jewry during the Thirty Years War," *Central European History* 16.1 (1983), 3–30.

"Spanish Wool Exports and the European Economy, 1610–40," *The Economic History Review*, New Series 33.2 (1980), 193–211.

Jansson, Karin. "Soldaten und Vergewaltigung in Schweden des 17. Jahrhunderts," in Benigna von Krusenstjern and Hans Medick, eds., *Zwischen Alltag und Katastrophe – Der Dreißigjährige Krieg aus der Nähe*. Göttingen: Vandenhoeck & Ruprecht, 2001, 195–225.

Jeggle, Christoff. "Labeling with Numbers? Weavers, Merchants and the Valuation of Linen in Seventeenth-Century Münster," in Bert de Munck and Dries Lyna, eds., *Concepts of Value in European Material Culture, 1500–1900*. Surrey: Ashgate, 2015, 33–56.

Jones, Howard. *My Lai: Vietnam, 1968, and the Descent into Darkness*. Oxford: Oxford University Press, 2017.

Jordan, Reinhard. *Chronik der Stadt Mühlhäusen in Thüringen*, Vol 3. Mühlhausen: Dannischer Buchhandlerei, 1905.

Jungklaus, Bettina. "A Mass Grave from the Thirty Years War on Friedländer Tor Neubrandenburg," in *Proccedings of the Battlefield and Mass Grave Spectra: Interdisciplinary Evaluation of Locations of Violence* conference. Brandenburg an der Havel, November 21, 2011.

Jungklaus, Bettina and B. Prehn. "Ein Soldatenmassengrab vom Friedländer Tor in Neubrandenburg aus dem Jahre 1631 und dessen anthropologische Untersuchung," in *Heimatgeschichtliches Jahrbuch des Regionalmuseums Neubrandenburg*, 35. Neubrandenburg: Regionalmuseum Neubrandenburg, 2011, Vol. 20, 10–33.

Kaiser, Michael. "Außreiser und Meuterer im Dreißigjährigen Krieg," in Ulrich Bröckling and Michael Sikora, eds., *Armeen und ihre Deserteure. Vernachlässigte Kapitel einer Militärgeschichte der Neuzeit*. Göttingen: Vandenhoeck und Ruprecht, 1998, 49–71.

Kalyvas, Stathis. *The Logic of Violence in Civil War*. Cambridge: Cambridge University Press, 2006.

Kamen, Henry. *Spain's Road to Empire: The Making of a World Power 1492–1763*. London: Allen Lane, 2002.

Kapser, Cordula. *Die bayerische Kriegsorganisation in der zweiten Hälfte des dreissigjährigen Krieges 1635–1648/49*. Münster: Aschendorff Verlag, 1997.

Keegan, John. *The Face of Battle: A Study of Agincourt, Waterloo, and the Somme*. London: Penguin Books, 1976.

A History of Warfare. New York: Random House, 1993.

Keirnan, V. G. *The Duel in European History: Honor and the Reign of Aristocracy*, 2nd ed. London: Zed Books, 2016.

Kiessling, Alois and Max Matthes. *Textil-Fachwörterbuch*. Berlin: Schiele & Schön, 1993.

Kindleberger, Charles P. "The Economic Crisis of 1618 to 1623," *The Journal of Economic History* 51.1 (1991), 149–175.

Kirk, Thomas Allison. *Genoa and the Sea: Policy and Power in an Early Modern Maritime Republic 1559–1682*. Baltimore: The Johns Hopkins University Press, 2005.

Kituai, August. *My Gun, My Brother: The World of the Papua New Guinea Colonial Police, 1920–1960*. Honolulu: University of Hawaii Press, 1998.

Kleinhagenbrock, F. "Die Wahrnehmung und Deutung des Westfälischen Friedens durch Untertanen der Reichsstände," in Inken Schmidt-Voges, Siegrid Westphal, Volker Arnke and Tobias Bartke, eds., *Pax perpetua. Neuere Forschungen zum Frieden in der Frühen Neuzeit*. Munich: De Gruyter, 2010, 177–193.

Konze, Marlies and Renate Samaritan. "Der Stralsunder Laufgraben von 1628 – verschüttete Söldner und Waffen in situ. Festungsbau im Süden der Hansestadt (Quartier Frankenhof) im Spiegel archäologischer Befunde und historischer Quellen," *Forschungen zur Archäologie im Land Brandenburg* 15 (2014), 197–231.

Kouřil, Milos. *Documenta Bohemica bellum tricennale illustrantia, Tomus III: Der Kampf des Hauses Habsburg gegen die Niederlande & ihre Verbündeten: Quellen zur Geschichte des Pfälzisch-Niederländisch-Ungarischen Krieges, 1621–1625*. Prague: Academica, 1976.

Král von Dobrá Voda, Adalbert Ritter. *Der Adel von Böhmen, Mähren und Schlesien*. Prague: I. Taussig, 1904.

Kramer, Johannes. *Etymologisches Wörterbuch des Dolomitenladinischen*. Hamburg: Helmut Buske Verlag, 1990.

Kroener, Bernhard. *Les Routes et les Étapes: Die Versorgung der französischen Armeen in Nordostfrankreich (1635–1661): Ein Beitrag zur Verwaltungsgeschichte des Ancien Régime*. Münster: Aschendorff Verlag, 1980.

Kroll, Stefan. *Soldaten im 18. Jahrhundert zwischen Friedensalltag und Kriegserfahrung: Lebenswelten und Kultur in der kursächsischen Armee 1728–1796*. Paderborn: Schöningh Paderborn, 2006.

von Krusenstjern, Benigna and Hans Medick, eds. *Zwischen Alltag und Katastrophe: Der Dreißigjährige Krieg aus der Nähe*. Göttingen: Vandenhoeck & Ruprecht, 1998.

Lappa, Daphne. "Religious Conversions within the Venetian Military Milieu (17th and 18th Centuries)," *Studi Veneziani* LXVII (2013), 183–200.

Leach, Edmund. *Social Anthropology*. Glasgow: William Collins Sons, 1982.

Lehmann, Christian. *Die Kriegschronik: Sachsen mit Erzgebirge*, ed. Hendrik Heidler. Norderstedt: Books on Demand, 2009.

Lehmann, Johannes F. *In Abgrund der Wut: Zur Kultur und Literaturgeschichte des Zorns*. Freiburg im Breisigau: Rombach Verlag, 2012.

"Feeling Rage: The Transformation of the Concept of Anger in the Eighteenth Century," in Karl A. E. Enenkel and Anita Traninger, eds., *Discourses of Anger in the Early Modern Period*. Leiden: Brill, 2015, 16–48.

Lemire, Beverly. *Global Trade and the Transformation of Consumer Cultures: The Material World Remade, c. 1500–1820*. Cambridge: Cambridge University Press, 2018.

Lewis, Margaret Brannon. *Infanticide and Abortion in Early Modern Germany*. London: Routledge, 2016.

Lifton, Robert Jay. "Haditha: In an 'Atrocity-Producing Situation' – Who Is to Blame?" *Editor & Publisher*, 2006.

Home from the War: Learning from Vietnam Veterans. New York: Simon and Schuster, 1973.

Lorenz, Maron. *Das Rad der Gewalt: Miliär und Zivilbevölkerung in Norddeutschland nach dem Dreißigjährigen Krieg*. Cologne: Böhlau Verlag, 2007.

Loriga, Sabina. *Soldats: Un laboratoire disciplinaire: l'armée piémontaise au XVIII siècle*. Paris: Les Belles Lettres, 2007.

de Luca, Giuseppe and Marcella Lorenzini. "Conflicts, Financial Innovations, and Economic Trends in the Italian States during the Thirty Years War," in Lila Constable and Larry Neal, eds., *Financial Innovation and Resilience: A Comparative Perspective on the Public Banks of Naples (1462–1808)*. London: Palgrave Macmillan, 2019, 165–186.

Lucht, Antje. *Fahnen und Standarten aus der Zeit des Dreissigjährigen Krieges 1618–1648, Vol 2: Die Katholische Liega und die Kaiserliche Armee*. Freiberg: Buvin Verlag, 2015.

Lund, Erik A. *War for the Every Day: Generals, Knowledge, and Warfare in Early Modern Europe, 1680–1740*. Westport: Greenwood Press, 1999.

Lynn, John. *Giant of the Grand Siècle: The French Army, 1610–1715*. Cambridge: Cambridge University Press, 2006.

"How War Fed War: The Tax of Violence and Contributions during the Grand Siècle," *Journal of Modern History* 65 (1993), 286–310.

Women, Armies, and Warfare in Early Modern Europe. Cambridge: Cambridge University Press, 2008.

Maddern, Philippa. *Violence and Social Order: East Anglia, 1422–42*. Oxford: Clarendon Press, 1992.

Maffi, Davide. *Il Baluardo della Corona: Guerra, esercito, finanze e società nella Lombardia seicentesca (1630–1660)*. Florence: Le Monnier Università Storia, 2007.

Mann, Golo. *Wallenstein: Sein Leben Erzählt*. Frankfurt am Main: S. Fischer Verlag, 1986.

Marshall, S. L. A. *Men against Fire: The Problem of Battle Command*. New York: William Morrow and Company, 1947.

Martines, Lauro. *Furies: War in Europe 1450–1700*. New York: Bloomsbury Press, 2013.

Mazur, Peter. *Conversion to Catholicism in Early Modern Italy*. New York: Routledge, 2016.

Mazzaoui, Maureen Fennell. "The First European Cotton Industry: Italy and Germany, 1100–1600," in Giorgio Riello and Prasannan Parthasarathi, eds., *The Spinning World: A Global History of Cotton Textiles, 1200–1850*. Oxford: Oxford University Press, 2009, 63–87.

McMahon, Darrin M. *Happiness: A History*. New York: Atlantic, 2006.

McNeill, William. *The Pursuit of Power: Technology, Armed Force, and Society since AD 1000*. Oxford: Oxford University Press, 1982.

McShane, Clay and Joel A. Tarr. *The Horse in the City: Living Machines in the Nineteenth Century*. Baltimore: The Johns Hopkins University Press, 2007.

McVay, Pamela. "Brawling Behaviors in the Dutch Colonial Empire: Changing Norms of Fairness?," in Tonio Andrade and William Reger, eds., *The Limits of Empire: European Imperial Formations in Early Modern World History, Essays in honor of Geoffrey Parker*. New York: Routledge, 2016, 237–255.

Medick, Hans. *Der Dreißigjährige Krieg: Zeugnisse vom Leben mit Gewalt*. Göttingen: Wallstein Verlag, 2018.

Möller, Hans-Michael. *Das Regiment der Landsknechte: Untersuchungen zur Verfassung, Recht, und Selbstverständnis in deutschen Söldnerherren des 16. Jahrhunderts.* Wiesbaden: Fritz Steiner Verlag, 1976.
Moote, A. Lloyd. *Louis XIII, the Just.* Berkeley: University of California Press, 1989.
Mortimer, Geoff. *Eyewitness Accounts of the Thirty Years War 1618–1648.* New York: Palgrave Macmillan, 2002.
Muldrew, Craig. *The Economy of Obligation: The Culture of Credit and Social Relations in Early Modern England.* Basingstoke: Palgrave, 1998.
Neal, Derek. *The Masculine Self in Late Medieval England.* Chicago: The University of Chicago Press, 2008.
Nicklisch, Nicole, Frank Ramsthaler, Harald Meller, Susanne Friederich and Kurt W. Alt. "The Face of War: Trauma Analysis of a Mass Grave from the Battle of Lützen (1632)," *PLoS One* 12.5 (2017).
Nowosadtko, Jutta. "Soldiers as Day-Laborers, Tinkers, and Competitors. Trade Activities in the Garrisons of the Eighteenth Century Using the Example of Prince-Bishopric Münster," in Thomas Buchner and Philip R. Hoffmann-Rehnitz, eds., *Shadow Economies and Irregular Work in Urban Europe: 16th to Early 20th Centuries.* Münster: LIT Verlag, 2011, 165–181.
Nye, Robert. *Masculinity and Male Codes of Honor in Modern France.* Berkeley: University of California Press, 1998.
Oestrich, Gerhard. *Neostoicism and the Early Modern State*, ed. Brigitta Oestrich and H. G. Koenigsberger, tr. David McLintock. Cambridge: Cambridge University Press, 1982.
Ogilvie, Sheilagh. *A Bitter Living: Women, Markets, and Social Capital in Early Modern Germany.* Oxford: Oxford University Press, 2003.
  "Germany and the Seventeenth-Century Crisis," in Geoffrey Parker and Lesley Smith, eds., *The General Crisis of the Seventeenth Century*, 2nd ed. New York: Routledge, 2005, 57–86.
Ongaro, Giulio. *Peasants and Soldiers: The Management of the Venetian Military Structure in the Mainland Dominion between the 16th and 17th Centuries.* New York: Routledge, 2017.
Ongaro, Giulio and Simone Signaroli. *I cannoni di Guspessa. I comuni di Edolo, Cortenedolo e Mu alle soglie della Guerra dei Trent'Anni (1624–1625).* Valle Camonica: Pubblicazioni del Servizio Archivistico Comprensoriale di Valle Camonica, 2016.
Orlin, Lena Cowen. *Locating Privacy in Tudor London.* Oxford: Oxford University Press, 2007.
Osment, Steven. *When Fathers Ruled: Family Life in Reformation Europe.* Cambridge, MA: Harvard University Press, 1983.
Outram, Quentin. "Demographic Impact of Early Modern Warfare," *Social Science History* 26 (2002), 245–272.
Padjera, Emil. "Die bastionäre Befestigung von Frankfurt aM," in *Archiv für Frankfurts Geschichte und Kunst, Band 31* 3.12 (1920), 230–302.
Parker, Geoffrey. *The Army of Flanders and the Spanish Road 1567–1659: The Logistics of Spanish Victory and Defeat in the Low Countries' Wars.* Cambridge: Cambridge University Press, 1972.

Global Crisis: War, Climate, and Catastrophe in the Seventeenth Century. New Haven: Yale University Press, 2014.

"Mutiny and Discontent in the Spanish Army of Flanders, 1572–1607," *Past & Present* 58 (1973), 38–52.

"The Soldier," in Rosario Villari, ed., *Baroque Personae.* Chicago: University of Chicago Press, 1995, 32–56.

Parker, Geoffrey and Lesley Smith, eds. *The General Crisis of the Seventeenth Century,* 2nd ed. New York: Routledge, 2005.

Parrott, David. *The Business of War: Military Enterprise and Military Revolution in Early Modern Europe.* Cambridge: Cambridge University Press, 2012.

"Foreword," in Eduardo de Mesa, *The Irish in the Spanish Armies in the Seventeenth Century.* New York: Boydell Press, 2014.

"France's War against the Habsburgs, 1624–1659: The Politics of Military Failure," in Enrique García Hernán and Davide Maffi, eds., *Guerra y Sociedad en La Monarquía Hispánica: Politica, Estrategia y Cultura en la Europa Moderna (1500–1700),* Vol. 1. Madrid: Laberinto, 2006, 31–49.

Richelieu's Army: War, Government, and Society in France, 1624–1642. Cambridge: Cambridge University Press, 2006.

"Strategy and Tactics in the Thirty Years War: The 'Military Revolution'," in Clifford J. Rogers, ed., *The Military Revolution Debate: Readings on the Military Transformation of Early Modern Europe.* New York: Routledge, 1995, 227–252.

Pastoreau, Michel, trans. Joy Gladding. *Green: The History of a Color.* Princeton: Princeton University Press, 2014.

Pedlow, Gregory W. *The Survival of the Hessian Nobility, 1770–1870.* Princeton: Princeton Legacy Library, 1988.

Perjés, Geza. "Army Provisioning, Logistics and Strategy in the Second Half of the 17th Century," *Acta Historica Academiae Scientiarum Hungaricae* XVI (1970), 7–51.

Peyronel, Susanna. "Frontiere religiose e soldati in antico regime: il caso di Crema nel Seicento," in Claudio Donati, ed., *Alle frontiere della Lombardia: politica, guerra e religione nell'età moderna.* Milan: FrancoAngeli, 2006, 19–40.

Pezzolo, Luciano. "Professione militare e famiglia in Italia tra tardo medioevo e prima età moderna," in Anna Bellavitis and Isabelle Chabot, eds., *La Justice des familles: Autour de la transmission des biens, des savoirs et des pouvoirs.* Rome: École française de Rome, 2011, 341–366.

Pfister, Ulrich. "Consumer prices and wages in Germany, 1500–1850," *Westfälische Wilhelms-Universität Münster Historisches Seminar,* March 2010.

Pieth, Friedrich. "Der Dreibündengeneral Rudolf v. Salis und ein österreichischer Bericht über den Einfall des Grafen Alwig v. Sulz in Graubünder 1622," *Bündnerisches Monatsblatt: Zeitschrift für bündnerische Geschichte, Landes- und Volkskunde* 4 (1915), 113–115.

"Der Dreibündengeneral Rudolf v. Salis und ein österreichischer Bericht über den Einfall des Grafen Alwig v. Sulz in Graubünder 1622: Fortsetzung und Schluß," *Bündnerisches Monatsblatt : Zeitschrift für bündnerische Geschichte, Landes- und Volkskunde* 5 (1915), 158–164.

Pohl, Jürgen. *"Die Profiantirung der Keyserlichen Armaden Ahnbelangendt:" Studien zur Versorgung der Kaiserlichen Armee 1634/1635*. Vienna: F. Berger & Söhne, 1994.
Pohl-Zucker, Susanne. *Making Manslaughter: Process, Punishment and Restitution in Württemberg and Zürich, 1376–1700*. Leiden: Brill, 2017.
Post, W. D. *Inventaris van het archief van de familie Snouckaert van Schauburg, 1487–1986*. Den Haag: Nationaal Archief, 1986.
Rediker, Marcus. "The Poetics of History from Below," *Perspectives on History* (2010), available at: www.historians.org/research-and-publications/perspectives-on-history/september-2010/the-poetics-of-history-from-below, last accessed March 11, 2024.
Villains of All Nations: Atlantic Pirates in the Golden Age. Boston: Beacon Press, 2004.
Redlich, Fritz. *De Praeda Militari: Looting and Booty, 1500–1816*. Wiesbaden: Franz Steiner Verlag, 1956.
The German Military Enterpriser and his Work Force, 2 vols. Wiesbaden: Franz Steiner Verlag, 1964–1965.
Garcia, Luis Antonio Ribot. "Soldados españoles en Italia. El Castillo de Milán a finales del siglo XVI," in Enrique Garcia Hernan and Davide Maffi, eds., *Guerra y sociedad en la monarquía hispánica: política, estrategia y cultura en la Europa Moderna, 1500–1700, Volume 1*. Madrid: Laberinto, 2006, 401–444.
Riley, James C. "A Widening Market in Consumer Goods," in Euan Cameron, ed., *Early Modern Europe: An Oxford History*, Oxford: Oxford University Press, 2001.
Roberts, Michael. "The Military Revolution, 1560–1660," reprinted in Clifford J. Rogers, ed., *The Military Revolution Debate: Readings on the Military Transformation of Early Modern Europe*. Abingdon: Routledge, 1995, 13–36.
Romano, Ruggiero. "Between the Sixteenth and Seventeenth Centuries: The Economic Crisis of 1619–22," in Geoffrey Parker and Lesley Smith, eds., *The General Crisis of the Seventeenth Century*. Abingdon: Routledge, 1997, 165–225.
Roper, Lyndal. *The Holy Household: Women and Morals in Reformation Augsburg*. Oxford: Oxford University Press, 1989.
Rowlands, Guy. *The Dynastic State and the Army under Louis XIV: Royal Service and Private Interest 1661–1701*. Cambridge: Cambridge University Press, 2002.
"Review of *Giant of the Grand Siècle* and *The Wars of Louis XIV*, by John Lynn," *French History* 14 (2000), 450–454.
Rublack, Ulinka. *Dressing Up: Cultural Identity in Renaissance Europe*. Oxford: Oxford University Press, 2011.
Ruff, Julius R. *Violence in Early Modern Europe 1500–1800*. Cambridge: Cambridge University Press, 2001.
Sabean, David Warren. *Kinship in Neckarhausen, 1700–1870*. Cambridge: Cambridge University Press, 1997.
Power in the Blood: Popular Culture and Village Discourse in Early Modern Germany. Cambridge: Cambridge University Press, 1984.

Property, Production, and Family in Neckarhausen, 1700–1870. Cambridge: Cambridge University Press, 1990.

Salm, Hubert. *Armeefinanzierung im Dreißigjährigen Krieg: Die Niederrheinisch-Westfälische Reichskreis 1635–1650.* Münster: Aschendorff Verlag, 1990.

Sandberg, Brian. "The Magazine of All Their Pillaging: Armies as Sites of Second-Hand Exchange during the French Wars of Religion," in Laurence Fontaine, ed., *Alternative Exchanges: Second-Hand Circulation from the Sixteenth Century to the Present.* New York: Berghahn Books, 2008, 76–96.

Sargent, Thomas J. and François R. Velde. *The Big Problem of Small Change.* Princeton: Princeton University Press, 2002.

Schennach, Martin Paul. "Lokale Obrigkeiten und Soldaten. Militärgerichtsbarkeit in Tirol in der ersten Hälfte des 17. Jahrhunderts," in Andrea Griesebner, Martin Scheutz and Herwig Weigl, eds., *Justiz und Gerechtigkeit. Historische Beiträge (16.–19. Jahrhundert).* Vienna: Studienverlag, 2002, 199–218.

Schilling, Heinz. *Die Stadt in der Frühen Neuzeit.* Munich: R. Oldenbourg Verlag, 2004.

Schirmer, Uwe. *Kursächsische Staatsfinanzen (1456–1656): Structuren – Verfassung – Functionseliten.* Stuttgart: Franz Steiner Verlag, 2006.

Schlumbohm, Jürgen. "Gesetze, die nicht durchgesetzt werden: ein Strukturmerkmal des frühneuzeitlichen Staates?," *Geschichte und Gesellschaft* 23.4 (1997), 647–663.

Schöltz, Susanne. "Female Traders and Practices of Illicit Exchange. Observations on Leipzig's Retail Trade between the Sixteenth and Nineteenth Century," in Thomas Buchner and Philip R. Hoffmann-Rehnitz, eds., *Shadow Economies and Irregular Work in Urban Europe: 16th to Early 20th Centuries.* Münster: LIT Verlag, 2011, 127–140.

Sella, Domenico. *Crisis and Continuity: The Economy of Spanish Lombardy in the Seventeenth Century.* Cambridge, MA: Harvard University Press, 1979.

Sender, Ferdinand. *Georg Friedrich Greiffenclau von Vollrads 1573–1629. Ein Prälat aus der mittelrheinischen Ritterschaft. Aufstieg und Regierungsantritt in Mainz.* Mainz: Gesellschaft für Mittelrheinische Kirchengeschichte, 1977.

Sennewald, Roland. *Die Kursachsen im Dreißigjährigen Krieg: Band I: Das kursächsische Heer im Dreißigjährigen Krieg.* Berlin: Zeughaus Verlag, 2013.

Die Kursachsen im Dreißigjährigen Krieg: Band II: Die Kursächsischen Feldzeichen im Dreißigjährigen Krieg 1618–1648. Berlin: Zeughaus Verlag, 2013.

Shaw, W. A. *The History of Currency.* New York: G. P. Putnam's Sons, 1896.

Shils, E. A. and Morris Janowitz. "Cohesion and Disintegration in the Wehrmacht in World War II," *The Public Opinion Quarterly* 12.2 (1948), 280–315.

Showalter, Dennis and William J. Astore, *Soldiers' Lives through History: The Early Modern World.* Westport, CT: Greenwood, 2007.

Spicer, Joneath. "The Renaissance Elbow," in Jan Bremmer and Hermann Roodenburg, eds., *A Cultural History of Gesture: From Antiquity to the Present Day.* Cambridge: Polity Press, 1991, 84–128.

Spierenburg, Pieter. "Men Fighting Men: Europe from a Global Perspective," in Robert Antony, Stuart Carroll and Caroline Dodds, eds., *The Cambridge World History of Violence, Vol. III, 1500–1800.* Cambridge: Cambridge University Press, 2020, 292–310.

Stadler, Barbara. *Pappenheim und die Zeit des Dreissigjährigen Krieges.* Winterthur: Gemsberg-Verlag, 1991.
Staiano-Daniels, Lucian. "A Brief Introduction to Seventeenth-Century Military Manuscripts and Military Literacy," *Manuscript Studies* 5.1 (2020), 142–163.
"Determining Early Modern Army Strength: The Case of Electoral Saxony," *Journal of Military History* 83.4 (2019), 1000–1020.
"Masters in the Things of War: Rethinking Military Justice during the Thirty Years War," *German History* 39.4 (2021), 497–518.
"Scribes and Soldiers: A Brief Introduction to Military Manuscripts and Military Literacy," *Manuscript Studies* 5.1 (2021), 142–163.
"Two Weeks in Summer: Soldiers and Others in Occupied Hesse-Cassel 14–25 July 1625," *War in History* 30.2 (2022), 1–25.
"What Is 'Experience' and Why Is Military History Obsessed with It?," paper presented at the *Interpreting Translation, Taste, and Obsession at Historical Epistemology Conference: In Honor of David Sabean,* UCLA, May 18, 2018.
Steensgaard, Niels. "The Seventeenth-Century Crisis and the Unity of Eurasian History," *Modern Asian Studies* XXIV (1990), 683–697.
Stieve, Felix. "Mansfeld, Graf Bruno III. Von," in Historische Kommission bei der Bayerischen Akademie des Wissenschaften, ed., *Allgemeine Deutsche Biographie,* Vol 20. Leipzig: Duncker & Humblot, 1884, 221–222.
Stone, Lawrence. *The Family, Sex, and Marriage in England, 1500–1800.* New York: Harper and Row, 1977.
Storrs, Christopher, ed. *The Fiscal-Military State in Eighteenth-Century Europe: Essays in Honor of P. G. M. Dickson.* Aldershot: Ashgate, 2009.
Stouffer, Samuel. *Studies in Social Psychology in World War II: The American Soldier.* Princeton: Princeton University Press, 1949.
Stoyle, Mark. *Soldiers and Strangers: An Ethnic History of the English Civil War.* New Haven: Yale University Press, 2005.
Stradling, R. A. *Spain's Struggle for Europe, 1598–1668.* London: The Hambeldon Press, 1994.
Stuart, Kathy. *Defiled Trades and Social Outcasts: Honor and Ritual Pollution in Early Modern Germany.* Cambridge: Cambridge University Press, 2006.
Swart, Erik. "From "Landsknecht" to "Soldier": The Low German Foot Soldiers of the Low Countries in the Second Half of the Sixteenth Century," *International Review of Social History* 51 (2006), 75–92.
Tallett, Frank. "Soldiers in Western Europe, c. 1500–1790," in Erik-Jan Zürcher, ed., *Fighting for a Living: A Comparative Study of Military Labor 1500–2000.* Amsterdam: Amsterdam University Press, 2010.
War and Society in Early Modern Europe: 1495–1715. New York: Routledge, 1992.
Teibenbacher, Peter, Diether Kramer and Wolfgang Göderle. "An Inventory of Austrian Census Materials, 1857–1910. Final Report," working paper for the Max Planck Institute for Demographic Research WP2012-007, December 2012.
Teschke, Benno. *The Myth of 1648: Class, Geopolitics, and the Making of Modern International Relations.* Brooklyn: Verso, 2003.
Thomas, Elizabeth Marshall. *The Harmless People.* New York: Alfred Knopf, 1959.

Thomas, Keith. "Work and Leisure," *Past and Present* 29 (1964), 50–66.
Thompson, E. P. "History from Below," *The Times Literary Supplement* (1966), 279.
"The Moral Economy of the English Crowd in the Eighteenth Century," *Past and Present* 50 (1971), 76–136.
Thüringer Verband der Verfolgten des Naziregimes – Bund der Antifaschisten und Studienkreis deutscher Widerstand, ed. *Heimatgeschichtlicher Wegweiser zu Stätten des Widerstandes und der Verfolgung 1933–1945, Reihe: Heimatgeschichtliche Wegweiser Band 8: Thüringen*. Erfurt: Thüringer Verband der Verfolgten des Naziregimes – Bund der Antifaschisten und Studienkreis deutscher Widerstand, 2003.
Tilly, Charles. "Reflections on the History of European State-Making," in Charles Tilly, ed., *The Formation of National States in Western Europe*. Princeton: Princeton University Press, 1975, 3–83.
Tlusty, Barbara. "Bravado, Military Culture, and the Performance of Masculine Magic in Early Modern Germany," in the panel *Masculinity and Military Culture*, 8th Annual FNI Conference, *Rethinking Europe: War and Peace in the Early Modern German Lands*, March 9, 2018.
The Martial Ethic in Early Modern Germany: Civil Duty and the Right of Arms. New York: Palgrave Macmillan, 2011.
"The Public House and Military Culture in Germany, 1500–1648," in Beat Kümin and Barbara Tlusty, eds., *The World of the Tavern: Public Houses in Early Modern Europe*. London: Routledge, 2002, 136–156.
Turnbull, Colin. *The Forest People: A Sudy of the Pygmies of the Congo*. New York: Simon and Schuster, 1961.
The Mountain People. New York: Simon and Schuster, 1972.
Vorel, Petr. *Páni z Pernštejna. Vzestup a pád rodu zubří hlavy v dějinách Čech a Moravy*. Prague: Rybka, 1999.
de Vries, Jan. "Between Purchasing Power and the World of Goods: Understanding the Household Economy in Early Modem Europe," in J. Brewer and R. Porter, eds., *Consumption and the World of Goods*. London: Routledge, 1993, 85–132.
"The Economic Crisis of the Seventeenth Century after Fifty Years," *Journal of Interdisciplinary History* 40.2 (2009), 151–194.
"The Industrial Revolution and the Industrious Revolution," *Journal of Economic History*, 54 (1994), 249–270.
The Industrious Revolution: Consumer Behavior and the Household Economy, 1650 to the Present. Cambridge: Cambridge University Press, 2008.
"Luxury in the Dutch Golden Age in Theory and Practice," in Maxine Berg and Elizabeth Eger, eds., *Luxury in the Eighteenth Century: Debates, Desires, and Delectable Goods*. New York: Palgrave Macmillan, 2003, 41–56.
Walker, Garthine. "Sexual Violence and Rape in Europe, 1500–1750," in Sarah Toulalan and Kate Fisher, eds., *The Routledge History of Sex and the Body: 1500 to the Present*. New York: Routledge, 2015, 429–443.
Wedgwood, C. V. *The Thirty Years War*. New York: New York Review Books Classics, 2005, first edition 1938.

Wendland, Andreas. *Der Nutzen der Pässe und die Gefährdung der Seelen: Spanien, Mailand und der Kampf ums Weltlin (1620–1641)*. Zürich: Chronos Verlag, 1995.

Whitman, James. *The Verdict of Battle: The Law of Victory and the Making of Modern War*. Cambridge: Harvard University Press, 2012.

Wiesener, Merry. "Manhood, Patriarchy, and Gender in Early Modern History," in Amy E. Leonard and Karen L. Nelson, eds., *Masculinities, Childhood, Violence: Attending to Early Modern Women – and Men*. Newark, NJ: University of Delaware Press, 2011.

"Wandervogels and Women: Journeymens' Concepts of Masculinity in Early Modern Germany," *Journal of Social History* 24.4 (1991), 767–782.

Wilson, Peter. *Europe's Tragedy: A New History of the Thirty Years War*. London: Penguin Books, 2009.

"Foreign Military Labor in Europe's Transition to Modernity," *European Review of History: Revue européenne d'histoire*, 27.1–2 (2020), 12–32.

Lützen. Oxford: Oxford University Press, 2018.

"Meaningless Conflict? The Character of the Thirty Years War," in F. C. Schneid, ed., *The Projection and Limitation of Imperial Powers 1618–1850*. Leiden: Brill, 2012, 12–33.

"'Mercenary' Contracts as Fiscal-Military Instruments," in Svante Norrhem and Erik Thomson, eds., *Subsidies, Diplomacy, and State Formation in Europe, 1494–1789: Economies of Allegiance*. Lund: Lund University Press, 2020, 68–92.

"On the Role of Religion in the Thirty Years War," *Institute for Historical Research* 30 (2008), 473–514.

Wilson, Peter and Marianne Klerk. "The Business of War Untangled: Cities as Fiscal-Military Hubs in Europe (1530s–1860s)," *War in History* 29.1 (2020), 1–24.

Wuttke, Robert. "Zur Kipper- und Wipperzeit in Kursachsen," *Neues Archiv für Säcsische Geschichte und Altertumskunde* 15 (1894), 119–156.

van Zanden, Jan. "Wages and the Standard of Living in Europe, 1500–1800," *European Review of Economic History* 3.2 (1999), 175–197.

Zunckel, Julia. *Rüstungsgeschäfte im Dreißigjährigen Krieg: Unternehmerkräfte, Militärgüter, und Marktstrategien im Handel zwischen Genua, Amsterdam, und Hamburg*. Berlin: Duncker und Humblot, 1997.

Zweierlein, Cornel. "The Thirty Years War: A Religious War? Religion and Machiavellianism at the Turning Point of 1635," in Olaf Asbach and Peter Schröder, eds., *The Ashgate Research Companion to the Thirty Years War*. London: Routledge, 2014, 240–242.

Index

abortion, 120
Albrecht, Hans, 32
Alessandria, financing the regiment, 38
Andreas, Michael, 84
The Angel (tavern), 32, 80, 82, 135, 186
  drinkers sit by function, not rank, 83
Apollo, von (*nom de guerre*), 85
Appelt, Phillip, 15, 40
Aquinas, Thomas, 126, 137
armies
  as nodes of circulation for weapons or goods, 29
  once dispersed, not easily reconstituted, 188
Armin, von, military dynasty, 94
arquebus, 119, 182
arquebusiers, 94
  less honorable than cuirassiers, 89
  pay rates of, 150, 158
Articles of War, oaths to, 19
Aschenbacher, Samuel, 37
attrition, rate calculated from roll-calls, 105
Augsburg, occupation of, 29
Augustus I, Elector of Saxony, 27
Augustus II, the Strong, Elector of Saxony, 12

backpacks, wicker, 128
Balbi, Steffano, 37–38
Bamberg, Bishop of, 14
banking and loans, increase of, 25
Bartelt (boy servant), 28
Bassompierre, François de, 10
Bauer, Hans Harold von (joke name?), 92
Beck, Johann, 191
Beer, Franz, 37
beer, gifts of, 15, 177
Benedict the Rat, 115
Bernardo the Cat (soldier), 19
Bernhardt, Samuel, 81
Bernleben, David von, 144
Beyer, Urban (soldier), 83
Beyer, Wendel (merchant), 61, 76
Binder, Jacob, 188

Birckner, Adam, 146
black money (fiat coinage), 27
Blanckenberg, Mattheus, 34
blasphemy, proof of toughness, 100
Bogislav of Chemnitz, 81
Bohemian Estates, 12
Bötger, Jacob, 15, 40
Brandenburg, Electorate of, 160
Breda, siege of, 8
Breitenbach, Julius Caesar von, 95
Breitenbach, von, military dynasty, 95
Bremio, Gioanni Domenico, 105
Bresciani, Giuseppe, 102
building trades as benchmark for pay, 154
Buquoy, Count of, 8
Busto Arsizio, 18

Calvinist language in a testament, 98
Camargo, Theodoro de, 8, 34, 78
  career, 9, 133
  character, 123, 133
  concept of honor regarding his wife, 122
  death, 133
  feared his wife would poison him, 123 rightly, 123
  as judge, 67, 132, 140
  married life, 121, 123
  murders his wife, 128
    acquittal a foregone conclusion, 128
Camargo, Theodoro de, son of preceding, 130
cambric, 62
capitulation, honorable and dishonorable, 138
Capoletto, Camillo, 18, 37
Carpzov, Johann Benedict, 96
Castone, Giovanni Battista, 38, 162, 171, 178
Catholics and Protestants fight over Switzerland, 10
children as camp followers, 129
Christof the Drummer, 145
cloth
  grades of, 73

Index

supply of, 63
types of, 62
clothing
  cotton vs wool, 164
  made from stolen fabric, 67
  soldiers' symbolized freedom, not obedience, 65
Coeuvres, Marquis de, 10
cohesion, small-group, 73
credit and debt, networks of, 37
Cremona, financing the regiment, 38
crime scene, murdered wife, 118
Croat dragoons, modern bigotry against, 48
Crow, Anthony, 115
currency
  debasement of, 27–28, 155, 157
  exchange rate manipulations, 28
  gold, silver, and tin, 27–28
  soldiers used more cash, 29

Daumer, Daniel, 187
debts, officers and, 37
Deckert, Heinrich, 32
Denmark, king and army of, 171
desertion, 34
  effects of, 33
  even officers deserted, 40
  frequency of, 34, 40, 56, 198
  letters excusing, 40
  as negotiation, 40
  not clearly distinguished from absence with leave, 33
  punishment of, 34, 132, 134
  reasons for, 33, 192
Devil, Hans, 100
  his boy servant, 22
Devil, The, making a pact with, 100
Dionysius the Areopagite, 137
dragoons, least prestigious branch, 85
Dransdorf, August Adolf von, 165
Dransdorf, Christof von, 165
Dransdorf, Wolf Heinrich von, 35, 100, 167, 198
Drescher, Gregor, 66
Dressler, Georg, 39
drill, military, never mentioned by Mansfelders, 80, 196
drums
  cavalry kettledrums, 89
  drummer bangs his drum while officers fire out the window, 21
drunkenness
  leads to disaster, 22, 135
  less dishonorable than lying, 140
  universal in the regiment, 140

duels, noble vs. commoner, 85
dynasties, military, 94

Eckert, Jonas, 85, 198
economic crisis of the early seventeenth century, 25, 39, 64, 157, 161
economy, valuables sold for pitiful sums, 29
egualanza generale, 16
Elector of Saxony, 9, 50, 76, 129, 153, 170
Electoral Field Life Guard (Life Regiment), 96
English Civil War, 48
ethnography, defamiliarization in, 1
evidence, documentary
  for the Mansfeld Regiment, 5
  for other soldiers and armies, 6
experience, importance of, 81

fairness, concept of, 31
family economy, soldier and partner, 156
feathers in hats, symbolism of, 65
Ferdinand II, 49
Feria, Duke of, 11, 13, 16, 18, 37–38, 105, 127, 161–162, 168, 181
Fernandez de Córdoba, Gonzalo, 38, 120, 162, 168, 180
fertility, effects of soldiers' presence on, 110
finance
  military, international, 7
  public and private, 25, 167
financing the regiment, 39
fiscal military state, growth of, 196
flag bearers
  high proportion of nobles, 91
  most honorable officers, 79
  stereotypically flamboyant, 141
flag, company
  ripped down in mutinies, 173
  ripped down when a unit dissolves, 139
  Schutze's confiscated while in court, 143
  symbolism of, 139
Fortuna, Gideon de la (*nom de guerre*), 85
Frankfurt, refuses to help the regiment, 177
friendships across religious lines, 57
Friese, Friedrich (chronicler), 59
Fritzsch, Jacob, 104
Fugger, Ott, 119
Funcke, Simon, 130
fustian (*Parchent*), 62, 64

Gallarate, 18
gallows and withered trees, for hangings, 34
Gammert, Juan, 34–35, 133–134
Gattone, Bartolomeo, "The Bag", 182
Gauert, Heinrich, 21

Gebler, Hans, 32
gender roles and the soldier, 122
Genoa, campaign against, 11
gentlemen volunteers, 91
geopolitics of the regiment's campaign, 11
Geyer, Hans, 34
Goldstein, Joachim, Chancellor of Merseburg, 76
Golzer, Barthel, 164, 167
Gonzaga, Ferdinando, Duke of Mantua, 189
Gray League, or *Grisons*, 9
Greiffenklau, Georg Friedrich von, Archbishop, 176
Grimmelshausen, Hans Jacob von, 129
Grinzelman, Barthel, 197
Grünthal, Wolf Heinrich von, 150
Gruppach, Melchior von, 66, 96
Guarde, Victoria
  burial of, 124
  character, 133, 196
  family, 119, 123
  her abortion, 120
  her driver, 55
  her money and rich possessions, 118, 121, 126
  her servants testify, 126
  local reaction to her murder, 124
  married life, 121, 123
  murdered by her husband, 128
gulden, as money of account, 27

Habsburgs, Spanish and Imperial, 9
Hagendorf, Anna Maria, 28, 156
Hagendorf, Elizabeth, 130
Hagendorf, Peter
  as source, 3, 11
  called his things "his linens", 28
  career, 29, 42, 97
  family, 130–131
  his side hustle, 155
  his travels, 43
  shared in cloth stolen while he was wounded, 69
halberdiers
  more honorable than musketeers, less so than pikemen, 79
  noble, 91
  pay rates of, 150
Hammer, Jacob, 78
Hanau
  Count of, 192
  Sulz's regiment in, 193
hangers-on, camp followers, 82
Haugwitz, Lieutenant Colonel, 85

health, soldiers'
  bad knees, ankles, and hips, 43
  death and sickness rates calculated, 105
health, soldiers' and civilians', 115
  baptisms of soldiers' children, 116
  destitute men buried for free, 115
  statistics, difficulty of interpreting, 110
Hedeler, Stefan, 85
Heimberger, Hans, 34
Hennig, Heinrich, 51
Henri IV, King of France, 10
Hesse, Margrave of, 35
Hevel, Michael, 34, 36, 40, 98
  argues, 27
Heyl, Hans Georg, 83
Hildebrand, Cilian, 146
historical arguments reconsidered, 195
  neo-Darwinian theory of military masculinity, 122
  that cavalry was recruited from more rural areas, 53
  that German forces became more ethnically diverse during the war, 51
  that mercenaries were rootless or marginalized, 7, 42, 47, 54, 197
  that military cohesion requires physical proximity, 71
  that military discipline and control increased, 2, 4, 7
  that seventeenth century soldiers were trained with standard drills, 80
  that social networks coincide with small military units, 71
  that the war grew crueller with time, 48, 197
  on the symbolism and effect of uniforms, 64
historical background of the Mansfeld Regiment's campaign, 11
history from below, soldiers an ideal topic for, 4
Hoffahne, Saxon, 42, 154, 158
homicide, anger as excuse for, 127
honor
  any connection with an executioner dishonorable, 165
  capitulation, honorable and dishonorable, 138
  and dishonor, contagious, 166
  dishonor of calling a superior *du*, 83
  insults lead to swords, then lawsuit, 83
  punishment more shameful than crime, 165
  and respect shown by gifts of stolen cloth, 69

Index

some weapons more honorable than others, 79
horn, of cuckoldry, 167
horses, abundance of even in cities, 52
Hubrich, Christian, 142, 144

inquest, into theft of fabric, 66
Inquisition, The, 101
Inquisitor of Milan, 102
insubordination, 145
insults, verbal, 140, 143
  multilingual, 136
  rarely religious, 100
intermarriage of military families, 129
iron century, seventeenth century as, 156
Isabella, Infanta, 8

Japsch, Maz, 35
Jewish soldiers, 99
Johann Georg I, Elector of Saxony, 12–13, 27, 160
Johann Georg II, Elector of Saxony, 165
Johann Georg III, Elector of Saxony, 160
jokes on one's deathbed, 198
Jude, Martin, 99
Jungnickel, Hans, cuts Georg Reinsberger for shoving his woman, 30

kelsch, golsch (*Colschen*), cloth, 62
Kettel, Christoff, 22
Kirchhof, Hans Wilhelm, 137
Kirchner, Peter, 118
Kleiben, Michael, 100, 186
Kley, Hans, 186
Kochstetter, Hans Reinhardt, 164
Koenig, H. E., 33
Koenig, Jonas Ernst, 51
Korn, Nicholas, 84
Krahe, Carl von, 47
Krakow, Stach, xvii, 40, 43, 116, 146, 193
Krause, Tobias, 100
Kreis, Upper Saxon, 26
Kronberg, Johann Schweikhard von, 175

Laiber, Matthias, 134
Landsknechts, 31, 40
lanterns, for watchmen, 59
Lauerwald, Bernard, 189
Lauren, Georg, 35, 164, 167
  shames Wolf Heinrich von Dransdorf's wife, 166
lawsuits, between officers, 83–84, 167
League of God's House, 9
League of the Ten Jurisdictions, 9
League, Gray (*Grisons*), 9

Legnano, badly hit by the Mansfelders' presence, 106
Leopold, Archduke of Further Austria, 15, 195
Leopold, Hans, rapid promotion of, 93
lice, abundance of, 164
lieutenant, increase in status of, 157
Life Regiment (Electoral Field Life Guard), 96
Lipsius, Justus, neo-Stoic philosopher, 85, 196
Lipsius, Justus Wilhelm, pikeman, 85, 196
lire, as money of account, 27
Locke, John, 127
Löhlen, Hans and Andreas, 54
Löhr, Simon, 32
loot from the sack of Mantella and Roberti, 181
looting and stealing, partial compensation for low wages, 159
Löser, Eustachius (Stach), 39, 51, 78, 93, 96, 139
  death, 56
  friendship with von Pernstein, 57
  Mansfeld writes to him about Wallenstein, 172
  his plundered Turkish horse, 169
Louis XIII, King of France, 10
loyalties, mixed, 13
Lusatia, Upper and Lower, 13, 45
Luther, Martin, 11
Lutheran troops offend Italians, 102
Lützen, battle of, 56, 94, 133

Madrid, Treaty of, 10
Magdeburg
  Margrave of, 45
  sack of, 28, 69, 130
Mansfeld Regiment, 4, 100, 172
  ambushed by peasant militia, 178
  collapse of, 104, 163, 169, 174–175, 189
  devastating effects on local civilians, 105, 182
  far-flung contacts, 18
  on the march, 16, 174
  material contexts of, 195
  no specific uniforms, 66
  not necessarily better-armed than civilians, 102
  officers of, 78, 96
  one of the "two old regiments", 77
  possibly to be combined with Sulz Regiment, 195
  quarters in Italy, 18
  religion in, 99
  sack of Mantella and Roberti, 182
  social structure of, 82, 195
  structural weakness of, 196

Index

Mansfeld, Bruno von, 12, 56
Mansfeld, fortress of, 11
Mansfeld, Wolf von, 4, 13, 45
  conversion to Catholicism, 12
  and the end of the Mansfeld Regiment, 189
  greed and selfishness, 75, 161, 169
  hating and hated by Wallenstein, 171
  heads home when regiment is sworn in, 20
  letters, 75, 77, 127, 172, 199
  origin and family, 12
  takes command of Sulz's regiment, 193
Mantella and Roberti, sack of, 182
  case closed without comment, 181
  soldiers' testimony, 181
Maximilian II, Holy Roman Emperor, 13
Mazza, Gian Paolo, 191
Meder, Michael, 166
Medringer, Andreas, 66, 83
Melhorn, Andreas, 136
Metsch family, military dynasty, 95
Metzsch, Hans Georg, casually joined the enemy, 97
Meylig, Barthel, 186
Michael the Surgeon, 100
microhistory, 2, 4
Milan, 10, 24, 26
  financing the regiment, 38–39
military justice, not always harsh and arbitrary, 31
Miltirz, Bernhard, 156
mints, large number of, 26
miscarriages, possible effect of soldiers' presence, 110
money of account, xiii, 27
money-making, as part of honor, 122
Montferrat, peasant militia of, 178
Monzón, Treaty, 167
moral economy of violence, 124
Moser, Captain, 33
  his flag-bearer, 137, 143
motivation, why men fight, 73
  complex, and historically contingent, 70, 72
murders and accidental killings
  of Hans Heinrich Tauerling, 22–23
  of Victoria Guarde, 128
musket salvoes, fired for officers leaving quarters, 21
musketeers
  less honorable than halberdiers or pikemen, 79
  noblemen as, 91
  pay rates of, 150
mutinies
  examples, 31, 33, 174
  as a form of economic negotiation, 26, 31

Naples, economy of, 24
Naubrandt, Petrus (priest), 185
Netherlands, Spanish, 8
Neuhäusel, Battle of, 8
nobles and commoners
  all ranks open to both, 92
  differences less in the military, 77, 90
  nobles never served commoners, 89
  proportion of nobles in the cavalry, 90
  proportion of nobles in the infantry, 91
  young nobles serve in ranks for experience, 91
noms de guerre, 85
Nuremburg, feeds the cavalry, but gives no money, 15

oats, cost of, 154
Obersteuerkollegium, 160
obligations, reciprocal
  expressed with stolen cloth, 69
Ocampo, Francisco, 77
officers
  changed roles often, 78
  not a rank, but a defined task, 78
  reformed, 149
Olivares, Count-Duke of, 190
Ossa zu Dehla, Wolf Rudolf von, 43, 192, 195, 199
  tracks religion, punishes Protestant towns, 194
Ovid, 120

Pappenheim, Count of, 11
Paritzsch, Abraham, "Tartar", 154
Parma, Duchy of, 47, 56
Parma, Duke of, 53
Paudiz, Hans Wilhelm von, 85
pay, soldiers'
  archival sources for, 146
  back pay had to be paid before a unit could be dismissed, 163
  cavalry, 154, 158
  vs civilian wages, 156
  evidence from contracts, 160
  haggled over, 147
  infantry, 146–147, 152–153
  Mansfelders paid less than other regiments, 163
  not always proportional to skills and experience, 155
  and social status, 154
  solid currency may compensate for low wages, 159
  sometimes supplemented by free food, 163

Index

supplemented by cash from officers, 147
variation over time, 161
Paz, Lucas, 163
pardoned, 162
Peace of Prague, 50
peasantry
 abused by drunken gang of soldiers, 186
 not the main source of recruits, 53
Pellegrini, Margarita, 125
Pelz, Adam, betrayed by his fustian pants, 67
Pernstein, Vratislav Eusebius von, 78
 abandons the regiment for a job with Wallenstein, 170
 friendship with Löser, 57
 investigates sack of Mantella and Roberti, 182
 writes to Mansfeld about cavalry's lack of money, 169
Philip IV, king of Spain, 5, 23, 172, 190
Philip, Heinrich, from Steinsdorf, 150
pikemen
 source of lower officers, 93
 status and pay of, 79, 150, 152
pillage economy, 30
plague death, possible, 114
Pohl, Mattheus, 136
Pomerania, Saxon losses in, 93, 161
Pönisch, Hans, 186
Pope and Catholicism, Lutheran soldiers insult them when drunk, 102
Pranckh, Maria Cordula, Freiin von, 130–131
prices, calculation of by economists, 157
prisoner, pays for his food and drink, 76
Protestant Union, 194
Protestants and Catholics fight over Switzerland, 10

quartering, difficulties of, 16
quartermasters, 59, 61

Rammingen, burning of, 23
ranks, military, 92–93
 elite pikemen a source of lower officers, 93
 inconsistent and idiosyncratic, 78
 list of officers in the Mansfeld Regiment, 78
 "making it" as a soldier, 92
rape, by soldiers, 180, 185
Rasini, Antonio, 102, 119, 123–124, 126, 182
Rathaus, Dresden, 76
recruiting
 based on regional and local ties, 51, 56, 197

both horse and foot more urban than civilians, 53
Central European mercenaries always international, 49
geographical spread, 47
German-speakers predominate even in non-German areas, 51
many joined armies hostile to their princes, 45
not more international as war proceeded, 51
origins of soldiers in the Mansfeld Regiment, 55
peasants underrepresented, 53
recruiting-sergeants showed the handsomest and best-dressed soldiers, 64
Saxony and Sweden compete for the same recruits, 50
traveling units picked up recruits along the way, 55
Red Vincent, soldier, 19
Redlich, Fritz, 3
re-feudalization of northern Italy, alleged, 25
regiments
 composition fluctuated continually, 56
 dismissed without settling of accounts, 192
 recruited at the commander's expense, 192
 traveled further than soldiers might have on their own, 56
Reinsberger, Georg, 30
religious ceremonies in camp, 131
religious differences, difficult to track, 99
respect and honor, shown by gifts of stolen cloth, 69
Revelheimer, Christoff, 22, 55
Ritter, Hans, 100
roll call
 infantry listed by seniority, 47
 some names are probably nicknames
 Georg Ungar ("the Hungarian"), 51
 Hans Devil, 100
Rosario, Count, 125
Ross, Georg, 83
Roth, Augustus, 40
Rudolph II, Holy Roman Emperor, 56

Sachsen, Franz Albrecht von, 158
Sachsen-Lauenburg, Duke Carl of, 56
Salvaterra, Giovanni, 37, 39
Sannazaro, Giovanni Battista, 107, 178, 181
Sanner, Elizabeth, 116
sausage for meat, causes a mutiny, 33

Saxon Life Regiment, 50
Saxon State Archives, 42, 66, 92, 146
Saxony, Electoral, 66
  balanced between Catholic and Protestant, 13
  currency debasement in, 26
  most powerful Protestant state in the Empire, 12
  role in the Thirty Years War, 13
Schaumburg Regiment, 124
Schingo, Hans Wolf von, 66, 142
Schleinitz, Hauboldt von, 150
Schlüssel, Sebastian, 40
Schmaliner, Georg, 163
Schmidt, David, refuses to lie under oath for Steter, 142
Schneeberg, Andreas Melchior von, 66, 68
Schneider, Georg, 100
Schobinger, Hans Jacob, 61, 76
Schrauttenbach, Johann Wolf von, 35
Schutze, Hieronymus Sebastian, 60, 66, 90, 135
  character of, 66, 141
  distribution of stolen cloth shows social networks, 76
  feud with Felix Steter, 136, 143
  jumps a table on horseback inside a tavern, 135
  shoots his friend dead while drunk, 22
  trial for murder, 23
Ségers, Anna Luisa, 125
seignorage, 26, 28
self-defense, pleas of, 145
sheep, theft of, hanging the punishment for, 34
shooting pistols out the window while drunk, 22
Silbernagel, Johann, 27, 34
slang, military, 32, 43
  "to be in," be in winter quarters, 43
  "to go on," remain in the army, 32
  "to go out," to go to war, 32
  "to go out, march out," to go to war, go on campaign, 43
  auf dem garten, "on the guard," without a master, 35
  Außreisen, "run away," desert, 33
  Bestallungen, contracts to order troops, 146
  billy goat, derogatory for soldier, 6
  chef-de-file, "chief of the line", 80
  chef-de-serre-file, "chief of the back of the line", 80
  Die Kriegsleute, "War People" (soldiers), 1
  Das Kriegsvolk, "War People" (soldiers), 1
  Die Leute, "people" (soldiers), 1
  Die Volk, "people" (soldiers), 1
  Dienst, "service," of soldiers to commanders, 35
  Doppelsöldner, "double mercenary," pikeman, 150
  Entloffen, "stray away," desert, 33
  frisch, "brisk", 65, 196
  Garteknecht, soldier without a master, 35
  Gefreiter, "freed (from watch duty)," squad leader, 58, 80
  helle haufen, "bright band," elite, 65
  honored, a debt that has been paid, 36
  Hurenwebel, "whore sergeant," officer in charge of the baggage train, 78
  Impresarius, recruiting agent, 162
  la gente, "people" (soldiers), 1
  lancepassades, "broken lances," experienced soldiers, 80
  les gens, "people" (soldiers), 1
  les gens de guerre, "War People" (soldiers), 1
  Personen, "persons" (soldiers), 1
  Pflicht, "duty," of soldiers to commanders, 35
  Pigknir von Adelsburch, "noble pikeman", 150
  polyglot, 6
  Rechtschaffener Kerl, "righteous guy", 40–41
  redlich, "upright", 41, 134
  salva guardia, letter of safe conduct for property, 59, 192
  sexual insults, 6
  Soldaten, "soldiers", 1, 74
  Söldner, "mercenaries", 1
  Streng und Mannlich, "stern and manly", 121
  terms for different kinds of soldier's pay, 36
  Ungelegenheit, "inconvenience," euphemism for looting, rape, murder, and torture, 181
  Vertheil, "money to distribute", 153
  wacker, "fresh and alert", 65, 196
  Zurechnen, "to make it", 146
social cohesion, leads some soldiers to crime, 179
social contract, implicit, 40
social distance
  between Catholic Mansfelders and local Catholics, 116
  between common soldiers and minor officers not large, 82
social mobility, 92–93
  greater in the army than civilian life, 77
  "making oneself" as a soldier, 92
social networks, military, 43, 71, 82, 132

Index

social organization of the Mansfeld Regiment, 195
soldiers
  archival sources for, 42
  ate more meat than civilians, 32
  attrition from disease and other causes, 104
  call civilians "insubordinate" for lack of better vocabulary, 177
  carried their own legal documents, 36
  common soldiers killed one another, officers sued, 198
  conspicuous consumption a sign of inner fire, 197
  deeply conscious of law, 187
  everyone drank too much, 198
  exempt from sumptuary laws, 65
  feared and hated by non-soldiers, 4
  few could afford luxuries, 197
  fight pitched battles with locals, 102
  Jewish, 99
  lacked small change to pay debts, 27
  long careers of, 94
    evidence from lists of deserters, 97
    some switched sides, 97
  more often killed by peasants than enemy soldiers, 33
  motivated by honor, not just money, 35, 39, 197
  paid extra for digging trenches and gathering wood, 30
  paid in non-debased money, 27
  previous occupations of, 41
  seen as hyper masculine and socially marginal, 121
  soldiering as part-time job, 30
  some were criminals, 198
  sometimes lacked armor and decent clothes, 34
  stereotyped as lazy, 155
  wealth before enlisting untraceable, 85
sources, archival
  cavalry records possibly lost in a fire, 18
  infantry rolls better organized than cavalry, 42
  in Italy, 19, 115
  local, for the disintegration of the regiment, 175
  Saxon State Archives, 42, 66, 92, 146
  vaguer about locations, the further from Saxony, 51
Spain, allied with Protestant non-Calvinist powers, 13
Spinner-Lords of St. Gallen, 58, 62, 74
Spinola, Ambrogio, 120
Spinola, Don Philip, 171

Spizer, Stefan, kills a tailor for insulting him, 6
squad leaders, 80
Starschedel, Dietrich von, the Elder, 93
state, changes in the idea of, 196
Steiner, Mattheus, 20, 34, 78, 92, 173
  compensates Swiss cloth merchants, 74
  has soldiers tortured, 75, 187
  his possible family, 116
  as judge, 118, 134
  kept detailed records that survive, 5, 36, 57, 74, 76
  omissions from his records, 100–101, 117
Steinnetze, Jobst, 33, 183
Steter, Felix, 64
  beaten, along with his wife, 144
  feud with Hieronymus Sebastian Schutze, 136, 143
  kicked by horse inside tavern, 135
  many disputes with other officers, 136
  picks fight with Winckelmann, 145
  stabs Winckelmann, 144
  threatens to take Schutze's flag, 139
stiletto
  used to attack a fellow officer, 144
  used to murder one's wife, 119, 123
Stocker, Erhart, 81
Stoffel, Prince von Schlauendorff, 89
Stum, Wilhelm, 125
Sulz, Alwig von
  begs the Emperor for money, 193, 199
  complains of devastation with no hint of guilt, 199
  diverts money meant for his troops, 191
  false report of his death, 193
  his third-in-command, 59–61, 63
  Mansfeld takes command of his regiment, 193
  musters a second regiment, 195, 199
  and the theft of fabric in Beringen, 58, 63
Sulz Regiment, 77, 195
supply, military
  decentralized, 63
  from in-kind to cash, 17
  Italian suppliers of cloth, 64
  uniforms, 63
Sweden, role in the war, 50

Taube, Dietrich von, 99
Taube, Hans von, 93
Tauerling, Hans Heinrich, 22–23, 69, 95, 135
teeth, soldiers', isotopes, 43
Teichmeyer, Heinrich, 104, 136, 143, 146
  death, burial, legacies, 29, 98, 103
Tertullian, 120

theft of fabric in Beringen
  discovery, 61
  investigation, 69
  judgment, 76
  officers gave cloth, soldiers sold and traded it, 68
  some set aside for sick men, 67
  value of fabric stolen and recovered, 61, 73
  who gave what to whom, 69
theories
  of masculinity, warfare, violence, 122
  of military motivation, 73
thick description, 7
Thirty Years War, phases of, 161
Three Leagues or *Bünde*, 9
Tiel, Christoff, 156
trade in second-hand arms, 173
transit, military, 18
travel, difficulties of, 16
trees, used for hangings, 132
  specified as withered, 34, 133
Treutler, Valentin von, 85, 198

Ulleben, Captain, 184
Ungar, Georg, 51
uniforms
  development of, 66
  express inner fire, dash, courage, 65
  massive scale of the cloth trade, 62
  and proto-uniforms, 66
  soldiers given only the cloth, 64, 66
  supply of cloth, 63
  symbolized freedom, not obedience, 65

Val de Fuentes, Marquis de, 20
Valtelline, control of, 9
Venice, economy of, 24
Venus, Friedrich (*nom de guerre*), 85
Vincenzo II, Duke of Mantua, 189
violence
  military vs. civilian, 185
  public vs. private, 132
Visconti, Cesare, 186
Vitzthum von Eckstedt, August, 164, 173
Vitzthum von Eckstedt, August and Dam, 96, 103, 189
Vitzthum von Eckstedt, Dam, 38, 162, 174, 187
  company rolls of, 50, 99, 105, 135
  deals with final collapse of regiment, 189
  lobbies for food in Germany, 175, 177
  victim of currency manipulation, 28, 169
  witness to Victoria Guarde's murder, 118
vocabulary, economic
  honored, a debt that has been paid, 36
  Interimsmünze, "interim money", 26

Kipper- und Wipper Zeit, period of debasement and inflation, 26, 28, 155, 157
Reichsgoldgulden, money of account, 27
Usualmünze, "customary money", 26

Wagner, Jakob, 29
Wagner, Marcus, 178, 180
Wallenstein, Albrecht von, Duke of Friedland, 191, 193
  hating and hated by Mansfeld, 171
  hires von Pernstein, 170
  Mansfeld contacts, 171
Wallhausen, Johann Jacobi von, 78
Wallnitz, Adam Adrian von, 91
weapons, more and less honorable, 79
wheellock arquebus, 182
wheellock pistol, 22
William of Orange, 31
William the Silent, 13
Winckelmann, Wolfgang, 25, 61
  career, 76, 78
  inventory of his possessions, 29
  letter from Mansfeld, 75
  poor despite his diligent embezzling, 196
  stabbed by Felix Steter, 144
  and the theft of fabric in Beringen, 61
  usually procured fabric for the regiment, 63
  willing to sue his lieutenant, or kill him, 145
Winckelmann's company, 36, 67, 97, 103–104
  and the theft of fabric in Beringen, 54, 58
  wine and beer, supplied to imprisoned officer, 76
Wittstock, Battle of, 43, 93, 161
women
  as camp followers
    carried everything for the men, 128
    disapproval of, 31
    a dispute leads to violence by their men, 30
    first-hand accounts of, 131
    led little dogs on ropes, 128
    social networks of, 132
    their economic roles, 30, 128, 156
    types of work, 156
  control of, as part of being a man of honor, 122
  officer shamed for wife's previous lover, 166
  wrath and revenge, 127
Würzburg, Bishop of, 14

Zader, Jacob, 54
Zeckel, Friedrich, 37
Zeutzsch, Joachim von, 92, 146

Printed in the United States
by Baker & Taylor Publisher Services